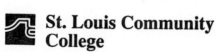

The Corinthian Body

The Corinthian Body   *Dale B. Martin*

Yale University Press   *New Haven and London*

Designed by Deborah Dutton.
Set in Janson type by Tseng Information Systems, Inc. Durham, North Carolina.

Printed in the United States of America by Book Crafters, Inc., Chelsea, Michigan.

Library of Congress Cataloging-in-Publication Data

Martin, Dale B., 1954–
    The Corinthian body / Dale B. Martin.
        p.   cm.
    Includes bibliographical references and index.
    ISBN 0-300-06205-2 (alk. paper)
    1. Bible. N.T.   Corinthians, 1st—Criticism, interpretation, etc.   2. Body,
Human—Religious aspects.   3. Body, Human, in literature.   4.Civilization,
Greco-Roman.   I. Title.
BS2675.6.B63M37   1995
233'.5—dc20   94-44947
                                                                          CIP

A catalogue record for this book is available from the British Library.

The paper in this book meets the guidelines for permanence and durability of the
Committee on Production Guidelines for Book Longevity of the Council on Library
Resources.

10   9   8   7   6   5   4   3   2   1

For Elizabeth A. Clark

Contents

Acknowledgments

For me, the most pleasurable part of writing a book is also the last: composing the acknowledgments and thanking all the people who have made it possible. At the top of the list are the colleagues and friends who read the entire manuscript, sometimes more than once, and offered invaluable advice, criticism, and encouragement; I am especially grateful to S. Scott Bartchy, Bart Ehrman, Susan R. Garrett, and Mary McClintock Fulkerson. Jerry Sumney and Troels Engberg-Petersen also kindly read parts of the manuscript at different stages. Judith Farquhar, a newly discovered friend at the University of North Carolina at Chapel Hill, introduced me to much material and saved me from mistakes in medical anthropology and cultural theory. Several scholars selflessly made their own work available to me before publication: Daniel Boyarin, Gail Paterson Corrington, Will Deming, David Kuck, Alan Mitchell, and Ben Witherington.

One of the great pleasures of working at a place like Duke University is the chance to learn from excellent graduate students. In that capacity, Melissa Aubin, Stephen Shoemaker, and Gregory Tatum read the manuscript and came back to me with sage questions and criticisms. I am especially grateful for the tireless work of my graduate research assistants: John Brogan helped with the early stages of the study, and Mary Hinkle to bring it to completion, volunteering along the way many excellent suggestions. I am also grateful to students in seminars taught by Bart Ehrman at UNC–Chapel Hill and Richard

Hays at Duke Divinity School who read and discussed parts of the manuscript while it was in preparation.

Certain organizations have provided support along the way. Portions of the work were read to the Ideology Group and Pauline Epistles Section of the Society of Biblical Literature and at the Association of New Zealand and Australian Theological Schools. The final draft benefited from discussions of those groups. Much of the material in Chapter 4 was previously published in the *Journal of the American Academy of Religion*, whose editors I thank for publishing the article in the first place and for permission to republish it here. I am grateful for financial support provided by the Duke University Research Council and for a Fellowship for University Teachers from the National Endowment for the Humanities. None of this support would have been possible without the advocacy and mentorship of the Chair of my department, Hans Hillerbrand.

The book is dedicated to the person perhaps most important in the past few years for my development as a scholar and member of the academic community: my colleague, mentor, and, most important, friend Elizabeth Clark.

Preface

The world of culture and literature is essentially as boundless as the universe. We are speaking not about its geographical breadth (this is limited), but about its semantic depths, which are as bottomless as the depths of matter. The infinite diversity of interpretations, images, figurative semantic combinations, materials and their interpretations, and so forth. We have narrowed it terribly by selecting and by modernizing what has been selected. We impoverish the past and do not enrich ourselves. We are suffocating in the captivity of narrow and homogeneous interpretations.

—*Mikhail Bakhtin, "From Notes Made in 1970–71"*

Although it is perhaps futile (and certainly arrogant) to tell readers how they should read one's book, I will nevertheless suggest two ways of reading *The Corinthian Body*. It may be read as (primarily) an interpretation of 1 Corinthians that (secondarily) concentrates on the ancient construction of the body as the focal point for textual and historical analysis or as (primarily) an exploration of ancient ideologies of the body that (secondarily) takes 1 Corinthians as a convenient window onto, or excuse to enter, the Greco-Roman world of the body. This points up what the book is *not*: either a full commentary on 1 Corinthians (for it does not address many important exegetical questions about the letter and goes beyond a simple explication of the text) or a comprehensive study of how the ancients saw the body (for I have limited myself to some extent to the corporeal issues raised by 1 Corinthians). My hope is that this dual focus will be deemed a strength, although I realize that some readers may wish for more detailed exegesis of the letter, and others may wonder why I did not address different issues regarding the body. The former may want to spend less time on Chapters 1 and 6, whereas the latter may find those two chapters the most interesting.

I have thus had two audiences in mind while writing: New Testament scholars and historians of the ancient Mediterranean. I hope this book may convince classical historians, if they need convincing, that the study of early Christian literature provides a fascinating and fruitful entrée into ancient culture from a standpoint that is not elite, which is something of a rarity. Yet I also hope to encourage biblical scholars to seek a fuller contextualization of early Christian texts, taking into account aspects of culture that rarely strike modern exegetes as having any "religious" relevance whatsoever. Each group may think I have indulged in overkill, spending far too much time analyzing either Greco-Roman science and superstition or Paul's exegetical conundrums. Yet the detail with regard to both is necessary, I would argue, in order to establish a textured contextualization of both Greco-Roman culture and the early Christian subculture.

The book ranges through fields normally thought to be far removed from religion in general and from Paul's letters to the Corinthians in particular. I devote much space to Greco-Roman medicine, magic, pharmacology, physiognomy, and philosophy. Moreover, long stretches of the book make only passing reference to Paul. To understand the method in this madness, the reader would do well to keep in mind that I wish to take issue with certain of my scholarly parents—or, more precisely, grandparents and great-grandparents: the *religionsgeschichtliche Schule*, which searched Jewish and Greco-Roman sources for "parallels" to early Christian language or practice, but did so in a way that I see as being too narrow. Concentrating mainly on aspects of ancient society they considered representative of "religion," these scholars were usually looking for the origins of Christian language or for influences from non-Christian sources that threw light on the development of Christian liturgical practice and theology. Early Christianity was portrayed against a background of Greco-Roman or Jewish religion and culture and was "explained" in terms of what it had borrowed from the surrounding cultures.[1]

My goals are rather different. I have little interest in the origins of any particular Christian practice or belief and in any case do not see origin as furnishing the meaning of language.[2] Nor am I particularly interested in finding influences on Paul. I am certainly not arguing that philosophical writings, much less Greco-Roman medical theory, had any direct influence on Paul's theology or ideology of the body. I concentrate on that literature merely in an attempt to discern different ideologies of the body at work in Greco-Roman culture. My goal is to sketch the logic underlying these ancient discourses about the body and see how the different Greco-Roman concepts of the body and its components relate to one another. Thus, I go to great lengths to describe Greek medical theories regarding the role of *pneuma* (usually, but misleadingly, translated "spirit" in religious texts) in and around the human body. I do this not because I think Paul ever read these medical texts—I'm fairly sure he did not—or because there is any direct relation between what they say and what he says, but because I am interested in comparing the unspoken assumptions about the body underlying the two kinds of texts, Paul's and the doctors'. By locating pneuma on the terrain of medical and other upper-class discourses, I provide a context in which its role in Paul's rhetoric may be perceived anew. I do not wish to argue that Paul's ideas *came from* Greek medical theories or the practices and language of magic or physiognomy. What I *will* argue, though, is that each of these discourses is driven by unspoken logics of corporeal construction and is implicated in particular ideologies that construe the body in certain ways as a result of certain societal interests. Paul's own logic of the body at times reflects these logics and at times differs from them. But since comparison of ideological systems is my goal, not tracing backgrounds or influences, more than a passing glance at the other discourses is necessary: we must dwell with, and on them long enough to understand their controlling logics.

I should also perhaps explain what may appear to be an indiscriminate use of Greek, Roman, and Jewish sources to construct Greco-Roman ideologies. I use the term *Greco-Roman* as a chronological and geographical designation to refer to the urban culture of the eastern Mediterranean during the period from approximately 300 B.C.E. to 300 C.E. I draw on classical Greek sources (for example, those from fifth- to fourth-century B.C.E. Athens) as well as Roman sources, but only when I believe that the older sources are relevant for first-century C.E. culture in the eastern Mediterranean, the city of Corinth being my primary focus. In what is perhaps a controversial practice, I also sometimes use Jewish sources to reconstruct Greco-Roman culture; for, on my reckoning, the Judaism of this period, certainly in its manifestations in Greek and Roman cities, but also in Palestine, is a Greco-Roman religion, having been indelibly affected by the dominant culture of Hellenism and to a lesser extent that of Rome. I thus take Judaism to be an ethnic subculture within the hegemonic culture of the Hellenistic Mediterranean. Any firm distinction between "Greco-Roman" and "Jewish" in this period is therefore historically misleading, even if, for some people, it is theologically important.

A third caveat: in this book, *ideology*—a controversial and slippery word— refers to the relation between language and social structures of power. It is the linguistic, symbolic matrix that makes sense of and supports a particular exercise of power and the power structures that exist. Ideology is more than simply "ideas"; more too than beliefs, which term evokes a supposed genealogy of beliefs or the "intertextuality" of a belief in relation to similar beliefs (desiderata pursued by the history-of-religions movement). An ideological study raises questions about the connections between language and social power relations, about the actual or potential consequences of linguistic events, about who wins and who loses given the possibility of triumph of one position over another. In its concern for the outcome of linguistic events, ideological analysis examines language as rhetoric—that is, as the attempt to persuade.

Ideology, in my usage, is a more serviceable concept than "ideas," "theology," or "beliefs," because it avoids reference to authorial intention: the person who uses ideology or is influenced by it need not be aware that this is the case. For example, a woman may have no intention of promoting patriarchal ideology when she habitually submits to her husband and to male leaders of her church "for her own good," but her intentions do not preclude an analysis of her behavior as an expression of patriarchal ideology. Workers may sincerely believe that they are "freely contracting" their labor in exchange for a fair wage, but this does not rule out the possibility that they are subscribing to a capitalist rhetoric that keeps them in a position of powerlessness regarding the conditions, ownership, and products of their labor. Ideologies diffuse themselves throughout societies and classes even when they are not recognized. Moreover, ideology is a more useful term than "propaganda," since the latter has connotations of being imposed from above, by those in power, whereas "ideology" connotes, in Miriam Griffin's words, "a kind of collusion of belief and expression, not altogether conscious, between those above and those below."[3] For instance, when I say (as I do in Chapter 9) that Paul threatens women with the "angelic phallus," I am not making any claim about Paul's own interpretation of his statement. Although Paul's authorial intentions (insofar as they may be constructed) are not entirely irrelevant, they are not decisive for establishing the correctness of my interpretation. I may indeed wish to speculate about what Paul *thought* he was doing, but that speculation does not have the power to settle the question of what he was *actually* doing.

The word *speculation* in the previous sentence suggests the need for a further caveat concerning my use of "ideology." Unlike some older Marxist users of the term, I do not equate ideology with "false consciousness," as against something called "truth." Like other contemporary scholars who wish to retain the term *ideology*, I am skeptical of any claim that someone (including a leftist scholar!) can stand outside ideology and correct a false consciousness by means of "reality," "history," "science," or any other discourse that claims a privileged Archimedean point of objectivity. Indeed, it is preferable to think of the term *ideology* not as referring to something "out there" but as signaling that a certain kind of analysis is taking place. By calling a statement *ideology*, I indicate the *way* I want to look at it, without implying that I intend to replace some false statement with an objectively true alternative; I mean only that I will examine it *as it relates to the (usually) asymmetrical social relations of power and domination*.[4] In fact, I am willing to conceive of liberating "counterideologies" employed by subordinated groups to oppose the oppressive ideologies of the dominant class or powerful social groups. But in my usage *ideology* usually refers to the system of symbols that supports and enforces the power structures of the dominant class and ruling groups; it therefore retains a generally negative tone with good reason, without implying that it can be overcome by recourse to some objective truth.

With these caveats in mind, let me outline the book's main theses. I argue that the theological differences reflected in 1 Corinthians all resulted from conflicts between various groups in the local church rooted in different ideological constructions of the body. Whereas Paul and (probably) the majority of the Corinthian Christians saw the body as a dangerously permeable entity threatened by polluting agents, a minority in the Corinthian church (which, following several other scholars, I call "the Strong") stressed the hierarchical arrangement of the body and the proper balance of its constituents, without evincing much concern over body boundaries or pollution. The different stances taken by Paul and this minority group on various subjects—rhetoric and philosophy, eating meat that had been sacrificed to idols, prostitution, sexual desire, marriage, speaking in tongues, the resurrection of the body, and the veiling of women during prophecy—spring from their different assumptions regarding both the individual human body and the social body—in this case, the church as the body of Christ. Furthermore, these positions correlate with socioeconomic status, the Strong being the higher-status group, who enjoy a relatively secure economic position and high level of education, and Paul, like many members of the Corinthian church, being among the less educated, less well-off inhabitants of the Roman Empire. This is not to say that Paul *came from* a lower-class background; for, as I have argued elsewhere, I believe that he grew up in a relatively privileged milieu and viewed his manual labor as voluntary self-abasement for the sake of his ministry.[5] But, for whatever reason, his view of the body is more in harmony with views generally held by lower-status, less-educated members of Greco-Roman society. And the same class lines that divided urban society at large also divided the Corinthian church.

Many scholars of early Christianity in the past several years have rejected "class" as a viable category for the analysis of ancient culture. They point out that the economic groups in ancient society do not fit the categories of class that have been used by Marxists and sociologists analyzing modern industrial, and particularly capitalist, societies and argue that status is a more useful category than class for the historical study of Roman society.[6] While agreeing with them about the importance of status, a more informal and fluid category than class, I nevertheless believe that the socioeconomic issues addressed by class analysis are entirely relevant to ancient Mediterranean society.

Modern American scholars reject "class," I believe, because they assume that it necessarily—and primarily—refers to economic level: that people are assigned to different classes according to how much money they possess. But, historically, class is not a matter of rich or poor or something in between (though possession of economic power is likely to be correlated with class). Rather, it should be seen as relational, as concerned with relationships between groups of people in a society. The classical historian G. E. M. de Ste. Croix, for example, defines class as "the collective social expression of the fact of exploitation, the way in which exploitation is embodied in a social structure."[7] One is a member of the upper class if one "is able to exploit, and does exploit, the labour of others."[8] Since class is a relation, those who live off the surplus labor value of others (no matter how wealthy or otherwise they are) are members of the propertied, or upper, class, whereas those whose labor provides the surplus value that supports the livelihood of others are members of the exploited class or classes.[9]

It is economic *relationship*, rather than wealth per se, that is important for an analysis of early Christianity. Almost all New Testament scholars admit that although we have evidence that some early Christians enjoyed a high status relative to manual laborers, artisans, the destitute—the majority of the inhabitants of the Roman Empire—probably none of them could be called members of the highest class of the Empire. The official ruling class of Roman society was a minute fraction of the population, made up of members of the three highest Roman *ordines* ("orders")—senators, equestrians, and decurions—along with local aristocracies in the provinces. Below them were the *humiliores*, an economically wide-ranging category that included people who controlled considerable amounts of money (for example, many merchants) and both freeborn and freed, all of whom depended on the labor of others for their livelihood. Below that were the "poor": artisans, construction workers, and owners of small business establishments like bars, baths, and brothels. And further down still were the destitute poor: unskilled laborers, those who made do with the occasional day job, and the unemployed.[10]

When in my discussion of the Corinthian debate I occasionally call Paul's opponents at Corinth "upper-class," this should not be taken to imply that any of them were members of the true elite; it is doubtful that any of them was of the equestrian or decurion order, much less the senatorial. My guess is that the more affluent members of Paul's churches were in that middle area between the true elite and the poor. Some were certainly heads of households (*patresfamilias*), meaning that their households included both freed persons and slaves; and they probably made their living off the surplus labor value of their dependents, which would place them, on my reckoning, in the upper class—even though significantly below members of the acknowledged high orders of Roman society. What we have in the Corinthian church, then, is a division between those who to a great extent controlled their own economic destiny and those who did not. Thus, although the Corinthian church contained no one from the highest levels of Greco-Roman culture—which, incidentally, produced most of the extant literature of the period—it did comprise a range of socioeconomic positions, which, I will maintain, prompted theological conflicts. These conflicts stemmed from conflicts over ideology, differences in world view that correlate with different class positions.

All those conflicts, I will argue, are consequences of a more fundamental, though never explicitly acknowledged, conflict regarding the construction of the body. To explore this conflict, I have divided the book into two parts, the first centering on the hierarchy of the body, the second on sources of pollution. Each part begins with a chapter sketching Greco-Roman concepts and then proceeds to an analysis of the relevant debates in 1 Corinthians. Thus Part I starts with a chapter delineating the hierarchical construction of the body in Greco-Roman thought. Then the various issues in 1 Corinthians that revolve around issues of hierarchy are explored: the role of rhetoric and philosophy in hierarchical society, the hierarchy of the social body and the socioeconomic divisions of the Corinthian church, speaking in tongues, and the resurrection of the body. In this first part I argue that Paul takes issue with the corporeal hierarchy of upper-class ideology, substituting in its place a topsy-turvy value system that reflects, in his view, the logic of apocalypticism and loyalty to a crucified Messiah.

The second part of the book begins with an analysis of disease etiologies in Greco-Roman culture, so furnishing an entrée into notions of pollution and the boundaries of the body. In subsequent chapters other theological issues of 1 Corinthians—prostitution and "polluting" sex, eating meat that has been sacrificed to idols, diseases stemming from the Lord's Supper, the control of desire, and the veiling of women—are explored in terms of different concepts of the susceptibility of the body, both individual and social, to pollution. It turns out that Paul and certain other members of the church are more concerned about pollution and the boundaries of the body than members of higher status and better education. Yet, as I will make clear, issues of hierarchy and pollution cannot be separated altogether: the hierarchical concept of the body that supports and maintains the power structure of Greco-Roman society—and hence the power of the Strong in the Corinthian church—is itself what makes this group relatively unconcerned about boundaries and pollution. But now I am getting ahead of myself: explicating these connections must await the unveiling, ideological and theological, of the Corinthian body.

Abbreviations

ANF	*The Ante-Nicene Fathers*
CIJ	*Corpus inscriptionum iudaicarum*
EG	*Epigrammata Graeca ex Lapidibus Conlecta*, ed. G. Kaibel, Berlin, 1878.
HP	A. A. Long and D. N. Sedley, *The Hellenistic Philosophers*
IG	*Inscriptiones graecae*, 1873–
JSNT	*Journal for the Study of the New Testament*
JSOT	*Journal for the Study of the Old Testament*
LSJ	H. G. Liddell and R. Scott, *A Greek–English Lexicon*, 2d ed. by H. S. Jones, 1924–1940. Oxford: Clarendon Press.
NRSV	The New Revised Standard Version
PGM	K. Preisendanz, ed., *Papyri Graecae Magicae*
SEG	J. J. E. Hondius, et al., eds., *Supplementum epigraphicum graecum* 1923–
SVF	J. von Arnim, ed., *Stoicorum Veterum Fragmenta*, 1903–24
TAM	E. Kalinka and R. Herberdey, eds., *Tituli Asiae Minoris*, Vienna: A. Hoelderi, 1901–
TDNT	*Theological Dictionary of the New Testament*, ed. Gerhard Kittel and Geoffrey W. Bromiley. Grand Rapids, Mich.: Eerdmans.

I *Hierarchy*

1 *The Body in Greco-Roman Culture*

Different societies construct the human body differently. When we as modern persons read ancient documents, especially the Bible, and come across words like *body* and *soul*, *spiritual* and *physical*, we naturally take them to mean about what they mean in modern culture. In this chapter I will attempt to show how Greco-Roman constructions of the body were significantly different from our own. Categories and dichotomies that have shaped modern conceptions of the body for the past few centuries—dichotomies like natural/supernatural, physical/spiritual (or, for those embarrassed by the spiritual side of the pair, physical/psychological)—did not exist in the ancient world as dichotomies. Other dualisms, moreover, functioned quite differently for the ancients than a mere translation of the terms into English would indicate. For example, the Greeks made elaborate use of a body/soul dualism and argued about the possibility of a material/immaterial dualism (a few accepting a form of the latter, most not). But it seems that what the ancients *meant* by "soul" or "matter" in these discussions differed considerably from what we moderns mean by such terms. Perhaps the most interesting way to proceed toward an understanding of the ancient body is to try to wipe clean our slate of corporeal vocabulary and attempt the (ultimately impossible) task of taking an imaginative leap into the past, recognizing that even "things" like bodies, minds, and matter will not only look, but actually be, quite different in a world so unlike our own.

Ironically, the best place to start our imaginative time travel is not with the ancients themselves but with the philosopher who marks the watershed of Western conceptualization, René Descartes. The modern world is a complex historical phenomenon, owing its constitution to innumerable factors: thousands of thinkers, as well as economic, political, and social forces. It would be grossly misleading and naive to attribute the construction of our forms of knowledge to any one human being or any grouping of "great minds."[1] But a quick look at Descartes will bring into focus the assumptions that have ruled much of our reading of ancient writers, biblical writers in particular. Even for those of us who have never studied Descartes himself, some of the ways in which he defined the human situation provide the lens through which we see ourselves and nature. In particular, the relations between body and mind (or soul), physical and spiritual (or psychological), matter and nonmatter, nature and supernature, were delineated by Descartes in ways from which modern mentalities have only recently begun to escape. It is practically a truism that "the boundaries between mind and body were redrawn by Descartes."[2]

We should keep in mind that Descartes viewed his writings on metaphysics as a preliminary to his more important goal of fashioning a method for the scientific study of nature. A devout Catholic, Descartes sought a scientific methodology that could be used to study the world without threatening the Church's claim to exclusive jurisdiction in religious matters such as the reality of the divine, the revelation of Scripture, the possibility of volition, and the immortality of the soul. Descartes sought a realm of reality distinct from that of revelation and the divine, a realm that could be analyzed "rationally"—that is, without interference from the truths of revelation.[3] We might excusably exaggerate a bit and say that Descartes *invented* the category of "nature" as a closed, self-contained system, over against which he could oppose mind, soul, the spiritual, the psychological, and the divine. In fact, Descartes quite self-consciously redefined "nature" to exclude those aspects of reality that he believed could not (and should not) be studied in terms of physical mechanism. As he states in his *Meditations on the First Philosophy*, "Nature is here taken in a narrower sense than when it signifies the sum of all the things which God has given me; seeing that in that meaning the notion comprehends much that belongs only to the mind [to which I am not here to be understood as referring when I use the term nature]."[4] This is important, for, as we will see, it is precisely Descartes's rejected "sum of all things" that was the normal *ancient* meaning of the Greek term *physis* (nature).

By constructing the category of nature to include only those parts of the universe that could be observed "scientifically," Descartes left an entire realm in need of a new category—hence the necessity of the "supernatural," a realm taken by Descartes to be real enough but one that cannot be analyzed by the rational means used to analyze the (newly invented) physical world. To the nonphysical realm belong all those aspects of reality that exercise volition and true freedom: God, the soul or mind, the "I" of the human self. There could be no ontological relation, therefore, between the "I" and the material world. According to Descartes, "I thence concluded that I was a substance whose whole essence or nature consists only in thinking, and which, that it may exist, has no need of place, nor is dependent on any material thing: so that 'I,' that is to say, the mind by which I am what I am, is wholly distinct from the body and is even more easily known than the latter, and is such, that although the latter were not, it would still continue to be all that it is."[5] For Descartes, the "I" is identified with the mind (*mens*) or the soul (*animus*)—the two could be used interchangeably.[6]

The body, on the other hand, lacks volition and occupies a firm place within mechanistic, physical nature. "By body I understand all that can be terminated by a certain figure; that can be comprised in a certain place, and so fill a certain space as therefrom to exclude every other body; that can be perceived either by touch, sight, hearing, taste, or smell; that can be moved in different ways, not indeed by itself, but by something foreign to it by which it is touched [and from which it receives the impression]; for the power of self-motion, as likewise that of perceiving and thinking, I held as by no means pertaining to the nature of body; on the contrary, I was somewhat astonished to find such faculties existing in some bodies."[7] The body itself has no faculty of self-motion; it is a machine, like a clock, and therefore can be studied like a machine.[8]

Descartes briefly entertains the notion, known from Greek philosophy, that the soul may be "something extremely rare and subtile, like wind, or flame, or ether, spread through my grosser parts."[9] But he firmly rejects all such notions (precisely those of most ancient theorists), insisting that the "I" cannot be anything like "a thin and penetrating air diffused through all these members, or wind, or flame, or vapour, or breath, or any of all the things I can imagine."[10] Although a "substance," the soul or "I" is not corporeal and can have no participation in the physical, material, or natural realm. The mind is in the body only like a pilot in a vessel. True, the mind and the body are joined together in "a certain unity," otherwise the mind would not be able to experience pain. But there is a vast ontological difference between mind and body, and in the end, "all these sensations of hunger, thirst, pain, etc., are nothing more than certain confused modes of thinking, arising from the union and *apparent* fusion of mind and body."[11]

What is important in all this is not Descartes's body/soul dualism; that existed in some form throughout the ancient world, in philosophy, ethics, and even in popular thought. Rather, Descartes's importance for our purposes is his construction of that dualism as an ontological dualism (that is, his notion that these two things by their very substances partook of radically different realms of reality) and his linking of it to a larger dichotomous system that included several other categories. On one side were body, matter, nature, and the physical; on the other were soul or mind, nonmatter, the supernatural, and the spiritual or psychological. Though it still influences many modern minds, this was a system of which the ancients knew nothing. Descartes's radical separation of mind from body, his mechanistic view of the body and volitional view of the mind, his cloistering of nature as a separate ontological realm from soul, God, mind, or will, was in service of his interest in constructing a unified scientific method without exposing himself to accusations of heresy. Unfortunately, though helpful for the development of science and modern thought, Descartes's dichotomy has misled countless readers in their reading of ancient authors, Paul especially.[12]

The Ancient Philosophical Body

Reading a previous generation of biblical scholars, one could be pardoned for coming away with the notion that the ancient world had two different conceptions of the body, the Greek and the Hebrew.[13] Paul and other early Christians, it was thought, were unlike certain Greek philosophical figures, especially in their views of the body, because of their "Jewishness." This picture not only ignores the diversity within ancient Judaism, as well as the many Jews, like Philo of Alexandria, who held very "Greek" concepts of the body; it is also based on questionable assumptions about Greco-Roman culture. In the first place, Greco-Roman philosophy is assumed to share our modern notions of the body and reality, including the Cartesian dichotomies sketched above. Second, it is portrayed as more unified and more homogeneous than it actually was. Third, ancient philosophical writings are assumed to represent ideas widely held by other inhabitants of the Greco-Roman Mediterranean, even those (the vast majority) who were uneducated and seldom exposed to philosophical teachings. In what follows, I intend to critique each of these assumptions. Later, I will stress repeatedly that ancient philosophers—who represent a tiny fraction of the population—cannot be used to reconstruct views of the broader population. Popular views can be extracted from their writings only via a critical reading, which I will attempt occasionally—with regard, for instance, to lower-class views of disease, death, and "superstition." For the present, though, I will attend to the philosophers themselves, in order to illustrate both the diversity of ancient philosophical opinions and their distance from modern or Cartesian categories.

Too often in biblical scholars' treatments of Greco-Roman views, a certain kind of Platonism—with its radical separation of body and soul, its deprecation of "matter" (a term that, as we will discover, is much more problematic than is often assumed), and its belief in the immortality of the soul—is taken to constitute *the* Greek view. Even a glance at ancient philosophy, however, reveals that words like *sōma* (body), *psychē* (soul), *physis* (nature, or, as it is sometimes misleadingly translated, "the physical") and *hylē* (matter) meant for the ancients quite different things from what they mean to us; any straightforward translation of the terms into these English equivalents will be inadequate at best and completely inaccurate and misleading at worst.

To get an idea of the multiplicity of philosophical views of the body and to appreciate the difficulties of translation, the best place to begin is with Aristotle's *On the Soul*. This treatise is important for our purposes not so much for what Aristotle himself teaches about the soul or the body but because he relates—how accurately is another question—the views of many of his predecessors and contemporaries. Aristotle assumes, like practically all Greek and Roman thinkers, that the soul, as the basis of animate life, is part of nature (*physis*, 1. 1. 402a). Immediately, therefore, we see an important difference from Cartesianism, which holds that the study of nature (the *physical* sciences) excludes the study of the soul. For Aristotle, as for other ancient theorists, "psychology" cannot be divorced from physics. *Physis* includes "all that is."

The translation of *hylē* as "matter" also causes confusion. When Aristotle contrasts *hylē* to something, it is not to a Cartesian-like immaterial substance, but to *eidos*, "form," invoking thereby not a matter/nonmatter dichotomy but a form/content dichotomy (1. 1. 403b). Elsewhere, he opposes *hylē* to *logos*, meaning something like "structure" or "form" (2. 4. 416a18; cf. 2. 12. 424a17, 3. 12. 434a30), a concept that has no relation to the Cartesian "immaterial substance."

Aristotle, moreover, lists the views of several other thinkers about the nature of the soul. For Democritus it is fire and heat; for Leucippus it is composed of spherical atoms that move easily through other things; for Pythagoreans, "soul is identical with the particles in the air"; and others think that it is what makes these particles move (1. 2. 404a). Even Plato, according to Aristotle, held that the soul (or at least some part or kind of soul) is constructed out of the "elements" of the universe (*stoicheia*, 1. 2. 404b26). Another view, rejected by Aristotle but somewhat close to his own nevertheless, held that the soul was simply the "mixture" or "harmony" of the composites of the body (1. 4. 407b27–408a25). Aristotle's own view is that the soul is the "form" to the body's "content" or "matter."

What is most interesting for my purposes is not Aristotle's conception of the soul but the way he uses the terms *sōma* (body) and *hylē* (matter?). Whereas modern readers often take "incorporeal" to be equivalent to "nonmaterial," this is not Aristotle's view. Having outlined these various philosophical accounts of the soul, all of which identify it with some kind of stuff, Aristotle concludes: "But all, or almost all, distinguish the soul by three of its attributes, movement, perception, and incorporeality" (1. 2. 405b). In other words, the soul could be incorporeal and still be composed of "stuff." One could believe that the soul should not be called "body" but still understand it as occupying space, as having a "place" (1. 3. 406a). This means that the soul, though neither *hylē* nor *sōma*, cannot be placed in the Cartesian category of nonmatter, since for Descartes (and for the traditional modern understanding) something is "matter" or "physical" if it occupies space. Furthermore, elements like water and air, taken by Aristotle to be what we would call "matter," are nonetheless "noncorporeal" (*On Sense and Sensible Things* 5. 445a22–23). When Aristotle uses the word *hylē*, therefore, we misunderstand him if we translate it as anything like the modern term "matter."

But modern scholars seem unable to resist the temptation to read *hylē* as "matter" (in the modern sense), leading to all kinds of confusion. In one place, for example, where Aristotle is explaining why some theorists take fire to be the stuff of the soul, the English translation by W. S. Hett proceeds, "for this is composed of the lightest constituents, and of all the elements is the nearest to incorporeal" (1. 2. 405a, Loeb edition). The Greek, however, is *kai malista tōn stoicheiōn asōmaton*, more literally translated: "it is the most (or especially) noncorporeal of the elements." Hett's translation implies that Aristotle took fire to be corporeal (that is, material) but *almost* incorporeal, consisting of very "thin" matter. Aristotle actually seems to be saying that fire *is* incorporeal—even though he believes that fire is constituted by matter (in the modern sense of the term—that is, that it is "stuff" of some sort). Elsewhere, Aristotle records the opinion of others that the soul is "composed of very light parts." Hett's translation continues: "or as corporeal but less so than any other body" (1. 5. 409b20). Aristotle's Greek, however, is *to asōmatōtaton tōn allōn:* "the most incorporeal of the others" (to translate woodenly). In other words, Aristotle is saying that certain people believe the soul to be composed of very light parts and yet still to be incorporeal. Hett's mistranslation is due to the fact that he reads *hylē* as "matter" in a Cartesian sense and sees "incorporeality" as belonging to the "immaterial" side of a material/immaterial dichotomy, which does not accurately reflect Aristotle's own categories.

Our dichotomies are even more inappropriate for Epicureanism. The Epicureans held that "nothing that lacks body can act or be acted upon, nor can anything except void and emptiness provide place."[14] Thus, all entities that act or are acted upon are bodies. Mind and spirit are corporeal because they move the body, which they could not do without touch, and touch is not possible without body. According to Lucretius, the mind strikes the spirit, the spirit strikes the body, and so the body walks or moves.[15] "Nature" is taken to include noncorporeality, but only as "void, place, and room" (*kenon, topos, chōra*). Throughout the Epicurean texts, soul and mind are corporeal because body is taken to be the nature of all (of what we call) matter. The only alternative to matter is void, nothing, the place where things can be. Nevertheless, the void is still understood to be part of "nature." Although the Epicurean category of "body" comes quite close to the modern category of "matter," we must remember that the Epicureans used "body" to include other elements, such as air and water, that Aristotle and other philosophers would call "incorporeal"— yet nonetheless "stuff."

In Stoicism we encounter a complex philosophical system dependent on Aristotle but departing from him in important ways. Our Cartesian categories prove problematic here for different reasons, not least of which is the category of "nature." Seneca mentions the Stoic belief that nature (*natura*) includes things that exist (*sunt*) and things that do not exist (*non sunt*): that is, "things which enter the mind, such as Centaurs, giants, and whatever else falsely formed by thought takes on some image despite lacking substance."[16] For the Stoics, therefore, "nature" includes not only what we moderns would call nature but much else as well, such as anything that might be imagined to exist although no one believes that it actually exists. For the Stoics, furthermore, everything that "exists" is corporeal; only nonexistent "somethings" (like imagined things) can be said to be incorporeal.[17]

The relationship between hyle and soma in Stoicism is also confusing for modern readers. According to classical Stoicism (as reported by Diogenes Laertius), there are two "principles" of the universe, "that which acts and that which is acted upon." "That which is acted upon is unqualified substance, i.e. matter [*hylē*]; that which acts is the reason [*logos*] in it, i.e. god." (Again, as will soon become clear, the translation of *hylē* here as "matter" is misleading for the modern reader.) In addition to these "principles," the Stoics posit "elements." Whereas the principles are eternal and indestructible, it is expected that the

elements will dissolve in the conflagration that Stoics believe will bring an end
to the current world. The principles (which, it should be remembered, include both the gods and *hylē*) are bodies without form (*amorphous*), whereas the
elements are bodies *with* form.[18]

It should now be clear why "matter" is not a good translation of *hylē*. Hyle
is a principle, like the gods. It is not like stoicheia (the elements). It is more
permanent than the elements, and yet it is "body" (as are all these things). It
is not in opposition to anything conceived of as "noncorporeal substance" or
"nonmatter." In other words, although we may have difficulty discerning what
the Stoics thought hyle actually was, we can be certain that they saw it as
something quite different from the Cartesian or modern category "matter."

From other texts it appears that we may be closer to the Stoic conception if
we imagine *hylē* to stand for the more compact, dense, or heavy stuff that we
call matter. Galen reports that the Stoics taught that "the breathing substance
(*pneumatikēn ousian*) is what sustains, and the material substance (*hylikēn*) what
is sustained. And so they say that air and fire sustain, and earth and water are
sustained."[19] Plutarch writes that the Stoics held hyle to be "inert and motion-
less," given form and shape by "breath and aeriform tensions" (*pneumata kai
tonous aerōdeis*).[20] For the Stoics, hyle consists of earth and water and is sustained by air and fire. The logical translation of the word *hylē*, therefore, would
be something like "heavy matter" ("matter" being used here in the English
sense) as opposed to the "light matter" of air, fire, and (sometimes) ether.

To understand the Stoic conception of the human self, in particular the
soul, we must free ourselves of modern notions according to which soul and
body, mind and body, the psychological and the physical, occupy positions
on either side of an immaterial/material dichotomy and think instead of nature
as a spectrum. Hierocles, a Stoic philosopher who flourished around 100 C.E.,
explains that the human being is formed in pregnancy by the seed drawing
hyle from the mother's body and with it fashioning the embryo. He speaks
of the growing entity throughout as *physis* (a "piece of nature"? "physique"?)
and *pneuma* ("breath" or "spirit"). "In the early stages, the physique is breath
of a rather dense kind and considerably distant from soul; but later, when it is
close to birth, it becomes finer . . . So when it passes outside, it is adequate
for the environment, with the result that, having been hardened thereby, it is
capable of changing into soul." By the gradual process of gestation, physis has
become psyche in a progression along a continuous spectrum of what we, but
not they, would call matter.[21]

Throughout this brief survey, my purpose has been to show how modern
readers have construed ancient conceptions through the lenses of modern and

Cartesian categories and that modern notions (particularly those about "nature" and "matter") have led to misguided discussions of ancient notions of body and soul. If there is one Greek philosophy that comes close to the divorce between mind and body effected by Descartes, however, it is Platonism. Did not Plato and his followers anticipate Descartes in advocating a radical dualism between body and soul, the material and the immaterial?

Plato's *Phaedo* comes closer to Cartesianism than anything examined so far. It argues for a radical division between body and soul. The term *hylē* does not occur, but the realm of soma *appears* to include what Descartes would later call "matter": it is perceived by the senses rather than by pure intellectual activity; it includes everything that can be perceived by the senses; it is changeable and perishable (see *Phaedo* 81C; 82B). The soul, on the other hand, belongs to the divine realm of true existence, even though it is a "thing" and not just a "relation" like harmony. It is invisible, divine, immortal, and wise (79C; 81A). The soul is antithetical to the body, not simply, as the Stoics and others would later maintain, a "finer" kind of body. The realm of the soul is known only by the thinking of the mind and is hidden from the senses (66D; 79A; 82B).

Lest we overemphasize this Platonic dualism, however, we should note some complications in Plato's ideas. As is well known, Plato posited different kinds, or levels, of soul. A "weak" soul, for example, has difficulty escaping the body after death. Due to the impurity of the weak soul, it sinks back into another body and "grows into it, like seed that is sown. Therefore, it has no part in the communion with the divine and pure and absolute."[22] Aristotle maintained that Plato taught that the soul was composed of stoicheia (*On the Soul* 1. 2. 404b); and in the *Timaeus* Plato does seem to teach that the soul is composed of a mixing of the eternal, indivisible essence and some part of the "bodily" (should we say "physical"?) world (35A). Thus it is no surprise to find that the *Timaeus* also teaches that the divinities are material (in our sense of the word) insofar as they are made of fire and are spherical (40A) and that Plato can call the entire universe a single, living, visible creature and god (92C; see also 69C).

The *Timaeus* teaches that there are three distinct forms of soul, the highest being nearest to the divine, the lowest more inextricably mingled with the body. It is this lower aspect of the soul that is difficult to separate from the body and is what we would call the "physical." In spite of the dualism for which he is well known, therefore, Plato maintains that quite a few ailments that we would think of as psychological, ethical, or spiritual are actually physiological at base. Sexual incontinence, for example, "is generally a mental disease caused by a single substance (the marrow) which overflows and floods the body because of the porousness of the bones." All kinds of pains can alter the mind. "Acid and saline phlegm and bitter bilious humours roam about the body, and if they are trapped inside and can get no outlet the vapour that rises from them mixes with the movement of the soul, and the resultant confusion causes a great variety of disorders of different intensity and extent, which attack the three areas where the soul is located with different effects, producing various types of irritability and depression, of rashness and timidity, of forgetfulness and dullness" (86D). An Epicurean or Stoic could not have put it more "materialistically." Even in Plato, therefore, the most dualistic of ancient philosophers, we find something quite different from the radical ontological dichotomy between mind and body, matter and nonmatter, familiar from Descartes. We are still dealing with something more like a spectrum of essences than a dichotomy of realms.

Inasmuch as my goal is to examine early Christianity and debates going on in the churches of Paul, Plato's own positions are less important than the ways in which Plato was being read and appropriated in and around the first century C.E. When we analyze the Platonism—or perhaps we should say the Platonisms—that were around at that time, we encounter self-styled Platonists whose ideas of body and soul look to us remarkably like the monism of Aristotle and the Stoics.[23] According to recent historical reconstructions, the Platonic academy as an institution disappeared after 88 B.C.E.[24] One of the last important figures of Academic Platonism, Antiochus of Ascalon (ca. 130–67 B.C.E.), promoted a form of Platonism consciously adjusted to Stoic doctrines. As Robert Berchman explains, "With Antiochus the Platonic distinction between Being and Becoming is reduced to the Stoic distinction between that which is active and that which is passive. God is the active principle in the cosmos, and matter is the passive principle. There is no distinction between sensible and intelligible, corporeal and incorporeal. In this tradition there is no ontological dualism, only a modified ontological monism."[25] Thus, by the first century C.E., there existed a "Platonic tradition" that no longer subscribed to the radical dualism of Plato.

The nature of Platonism in the first century is difficult to determine because we have so few extant writings of Platonists from that period. This is due to at least two causes. First, though Platonism experienced something of a revival in the late Republic and early Empire, it does not seem to have been nearly as popular in the first century as during certain earlier and later times. By all appearances, Stoicism commanded far greater loyalty and influence.[26] Secondly, few writings of those who considered themselves Platonists survive. The most valuable witness we have is Philo of Alexandria, simply because so many of his writings were preserved by later Christian scribes. According to Berchman, Philo would have been familiar with Antiochus's "Stoicized" version of Platonism, and Philo's own Platonism has many Stoic elements.[27] Philo did attempt to preserve, however, the dualism of corporeal and incorporeal from early Platonism.

In spite of this dualism, Philo's concept of the self is more complex than is apparent on a quick reading. Like Plato, he posits three parts of the soul: the nutritive, the sense-perceptive, and the rational. The substance of the rational is the divine pneuma, but the substance of the sense-perceptive and vital (nutritive) parts is the blood.[28] The substance of the rational soul is difficult to imagine in modern terms. Philo did not call it *hylē* ("matter"), yet he seems to believe that it is made up of "ether" or fire. The soul of the wise man, for example, both comes from and will return to the ether (*Questions on Genesis* 3. 10–11). Elsewhere, Philo puts forward the (rather Stoic) view that the soul is made of the same substance as the "divinities," the heavenly bodies, and in still another place he makes clear that this substance is "ether" (or perhaps a fine sort of fire).[29] Philo holds "an essentially Stoic view of the heavens," in John Dillon's words, and therefore believes that the soul is composed of the same stuff as the heavenly bodies, which, though not called matter by Philo, still would not fit the Cartesian category of "nonmatter."[30]

Philo's appropriation of popular medical and scientific views of the function of pneuma is also important in this context, since most modern readers take *pneuma*, usually translated as "spirit," as an unproblematically "immaterial" thing. Later in this chapter I will give sustained attention to ancient accounts of the function of pneuma both inside and outside the body; at this point, I would merely like to draw attention to Philo's "Stoicism" and his use of certain notions as evidence that he is far removed from the Cartesian world view in terms of which many people today tend to read him.

In the first century, most medical theorists—and anyone speculating on the physiology of the body—seem to have accepted the originally Stoic idea that pneuma (usually understood as a very rarified form of air) was the stuff of perception.[31] The body was able to see, hear, and feel due to the presence of the stuff of pneuma carried throughout the body by means of veins, arteries, or perhaps (in the opinion of some) nerves. Philo completely accepts these views, explaining that the pneuma "does not occupy any place by itself alone without the blood but is carried along and mixed together with the blood. For the arteries, the vessels of breath, contain not only air by itself, unmixed and pure, but also blood, though perhaps a small amount. For there are two kinds of vessels, veins and arteries; the veins have more blood than breath (*pneuma*) whereas the arteries have more breath than blood, but the mixture in both kinds of vessel is differentiated by the greater or less (amount of blood and breath)." [32] In Philo, therefore, neither "soul" nor "spirit" should necessarily be understood as "immaterial substance" in the sense promulgated by Descartes and assumed by many modern interpreters.

Other Platonists immediately after the time of Paul confirm the picture of a Stoicized Platonism sketched here. Plutarch uses a traditional moral-philosophical contrast between body and soul for ethical purposes.[33] But elsewhere it becomes clear that this dualism is not equivalent to a material/immaterial one. In fact, in his *Concerning the Face which Appears in the Orb of the Moon* Plutarch seems to have adopted a Stoic view of the corporeality of the soul: "The soul is a mixed and intermediate thing, even as the moon has been created by god a compound and blend of the things above and below and therefore stands to the sun in the relation of earth to moon" (945D).[34] Plutarch's fanciful account of a man's vision (soul journey?) in *On the Sign of Socrates* also strikes the modern reader as "materialistic" in its psychology. "It seemed to him," writes Plutarch, that "he heard a crash and was struck on the head, and that the sutures parted and released his soul. As it withdrew and mingled joyfully with air that was translucent and pure, it felt in the first place that now, after long being cramped, it had again found relief, and was growing larger than before, spreading out like a sail" (590B). The soul then goes on something like a "heavenly journey," conversing with daimons at the higher levels of the universe.

Well into the second century we encounter more of the same: thinkers very much influenced by Platonism but whose concepts of the body are a far cry from reflecting the kind of radical dichotomy between material and immaterial expected of Platonism by modern readers. Ptolemy was an astronomer and geographer who lived from about 83 to 161 c.e. Although familiar with the debates among the various philosophical sects of his day and earlier, he refused to align himself firmly with any of them. But while he demurs from stating whether or not the soul is corporeal, his views of it are very much what we would call material. At death, "the soul is so constituted as to scatter immediately to its proper elements [*stoicheia*], like water or breath released from a container, because of the preponderance of finer particles." [35] Note how similar this sounds to Plutarch's description of the escape of the soul from the brain of the man who went on a heavenly journey. For Ptolemy, as for other thinkers, materiality is a spectrum of more or less, not a position in a dichotomy with nonmatter. Earth and water are "more material" (*hylikōtera*) than fire and air and therefore more passive. "Ether" is always "active" (implying that it is not hyle at all? 13. 2–4). Of the senses, touch is "more material" than the others (14. 2). Galen also, to whom we will return later in this chapter, very much considered himself a disciple of Plato; yet he refused to speculate on the precise question of the corporeality of the soul. He did, however, reject the notion that it was immaterial.[36]

In sum, my two basic points are these: that we must recognize both that first-century Platonism was more complex and less Cartesian than many of us assume it to have been and that Platonism was itself a minority position in this period.[37] The kind of popular philosophy that seems to have influenced early Christians, Paul in particular, was of a general moral sort and much more related to Stoic than Platonic concepts. Most important, an ontological dualism in the Cartesian sense is not found in the ancient world. A Platonic dualism of soul/body was discussed in some philosophical circles (although some kind of Stoic monism seems to have been more widespread), but it was quite different from Cartesian or modern views. For most ancient philosophers, to say that something was incorporeal was *not* to say that it was immaterial. Furthermore, to say that something was not composed of hyle did not mean it was immaterial in the modern sense of the word. Air, water, and especially ether could all be described as substances not included in the category hyle, yet we moderns would be hard pressed to think of them as "immaterial substances." In other words, *all* the Cartesian oppositions—matter versus nonmatter, physical versus spiritual, corporeal (or physical) versus psychological, nature versus supernature—are misleading when retrojected into ancient language. A "one world" model is much closer to the ancient conception, and, instead of an ontological dualism, we should think of a hierarchy of essence. To outline the nature of that hierarchy I will now leave the philosophers for the most part, and make use of other sources that, I hope, will lead us from the rather rarified air of philosophical discourse to discourses that may reflect more widely disseminated ideologies of the body in Greco-Roman culture.

Inside and Outside the Microcosmic Body

For most modern thinkers the individual human body is a different sort of thing from the things that surround it. In the modern world we may talk about the "social body," but for most of us the phrase is a metaphor; the social body is simply the aggregate of many individual bodies. And it is the individual aspect that, in the end, counts. We may also speak of the earth as a body or, more rarely in the modern era, imagine the human body as a microcosm that reproduces the macrocosm of the universe. But again, these modes of speech usually function as metaphors. We do not *really* think that the human body is simply the cosmos writ small or that each individual body is merely a reproduction of the same elements and dynamics that surround us.

But in the ancient world, the human body was not *like* a microcosm; it *was* a microcosm—a small version of the universe at large. As Leonard Barkan says, "The cosmological view of the individual man . . . characterized the study of natural philosophy at least until the Copernican Revolution."[38] The pre-Socratic philosophers based much on the assumption that human beings, body and soul, are made of the same stuff as the world around them. Empedocles taught that blood is the substance we think with, while Anaximenes argued that it was air, the substance that surrounds us and holds the world together.[39] These assumptions are found outside philosophical circles as well, as demonstrated in a study of Greek tragedy by Ruth Padel. Padel studied the function of "inner body" language for what we would call "psychological" description in a variety of classical Greek texts. As a translation of the multivalent Greek word *splanchna* (usually translated by scholars of religion as "compassion," "mercy," or some other term referring to an emotional or psychological state), Padel uses the accurately ambiguous English word "innards." Innards, however, are constituted of the same stuff as the rest of the cosmos: "*Splanchna* are made of the same fabric as the physical universe. They also match and mirror qualities of the divinity that runs and pervades that universe. This correspondence was articulated by the Greeks themselves."[40]

The most famous account of the microcosmic body in the ancient world is found in Plato's *Timaeus*, which portrays not only the human body as a cosmos but, conversely, the cosmos as a body. In the *Timaeus* the cosmos is a tangible body (28B), a "single living thing," a "visible living creature," and a "visible god" (69C; 92C). Plato followed pre-Socratic philosophers and Hippocratic medical theory in assuming that the human self (body and soul) was composed of the same elements as the universe: air (pneuma), earth, water, and fire.[41] Thus the dynamics that one saw at work in the external cosmos could be read onto and into the human body, the inner body being buffeted by the same weather as the outer body. Furthermore, the inner body was susceptible to movements of the outer elements in ways that seem strange to us. The Hippocratic text *Breaths* (*Peri Physōn*), for example, explains that too violent movement of air—that is, wind—uproots trees, swells the sea, and causes apoplexy.[42] As Padel puts it, "Air is both wind—breath in the world—and breath within a human being. It is part of the patterned system within and without."[43]

The body-as-microcosm was not a mere philosophical or literary *topos;* it ruled the care and economy of the self in everyday situations—in medical treatment, for example. Galen reports that Diogenes the Babylonian (ca. 240–152 B.C.E.) believed that the soul was fed by vapors of the blood, as stars are fed by vapors of the earth. Galen and other physicians attempted to manipulate the "weather" inside the body so as to retain or restore the ecological balance necessary for health.[44] Papyri demonstrate that "magical" as well as "medical" therapy depended on the link between the microcosm and the macrocosm. One magical spell, for example, mentions that Orion causes the Nile "to roll down and mingle with the sea," producing life in the same way as does the flow of "man's seed in sexual intercourse." Others mention the common belief that the human body has 365 members, in reflection of its cosmic structure. In another spell, intended to enable the magician to ascend into heaven and learn esoteric mysteries, the invocation begins by recalling the identity of the magician's bodily elements with the cosmic elements (the "nonsense" words and strings of letters are magical terms that are part of the spell): "First origin of my origin, *aeēiouō*, first beginning of my beginning, *ppp sss phr[e]*, spirit of spirit [that is, pneuma, one of the four elements], the first of the spirit in me, *mmm*, fire given by god to my mixture of the mixtures in me, *ōōō aaa eee*, earthy material, the first of the earthy material in me, *uē uōē*, my complete body . . ."[45] The spell continues with elaborate instructions for proceeding through the potentially hostile forces of the upper realms of the cosmos, the presupposition seeming to be that the magician has a right to such space travel because of the identity of his bodily elements with the elements through which he desires to ascend.

As is already apparent, construing the body as really (not just figuratively) a microcosm blurs any boundary between the inner body and the outer body. The workings of the internal body are not just an imitation of the mechanics of the universe; rather, they are part of it, constantly influenced by it. One of the important ways in which this assumption was expressed was through the concept of *poroi* ("channels," "ways," "passages"), the word from which we get the modern "pores." Empedocles was the early philosopher who, more than anyone else, promoted the doctrine of *poroi*. Blood and air flow into and through the body by means of poroi. Our bodies perceive "when something fits into the *poroi* of any of the senses." The existence of poroi of different sizes explains why the sense of taste cannot smell, the sense of smell cannot experience touch, the sense of sight cannot perceive taste: "One sense cannot judge the objects of another, since the passages of some are too wide, of others too narrow, for the object perceived."[46] *Poroi* are channels that enable external material to enter and pervade the body and constitute passageways within the body for psychic and nutritive (or destructive) matter. The Hippocratics made much use of poroi, as is summarized by Padel:

> For the doctors, this explains why "souls" suffer "irascibility, idleness, craftiness, simplicity." Why are souls "quarrelsome" or "benevolent"? Because of "the nature of the *poroi* through which the soul passes (*poreuetai*)." Soul is affected by the "nature of the vessels through which it goes, the nature of the objects it meets and with which it mixes." The Hippocratics use *poroi* with zest. Sweating is caused by air in the body condensing when it hits particular pores, flowing through them to reach the body's outer surface. Dropsy occurs when breaths have dilated the *poroi* by passing through the flesh; moisture follows the breaths into the *poroi*, the body becomes sodden, the legs swell. In a sense, "all Greek medical theories are about *poroi*. The human body is simply a system of *poroi*." *Poroi* begin Western medical portraiture of the infinitely penetrable body.[47]

The concept of poroi in medical theory is one expression of the ancient assumption that the human body is of a piece with the elements surrounding and pervading it and that the surface of the body is not a sealed boundary.

Another way in which the absence of a firm boundary between the inner and outer body is reflected in ancient conceptions is seen in the way the ancients assume that one can read the nature of the inner body on the external surface of the body. In the ancient world, physiognomy, the art of interpreting a person's character and inner state on the basis of visible, physiological characteristics, was a respected science, practiced by specialists and trusted by philosophers, doctors, rhetoricians, and the wider, uneducated populace. As a distinct scientific discipline and technique, it dates from at least the time of Aristotle and continues throughout antiquity. As Sextus Empiricus (second century C.E.) said, "For the body is a sort of outline sketch of the soul, as is also shown by the science of physiognomics."[48]

The Pseudo-Aristotelian *Physiognomics* is the earliest surviving text of this sort, probably dating from the third century B.C.E. The author explains the method: "The physiognomist draws his data from movements, shapes and colours, and from habits as appearing in the face, from the growth of hair, from the smoothness of skin, from voice, from the condition of the flesh, from parts of the body, and from the general character of the body" (806a28–33). The author works with a sort of body/soul dualism, but for him this does not involve an ontological dichotomy between the two; rather, the surface of the body is an expression of the forces and movements inside the body—that is, the soul. Thus madness (*mania*) may be thought of as a disease of the soul that should be treated by attention to the body: "Madness appears to be an affection of the soul, and yet physicians by purging the body with drugs, and in addition to these by prescribing certain modes of life can free the soul from madness. By treatment of the body the form of the body is released [recalling the Aristotelian doctrine that the soul is the 'form' of the body], and the soul is freed from its madness" (808a34–38).

Treatment aside—which, after all, was the domain of physicians and magicians—physiognomists could confidently predict a person's character by reading the body, because the physical makeup of the person's body necessarily constructed and constrained those essences and substances that we would call "psychological" states. Our own divisions between the "physical" and the "psychological" are strikingly absent in these texts. For example, the author explains the rationale that supports his rule that the distance from the navel to the chest determines a person's character: "Those in whom the distance from navel to chest is greater than the distance from the chest to the neck are gluttonous and insensitive [*anaisthētoi*, "insensate," meaning not simply that the person lacks compassion, but that he or she actually is less capable of sensation]; gluttonous because the receptacle into which they admit their food is large, and insensitive because the senses have a more cramped space, corresponding to the size of the food receptacle, so that the senses are oppressed owing to the excess or defect of the food supply" (*Physiognomics* 810b16). The senses are located and operate in a particular region of the body's trunk; they are not able to function properly when overly constrained, and hence a certain construction of the trunk will adversely affect a person's capacity for perception and emotion.

Centuries later the physician Galen made use of physiognomic theories. Galen follows Aristotle, for example, in linking the nature of the blood to the state of the soul and both to the surface of the body. As Elizabeth Evans writes, "Blood is conceived of as hot or cold, thick or thin, moist or dry, swift or slow. These qualities in the blood characterize the physiology of the soul and its activities. Such activities in turn affect the behavior of man and his outward appearance."[49] In what appears to us a curious mixture of medical and physiognomic concepts (of course, to Galen and his fellow scientists it would not have seemed curious in the least), Galen writes of the "emotional" problems attending excessive heat. "For if very much heat dominates, straightway there is bitter anger and madness and rashness. In such people the thorax is shaggy, and especially the chest and the parts near the praecordia. In general, even the whole body becomes warm when the heart is warm, unless the liver is sharply opposed to it."[50] This is not an aberrant theoretical position for Galen; he wrote an entire handbook proving "That the faculties of the mind follow the mixtures of the body."[51]

We shall have cause to return to the physiognomists later. At this point, I wish to emphasize only the close connection in ancient "common sense" between the internal processes of the body that we moderns might classify as "psychological" and the external aspects that we would distinguish as "physical." This is not simply to imply that ancient, like modern, medicine recognized the importance of psychosomatic conditions. In fact, the English word indicates that we moderns consider a psychosomatic illness to be something of an anomaly, a state whose explanation necessitates the combination of two normally discrete methodological and therapeutic realms. But for the ancients, no such discrete realms existed for the placement of the body and its workings, external or internal; the differentiation between inner and outer body was fluid and permeable. Moreover, the modern boundary between the psychological and the physiological is anachronistic with regard to ancient language and concepts.

To modern readers, it sometimes appears that ancient writers speak of "nonphysical" emotions by using "physical" language metaphorically or by means of analogy. In discussing Greek tragedy and medicine, Ruth Padel admits that to us it may seem as if the ancients were drawing an "analogy" from the physical to the psychological; but, she says, "I would stress that any 'analogy' is in *our* minds, not in Greek mentality, for to say that *Greek* imagination made an analogy between psychic and physical would anachronistically imply that it drew that distinction."[52] Elsewhere, addressing what she foresees will be an objection to her "literal"-sounding interpretation of the internal stuff of emotion in Greek thought, she continues:

> When I speak of innards, I mean all this equipment of feeling and thinking. The poets treat words fluidly as organs, vessels, liquid, breath. But I am not suggesting that tragedians "blurred" distinctions we make between mind and body, or that these words were ambiguous, or that the psychological "overlapped" the physical in Greek thought. These metaphors of blur and overlap would imply that the Greeks perceived two different things to blur, two meanings to slip between. If the distinctions and meanings are ours, not theirs, then there were no two things for them to blur or be ambiguous about. It is not useful to project semantic fields of our own words, like heart, soul, mind, or spirit, or to talk in terms of slippage.[53]

Rather than trying to force ancient language into our conceptual schemes, we would do better to try to imagine how ancient Greeks and Romans could see as "natural" what seems to us bizarre: the nonexistence of the "individual," the fluidity of the elements that make up the "self," and the essential continuity of the human body with its surroundings.

The Pneumatic Body

As we have seen, the ancients by and large view the self as a continuum of substances which all, somewhat automatically, interact with and upon one another.[54] One avenue by which we may enter into the ancient construction of the self is through an analysis of the role of pneuma in the Greco-Roman body. From the pre-Socratics well into late antiquity, pneuma is an important category in the composition of the cosmos and the human body. It plays a role in philosophy, medical theory, and even popular thought and speech. For most ancient theorists, pneuma is a kind of "stuff" that is the agent of perception, motion, and life itself; it pervades other forms of stuff and, together with those other forms, constitutes the self.

Pneuma was considered to exist all around us; it was sometimes spoken of as identical with air or wind, or perhaps as what one would end up with if the surrounding air were refined to its most primary substance. The pre-Socratic Diogenes of Apollonia, for example, attributed sense perception, thought, and motion to air.[55] Apparently, the role of pneuma grew in importance under the influence of the Stoics. Chrysippus defined pneuma as "moved air" and conceived of it as "a mixture of air and fire, a special kind of warm air."[56] Pneuma pervades and defines external reality; it is that "airy tension" that gives form and quality (for example, hard, soft, dense, white) to external objects.[57]

Many theorists considered air the ultimate source of all pneuma, including the pneuma that moves throughout the human body as the agent of motion, life, and sensation. As Heinrich von Staden explains, "In the dynamic materialism of the Stoics a human being is viewed as a continuum of constantly moving and changing *pneuma*, a mixture of air and fire that is capable of varying degrees of tension or tautness in its parts." The psyche, a corporeal substance "composed of fine particles," spreads through the entire body, "blended with the rest of one's *pneuma*."[58] Assumptions such as these are not limited to Stoics, however. Other theorists held that since pneuma is the source of life, fetuses (which, of course, have no access to air until birth) can be considered to have "natural motion" (*kinēsis physikē*) but not "pneumatic motion": in the words of (pseudo?) Plutarch, citing Herophilus (an Alexandrian physician of the third century B.C.E.), "They become living beings (*zōa*) whenever they are poured forth and take in some air." [59] Artemidorus shows that the connection between internal and external pneuma was presupposed in popular thought as well; his *Dream Handbook* mentions in passing that "our spirit [*pneuma*] has something in common with the atmosphere and the outer air" (2. 60). And Dio Chrysostom, certainly no orthodox Stoic, could speak of pneuma as the substance that is sucked in by people for nourishment (*Discourse* 12. 30).

In both scientific theory and popular thought, then, pneuma was the life-giving material for the members of the body, nourishing the body through a complex interaction of elements. It was commonly believed that the arteries carried pneuma, either alone or mixed with blood. [60] In the theories of physicians as diverse as Erasistratus and Galen (it should be remembered that Galen seemed to consider himself a follower more of Plato than any other philosophical sect or figure) pneuma traveled in the arteries to provide nourishment to the different parts of the body. [61] Owsei Temkin explains how in Galen's theory the "inborn *pneuma*" (*to symphytos pneuma*) or "vital spirit" (*pneuma zōtikon*) is sustained by the external air and in turn sustains the body: "In the lungs the inhaled air is digested as food is in the liver. Through the pulmonary veins this product reaches the heart. Here as well as in the arteries it is further assimilated and transported to the various parts of the body. For special purposes, however, additional refinement is needed, above all for the nourishment of the psychic pneuma. The arteries of the rete mirabile serve this purpose which is realized in the ventricles of the brain." [62] The outside air (which either is or contains pneuma) sustains the inner pneuma by inhalation. The *pneuma zōtikon* provides life to the different parts of the body and is itself further refined in order to nourish the *pneuma psychikon*. The body is a refinery for processing, among other things, pneuma. Connections between these different forms of matter, at different levels of refinement, are generally assumed. [63]

The fluidity of the category of pneuma enabled it to function in a wide variety of ways in ancient physiological systems, from medical explanations of disease to scientific explanations of sense perception. Aetius (ca. 100 C.E.), for example, spoke of hearing as "breath" that extends from the "commanding center" of the body to the ears; all the other "faculties," including even "seed" and "voice," are essentially pneumata that extend from the commanding center to the pertinent part of the body. [64] The most common discourse in which pneuma played an important role, however, was that of optics.

Different theorists, and the different philosophical schools in particular, disagreed about how pneuma actually functioned in the optical system. Plato seems to have taught that the physical body of an emission from an object "touches" the eye and that this touching is transmitted to the soul. A first-century B.C.E. treatise attributed to Geminus explains that "the intervening air [between the object and the eye] is extended together with, or carried along with, the raylike *pneuma* of the eye."[65] The Stoics attributed sight to the stretching of the "innate *pneuma*." In the words of David Hahm, "Stoic theory postulates a state of density or of tension being impressed on the base of the cone of tensed, visual air. This state is communicated back to the *pneuma* of the eyes and through it to the principal part of the soul where a presentation arises."[66] Or, as Heinrich von Staden explains using different terminology, "Presentations are part of a corporeal process—they are pneumatic alterations in the cardiac command center."[67]

In about the third century B.C.E. Herophilus discovered the nerves leading from the brain to the eyes and believed that these "ducts" contained pneuma.[68] The pneuma outside the body acted upon the pneuma in the eyes, which then acted upon the pneuma in the nerves and on into the brain. The function of the nerves, according to many physicians, was precisely to carry pneuma to and from different parts of the body, the pneuma acting as messenger from the "soul," or whatever the command center was called, to the limbs and organs of sense and from the extremities back to the seat of sensation.[69] Galen, who believed that the brain was the seat of sensation (not a universal opinion), taught that the brain extended itself throughout the body by means of the nerves, which held the "psychic *pneuma*," the stuff of sensation.[70]

In theories of disease too the link between the outer pneuma and the inner pneuma was important. Hippocratic texts speak of the pneuma as upsetting the body in fever because it "condenses and flows as water."[71] Diseases may come "from the *pneuma* by which, taking in, we live."[72] The whole body is endangered when the pneuma is corrupted by the inhalation of bad air, and the pneuma may be affected by poison from things like snakebites. According to Galen, psychological stress, severe pain, excessive movement, or any number of bodily ailments can corrupt the substance of the pneuma.[73]

How Galen conceives of the precise nature of the pneuma is unclear. At times he speaks of it as a vaporous substance; at other times, as Rudolph Siegel puts it, "as a subtle homogeneous fluid of varying viscosity, like oil of different grades."[74] In any case, since the organ of sensation and thought is the "cerebral *pneuma*," the mind itself may be altered by "metabolic changes" in the pneuma.[75] In his *Method of Treatment*, therefore, Galen warns against any therapy that would corrupt, weaken, or disperse the pneuma, and he notes that the physician must be sure that the air surrounding the patient is pure to avoid pollution of the pneuma.[76] What was true of Galen was true of many others as well: the pneuma was considered the stuff of rationality, thought, and sensation, and as such it was dangerously susceptible to pollution and corruption. It was not safely cloistered in a separate ontology; rather, it permeated other forms of nature and therefore could be acted upon, damaged, and even altered by other natural elements.[77]

The principle whereby the pneuma was affected by other elements is illuminated by the famous doctrine of the "sympathy" of the elements of the cosmos. In Stoic thought, the classical home of the doctrine of *sympatheia*, perceptions are both possible and reliable because of this sympathy.[78] The concept, shorn of its particularly Stoic aspects, informed other, non-Stoic theories. According to Edward N. Lee, for example, Epicurus also depended on a concept of sympatheia to explain perception.[79] And John Scarborough argues that all Roman medicine presupposed that "there was a kind of sympathy and antipathy in all nature."[80] Thus most theorists assumed commonalities both between the pneuma inside the body and external pneumata and between the pneuma and other elements of nature.

To many modern readers, these ancient explanations of sense perception appear remarkably mechanical.[81] Temkin delineates two different models of perception theory: a "mechanistic" model, attributed to Erasistratus and Asclepiades, and a "psychological" model (I think the term "anthropomorphic" is more descriptive), advocated by Galen in opposition to the earlier mechanistic theories.[82] I have already given examples of mechanistic ways of talking about the activities of the pneuma. Other theorists, however, speak of the different human elements as if they were agents. Aristotle explains that nearsightedness results when a person's sight is "weak" and "thin" and is therefore unable to "push aside" the surrounding air to penetrate to the object; instead, it is reflected off the air and back to the person, preventing vision.[83] Two centuries after Aristotle, Hipparchus compared visual rays to hands that "reach out" and bring the image of the object back to the "visual perceptor" (*to horatikon*).[84] The Epicurean Lucretius explains why a person looking out from darkness can see into the light, whereas a person looking from the light cannot see into a dark room. In the first case the dark air, which is denser, enters the eyes first and "besieges" the passages of perception; the light air then follows and "cleans out" the passages to enable sight. The person in the light, on the other hand, receives the light air first; but then the dark air follows and "besieges" the passages, thus preventing the films given off by objects in the dark room from entering the passages and being perceived.[85] All these theorists resort to anthropomorphic imagery to explain the processes of sensation.

This combination of mechanical and anthropomorphic imagery in ancient theories of sensation may strike modern readers as odd, but without it we cannot understand how the ancients constructed the body or the "self." Sensations affected the entire human being precisely because the various human elements were interconnected, each acting on and reacting to one another like cogs in a machine or soldiers in a battle. In most of Greco-Roman culture a human being was a confused commingling of substances. A few philosophers, Platonists perhaps, may have emphasized a dualism between the body and the soul.[86] But such theorists represented a small minority. In the absence of such an ontological dualism, for most people of Greco-Roman culture the human body was of a piece with its environment. The self was a precarious, temporary state of affairs, constituted by forces surrounding and pervading the body, like the radio waves that bounce around and through the bodies of modern urbanites. In such a maelstrom of cosmological forces, the individualism of modern conceptions disappears, and the body is perceived as a location in a continuum of cosmic movement. The body—or the "self"—is an unstable point of transition, not a discrete, permanent, solid entity.

The Malleable Body

Upper-class ideology of the body was not altogether consistent. On the one hand, it insisted that a person's character was set from birth. Thus Greco-Roman novels or romances never tire of showing how true nobility necessarily manifests itself on the body. No matter what servile conditions the hero or heroine falls into, a discerning person will always be able to recognize the aristocratic nature registered on the body of the main character, who was, of course, always a young man or woman of excellent breeding. Conversely, a servile nature could not be hidden by the trappings of a superior class.[87]

On the other hand, documents written by and for the upper class show much concern with the procedures whereby the young body may be formed to reflect the corporeal esthetics of its own class. Would-be mothers were instructed on how to make sure that their babies would be born with the proper appearance and character; nurses were taught to bathe and swaddle the infant so that its tiny body would assume the appropriate aristocratic beauty; and athletic trainers were advised by doctors and other scientists on the techniques of massage that would assure the correct formation of the adolescent male body. The goal of upper-class ideology was not utter consistency but the maintenance of the hierarchical structure of society, the power of the ruling class and its control over the human body. In terms of that goal, apparently, its ideology of the body was eminently successful.

Take, for example, the physician Soranus, who practiced at the end of the first and beginning of the second century. Among other things, he wrote a *Gynecology* dealing with all sorts of female health issues, including childbirth and the care of the newborn. The book is written with a broader audience in mind than simply other doctors, midwives, or nurses. We should see its audience as including educated (and therefore, for the most part, upper-class) lay people, especially the conscientious *paterfamilias* who considered the health, education, and well-being of his household his personal business. Soranus's *Gynecology* thus both reflects and influenced upper-class constructions of the body.[88]

The proper formation of the body began before birth, even before conception. Reflecting quite common ideas, Soranus tells young women that they must be careful about what they look at during sex: women who gazed on monkeys during intercourse have borne children who resembled monkeys. Women should also be sober during coitus, since drunkenness may produce "strange phantasies" in the mind, which may then imprint themselves on the body of the resulting fetus.[89]

The real task of shaping the aristocratic body, however, began at birth. After a bath, which itself is carefully prescribed, the nurse is to hold the newborn upside down by the ankles so that the body will be straightened, the sinews untangled, and "the spine given the right curves." Next comes a massage: every part of the body must be "modeled" by the nurse's hands. The nurse should use the ball of her thumb to "flatten out the hollows of the knees"; she should use her thumb to mold the valley that runs along the back up the spine; and using her thumb and forefinger, she must "hollow out the region around the buttocks." Of course, great care must be taken to mold the head of the infant correctly. "She should first, by rotatory movements with each hand, massage the little head round and round. Secondly, with her hands facing each other she should somehow mould it, now with one hand placed against the back of the head and the other against the forehead, now with one against the top of the head and the other under the chin. And she should dexterously bring the skull into good proportions, so that it may become neither too lengthy nor pointed."[90] She should massage the eyes and shape the nose, "raising it if flat, but pressing it if aquiline." Even the male infant's genitals must be manipulated. Thus, "If the infant is male and it looks as though it has no foreskin, she should gently draw the tip of the foreskin forward or even hold it together with a strand of wool to fasten it. For if gradually stretched and continuously drawn forward it easily stretches and assumes its normal length, covers the glans and becomes accustomed to keep the natural good shape" (2. 16. 34 [103]). Clearly, "natural" here has nothing to do with the way the body might grow if left to nature. What is "natural" is the body that conforms to the esthetic expectations of the upper class. One must, therefore, gently coerce the body into its "natural" form.

The instructions on swaddling and unswaddling infants also reveal the common sense about the malleability of the body. The midwife is told to wrap a broad bandage circularly around the thorax, "exerting an even pressure when swaddling males, but in females binding the parts of the breast more tightly, yet keeping the region of the loins loose, for in women this form is more becoming" (2. 9. 14–15 [29. 83–84]). One should not unswaddle too early, otherwise the body may not solidify in the proper, firm shape. "We deem it right to loosen them when the body has already become reasonably firm and when there is no longer fear of any of its parts being distorted. In some cases this comes about more quickly because of a better structure of the body, while in others it comes about more slowly because of a weaker physique" (2. 19. 42 [39. 111]). In other words, some bodies, due to their superior nature manifested already in infancy, become firmer and correctly formed more quickly; but others may overcome their weaker natures with appropriate care. A more reliable process assures that the child will become right-handed: the nurse simply unswaddles the right hand a few days before the left, keeping the left hand tied up.

These instructions of Soranus's *Gynecology* sound strange to us, perhaps even cruel; but they merely reflect the cultural common sense that the self is formable by society. All aspects of the body and the self are malleable and susceptible to formation by the nurse, midwife, or whoever is standing in for society at the time. From birth and even before, the body must be controlled, cultivated, and manipulated (quite literally), so that it will be well-formed, attractive, and healthy. The shape of the body and its inner constitution are thus subject to the molding of civilization. The idea of a self left to grow all by itself appears to have been unthinkable. The infant's bath is the early regimen of the self.

The manipulation of the young male body (at least that of upper-class males) continued through childhood and adolescence. Galen's *Hygiene (De sanitate tuenda)* is devoted entirely to the manipulation of the body (primarily that of the male) from youth to old age. It gives elaborate advice about how to maintain the proper temperature of the body, the healthy balance of fluids and humors, the regulated evacuation of impurities, and the distribution of nutritives.[91]

Book 2 is concerned with the formation of the adolescent male body through exercise and massage. Massage is advocated partly to relax the muscles and relieve fatigue, but its most important purposes are three: to soften or harden the flesh, to thin or thicken the skin, and to open the pores to enable proper evacuation through the pores and the bowels.

As in all of Galen's system, the goal of treatment is balance and moderation. If the body is too soft, it will be susceptible to the deleterious effects of external agents such as cold, moisture, or impure pneumata; if too hard, the immature body's growth will be restricted. If it is too thick (which here means that the pores are too constricted), excrements from within the body—such as moisture, vapors, inadequately digested food—will not be evacuated. But if the body (here meaning primarily the flesh and the skin) is too "thin," then the pores will be too open, and precious materials will flow out (2. 12, p. 93; see also 1. 10, p. 33). Fortunately, however, proper care—especially exercise, massage, breath control, and baths—can mold the body to the appropriate balance.

The body of the boy is actually altered by massage therapy. If the therapist wishes to thicken the body, he will massage it firmly and vigorously; if he wishes to soften it, he will massage it gently. But he must be careful, for too much gentle massage will dissipate or diminish the flesh (2. 4, p. 67). The therapist may also wish to thicken and toughen the skin so as to constrict the pores (both the pores on the surface of the body and the internal pores that allow passage for materials within the body), in which case he will massage it firmly and rub the skin with powder or certain "constricting oils" (2. 6, p. 72).[92] In all this, massage serves as a mechanism for controlling the boundary between the body and its environment. There is no attempt, however, to maintain a completely firm, impenetrable boundary. Some movement of materials through the body's surface and within its innards is necessary. So the youth must be taught to hold his breath and force it downward during some forms of massage. This will force impurities to pass through his internal organs and then out through his muscles and skin, while the massage therapist manipulates the body's surface to open the pores.

In one chapter Galen gives elaborate instructions on how to administer a young man's first cold bath, an important tool in forming the beautiful, healthy body. The normal male body should not be exposed to the cold bath until the young man has reached a certain age, about "the middle of its fourth seven years" (that is, about twenty-five). The reason for waiting so long is that the cold bath regimen hardens the body and thickens and toughens the skin, thus making growth difficult. The cold bath, therefore, should be administered only to youths whose growth is complete. The time should be the beginning of summer, on a windless, warm day, during the warmest part of the day, in a gymnasium of the "most moderate temperature." The youth should be courageous and cheerful. He should first be rubbed vigorously by several men using coarse muslin (or even gloves made of muslin to facilitate vigorous rubbing) and, perhaps, oil. He should then exercise quickly and leap immediately into the cold water, avoiding getting wet gradually lest he shiver. Afterwards, he should be rubbed with oil by several masseurs and then eat more food than usual but take no drink. Galen advises that the same regimen be repeated for several days, although the desired alteration of the youthful body will be noticeable even after the first day: "On the following day they come to their exercise in better condition, having the same body weight as on the day before, but more compact and muscular and better-toned, and their skin thicker and tougher" (3. 4, p. 112).

Throughout Galen's diverse, detailed prescriptions one goal repeatedly surfaces: the masculinization of the young body. As I will explore more fully below, all bodies (male and female, young and old) fall somewhere on a spectrum from moist to dry, cold to hot, soft to hard. Women and infants are moister, colder, and softer than men. Effeminate (soft, *malakos*) men are those whose constitutions (including what we would call both psychological and physiological) are too moist or soft. The manipulation of the young body of such a man, from a very young age until the time of the first cold bath, has as its goal the gradual drying and hardening of the body until it arrives at the proper balance of cold/hot, moist/dry, soft/hard that characterizes the flesh of the aristocratic adult male. To this end, Galen is sure of his methods, boasting in one case, "I once took a child of thirteen years, and then, looking out for him after that during all the time of his growing age in accordance with the aforesaid objectives, have produced a youth well-balanced and symmetrical" (5. 3, p. 198). Although Galen is speaking particularly of the youth's legs, here, as elsewhere, his rhetoric makes clear that his real concern is the complete man, the physiological molding of the ideal upper-class self.

The Hierarchical Body

It is difficult for people today, imbued as we are with a modern "common sense" concerning the value of democratic egalitarianism, to appreciate how hierarchical and status-conscious Greco-Roman culture was. But, as has been repeatedly pointed out by historians, Roman society was a steep-sided pyramid, with carefully defined grades and an insistence on the natural, immutable place each person was to occupy in the hierarchy.[93] Furthermore, as Mary Douglas says, "The social body constrains the way the physical body is perceived"—and no location of ancient ideology illustrates her point more clearly than Greco-Roman society's hierarchical construction of the body.[94]

As I have already noted, the "governing" part of the body, variously spoken of as the soul or mind, was the highest-status member of the body or, alternatively, was thought of as a separate entity that ruled over the body. In Plato's *Phaedo* the soul is to the body as master to slave or divine to mortal (80A). The Stoics pictured the functioning of the senses and their influence on the different parts of the body as a hierarchical chain of command. Calcidius, a fourth-century Christian writer, reports that Chrysippus taught that "the soul as a whole despatches the senses (which are its proper functions) like branches from the trunk-like commanding-faculty to be reporters of what they sense, while itself like a monarch passes judgement on their reports."[95] Plutarch speaks of the mind as if it were a superior, but benevolent, intellectual who must at times give in to the needs of the weaker body, characterized as a lower-class manual laborer. He advises that good health can be maintained only if the mind is willing to leave its own endeavors for periodic care and exercise of the body: "This is just what happens to the mind: if it is unwilling to relax a little and give up to the body in distress and need, a little later a fever or a vertigo attacks it, and it is compelled to give up its books and discussions and studies, and share with the body its sickness and weariness. . . . When the body shares most in the work and weariness of the mind we should repay it by giving it the most care and attention" (*Advice about Keeping Well* [*Moralia* 137D–E]). This ancient form of body/soul dualism thus—not coincidentally—reflects the class structure of society.

The other parts and functions of the body also reflect the social hierarchy. Plato explains that the human head is spherical because that is the shape of divinities and the head is the most divine part of the body, ruling the rest. In fact, the body is a mere vehicle for the head, designed to carry it about and keep it from rolling around on the ground (*Timaeus* 44D)! The trunk of the body is divided by the midriff, as a partition between the superior and the inferior innards, "rather as a house is divided into men and women's quarters" (70A; see 70D–71A for other images of the body's hierarchy). Ptolemy, writing in the first half of the second century, explained psychological functions as physiological operations in different geographical locations of the body, each of which has some status assignment: "Sensory motions take place in the corresponding sense organ, appetitive motions in the area below the liver, emotive motions in the area around the heart (these last include cases of pleasure, pain, fear, and anger), and only cognitive motions occur when the remaining parts of the body are at rest but the head is being filled, like effects 'distributed' from the permanent internal movement."[96]

This was not merely a philosophical topos; it occurs in more popular contexts as well. Artemidorus, for example, points out in his *Dream Handbook* that parts of the body have status significance in dreams. The head represents one's father, the foot a slave; or, in another scheme, the right hand represents male family members, the left hand female. In another context, Artemidorus has the eyes represent one's daughters and the feet one's slaves. The status of the penis is ambiguous: it may represent one's parents, wife, or children; or, since it is called the "essential" or "necessary" thing (*anagkaion, anagkē*), it may in a dream indicate "poverty, slavery, and bonds"—this because the Greek word *anagkē*, though often used euphemistically for "penis," also provoked thoughts of constraint and hence slavery in the minds of Greek speakers.[97] In other words, the interpretation of the different parts of the body is flexible, though in every case a hierarchy is assumed.

Body hierarchy often expressed itself in the ways in which Greco-Roman writers explained the dynamics of the body's innards. The body's parts, humors, fluids, and forces were pictured as agents or aspects of a social economy, and their interaction was described in the terms of political power struggles. Indeed, the ancient physician was an economist of the corporeal *polis*. Galen explains, for example, how nourishment is distributed to different parts of the body according to their different natures and status (here portrayed as strength and weakness). The different parts expel excrement by sending it to "some adjacent region," like modern states trying to export their toxic waste. The unequal levels of strength in the body can lead to the same kinds of problems as society experiences due to inequalities. "If therefore the affected part has a strong constitution of body it does not receive what is sent, so that it shows the patient continually suffering only in that part first affected; but if it is weaker than that from which the excrement was sent, it receives it, but again sends it to some one of the weaker parts, and that again to another, until the excrement arrives at some one of those having none weaker than they."[98] Galen is explaining, albeit none too clearly, that in order for the body to be healthy, excrement must be expelled. Since stronger parts can refuse to receive it from weaker parts, while weaker parts cannot refuse to receive it from stronger parts, the weaker parts are stuck with more of the excrement, thus making them more susceptible to disease: the body has its own social and economic pecking order. This fits nicely Galen's assumption, outlined elsewhere in the same work, that people of lower socioeconomic status, due to their lack of leisure and education, will of necessity have a more difficult time warding off disease and maintaining their health. They are the "weaker" members of the economic body.[99]

Hierarchy was also inscribed on the ancient body in the way sexuality was constructed. The human body—whether of a man or a woman—was understood to comprise male and female aspects. As Thomas Laqueur demonstrates, sexuality in the ancient world was construed less in terms of a dichotomy between male and female and more as a spectrum in which masculinity occupied one pole, femininity the other. Laqueur calls this the "one-sex" model, as opposed to our modern "two-sex" model. "Thus the old model, in which men and women were arrayed according to their degree of metaphysical perfection, their vital heat, along an axis whose telos was male, gave way by the late eighteenth century to a new model of radical dimorphism, of biological divergence. An anatomy and physiology of incommensurability replaced a metaphysics of hierarchy in the representation of woman in relation to man."[100]

As Laqueur emphasizes, the male–female continuum was always hierarchical. It is well known that Aristotelian theory held women to be incomplete males: their bodies had simply never achieved the level of dryness, heat, and solidity that constituted masculinity.[101] The very flesh of women is colder, moister, softer, and more porous than that of men. Some other theorists seem not to accept the notion that females are colder than males. But then some other factor comes into play to inscribe their physiological inferiority.[102] Regardless, female inferiority is physiological. According to Hippocratic theories, the state of the womb during gestation determines the sex and constitution of the child. A hot, dry womb will produce male infants and infants of strong constitution. Females and weak infants are produced by cold, wet wombs. The sexual partners will produce a male child if they follow a "hot" and "dry" diet, a female if a "cool" and "moist" diet ("hot" and "cool" here refer more to the kind of food and drink—that is, what kind of bodily reaction the food gives rise to—than to the mere temperature).[103] Female seed is thinner and takes longer to coagulate. According to the Hippocratic "On Generation," the female fetus takes about forty-two days to form, the male thirty, because "the female embryo coagulates and is differentiated later, since the female seed is both weaker and more fluid than the male." The male fetus begins to move at three months, the weaker female fetus only at four months.[104]

This hot/cold, dry/moist, hard/soft system does not relate simply to the division between men and women. Every body contains the same spectrum within it. The care of infants, in fact, is designed to emphasize as much as possible the higher, masculine end of the spectrum. Infants tend to be moister, old men drier; a healthy body will be one that maintains the right equilibrium for its age. Soranus advocates, therefore, that one not feed an infant on milk after the body has become "solid," because "the body becomes moist and therefore delicate if fed on milk for too long a time." [105] As is clear from these statements, too much moisture or softness indicates weakness. Galen's *Hygiene* explains the link between "moist conditions," physiology, and environment as follows: "In moist conditions one must suspect either untimely use of sex relations or weakening of the strength from some other cause; or thinning of the body from excessively gentle massage, or from too much bathing, or from the air of the house in which he lived being warmer than necessary" (5. 2, p. 193). Much of Galen's hygienic and therapeutic method reads like a training manual designed to maintain the right degree of heat, dryness, and compactness for the masculinization of the young man's body and to keep it from slipping down the precarious slope to femininity.

According to the ancient ideology, then, every human body, male or female, occupies some position on the spectrum male–female, a position that could be discerned by the carefully trained scientist. The Pseudo-Aristotelian *Physiognomy*, for example, describes the "low-spirited man" thus: "His face is wrinkled, his eyes are dry and weak, but at the same time weakness of eye signifies two things, softness [*malakos*] and effeminacy [*thēlu*] on the one hand, depression and lack of spirit on the other. He is stooping [*tapeinos*] in figure and feeble [*apēgoreukōs*] in his movements" (808a9–13). The man's weak eye is linked to softness of flesh and hence to the feminine. Contrary to modern heterosexist ideology, be it noted, effeminacy has no relation to homosexuality. The same text explains how to recognize men categorized as "charitable" types: they are "delicate-looking, pale-complexioned and bright-eyed; their nostrils are wrinkled and they are ever prone to tears. These characters are fond of women and inclined to have female children; they are amorous (*erōtikoi*) by nature, inclined to be reminiscent, of good dispositions and warm hearts" (808a34–38). Since this type of physiological condition is closer to the feminine end of the continuum, such men are weak, effeminate, overly fond of sex *with women*, and liable to produce female offspring.

Entire species, according to the *Physiognomy*, can be located on the male–female continuum. Lions are more male (regardless of whether the particular lion is male or female), panthers more female—"petty, thieving and, generally speaking, deceitful" (810a8). Ethnic groups, as well as people with different shades of skin color, may also be categorized in this way: dark-skinned people are cowardly, on analogy with Ethiopians and Egyptians; but overly light-skinned people are also cowardly, on analogy with women (812a13).

As with other aspects of the Greco-Roman body, the male–female hierarchy reflects the cosmic hierarchy. As such, the Greco-Roman fascination with active and passive roles in society is inscribed in the masculinization and feminization of the human body. According to Ptolemy, the universal elements may all be placed in some position on this active–passive axis: "Earth and water are more material and altogether passive, fire and air are more capable of causing movement and are both passive and active, *aither* is always in the same condition and is active only. Among the compounds too, we apply the term 'body' properly to what is more material and less active and 'soul' to what moves both itself and body. It is therefore reasonable that the body should be classed with the elements of earth and water and the soul with the elements of fire, air and *aither*."[106] As is now well known, sex in Greco-Roman society was construed as necessarily implicated in this active–passive system. Women are weaker than men and therefore rightly play no active role in sexual intercourse. Boys resemble women in physique, so may rightly play the passive role in sex with men. Even outside the specifically sexual arena, those persons, things, or forces understood as active were construed positively as masculine; those seen to be passive were, negatively, feminine.

Thus, all the various aspects of the self were hierarchically arranged. A firm social hierarchy existed within the body of the ancient person, favoring male over female, strength over weakness, superior over inferior. Each individual body, moreover, could be placed confidently at some location in the physiological hierarchy of nature. In other words, each body held its hierarchy within itself, and every body occupied its proper place in the hierarchy of society and nature. Health was threatened when that hierarchy was disrupted.

The Beautifully Balanced Body

Conveniently enough for upper-class ideology, the proper status to be assigned to any body was displayed on its surface. In popular Greco-Roman culture, bodies were direct expressions of status, usually pictured as a vertical spectrum stretching from inhuman or barbaric ugliness to divine beauty. The gods, of course, were beautiful; and people of aristocratic birth or upper-class origins were expected to manifest their proximity to the divine by possessing a natural beauty and nobility. This cultural common sense recurs repeatedly in novels. In Chariton's *Chareas and Callirhoe*, for example, Callirhoe, the aristo-cratic heroine, is regularly mistaken for an apparition of Aphrodite. Although it is not as much emphasized in the novels, the converse assumption was also made: people of lower status were expected to be misshapen and ugly.[107]

The connection of beauty with status comes out also in the physiognomies. The Pseudo-Aristotelian text begins its list of different physiognomic types with a series of dichotomies between good and bad types, all of which can be readily recognized by physical traits: the brave man and the coward, the "easy dispositioned" and the "insensitive," the orderly and the shameless, the high-spirited and the low-spirited. In each case the positive type is character-ized by typical Greco-Roman concepts of beauty, whereas the negative type is consistently unattractive.[108]

Rhetoricians seem to have read physiognomies carefully and to have used what they learned from them both to improve their own bodily appearance in performances and to attack their opponents. Maximus of Tyre mentions physiognomy in a discussion of the proper delivery of an oration.[109] Polemo at-tacked a rival sophist, Favorinus, Plutarch's friend, using physiognomic analy-sis, pointing to his weakness of body as proof of his weakness of character.[110] Bodily appearance was so important for Greco-Roman status attribution that physiognomy attained a place in rhetorical curricula, according to Elizabeth Evans, becoming "a commonplace in Greek and Roman treatment of rhetori-cal theory and practice."[111] The rhetorician, like any other upper-class man, naturally wants to distance himself from any perception of bodily weakness, since that would necessarily imply social weakness. In Evans's words, "Physi-cal excellence must be associated with the wise man, since no excellence can be granted to the common man."[112]

In this ideological configuration, the perfect body was taken to reside at the elite end of a spectrum. It was divinely beautiful and partook of no weak-ness, commonality, or ugliness. In collusion with this ideological common sense, however, was another, somewhat different way of configuring the per-fect body: namely, as a mean between unacceptable extremes. This placement of the body was part of a wider Greco-Roman ideology of moderation and the mean. Again, physiognomics proves revealing. The writer of the Pseudo-Aristotelian handbook explains that in most things the "mean" or "middle" (*meson*) is desirable. Chests should be neither too caved in nor too thrust out (810b33). Eyes should be neither too small nor too large: "Those who have small eyes are small-minded; this is appropriate and also applies to monkeys. The large-eyed are sluggish: witness cattle. Therefore, the best-natured must have neither large nor small eyes" (811b19). Dark-skinned as well as light-skinned people are cowardly; only men of moderate color are courageous (812a13). A body that is too cool may be too feminine; but excessive heat, evident from an overly ruddy complexion, indicates madness: "those who are excessively heated would naturally be insane" (812a22).

Galen's therapeutics is founded on the same presuppositions. He writes: "The best-blended person is between the extremes of thinness and fatness, softness and hardness, warmth and cold. In soul likewise he is midway between rashness and cowardice, slowness and recklessness, pity and envy. He is kind, affectionate, humane, and prudent."[113] Of course, he must not be *too* kind or affectionate. As Galen writes in *On the Passions and Errors of the Soul*, "In my opinion, excessive vehemence in loving or hating anything is also a passion; I think the saying 'moderation is best' is correct, since no immoderate action is good."[114] In line with this ideology, Galen urges that all activities, especially eating and sex, be policed according to the principle of moderation: "And to all who read this, both laymen and doctors, I would give the common advice not to eat, like most men, as dumb animals do, and be like them, but to judge by experience what foods and drinks are injurious to them and what and how much activities. And likewise also with regard to sex relations, to observe whether they are harmless to them or injurious, and at what interval of days they are harmless or harmful."[115]

It seems never to have occurred to these theorists to wonder how one could so confidently know what particular constitution occupied the "middle." After all, for most of us the middle is wherever *we* are. The egocentrism of the Greco-Roman upper class, however, should by now come as no surprise. The ideology of the mean, inscribed upon and within the human body, was one among many techniques that enabled the Greco-Roman upper class to maintain its power and the hierarchical structure of society. Then, as now and often throughout history, emphasis on moderation and the middle functioned conservatively to solidify the status quo as defined by the upper class. By retaining the power to define beauty, status, and nature, the upper class maintained its position as the creator of the Greco-Roman body.

I have referred in this chapter to *the* Greco-Roman concept of the body, misleadingly giving the impression, perhaps, that the ancient body was a stable, monolithic construction consonant with upper-class ideology. The perpetrators of this dominant ideology were not completely successful, however, in their attempts to insinuate their view of the body throughout society, and later in the book I will point to various aspects of ancient body construction that differed from the upper-class body outlined in this chapter. In Chapter 6, for example, I argue that concepts of disease held by uneducated, lower-class members of Greco-Roman society reflect a different construction of the body from that assumed by the medical and scientific writers and their educated readers. I have felt it important, though, to begin with a detailed description of the body as perceived by the upper class, because it is against this background that the Corinthian disputes over the body took place. Paul's own views concerning the body and the dangers to it sometimes reflect this ideology; but at other times he opposes this view with presuppositions about the body, its boundaries, and its dangers that must have appeared odd or incomprehensible to his more educated converts. At each point, we must keep in mind that at least some of Paul's first auditors—who, as we will see, show evidence of exposure to philosophical ideas and thus were probably of higher social standing than most members of the Corinthian congregation—assumed a construction of the body like that sketched above: a microcosmic body hierarchically arranged and beautifully balanced, formed by the *paideia* of cultured society to portray on its surface the nobility of its character.

We must not concentrate so much on the individual human body, however, that we forget that it was but an instance of the social body. The same dynamics and mechanics that were expected to operate within the individual body provided the political rhetoric for the operation of the body politic; and just as there were conflicting ideologies of the individual body, so there were conflicting views of the proper dynamics of the social body. Paul's wish to convince the Corinthian church of the validity of his own theological and ethical opinions would necessitate both appropriating and modifying their assumptions regarding the body—each of their bodies and their communal body. The rhetoric of the social body, especially as portrayed in speeches on concord or harmony, is the subject of the next chapter.

2 _The Rhetoric of the Body Politic_

"If one were to run through the entire list of citizens, I believe he would not discover even two men in Tarsus who think alike, but on the contrary, just as with certain incurable and distressing diseases which are accustomed to pervade the whole body, exempting no member of it from their inroads, so this state of discord, this almost complete estrangement of one from another, has invaded your entire body politic."[1] When Dio Chrysostom spoke these words in Tarsus, probably around the beginning of the second century, he was drawing on a long rhetorical tradition that portrayed the polis, the city-state, as a body, and strife, discord, or any civil disturbance as a disease that must be eradicated from it. Within "deliberative" rhetoric—that is, rhetoric urging a political body toward some course of action—a popular topic was concord, or unity. Indeed, _homonoia_ ("concord") speeches, as they were known in Greek (the Latin was _concordia_), became practically a genre unto themselves, with predictable patterns, set clichés and examples, and an identifiable ideology. Professional rhetoricians delivered homonoia speeches at times of crisis or sometimes, it seems, simply for entertainment; historians embedded such speeches in their narratives at appropriate places; and the topic could be modified slightly to provide material for letters.

As a recent study by Margaret M. Mitchell has demonstrated, 1 Corinthians may be categorized, according to Greco-Roman rhetorical genres, as a deliberative letter—one could say a speech in epistolary form—urging concord and following the traditional strategies and topoi of homonoia speeches. The thesis (the Greek technical term is *prothesis*) for the entire letter is found in 1 Corinthians 1:10: "I encourage you, brothers, by the name of our Lord Jesus Christ, that you all agree and that you allow no schisms to exist among yourselves, but that you be mended together in the same mind and the same opinion."[2] Sometimes in the letter Paul will explicitly recall his theme "that there be no ruptures (schisms) in the body," as he does in 12:25; but even when not so explicit, Paul's constant concern throughout the letter is the unity of the church, Christ's body. Many of the terms Paul employs are borrowed directly from Greek homonoia speeches, and his rhetorical strategy of urging the Corinthians to do what is beneficial and what will make for the common advantage, rather than exercising their complete autonomy, is that of homonoia speeches. Mitchell's work has so decisively demonstrated that 1 Corinthians fits the ancient rhetorical category of the homonoia speech that I will not belabor the point. Something that should be examined further, however, is the ideological function of homonoia speeches.

The Ideology of Concord

As Dio's words above indicate, homonoia speeches regularly took the polis, which could stand for any social group, to be a body, and rebellion, factionalism, or discord (*stasis*) to be a disease. Sometimes the ancients appear to have thought of discord as an invasive agent, attacking the body politic from without. Aelius Aristides—to modern scholars the most famous patient (or hypochondriac)—said in a speech on concord, "Everywhere faction is a terrible, disruptive thing, and like consumption. For having fastened itself to the body politic it drains off, sucks out, and depletes all its strength, and does not cease until it has entirely worn it away, using the sick themselves as a means for their own destruction."[3] More commonly, however, rhetoricians talk about strife in the political body as an illness resulting not from external infectious agents but from an imbalance in the body's internal constituents.[4] Just as illness is usually portrayed by medical writers as a disruption of the natural harmony and balance of the body's essences, humors, and states (hot/cold, moist/dry), so discord is usually envisaged as the disruption of the natural concord of the different groups and classes that make up the body politic.[5] Like the private body, the public body is a hierarchy, with different members (in this case, classes) assigned by Nature to positions in the body and to particular roles in the harmonious cooperation of the body's parts.[6]

Homonoia speeches always assume that the body is hierarchically constituted and that illness or social disruption occurs when that hierarchy is disrupted. Moreover, the particular form taken by social disruption is class conflict. Even when the social situation must have been more complex than a simple opposition between "rich" and "poor," the speeches, almost without fail, portray the conflict as between two groups in the ancient city: the small upper class (the "haves") and the large lower class (the "have-nots"), comprising for the most part the rest of the population. The complexity of the actual conflicts pitting various groups against one another over a variety of issues, which we can sometimes glimpse through the rhetoric of the speeches, is masked by the typical portrayal of social strife as one between the two dominant classes of ancient political thought.

Thus, in a speech to the Rhodians on concord, Aelius Aristides praises Solon, the quasi-legendary Greek forefather and lawgiver: "He was most of all proud of the fact that he brought the people together with the rich, so that they might dwell in harmony in their city, neither side being stronger than was expedient for all in common" (*Oration* 24. 14). When Dio speaks in Tarsus he addresses the *dēmos:* that is, the main body of citizens, as opposed to the small ruling class. At times, Dio concentrates on conflicts between the Council (*boulē*), which was understood to represent the interests of the small upper class, and the Assembly (*ekklēsia*) of the large lower class of citizens, the demos (*Discourse* 34. 16, 21).[7] In the same speech, Dio advises the demos on its conflicts with a different group, the city's linen-workers, who are apparently agitating for more civic privileges and possibly citizenship (34. 23). Still elsewhere in the same speech, Dio speaks of the conflicts between Tarsus and some smaller, neighboring towns (34. 10–11). The various conflicts are structured as one conflict, however, that between the strong and the weak. The simple class struggle between a small upper class and a large lower class thus provided the lens through which all sorts of social conflicts were viewed.

The ideological purpose of homonoia speeches was to mitigate conflict by reaffirming and solidifying the hierarchy of society. To this end, certain topoi (set examples) recur with tiresome regularity. A favorite device is to show how the political hierarchy of the city mirrors the harmonious hierarchy of the cosmos. The cosmos works well because each cosmic entity knows its place in the cosmic body. As Aelius Aristides says, "The sun proceeds in its course ever preserving its proper place, and the phases of the moon and the motion of the stars go on, and the revolutions and the positions of each in respect to one another and their proper distances, and again their harmonies are preserved, since agreement prevails among them, and there are no differences present nor do they arise, but all things have yielded to the law of nature and they use one will concerning all their duties, so that if imitation of the gods is an act of men of good sense, it would be the part of men of good sense to believe that they are all a unity, as far as is possible" (*Oration* 23. 77). As Dio points out, not only the heavenly bodies (sun, moon, and stars) but also the "elements" (*stoicheia*) of the cosmos embody concord (*Discourse* 38. 11). Air, earth, water, fire, and ether are all hierarchically arranged, "not only the more powerful (*ischyrotera*) and greater, but also those reputed to be the weaker" (*ta elattō*, 40. 35).[8]

The topos of the cosmos = polis could follow a reverse journey, being borrowed from homonoia contexts and appropriated for use in explaining physics. Thus the Pseudo-Aristotelian *On the Cosmos* explains the *synkrisis* (mixture) of the elements of the cosmos by appeal to commonplaces about concord, noting that opposite classes of people work together to make up the city. "It is as if men should wonder how a city survives, composed as it is of the most opposite classes (I mean rich and poor, young and old, weak and strong, bad and good). They do not recognize that the most wonderful thing of all about the harmonious working (*politikēs homonoias*) of a city-community is this: that out of plurality and diversity it achieves a homogeneous unity capable of admitting every variation and degree" (5.396b, trans. Furley). It is worth noting that in the joining of these hierarchically arranged opposites the hierarchy itself is not challenged. In fact, since opposites are necessary for each other's existence, it would appear that the weak and poor are necessary to balance the strong and rich—in the city as well as the cosmos. Homonoia has as its aim not equality or strength for all members but the preservation of the "natural" relation of strength to weakness.[9]

This same ideology is evident in another topos of homonoia speeches: the state as a household. The household lives harmoniously when the different members—paterfamilias, wife, children, slaves—all occupy their proper positions with mutual respect but submission to those above them in the familial pyramid.[10] The necessity of interdependence and mutuality between the different members does not in any way imply equality. According to Dio, in a concordant household the parents may even enjoy "friendship" (*philia*) with their children; but, contrary to the philosophical notion that friendship implies or necessitates equality, Dio has no intention of advocating equality between parents and their children, much less with their slaves or freed persons (*Discourse* 40. 41).

In homonoia speeches the point is sometimes made that those of higher status may need to yield in some matter to those of lower status and accommodate their demands to the needs of the "weaker" for the sake of concord and the good of the whole. As Aelius Aristides puts it, in a passage combining many of the elements we have already examined, "Let each side dispense with its envy and greed. I speak of the envy felt by the poor for the rich, and of the greed of the rich against the poor. In sum, imitate the form and fashion of a household. What is this? There are rulers in a household, the fathers of the sons and the masters of the slaves. How do these administer their households well? Whenever the rulers do not think they can do anything [they please], but voluntarily give up some of their authority, and the others accept as authoritative whatever their superiors decide" (*Oration* 24. 32–33). Thus, yielding to the other and giving up one's private interest for the sake of the common good is a regular theme of homonoia speeches, and sometimes this entails the stronger yielding to the weaker.[11]

As the above quotation from Aelius Aristides shows, however, this momentary yielding constitutes no challenge to the normal and natural hierarchy of the political body, any more than a momentary acquiescence to his son's importuning would mean a surrender of the father's power. Indeed, there existed in the Greco-Roman world a conservative ideology, which may be called benevolent patriarchalism, that maintained social hierarchy by urging the lower class to submit to those in authority and the higher class to rule benevolently and gently, accommodating its own demands in order to protect the interests of those lower down the social scale.[12] Those of higher status might sometimes be encouraged to yield to those of lower status on a particular point; but within the context of benevolent patriarchalism this yielding was not to result in any actual status reversal or confusion. The upper class must continue to rule from a higher position of benevolent but firm strength.

Benevolent patriarchal ideology portrays itself as offering a middle way between two political extremes. In Greco-Roman political writings and speeches, democracy is portrayed as the excessive freedom of the masses and the enslavement of the upper class (the "natural" leaders) to the lower class, resulting in chaos. Tyranny, at the other extreme, is portrayed as excessively harsh and unbending rule whereby the upper class, an oligarchic faction, or a dictator rules without taking into account sufficiently the interests of the entire political body, including the masses. But when the stronger rules the weaker with restraint and the weaker submits to the stronger in self-control, the interests of the entire city are protected, and everybody lives happily ever after.

Dio Cassius, grandson of Dio Chrysostom, describes conflicts in Rome that were ancient even in his time (they took place in 495 B.C.E.) in such terms:

Those whose money gave them influence [*hoi ischyontes tois chrēmasin*] desired to surpass their inferiors in all respects as though they were their
sovereigns, and the weaker citizens [*hoi asthenesteroi*], sure of their own
equal rights, were unwilling to obey them even in the smallest particular. The one class [i.e., the lower], insatiate of freedom, sought to enjoy
also the possessions of the other; and this other class [the higher], uncontrolled in its desire for public honours, was bent also on subjecting the
persons of the former class. So it was that they sundered their former relations, wherein they had been wont harmoniously to assist each other
with material profit, and no longer made distinctions between the citizen
and the foreigner. Indeed, both classes disdained moderation, the one setting its heart upon an extreme of authority, the other upon an extreme of
resistance to servitude [*ethelodouleia*].[13]

It should be noted that moderation is expected to be differently embodied
when practiced by the two classes. For the upper class, moderation consists
in being satisfied with its superior position and the general obedience of the
lower class but resisting the temptation to attain ever more honors and an even
greater share of the economic pie. For the lower class, moderation consists in
being satisfied with citizenship and some freedom but resisting the temptation
to struggle for economic equality, portrayed by the ancient ideology as envy
of the riches of the upper class. Far from being a *moderate* ideology, therefore,
benevolent patriarchalism was consistently quite conservative, geared to maintaining the class structure by advocating only *moderate* exploitation of the lower
class.[14]

Ancient speakers on homonoia sometimes recognize the conservative ideological function of the advice that the strong should at times yield to the
weak. Plutarch, for example, explains how Theopompus modified his harsh
oligarchic Spartan constitution to admit some input from the ephors. He was
criticized for giving up power but defended his actions by claiming that *some*
sharing of power would give the monarchy greater longevity. Plutarch explains: "By renouncing excessive claims and freeing itself from jealous hate,
royalty [*basileia*] at Sparta escaped its perils, so that the Spartan kings did not
experience the fate which the Messenians and Argives inflicted upon their
kings, who were unwilling to yield at all or remit their power in favour of
the people" (*to dēmotikon*).[15] The moderation of benevolent patriarchalism was
opposed, on the one hand, to the radicalness of democracy, which would dangerously turn the natural status hierarchy upside-down, and, on the other, to
tyranny, which would endanger itself by inflexibility. Plutarch, among many

others, recognized the conservative goal of this benevolent treatment of inferiors: the lower classes would submit more readily if well treated.

As I have indicated, benevolent patriarchalism was not the only ideology around. Democratic rhetoric certainly existed, although we only have glimpses of what it must have been like, which is not surprising, since the surviving literature was almost all written by and for the upper class. Some texts do echo, albeit faintly, an oppositional rhetoric that challenged benevolent patriarchalism. In his speech *On the Peace*, for example, Isocrates (fourth century B.C.E.) addresses the people of Athens at a time when the constitution was democratic and the air filled with populist rhetoric. Throughout the speech, Isocrates tries to persuade the Athenian populace to ignore the demagogues and give up imperial pretentions; he says that justice requires the independence and self-rule of all the Greek city-states. He argues that it is not to the Athenians' *true* advantage to grasp for more and more power; they should be content with what they have. Isocrates makes the point—and seems able to assume agreement from his audience—that all the Athenians "once upon a time" believed that it was not just for the stronger to rule over the weaker (*tous kreittous tōn ēttonōn archein*). Isocrates appears to build his argument here on a rejection of the benevolent patriarchal dogma (which he elsewhere in the same speech accepts: §91) that the strong *ought* to rule over the weak. His momentary appropriation of the democratic theme that it is unjust for the strong to rule over the weak is probably viable only because he must make his case within a political climate imbued with democratic ideology.

Demosthenes (a younger contemporary of Isocrates) in a similar situation makes a similar move. In a letter attempting to persuade the demos to allow him to return to Athens, he uses the commonplace of the polis as a household. Contrary to normal usage, however, he puts himself and other leaders in the position of children and the populace in the position of parents, reversing the normal statuses of the topos. This is obviously due to the democratic forces with which Demosthenes has to deal. Elsewhere, he repeatedly aligns himself with the "democracy"—that is, the people—and likens his enemies to the traditional enemy of the people, the "oligarchs." [16] Since both Isocrates and Demosthenes are dealing with a democratic populace, the hierarchical assumptions of benevolent patriarchalism are, at least momentarily, either set aside or challenged.

In one text we find a spectrum of ideological positions when dealing with civic conflict. In his account of the strike of the Roman plebs, Dionysius of Halicarnassus (writing in the first century B.C.E. about an event that took place in 492 B.C.E.) presents several speeches, some by members of the Senate and a few by leaders of the sedition. One senator, urging the Senate to face the problem, delivers a typical homonoia speech, bemoaning the fact that Rome has been split into two cities, "one of which is ruled by poverty and necessity, and the other by satiety and insolence" (6. 36, trans. Cary). The next day, when the Senate convenes again, three speeches are given, advising different policies. Publius Verginius, who has a "democratic" reputation (*dēmotikos*), advocates a "middle" course (*meson*): the Senate should forgive the debts of the plebs who recently fought in a battle, as well as those of their families; but the rest of the people should still be responsible for their debts. Titus Larcius offers a still more liberal solution: all the people (*dēmos*) should be forgiven their debts, "for only thus can we make the whole state harmonious." The third speaker, Appius Claudius, is the most conservative, insisting that the Senate should never yield to the masses. Rather, a dictator should be appointed to act in the interests of the "common good" (*koinos*). In spite of the appeal to the common interest, this is actually a plan that will meet the demands of only the upper class. After all, anyone could (and usually had to) appeal to that chimera of "common interest."[17]

Later, Dionysius relates the speeches of the senatorial delegation sent to appeal to the plebs. The first is a conciliatory speech very much in the homonoia style, with many of its commonplaces. Lucius Junius, a leader of the plebs, answers with a "democratic" rejection of the envoys' offer in a speech that attacks the patricians and the Senate by claiming that they always act only in the interests of their own class, the rich. Throughout, he urges the plebs, whom he designates *hoi tapeinoi* (the "lowly" or "humble"), to stand up for their own interests. The scene ends with a conciliatory homonoia speech by Menenius Agrippa, a moderate senator, who relates the famous fable about the body that perished because the different members rebelled against the belly, representing the ruling class. Along the way, Menenius notes that the ignorant (the plebs) will always need prudent leadership, while the Senate "will always need multitudes willing to be ruled."[18] Menenius advocates a middle position, that of benevolent patriarchalism; he urges the maintenance of traditional hierarchical roles tempered with concern for the good of the lower class. This middle position is flanked on the democratic side by the speech of Lucius Junius and on the oligarchic side by the speech given before the Senate by Appius Claudius. The ideological lesson is that benevolent patriarchalism provides the only chance of success, because it avoids the extremes of excessive freedom and status disruption on the one side and excessive tyranny and oppression on the other.

As Dionysius's narrative implies, homonoia rhetoric could be addressed to higher- as well as lower-class audiences, with some modifications, of course. Two homonoia speeches by Dio Chrysostom are interesting, because they are addressed to two different audiences, one occupying the position of the stronger, the other that of the weaker. I have already mentioned Dio's speech at Tarsus. One of the goals of that speech was to resolve a conflict between Tarsus, a large, powerful city, and the smaller neighboring towns (34. 10–11). Dio argues that Tarsus is so strong that it can afford to be magnanimous and yield to the smaller towns in border disputes without fearing that its superior status will be threatened. With a tone of disdain, Dio says, "It may be true that, if Mallus because of the dunes and the pasturage on the sand were likely to become greater than Tarsus, you ought possibly to show so much concern; but as it is, disgrace and mockery are all you stand to gain from the objects of your quarrel" (34. 46). In Dio's view, the stronger should yield to the weaker as long as the condescension does not lead to an actual reversal of positions; indeed, if they do not yield at all, they will be perceived as small-minded and petty.[19] But Tarsus will be looked on "with admiration and affection" if it leads "mildly" and "considerately" (34. 47; cf. 34. 50).

One might expect that when he turns to the "lesser" in such a dispute, Dio would leave behind benevolent patriarchalism and employ a more democratic strategy; but such is not the case. In *Discourse* 38 he addresses Nicomedia about its dispute with Nicea, the greater of the two cities. In the first place, Dio insists to the Nicomedians that what they really want (what is in their "true" interest) is not just the *title* of "first city" but actually to *be* the first city (38. 30–31). He then explains that the way to achieve this is not by conflict with Nicea over the title but by being a better benefactor of the smaller cities in the area dependent upon Nicomedia—that is, by outdoing Nicea in benefaction (38. 32). Finally, he urges Nicomedia to show that it is concerned with the interests of *all* Bithynia, precisely the kind of concern expected of a well-off patron (38. 33). He nowhere questions the naturalness of hierarchy. For Dio, the real embarrassment would be to claim a status that one does not really, or "naturally," have (38. 38). As he says, evoking the traditional topos of speech versus deeds, "Titles are not guarantees of deeds, but deeds of titles" (38. 40, my trans.). There is nothing wrong with a man seeking recognition as "first" or "king" but only with reaching beyond himself and seeking the title without actually being "first." In line with benevolent patriarchalism everywhere in the ancient world, Dio does not object to the status hierarchy; he simply insists that words should fit facts and that the natural hierarchy should be recognized.[20]

As these texts demonstrate, Paul lived in a society with a long tradition of rhetorical treatments of concord. That tradition was heavily implicated, moreover, in a particular ideology of social control that I have called "benevolent patriarchalism." Beyond categorizing 1 Corinthians as a homonoia letter, therefore, we must examine the ideological significance of Paul's rhetoric against the backdrop of other treatments of concord in his culture. As I will argue below, Paul's appropriation of the rhetoric of unity is surprising and quite at odds with the dominant goal of homonoia speeches, which is to solidify the social hierarchy by averting lower-class challenges to the so-called natural status structures that prevail in society. Paul was well acquainted with the rhetoric of concord, but in 1 Corinthians he turns it against its usual role as a prop for upper-class ideology. To some extent my case here depends on the assumption that Paul was himself a rather skilled rhetorician. Is it possible that a Jewish leather-worker who calls himself a Pharisee and decries the use of rhetoric and worldly wisdom could actually have been rather well trained in Greco-Roman rhetoric? In order to answer this question, I must make a short detour to demonstrate the importance of Greco-Roman rhetoric for Paul's presentation of himself in 1 Corinthians.

The Status of Rhetoric

Several times in 1 Corinthians 1–4 Paul disparages rhetoric and insists that he is making no use of rhetorical skill and training in his preaching or letters. But he protests too much. In 1:17 he says that he preaches "not with rhetorical technique" (*ouk en sophia logou*). I have here translated the Greek to reflect recent research showing that Paul's language does not refer simply to philosophy (although in 1 Cor. 1–4 he wishes to impugn philosophy as well) but that he is attacking rhetoric in particular.[21] *Sophia*, most often translated "wisdom," also means what we would call "technique" or "skill." Coupled with *logos*, another word with a wide range of meanings in Greek but one that here probably refers to public speech, the term is meant to signal that Paul self-consciously eschewed rhetorical techniques in his presentation of his message in Corinth.[22] In 1:20 Paul links together the Hellenistic moral-philosophical sage (*sophos*), the Jewish "scribe" (*grammateus*), and the "debater" (*suzētētēs*, a rhetorically trained person who might join in actual or staged debates on any number of topics in a law court, a lecture hall, or a private home).[23] Paul distances himself from all three. In 2:1 and 2:4 he again claims that he first preached to the Corinthians without any "excellence of speech or skill (or wisdom, *sophia*)" and not in "persuasive and skillful speeches" (*en peithois sophias logois*). To anyone in

Greco-Roman society, the phrase would immediately recall the terminology of rhetorical training. In 2:13 Paul emphasizes that what he is rejecting is the kind of rhetoric "taught by humans"—that is, the persuasive speech learned in the schools and lecture halls of the rhetoricians. Paul closes this first section of the letter with a parting shot at rhetoric: "The kingdom of God is not a matter of speech, but of power" (4:20). With all his decrying of the use of rhetoric, am I being cynical in insinuating that Paul is here more than anywhere using his own rhetorical training quite skillfully? Not at all.

In fact, rhetorical deprecations of rhetoric were quite common. Cicero, for example, was certainly not the only one among the ancients to notice that Plato's denunciations of rhetoric were themselves rhetorically powerful.[24] In his own treatment of rhetoric, Cicero portrays Roman orators criticizing professional rhetoricians and teachers of rhetoric while still admitting that they themselves had benefited from rhetorical training.[25] It was even common for orators to include in their speeches feigned doubts about their own rhetorical abilities and to insist on their naiveté with regard to rhetorical sophistication. Thus Isocrates attempts to disarm skeptical hearers with expressions of self-doubt about his ability to persuade.[26] Dio Chrysostom, perhaps the most famous orator of his time, pretends to be embarrassed about his lack of speaking ability and to wonder why he should be invited to lecture. All of his *Discourse* 42 (which was probably an introduction to some other speech) is devoted to winning over the audience by mock humility about his rhetorical skills.

What should we make, then, of Paul's confession in 2 Corinthians 11:6 that he is a "layman with regard to speech" (*idiōtēs tō logō*)? The phrase is usually taken to mean that Paul is claiming to have had no rhetorical training whatsoever. The Revised Standard Version renders it "unskilled in speaking," which the New Revised Standard Version has changed to "untrained in speech." But both these translations are misleading, as is apparent when we compare similar demurrals by orators themselves. Isocrates uses the term *idiōtēs* to refer to persons who have been trained in his own rhetorical school. He points out that the majority of his pupils are *idiōtai*—that is, not professional rhetors or teachers of rhetoric. This does not mean, obviously, that they are untrained in rhetoric. Of his former students he says, "Some of them have been turned out competent champions and others able teachers; while those who have preferred to live in private (*idiōteuein*) have become more gracious in their social intercourse than before, and keener judges of discourses and more prudent counsellors than most."[27] Elsewhere, Isocrates uses the term to refer to one who has studied philosophy but not become a professional philosopher or a public figure.[28] Even Dio Chrysostom, in his self-deprecating comments on his own rhetorical abilities, calls himself an *idiōtēs* in rhetoric.[29] When Paul calls himself a "layman with regard to speech," therefore, he is saying that he is not a professional orator or a teacher of rhetoric; but he is not denying that he has had a rhetorical education. In fact, in both his disparagement of rhetoric and his claim to be only a layman, Paul stands in a great tradition of rhetorical disavowals of rhetorical activity.[30]

As a matter of fact, it would have been impossible for an urban person of Paul's day to avoid exposure to a great deal of rhetoric. It was ubiquitous in the Greco-Roman city; speeches, and even professional rhetorical displays, were regular events in temples, theaters, council chambers, lecture halls, and at public festivals and games.[31] Furthermore, anyone who received any Greek education whatsoever would thereby receive at least a modicum of rhetorical education. The most elementary education was that offered by the *grammatikos* or the *ludi magister*, who traditionally taught reading, writing, and literature, with a concentration on poetry as the primary body of literature taught to children. Children might also be taught by a *calculator*—that is, a teacher of elementary arithmetic.[32] Though it was not their primary duty, these teachers included some rhetorical training even in their elementary lessons, perhaps having children memorize short set speeches and learning the elementary categories of rhetorical taxonomies. Suetonius informs us, for example, that aspects of rhetorical education like stock problems, paraphrase, addresses, and character sketches were included in the elementary curriculum. Quintilian, seeking to defend the turf of the teacher of rhetoric, objects to grammarians usurping the higher curricula of the rhetorician. He says that "teachers of literature"—that is, those teaching the elementary subjects—should *not* include rhetorical exercises like *prosopopoeia* (an exercise in which the student assumes the persona of a stock character and gives a speech in his or her assumed style) or *suasoria* (speeches designed to persuade an audience to a particular action). Declamation also, according to Quintilian, should be reserved for rhetorical, not grammatical, school.[33] Quintilian's objections demonstrate that, despite his protestations, some rhetorical teaching went on even at the elementary level of education.

Rhetorical training proper, however, began when the schooling under the grammatikos ended.[34] People who could afford it, and certainly everyone in the upper class, would have arranged for their sons to receive a rhetorical education, sometimes privately but probably more often by attendance at a school maintained by a professional teacher of rhetoric. While the students were exposed to literature, history, science, perhaps mathematics, and other subjects known to the Romans as the "liberal arts," the main activity of the schools was instruction in public speaking. Students would learn rhetorical theory, memorize speeches and imitate their teacher, and compose speeches on a variety of themes and in a variety of styles. The other subjects covered were also approached, most often, through the method of rhetoric. A discussion of science or political philosophy might come in the form of a speech on the lips of a famous man of the past or of a debate between students. Thus, training in rhetoric provided both the main subject and the organizing structure of all secondary education. Tacitus gives us a glimpse of the situation when he has a character in his *Dialogue on Orators* complain that, whereas in Cicero's day students learned history, philosophy, law, music, geometry, grammar— that is, all the liberal arts—in his own time they study nothing but rhetoric (30). As Tacitus and many others make clear, some educated people of Paul's day would have been exposed to some philosophical training, but all educated people would have been drilled in rhetoric; for Greco-Roman education *was* rhetorical education.

In the highly stratified Greco-Roman society, this meant that rhetorical education and ability were an indispensable status indicator. It is difficult for us today, with our ingrained notion of "mere rhetoric" (and our sometimes incoherent political leaders), to appreciate fully the high status assigned to rhetoric in the ancient city. Although rhetoricians were usually persons born into the upper class, in a few cases men were able to advance themselves somewhat by means of their rhetorical ability, either, like Cicero, by actually practicing as advocates or by becoming celebrated orators or teachers of oratory. In any case, numerous inscriptions survive that testify to the high status accorded sophists and rhetoricians.[35] Inscriptions from Delphi, for instance, honor rhetors and sophists, along with other "men of letters" such as poets, historians, and philosophers; the inscriptions are dated from the fourth century B.C.E. to the second century C.E.[36] Other inscriptions show that rhetors, along with historians, musicians, poets, and performers, served as ambassadors between Greek cities for several centuries. A first-century B.C.E. inscription from Antioch honors Diotrephes, a rhetor who was obviously important as a local leader and benefactor. We also know, from Delphic epigraphic evidence, of an honored family of sophists, the family of Titus Flavius Phylax (around 100 C.E.).[37]

These various sources show that professional rhetoricians, whether declaimers themselves or teachers, enjoyed high status throughout our period, and also that possession of *some* rhetorical ability and education was necessary for any man who aspired to respectability. As Bowie says, "It is true that a command of rhetoric was of great importance, but that could be assumed in a much wider range of the educated upper classes than rhetors and sophists." [38] We thus find even merchants and businessmen, who were not considered respectable by the truly high class—that is, the nonlaboring and landowning class—letting us know in their inscriptions that they were eloquent speakers as well as successful businessmen. [39] It is also understandable that Plutarch, for example, should express the cultural common sense that the upper-class gentleman will be an accomplished speaker (or at least a well-trained one) and that "weakness of speech" correlates with other indicators of low status. He notes that the Stoic *sophos* or sage will be "handsome (*kalos*), gracious, liberal, eminent, rich, eloquent (*deinos eipein*), learned, philanthropic," and that his opposite will be a man who is "ugly (*aischros*), graceless, illiberal (that is, servile), dishonored, needy, a poor speaker (*asthenēs peri logon*), unlearned, misanthropic." [40] Elsewhere, referring to popular Stoic discourse, he notes that the moral-philosophical *sophos* will be "an orator, a poet, a general, a rich man, and a king." [41] Oratorical ability occupies a place alongside beauty and wealth in characterizing the truly noble man. It was as inconceivable, at least according to this dominant ideology, that a true aristocrat would be ignorant of rhetoric as that he would be ugly or poor. As Samuel Ijsseling puts it, "In considering the power structure in ancient Greece [and, one might add, imperial Rome] one must keep in mind the rather sharp distinction between those who could speak well (the powerful) and those who could not (the powerless)." [42]

In recent years a developing consensus has emerged that Paul must have had some sort of rhetorical education. [43] Ascertaining Paul's social class is a notorious problem, but we do have some indicators. If he was a Roman citizen, as the author of Acts claims (Acts 22:27), that in itself is an important status indicator, given that he was a Jew from the provincial city of Tarsus and that in the middle of the first century Roman citizenship was not easy to come by for eastern provincials. Although citizenship alone does not indicate a particular class position, it is one piece of evidence that Paul was not from the lower classes. On the other hand, he was a leather-worker who supported himself by manual labor during his missionary activity, which by itself suggests a position among the lower classes. [44] I have argued elsewhere, however, that Paul's *attitude* toward his labor suggests an upper-class background, or at least a social level such that he could have expected never to work at a handcraft. Paul speaks of his manual labor as demeaning and humiliating; he portrays it as something he took on as part of an intentional strategy of social self-lowering. He became a manual laborer in order to appeal to manual laborers. [45] All this suggests that Paul came from a social level that, while not of the highest (equal to the senatorial, equestrian, or decurion orders in the Roman system), would have allowed—indeed, mandated—a rhetorical education. In the end, though, the best evidence for Paul's class background comes from his letters themselves. In the past several years, study after study has shown that Paul's letters follow common rhetorical conventions, contain rhetorical topoi, figures, and techniques, and are readily analyzable as pieces of Greco-Roman rhetoric. To more and more scholars, who have become more and more cognizant of Greco-Roman rhetoric, it is inconceivable that Paul's letters could have been written by someone uneducated in the rhetorical systems of his day. Paul's rhetorical education is evident on every page, and that education is one piece of evidence that he came from a family of relatively high status.[46]

It might be objected that Paul's opponents focus precisely on his rhetorical abilities, or lack thereof, to criticize him. It is true that the criticisms of Paul evident from the Corinthian correspondence are rhetorical criticisms; that is, they assume criteria of success and failure that make sense only within the discourse of Greco-Roman rhetoric. But we must analyze those criticisms more thoroughly to ascertain what they actually tell us about Paul's rhetorical abilities and education.

There is no evidence that Paul is being directly attacked by anyone in Corinth at the time he wrote 1 Corinthians. He does sound apologetic sometimes, as when he defends his decision to accept no money from the Corinthian Christians. But his apologia in 1 Corinthians 9 is not a real apology; which is to say, it is not a response to an actual attack already mounted by persons at Corinth. Rather, it is a digression in which he uses the form of an apology to present his own actions as a model for the behavior he is advocating in chapters 8 and 10. Thus he urges the Strong at Corinth to imitate him and give up their prerogatives for the sake of weaker Christians.[47] Elsewhere in 1 Corinthians Paul sometimes sounds as if he is defending himself, as when he says repeatedly that he is *not* using skillful rhetoric. But mock apologies and demurrals, as I have already noted, were not unusual in Greco-Roman speeches; they served to disarm potential critics and predispose the audience to be more favorably inclined toward the speaker.[48] They do not constitute evidence of an actual situation of apology. We should therefore not look to 1 Corinthians for signs of direct criticisms or open attacks on Paul by people at Corinth.

By the time Paul wrote 2 Corinthians, however, the situation had changed. He had been openly opposed by some people at Corinth.[49] His authority had been directly challenged, and he had been forced into a public confrontation with at least some people in the church there. Furthermore, when he wrote 2 Corinthians 10–13, which I take to be part of a separate letter, he was forced to defend himself vigorously against criticisms originating with Christian missionaries recently arrived at Corinth, people Paul calls the "super" (or "superfluous") apostles.[50] The criticisms to which Paul responds in 2 Corinthians 10–13, moreover, are directly related to his rhetorical performance.

In 2 Corinthians 10:1 Paul says, "I, Paul, myself appeal to you through the gentleness and meekness of Christ, I who am 'lowly among you when in person but bold toward you when away.'" The last phrase sounds as if Paul is quoting back to the Corinthians a criticism he has heard of himself. In 10:9 he denies that he is trying to frighten the Corinthians "by means of letters." And then we get what is obviously a quotation: "His letters, they say, are weighty and strong, but his bodily presence is weak and his speech despicable" (10:10). Paul responds by insisting that his strong epistolary persona will be evidenced later by his presence (10:11). His opponents are apparently criticizing him for a lack of consistency in his self-presentation. His letters, they admit, are rhetorically powerful, but his personal presence lacks the same power. In person, when actually speaking in Corinth, Paul appears weak, vacillating, and of low class.

Not surprisingly, these criticisms stem from values and ideologies taught in Greco-Roman rhetoric. According to rhetorical theory, letters are supposed to serve as a substitute for the bodily presence of the writer.[51] Any good speech should accurately reflect as far as possible the true persona of the speaker. Since letter writing was included in rhetorical education as a subspecies of speech making, students were taught similar rules for letters as for speeches: a well-written letter should accurately portray the writer and make the reader feel that the sender's voice is speaking. A discrepancy between the way people present themselves in a letter and the way they appear in person could be criticized as a failure of style due to lack of proper education. The discrepancy might be portrayed as a lack of consistency between "word" (the letter) and "deed" (the person's actual presence), and in rhetorical invective this was always grounds for criticism.[52]

Furthermore, it seems that what Paul's critics objected to about his presence was something directly related to his body. In Galatians 4:13–15 Paul admits that he has preached to the Galatians "in weakness (or disease) of flesh" (*di' astheneian tēs sarkos*). His next statement, that the Galatians have received him so graciously that they would have gouged out their eyes for him, has led some scholars to speculate that Paul may have suffered from some sort of eye disease that made his physical presence offensive or offputting. Whatever it was, Paul speaks of his personal presence in terms of such shame (Gal. 4:13–14) that it is clear that he regarded it as an embarrassment and a potential hindrance to rhetorical success. Then there is the "thorn in the flesh" about which Paul speaks in 2 Corinthians 12:7, where again he seems to be referring to some bodily disfigurement. In any case, it is a locus of shame and embarrassment for him. Paul himself seems to regard it as an indication of low status, one for which he must be content to let God's power compensate. Finally, we should note Paul's admission that he originally preached to the Corinthians in "weakness, fear, and trembling" (1 Cor. 2:3). As we have seen, this could be mock humility of the kind manifested by rhetors like Isocrates and Dio Chrysostom. But, given the other references to the weakness of his personal presence, especially those hurled at him by his opponents, which he seems only reluctantly to concede in 2 Corinthians 10–13, we would do well to assume that Paul is here referring to an actual condition: a physical deficiency that adversely affected his rhetorical performance.

Given the importance of the body, beauty, and strength for Greco-Roman rhetoric, this would be a real problem for Paul—if, that is, he wants to reach people who themselves subscribe to the values conveyed by Greco-Roman rhetorical education. As I pointed out in the last chapter, bodily appearance was so important for rhetoricians that they studied physiognomies in order to learn how to present themselves and how to attack the physical characteristics of their opponents. Part of rhetorical education and theory addressed appearance and bodily presentation, and the personal appearance of the sophist was of supreme importance. As D. A. Russell says, "His dress and manners are often noted, neat appearance or conspicuous extravagance being liked, and plebian roughness tolerated only as an eccentricity."[53] Thus Quintilian urges older men to cease declaiming when their bodies begin to weaken: "For the orator depends not merely on his knowledge, which increases with the years, but on his voice, lungs, and powers of endurance. And if these be broken or impaired by age or health, he must beware that he does not fall short in something of his high reputation as a master of oratory, that fatigue does not interrupt his eloquence, that he is not brought to realise that some of his words are inaudible, or to mourn that he is not what once he was" (*Rhetoric* 12. 11. 2–3, trans. Butler). Quintilian is not simply addressing the practical problems of being heard; rather, he is expressing the Greco-Roman common sense that strength and beauty of body are reflections of nobility of character. The speaker's message may be admirable, but if it is belied by his body, his message will be impugned because it does not match "reality," and he himself will become a target of ridicule. Words must fit deeds—which in this case means that one's speech must be underscored by one's body. A discrepancy between the content of the speech and the embodiment of the speaker disrupts the unified world of upper-class ideology.

This is the criticism to which Paul responds in 2 Corinthians 10–13. His critics point to his weakness of body (whether due to illness, disfigurement, or simply constitutional infirmity) as irrefutable evidence of weakness of character. His letters (strong) do not match his presence or speaking ability (weak). The strength he claims for himself does not match his embarrassing public persona. Even in 1 Corinthians, before such open criticisms have been voiced, Paul recognizes the potential problem—and offers himself as an instance of the surprising action of God, who works strength in weakness and overcomes the strong by means of the weak. At any rate, Paul's recognition of the problem and his concern to confront it head-on demonstrate that he is aware of the expectations raised by rhetorical training. His education had evidently alerted him to the problems he would face as one with distinct rhetorical talents (manifested by his letters and confirmed even by his opponents) burdened by a physical inability to embody these in a world saturated with the value systems of rhetoric, beauty, and strength.

The Rhetoric of Status

The best proof that Paul is being a skillful rhetorician in 1 Corinthians 1–4 is a rhetorical analysis of the text. This could be approached in many ways, but I will focus my analysis, for the most part, on an examination of the outline and intricate structure of Paul's argument in these chapters. The first four chapters of 1 Corinthians constitute a self-contained argument, containing in nuce all the important strategies and theological points that he will expound in the rest of the letter, when he turns from the general to the specific.[54] The following is a skeletal outline of chapters 1–4:

I. Introduction (1:1–9), ending with the thesis statement (1:10)
II. Initial statement of the problem of division and call to unity (1:11–17)
III. Two opposing realms of reality and their value and status systems (1:18–31)
IV. Paul's ministry as example of the "other" realm (2:1–16)
V. The status of the Corinthians in the different realms (3:1–23)
VI. An ironic contrast between the status of the apostles and "certain ones" at Corinth (4:1–21)

Throughout, Paul's primary concern is to promote unity in the Corinthian church, the body of Christ. But, as a careful analysis of his strategy will show, Paul is concerned not with divisions of just any sort; rather, his repeated stress of status considerations demonstrates that the problem of disunity at Corinth derives from issues related to status. I will argue, building on previous scholarship, that the Corinthian church was split along status lines, with higher-status members taking one position on several issues and lower-status members another. Paul's repeated allusions to rhetoric—his own disavowal of it and his allegations that others value it too highly—contribute to the conclusion that rhetoric and its associated status implications constitute a central aspect of the disputes within the Corinthian church.

Introduction and thesis statement (1:1–10)

Paul's introduction includes the traditional elements of a Greco-Roman letter greeting (vv. 1–3), along with "thanksgiving" (vv. 4–9) and the prothesis (v. 10). At the same time, it elicits three themes that will recur throughout chapters 1–4 and the rest of the letter. First, Paul emphasizes that "all" the Corinthians—in fact, all Christians—experience the blessings of Christ. After naming himself a "called apostle," Paul refers to the Corinthians as "called holy ones" (vv. 1–2). He then broadens the picture to include "*all* those who have called on the name of *our* Lord Jesus Christ in *every* place, *theirs* and *ours*" (my emphasis). The repetition of the Greek word for "all" (*pas*) in verse 5 serves two purposes: it provides a rhetorical flourish by repetition of the *p* sound, and it carries Paul's theme of "all-ness" through the section. Finally, in verse 9, he ends the "thanksgiving" with an *inclusio* through another reference to being *called* (see vv. 1–2) and introduces for the first time the word *koinōnia* (commonality, partnership, or fellowship): "God is trustworthy, through whom you were called into the partnership of his son Jesus Christ our Lord." Not coincidentally, in Greek the last word of the thanksgiving is the first-person plural pronoun "our."

The second major theme of the introduction is status. Paul does not broach the subject directly here but sprinkles the thanksgiving with terminology that he will later unpack to make points about status issues. He notes, for example, that grace has *already* been given to the Corinthians; they *all already* possess it. They "have been made rich" *already* and already possess *all* speech and *all* knowledge (v. 5). Like privileged possessors of valuable knowledge or initiates into an esoteric and exclusive mystery, the Corinthians possess the mystery of Christ (v. 6). And, in case he has left any privilege out, Paul assures them that they are lacking in no charism (special gift) at all (v. 7).

The third theme of the introduction appears at first surprising, because it is one that has no place in traditional homonoia speeches. Yet, as we will see, it is indispensable for Paul's arguments about status throughout 1 Corinthians. This is Paul's invocation of apocalypticism, with its attention to imminent eschatology and its own system of values and status. Paul's reference to the "mystery" of Christ would have had a certain kind of resonance for any Greek speaker, evoking the mystery cults that were so important in Greek culture and were simply taken for granted as an ancient and important element in the Mediterranean city. But the term would also carry a reference to apocalypticism, not so familiar to the typical Greek but an indispensable feature of early Christian proclamation, especially in Paul's version of the gospel. For Paul the apocalypticist, "mystery" refers to the apocalyptic narrative in which the expected revelation of the heavenly Christ will overturn the structures of the world. The apocalyptic overtone becomes obvious only in verses 7 and 8, where Paul notes that the Corinthians "await the apocalypse of our Lord Jesus Christ, who will indeed establish you to the very end absolutely without guilt [that is, "unindictable"] in the court of our Lord Jesus Christ." I have translated the Greek *hēmera* as "court" to reflect Paul's juridical language about the Corinthians' "unindictable" state. But the word also means "day," and invokes traditional apocalyptic language about the eschatological "Day of the Lord."[55] It would be a mistake for us to force a decision about *which* meaning is applicable here. Paul's language, especially in this introductory section but also throughout the letter, derives much of its power precisely from its polyvalence or, as Mikhail Bakhtin would put it, "heteroglossia."[56] As we will see more fully below, Paul wants to place two different worlds in opposition to one another: the world of Greco-Roman rhetoric and status, with its attendant upper-class ideology, and a somewhat hidden world of apocalyptic reality proclaimed in the gospel of Christ, which has its own, alternative system of values and status attribution, which in some sense "mirrors" the values of "this world" but in another sense counters and overturns those values. In order to speak about both worlds, Paul must use language that has currency in both realms. His language must oppose one world to the other, but, in order to communicate, it must also function as a bridge between the two discourses. The heteroglossic nature of his rhetoric, therefore, reflects his need to inject the truth of an apocalyptic realm and its discourse into the mist and delusion of a supposedly unified and monolithic discourse of "this world," the world of Greco-Roman, upper-class ideology.

Paul closes this carefully crafted introduction with an equally crafted statement of his thesis: "I appeal to you, brothers, through the name of *our* Lord Jesus Christ, that you *all* say the *same* thing and that there be no schisms among you, but that you be established in the *same* mind and the *same* opinion"

(1:10, my emphasis). As I have already pointed out, several elements of this statement—the emphasis on *all*, on speaking the same thing, having the same mind and opinion, the reference to schisms—derive from homonoia rhetoric. Expounding on this sentence will be the purpose of the rest of the letter.

Initial statement of the problem of division and call to unity (1:11–17)

Here Paul simply sets out the problem. He tells how he came to know of the divisions among the Corinthians and characterizes the situation in a manner typical of homonoia speeches: that is, by attributing schisms to divided loyalties toward different leaders. Scholarship has concentrated on attempting to outline the specific "parties" involved, much of it assuming that since Paul mentions four names, he must be referring to four distinct groups; and there has been much speculation about what kinds of theology characterized the different groups. As Margaret Mitchell has recently noted, however, this way of talking about *stasis*, or factiousness, was common in rhetoric on concord, and we need not assume that Paul is really thinking of four actual groups in Corinth.[57] In fact, as many other scholars have pointed out, when Paul finally gets down to addressing specific issues, he simplifies the situation to a division between two groups, one that seems to hold—or at least aspire to—high status and another that does not.[58] As I argued above in the section on homonoia rhetoric, speeches on concord often simplify political conflict to one between "rich" and "poor," possibly using other terms such as "strong" and "weak," terms which, in any case, refer to groups higher and lower respectively in a hierarchical dichotomy. Paul's terminology may indicate that the Corinthian division is indeed between those of higher versus those of lower status, but we should keep in mind that the situation may have been more complex than Paul's rhetoric would suggest.

The other important aspect of verses 11–17 lies in Paul's use of himself as an exemplar of the behavior he wishes to advocate. Paul repeatedly proposes himself as an exemplar and often calls upon the Corinthians, or at least some of them, to imitate him. Here, in an important first move designed to show that he is not seeking his own self-aggrandizement, Paul uses himself to argue for the relative unimportance of the apostles or other preachers in the grand scheme of the Gospel. Christ must be the focus, not some leader, not even Paul himself. Paul will later portray himself as the most important leader of the Corinthian church, their *father*, as opposed to other leaders whom he characterizes as mere pedagogues (a low-status role usually filled by slaves).[59] Paul's rhetorical move here constitutes an implied "from the greater to the lesser" strategy: if he, the founder and first leader of the church, deserves no such divisive loyalty, much less does any other leader. Furthermore, Paul's self-reference recalls the common homonoia practice whereby the speaker cites himself as an example of one who has not his own interests in mind but the interests of the entire body politic.[60]

Two opposing realms of reality, their values and status systems (1:18–31)

In the previous section (1:11–17) Paul says nothing that would be out of place in a traditional treatment of concord—until, that is, the last four words: "the cross of Christ." As is well known, making a crucified criminal the honored, central figure of devotion ran completely counter to common assumptions.[61] It therefore provides Paul with an appropriate jumping off place for introducing a system of values that he will oppose to that of the dominant culture. In 1:18–31 Paul sets up an opposition between two realms or worlds: the realm of "this world" or "this age" and the realm (Paul will later use the term "kingdom," 4:20) of God. These verses further break down into two parts; the first (vv. 18–25) sets up the two realms as opposed, the second (vv. 26–31) puts forward the Corinthians themselves as an example of God's alternative status system.

In opposition to the accomplished rhetoric of the educated Greek, Paul praises the "speech of the cross," a term that would have struck Paul's hearers as paradoxical and perhaps ridiculous, as Paul himself says when he calls it "foolishness to those who are perishing" (1:18). To make his point, he plays with status terms in a way that must have seemed counter-intuitive to most of the Corinthians. "Where is the wise man? Where is the scribe? Where is the debater of this realm?" The Corinthians might well have answered, "What do you mean, 'Where are they'? They are all around you, occupying comfortable positions of power in every city of the Empire!" Paul allows no such answer, however, immediately insisting that God has already shamed all such leaders by proclaiming salvation through a crucified man. He disrupts the intuitive status expectations of his audience by invoking a belief he knows they share: the belief that in Christ, who was crucified, they have a common source of salvation and a common paradigm of leadership.

Yet, Paul does not dispense with terms of high status; nor does he attack hierarchy and preach equality. Instead, he appropriates the terminology of status ("wisdom," "power") and claims it for the oppositional realm of apocalyptic discourse. In one sense, God has overthrown wisdom by choosing foolishness, tearing down the high by means of the low. But in another sense, God has revealed that his wisdom and strength make human qualities look foolish and weak by comparison (1:25). The apocalyptic world is not one in which hierarchies are dissolved into equality but one in which the values of the Greco-Roman world are acknowledged but then turned on their heads. The apocalyptic gospel reveals the instability of the values assumed by Greco-Roman culture, replacing them with a mirror world in which top is bottom and bottom top.

This is where we see the importance of apocalyptic for Paul's argument. In order to oppose the dominant ideology, with its value system and its ways of attributing status, Paul must advance an alternative system. He finds one, to some extent, ready to hand in the dualism of Jewish apocalypticism, which had for centuries countered the imperialistic ideologies of Greece and Rome with a narrative that depicted an alternative, hidden, and vastly more powerful empire: the kingdom of God. All power structures of the empires of "this world" were mere shadows of the truly real, cosmic empire that was currently hidden to all human beings except those granted the esoteric vision of its imminent inbreaking. Jewish apocalypticism thus provided Paul with an alternative realm to oppose to the apparently seamless, irresistible unity of the dominant Greco-Roman ideology. Furthermore, Jewish apocalypticism had a long tradition of revolutionary appropriations. For centuries, Jewish prophets had proclaimed that God, the *Jewish* God, would overturn the structures of power maintained by Hellenistic and Roman armies and governments.[62] Ultimately, the last would be first, and the first would be last. The strong would be removed from their thrones, and God would lift up the downtrodden. These apocalyptic themes did not always express themselves in an overt political or military revolution, although they did on occasion; but they were always present and available for a variety of theological and social uses. Paul makes use of them to challenge the status assumptions of Greco-Roman ideology and traditional rhetoric.

The image that Paul himself adds to this traditional apocalyptic portrait is that of the crucified Christ as the central icon of the Gospel. With all its sometimes revolutionary-sounding language, even apocalyptic had never proclaimed, as far as we know, that the catastrophe of the ages would find its impetus and center in the execution by crucifixion of a Jewish prophet. Yet Paul takes this, to the Greek and the Jew the most paradoxical aspect of Christian preaching, as the paradigm *par excellence* of the radically different value system of the other realm. Without apocalypticism and his interpretation of the cross in apocalyptic terms, Paul would have had no alternative world to oppose to the overpowering ideology of the Greco-Roman ruling class. But with it, Paul can propose the existence of a world that is more real than the one the Corinthians see around them.

To drive his point home, Paul uses the Corinthians themselves as proof of his argument. As has been thoroughly explored, Paul's terminology in verses 26–31 is full of status significance. Few of the Corinthians are "wise," "power-ful," or "well-born"; they are not among "the strong" (*ischyroi*). All these words are reserved traditionally for members of the upper class. In fact, according to upper-class ideology, even the term *hoi polloi sophoi, dynatoi, ischyroi* ("the many wise, powerful, strong") would have sounded like an oxymoron, since it was part of the definition of "wise, powerful, and aristocratic" that such people were few; the "elite," by definition, could not include the masses (*hoi polloi*). The terms Paul applies to the Corinthians, on the contrary, are those used of the lower classes: "foolish," "weak," "shameful," "low-born," "despised," "those who are not." Not only do these terms have theological implications; they each carry clear class connotations. Paul's use of them tells us several things. First, since Paul is able to say all this without defense or argument, he must have been right: although these house churches seem to have been fre-quented by something of a cross-section of Corinthian society, the majority of the members must have been from the lower class. Second, since he says "not many of you are . . .", there must have been *some* who were not members of the lower class.[63] Finally, since Paul infiltrates his rhetoric with so many status terms, much, if not all, of the conflict among the Corinthians must have cen-tered on issues of status. At any rate, the important rhetorical move contained in 1:26–31 is Paul's enlistment of most of his audience as a living example of the topsy-turvy status system of his alternative world, the "kingdom of God." Normal status designations, those characteristics of which one would normally "boast," mean nothing in the realm to which the Corinthians have already, to some extent, been transferred.

Paul's ministry as example of the "other" realm (2:1–16)

In the next section, which includes all of chapter 2, Paul turns the spotlight from the Corinthians to himself and his ministry; *he* is now the exemplar of the other realm and its different values. Furthermore, in this section Paul begins in earnest his rejection of rhetoric, which here becomes a symbol of the status and power designations of "this world." In opposition to the high-status rhetor or sophist, Paul portrays himself as of low status—when judged, that is, by the criteria of "this age." Unlike the Greek intellectual, he admits to knowing nothing except a story about a crucified man (2:2). Unlike the self-assured, confident rhetor, he speaks his message in "weakness, fear, and trembling" (2:3). He is not advocating powerlessness, however. In fact, his next statement takes a page from rhetorical method itself, which often used a contrast between "word" and "deed" to disparage a rival rhetorician. Paul's own message, he claims, is not in "persuasive, technically sophisticated rhetoric" (*en peithois sophias logois*) but in a "pneumatic demonstration of power" (2:4). Ultimately, what Paul wants to oppose to human power is not weakness but divine power (2:5)—that is, power belonging to the other realm.

At this point in his argument, Paul makes a subtle but important shift. He began this section with self-deprecation, claiming, apparently, only weakness and low status for himself. But from this point to the end of the chapter he uses high-status terms for himself and other Christians, though these terms are redefined and given different meanings by being transferred to the discourse of his alternative realm. Paul does have a message of "wisdom" (*sophia*), but it is apocalyptic wisdom, previously hidden by God and kept for its ultimate goal of bringing "glory" and "fame" to Christians (2:7).[64] This wisdom is qualitatively different from that taught by high-class Greek teachers of philosophy or rhetoric. It is not available to "the rulers of this age" (2:6, 8).

Scholars have debated whether Paul's term "rulers of this age" is meant to refer to the human political rulers of his time or to what we would call supernatural beings, such as demons or angels, understood in apocalypticism to rule over the cosmos until the end time.[65] Here again, as so often with Paul's language, it is misleading to insist on a decision between these options. In apocalypticism, *all* human rulers are stand-ins for cosmic agents.[66] For Paul, as for any self-respecting apocalypticist, the government officials who crucified Jesus were not acting on their own; rather, human agents are mere shadows of cosmic agents who engineer the events of this world like toys in a sandbox. Forcing a division between the natural and the supernatural realms is a modern conceit, one that takes too little account of the importance of apocalypticism for Paul's world view. For Paul, what we would call the supernatural is inextricably mingled with the natural, and the natural is driven by supernatural forces. In other words, although Paul invokes a dualism of "this world" and the "other world," this dualism has nothing to do with modern ontological categories of nature and supernature, and no concept of "mere" politics understood independently of higher cosmic conflicts is possible in Paul's thinking. For Paul, "this world" is not the closed system of nature but the dark, confused world of rebellion against God. Had the "rulers of this age," both human and demonic, possessed the apocalyptic knowledge vouchsafed to Christians like Paul, they would never have engineered the crucifixion of God's Son; that they did so demonstrates the foolishness of their wisdom and the poverty of their wealth.

Christians, however, possess esoteric knowledge communicated by the stuff of divine rationality, pneuma. Just as pneuma is the highest element in the human body, the element of human thought and the essence of life itself (2:11), so the divine pneuma is the substance of the communication of divine wisdom (2:10–11). The pneuma of "this world"—which, according to physicians and physicists, enabled perception and thought (see Chapter 1)—is only a weak and misleading (that is, sin-inducing) false copy of the pneuma shared by God and Christians. The latter is the pneuma with which Paul deals and which is the source of true wisdom: "taught pneumatically, pneumatically reckoning pneumatics" (*en didactois pneumatos, pneumatikois pneumatika sygkrinontes*, 2:13).[67] Other human beings *cannot* (not simply "will not") be receptors of the divine pneuma because they are not pneumatically constituted persons; rather, they are *psychikoi*—that is, possessors of mere animalistic life, not pneumatic life.[68] By now, Paul has turned the tables by introducing a completely different status mechanism and reserving the high-status indicator, the possession of pneumatic—hence divine—knowledge, for Christians only.

The last two sentences of this section complete Paul's move from low to high status in the chapter. When Paul says that "the pneumatic person judges everything but is judged by no one," he invokes the common sense that to submit to another's judgment is to submit to his or her higher authority (2:15). He makes the remarkable claim that all these Corinthians, whom he has so carefully characterized as of *low* status in the previous section, are of higher status than everyone else in the world. And as if that were not enough, Paul ends with another astounding claim to high status: carefully using the first-person plural pronoun in an emphatic position in the sentence and including all the Corinthians with himself in this privileged position, he says, "*We* have the very mind of Christ!" (2:16). With a rhetorical finesse that renders the change almost imperceptible, Paul has moved from portraying both the Corinthians and himself in completely low-status terms to lifting them all to the highest possible status. But along the way he has called into question any use of normal, upper-class status designations for the assignment of honor within the church.

The status of the Corinthians in the different realms (3:1–23)

Having set up his two realms and made a case for their conflicting status systems, Paul now turns more specifically to the problems of the Corinthians' factionalism. And, as he does throughout this section, he again shifts his status attributions. Having just placed the Corinthians in the highest cosmic status position, as people who possess the very mind of Christ (2:16), he abruptly, in 3:1, flips his rhetoric again and portrays them in low-status terms. Having delineated the two realms, only one of which functions by means of pneuma, and placed the Corinthian Christians in that realm, Paul suddenly turns the tables and now puts them on the other side of the divide. They are not, after all, "pneumatics" but "sarkics" (*sarx* referring to "flesh," albeit to much more than we usually mean by "flesh"; it refers both to the lower form of matter that constitutes the human self and, in Paul, to the realm of cosmic existence that is in opposition to God). The Corinthians are implicated in the lowest possible form of human existence. They are babies in need of milk rather than spiritual adults who could be fed pneumatic food. The sign that points to their low status is the existence of factionalism among them. Paul has deftly brought the attention of his hearers back to the central issue, division within their church, and he has done so in a way that retains his focus on status and the two opposing realms of the cosmos.[69]

Paul, we can be sure, will not leave the Corinthians in the low-status position to which he assigned them in 3:1–4. But, on the way to raising them once more, he problematizes the status positions of himself and other apostles and teachers. In 3:5–17 he relativizes the position of apostles: they are only workmen, planters or waterers, whereas the Corinthians are God's field, the object of his care. Or, modifying a rhetorical commonplace that portrayed the body politic as a house, Paul portrays the Corinthian church as God's temple and himself and other teachers as mere architects or builders. Again, therefore, Paul ends a section with a reversal of the status positions assigned at the beginning of the section. He began by apparently excluding the Corinthians from the realm of pneuma and assigning them to the realm of sarx. He ends by making them the very dwelling of the divine pneuma: "Do you not know that you are the temple of God and that the pneuma of God lives in you?" (3:16). The next sentence shows the reason for Paul's shift: the criterion for assigning this status to the Corinthians is the unity of their church. "If anyone destroys the temple of God, God will destroy him; for the temple of God is holy, which very thing you yourselves are" (3:17). The Corinthians, by implication, can retain the high position assigned to them only by avoiding the schisms that would destroy the house of God.

In the last few verses of this section (3:18–23), Paul again promises the Corinthians very high status—but only if they give up any desire for, or pretense of, the status symbols (in this case, the wisdom) of "this world." "If anyone among you seems to be a 'wise man' [*sophos*] in the terms of this aeon, let him become a fool in order that he may become wise" (3:18). With these words, Paul again begins with what looks like a gentle rebuke of the Corinthians for their desire for conventional status. He ends, though, by making the Corinthians the *owners* of all: Paul, Apollos, Cephas, the cosmos, life, death, the present, the future—everything. In the cosmic hierarchy thus established, Paul places himself and all leaders *below* the ordinary members of the church, who occupy a position below only God and Christ. Thus, Paul has again in the course of one section moved his audience from the lowest- to the highest-status position.

An ironic contrast between the apostles and "certain ones" at Corinth (4:1–21)

In this last major section of Paul's curious homonoia speech we have still more clues about the specific problems of division at Corinth. Paul again begins by relativizing the status of the apostles. They are mere servants, or *oikonomoi* ("stewards," a word that would probably evoke images of managerial slaves) of the mysteries of God.[70] But as slaves, they may be judged only by their master, so the Corinthians' opinion of him ultimately matters little (vv. 3–4). Like any slave, he must submit only to the judgment of his master, Christ.

Paul next explicitly points out that all this status talk about himself is intended to serve only as an example of the behavior he is urging on the Corinthians. Paul considers that the Corinthians—or, as we will presently see, *some* of them—are becoming "puffed up" and are becoming so by promoting one Christian teacher, their favorite, over the others. To counter this divisive activity, Paul lumps all the teachers, including himself and Apollos, in the same category and assigns that category the lowest possible status. He then ironically contrasts this to the high-status positions claimed by these Corinthians. "Already you are filled! Already you are rich! Already you reign like kings!" (4:8). By contrast, the apostles are characterized by low-status terms: "last of all," "consigned to execution," "a shameful spectacle [like war prisoners] paraded before angels and human beings alike." "We are foolish because of Christ while you are wise in Christ. We are weak while you are strong. You are famous while we are dishonored" (vv. 9–10). There follows a string of humiliating depictions of the apostles: they are hungry, thirsty, homeless, and naked poor, manual laborers, despised and reviled by everyone, the scum of the cosmos, the residue, or scapegoats, of the world.[71] The radical difference between the extremely low status of the apostles and the high status claimed by certain people at Corinth could not be more starkly drawn.

As noted above, the terms used by Paul to depict these Corinthians provide some clues to the nature of their self-portrayal. As has been thoroughly documented by other scholars, the popular Stoic "wise man" was depicted as the only person who was truly wealthy and truly a king. Because he knew how to attune his desires to those things which are "according to nature," he would always have everything he needed, since "nature," in this form of popular philosophy, always arranged everything aright. Furthermore, because he ruled the only thing over which any human being has any real control—that is, his self—he was the only true "king." In circles even modestly influenced by the popular philosophy of the first century, it was common to speak of the true sophos ("wise man") as "wealthy" and "a king." But the same terms also functioned more broadly in the terminology of patron–client structures of the Empire. Patrons were sometimes called *rex* ("king"), and anyone who claimed to be of high status would need to be able to demonstrate his wealth by his benefaction. In 4:6–13 Paul juxtaposes the extremely low status of the Christian apostles, himself more than any, with the traditional designations of high status known to Greco-Roman society and popular philosophy.

In the last few verses of chapters 1–4, however, Paul once again turns the tables and reverses the status positions. After his vivid depiction of the low status of the apostles and the supposed high status of the Corinthian "rich," he suddenly changes his tune and speaks of the Corinthians as children and himself as their father. He even claims a uniquely high-status position for himself by contrast with any other teacher or leader of the Corinthian church. He is their "father," whereas all other leaders are mere "pedagogues." In the Greco-Roman household, as we have seen, the pedagogue was a slave, often a slave considered useless for any really important task, who supervised the child and made sure (among other tasks) that the child got to and from school and other activities. Unlike what one might assume on the basis of the modern term *pedagogy*, the pedagogue was not a teacher, but only a caretaker. Here, at the end of his opening homonoia speech, then, Paul suddenly eschews low-status depictions of himself and claims the highest possible position (as father), consigning other teachers and leaders to lower positions. He implicitly claims a high-status position also by calling on the Corinthians to imitate him.[72]

Here we see how intricately constructed his rhetoric is. In 4:18, at the very end of the entire first part of the letter, we finally realize that Paul has a dual audience in mind: on the one hand, the entire Corinthian church, as is evident in his repeated invocations of "all"; on the other hand, some *portion* of the church. Earlier, we might have assumed that when Paul complains about those who are "puffed up," making high-status claims for themselves, he is addressing the whole church. But in 4:18 it becomes clear that it is "certain ones" (*tines*) who are making such claims. Up to this point, Paul has skillfully avoided any direct attack on *part* of the church because he is urging unity; comments directed to only one group would have tended to split the church more deeply by appearing to attack only one faction. Thus, it is only at the end of the large first section of the letter that we get a hint that Paul will direct most of his firepower at one group in the Corinthian church, the "certain ones" who are "puffed up."

Paul's vacillation in his own status claims and his call for the Corinthians to imitate him reflect his primary concern about the Corinthian Christians who are making high-status claims for themselves. What he calls on them to imitate is his own voluntary acceptance of low status. In order to urge such an action, however, he must make *some* claim of high status and leadership for himself—otherwise, according to Greco-Roman common sense, he would be an inappropriate model for behavior. Paul's rhetoric in chapters 1–4 constitutes a complex, skillful strategy whereby he both claims and denies high status to himself. He argues powerfully against the power of rhetoric. He uses assumptions about hierarchy and status to overturn the status expectations of Greco-Roman culture. And, ultimately, he claims the highest status for himself in order to convince those of high status in the Corinthian church to imitate him in accepting a position of low status.

In spite of his disavowals of the use of rhetoric, Paul's argument in 1 Corinthians 1–4 shows rhetorical finesse and power that prove beyond any doubt that he had received some kind of rhetorical training. He uses the structure of a homonoia speech to urge the Corinthian church to unite; and the form his argument takes, focusing so consistently on status, makes it clear that the factionalism of the church was due to divisions based on status differences among the members. The particular status assumptions at issue are those of the dominant ideology of Greco-Roman culture, and Paul counters high-status assumptions by dividing the cosmos into two realms, that of "this world" and an alternative reality defined by apocalypticism. This move marks a radical break with traditional homonoia speeches, which invoke a unified, stable cosmos. Paul, by contrast, opposes "this cosmos" with an "anti-cosmos" whose value and status system is an inversion of what the Corinthians see all around them.

Paul's own low status, and to a lesser degree that of all the apostles, is a reflection of the alternative status system according to which the strong are weak and the weak are strong. Paul's call to imitation, while initially appearing to be just another claim to high status, is directed primarily to the "certain ones" at Corinth who are "puffed up," "rich," and "reign like kings." The particular behavior that Paul advocates is self-lowering and status reversal, the opposite of what would be advocated in any normal homonoia speech. Paul thus uses homonoia rhetoric to an ideological end that is the opposite of that normally advocated by such rhetoric. By calling on any Corinthians who consider themselves to be of high status to imitate his own position of low status, Paul implicitly advocates what upper-class ideology feared the most: the disruption of the stable hierarchy of the political and cosmic body. In the next three chapters we will see how Paul pursues the goal he only hints at in 1 Corinthians 1–4: the disruption of the hierarchy of the Greco-Roman body and the reversal of status positions for the sake of unity.

3 *The Body's Economy*

Scholarship on 1 Corinthians has taken the divisions at Corinth to be along several different lines: libertines opposed to ascetics, Gnostics or "proto-Gnostics" opposed to non-Gnostic Christians, "enthusiasts" opposed to Paul, Jews opposed to Gentiles, followers of Apollos opposed to followers of Paul, or some combination thereof.[1] Arguing against these positions, I am proposing a simpler one, which, in agreement with recent research, claims that the Corinthian church was for the most part split along one major "fault line," with wealthier, higher-status Christians (along with their dependents or ideological allies) on one side and lower-status Christians on the other. Like previous scholars, I identify the higher-status group with those whom Paul calls the "Strong" and the lower-status group with those he labels the "Weak."[2]

Already in 4:18 we have seen evidence that some of Paul's rhetorical ammunition was unloaded on only part of the Corinthian church: the "certain ones" who were "puffed up." Paul begins the next section with another gentle swipe at the same group. Complaining that the Corinthian Christians have done nothing about a fellow Christian who has been sleeping with his stepmother, Paul says, "And you are puffed up!" (5:2). He targets the same proud group later when he says, "This boast of yours is not good!" (5:6). Paul's accusation that some Corinthians are "puffed up" surfaces later when he insists that "knowledge puffs up" (8:1). Here it becomes apparent that the Corinthians who so value *gnōsis* (knowledge) are those Paul was referring to in 4:18. As this chapter will show, these are the higher-status Christians.

The Social Location of the Corinthian Slogans

Commentators have long noted that Paul quotes back to the Corinthians slogans they have themselves used, thereby providing us with what little access we have to "their" side of the dispute:

> "Everything is permitted to me" (6:12; 10:23).
> "Food is for the stomach, and the stomach for food. [And God will destroy both the former and the latter]" (6:13).[3]
> "We all have knowledge" (8:1).
> "An idol is nothing in the cosmos, and there is no God but one" (8:4).

There are other possible slogans or Corinthian positions embedded in Paul's letter (such as 1 Cor. 7:1), and I will at times argue that they may provide us with more information about the Corinthian situation. But these few suffice for sketching a plausible social location for the Strong at Corinth. The Strong appear to have emphasized radical freedom, at least for those wise enough to know how to use it. They claim "gnosis," or knowledge, for themselves. That knowledge teaches them not to fear gods or daimons, and this lack of fear of the gods seems to be linked to a radical monotheism. They show no concern for purity regarding food, and this seems tied to a deprecation of the body. But beyond this minimalist sketch, what more can we say about the social and economic situation of Paul's Corinthian disputants?

Some scholars have held that these slogans indicate that Paul's "opponents" at Corinth were Gnostics.[4] It was believed that they, like Gnostics of the second through fourth centuries, were Christians who believed in a radical dualism of body and soul, with a deprecation of the body and materiality in general and a belief that salvation consists in the elevation of the soul or spirit by means of esoteric knowledge (gnosis). Their deprecation of the body could lead them to either asceticism or libertinism, according to how they saw fit to act on their belief that the deeds of the body were despicable or inconsequential. They claimed a higher wisdom than ordinary Christians and rejected the dietary superstitions of other, supposedly weaker Christians and any belief in the resurrection of the body, holding instead a belief in the immortality of the soul, or perhaps believing that they, as gnostic Christians, had already experienced a spiritual resurrection.

Most scholars now reject this older view.[5] For one thing, we have little evidence that Gnosticism, as a delineable social movement, existed in the middle
of the first century. The gnosticisms we can identify all come from the second
century or later. Some scholars get over this chronological problem by calling the Corinthians "proto-Gnostics."[6] But this only begs the question; one
could say that anyone in the first century who held certain philosophical ideas
(deprecation of the body, some form of anthropological dualism) was a proto-
Gnostic, but this brings one no closer to a historical reconstruction of their
social location. Furthermore, later Gnostics usually taught that their gnosis
was esoteric, being transmitted to them by private, specialized procedures and
concealed from the majority of Christians. The mass of humanity had no access
to real knowledge, and even most Christians were "psychics," not "Gnostics."
By contrast, the Strong at Corinth were apparently able to say that "we *all*
have knowledge" (8:1); in other words, they seem to have argued that even
weaker Christians could and should benefit from superior knowledge about
the gods and dietary rules. This does not sound like the rigid epistemological
hierarchy of later Gnosticism. Nor do the slogans of the Strong concerning the
body sound like later Gnosticism. The Strong do not claim that the body or
materiality is evil; they simply imply that it does not matter a great deal. They
show little concern that bodily activities, whether eating meat offered to idols
or visiting prostitutes, will pollute either themselves or the rest of the church.
Their position suggests not that the body is evil but merely that it is inferior,
and that sexual misdeeds on the part of some Christians are relatively unim-
portant for the spirituality of other Christians. Calling these slogans "Gnostic"
over-specifies their probable social location. As I will show, many other people
in the first century were exposed to these kinds of arguments, and limiting
their purview to Gnosticism is not historically defensible.

Other scholars are closer to the mark in arguing that the Corinthians' slogans
come from Cynic discourse.[7] Cynics spoke of radical freedom from convention.
They taught that the sophos, or "sage," was the only person who was truly
free: he alone could do whatever he willed, because his will was completely
attuned to nature. Thus he would never will to do anything that was outside
his own power or was contrary to nature. The sophos was the only person
who perfectly ruled the potential for agency. Because of his superior wisdom
and knowledge, he knew how to be content with whatever nature brought
him. Clearly, this kind of popular philosophy provides a viable context for the
slogans and position of the "certain ones" addressed in 1 Corinthians. In 4:8
Paul says that these Corinthians claim to be "kings, rich, and wise"; they pos-

sess wisdom superior to the masses and therefore know better than to entertain superstitious fears about the gods or conventional beliefs about pollution.

But calling these positions "Cynic" is again overly specific. As is well known, Stoics also used these kinds of slogans and taught this kind of moral philosophy. I would argue, moreover, that even limiting this discourse to Stoic circles is too specific. In the first century, phrases and doctrines that originated among early Cynics and later Stoics had attained a wide currency in the general marketplace of popular, moral philosophy in the Roman Empire. Such phrases could be found on the lips of philosophers who cannot really be categorized as Cynics or Stoics. Cicero did not consider himself a Stoic, but the phrases they used came easily to him; Philo thought of himself as a follower of Plato, but he wrote a rather Stoic-sounding essay proving "That Only the Good Man Is Free."[8] Furthermore, the goal of the educated upper-class person of the early Empire was not to adhere too closely to one philosophical school but to be able to show evidence of learning from several famous schools and traditions.[9] The educated Roman or Greek was expected to be able to mouth a few of the main catch-phrases or doctrines of the major traditions, but rigid school loyalty or even a great deal of familiarity with particulars was considered eccentric or excessive. All we can say about the Strong at Corinth, therefore, is that they had been exposed to general principles of moral philosophy stemming from Cynic and Stoic traditions; we cannot demonstrate that they were themselves Cynics or Stoics.

But even an admission of exposure to philosophical commonplaces carries some implications about the socioeconomic position of the Strong. Whereas inhabitants of the typical Greco-Roman city might occasionally hear a Cynic bawling out philosophical phrases on a street corner or in a market, and whereas people might also be exposed to philosophical rhetoric in speeches by professional orators on public occasions, the most common places for philosophical teaching or discussion were the philosophical schools and the households of the well-to-do. If the Corinthian Christians who spouted these platitudes had received formal philosophical training, that would provide firm evidence of their relatively high economic position. Anyone *could* attend lectures, and thus we know of a few cases in which persons of the lower class received a philosophical education. For example, Epictetus, while still a slave, was allowed by his master to attend the lectures of Musonius Rufus.[10] After his manumission, Epictetus himself established a school, taught for fees, and thus lifted himself out of the ranks of the lower class. Once he began capitalizing on his education and teaching philosophy himself, he never worked as a manual laborer. Thus, those people from the laboring classes who were able through whatever circumstance to procure a philosophical education were able, by means of that education, to move out of the lower classes. For the most part, however, only people of leisure and money would have been able to expose themselves to such an education.[11]

I mentioned also that persons may have been exposed to philosophy in the households of the well-to-do. Greco-Roman literature is full of references to "household philosophers" who seem to have been supported mainly by the benefaction of patrons. These philosophers might live in the household itself, or they might be "hangers-on," attending dinner parties, spending their days socializing with or advising the paterfamilias, or even educating the youth of the household.[12] But all this suggests a rather high-class position for the household. If a man desired to have a pet philosopher grace his table or drawing room, he would need to possess sufficient funds to support a household that at least aspired to elegance. In other words, knowledge of philosophical views on the part of some Corinthian Christians is good evidence that they had been exposed either to a philosophical education themselves or to the "salon" society of upper-class households. Either way, their knowledge of moral philosophy implies a higher-class position. We need not think of them as Cynics or Stoics themselves, but their knowledge of such traditions indicates the circles in which they moved.

My arguments here are not original; scholarship on 1 Corinthians for the past few decades has argued that a dominant minority within the Corinthian church were people of relatively high status, when compared, that is, to the rest of the Corinthian Christians. In a famous series of articles, Gerd Theissen in particular has attempted to place the Corinthian debates in socioeconomic perspective. In one, Theissen shows that the Corinthian controversy over the Lord's Supper (11:17–34) split the church along status lines. Paul speaks of those who "have not" (*hoi mē echontas*, 11:22) as opposed to those who "have" things like houses in which to eat and drink their fill. This recalls the way Greek rhetoric often referred to the two main classes of rich and poor.[13] In the church the "haves" (*hoi echontes*) arrived early (with more control over their time, they could arrive at the meetings well before any laborers, who owed their days to their employers or masters) and began, at their own leisure, the common meal, which probably included at some point a more formal breaking of bread and sharing of wine commemorating the death of Jesus. Thus they were being filled, perhaps even getting drunk, while others, as Paul says, were "going hungry" (11:21).

Theissen further explains that Greco-Roman dinner parties encoded and embodied status differentiation in all aspects of their enactment. It was considered natural that guests occupy places around the room according to their relative status and honor as decided by the host. And, as many ancient writers mention, different guests were often served different portions, with regard both to quantity and quality of food and wine, reflecting their status or proximity to the host; the host's most honored guests and closest friends would sit near him and receive better food and wine, while his friends of lesser status, his clients, and perhaps lower freedmen would occupy positions of descending status and receive portions of lesser quantity and quality. This practice of status discrimination was so expected that some authors comment when it is absent, expressing surprise that some particular host does *not* distinguish among his guests at dinner.[14]

Theissen explains that the Strong at Corinth, if they were indeed those Christians of higher status, accustomed to the conventions of dinner-party society, would naturally have expected some status differentiation at church common meals. After all, as patrons of the church, they were paying for most of the activity out of their own pockets; they hosted the house churches in their homes and provided most of the financial support for the church, as well as the food and drink for the common meals. Why shouldn't they and their special guests go ahead and enjoy the food and wine that they themselves had furnished?

Paul's solution to the Lord's Supper controversy also indicates that the problem was one of division between Christians of higher and lower status (rather than being a disagreement about the interpretation of the elements of the Lord's Supper or a simple deficiency in piety in its observance). Paul tells the "haves" to eat in private before they come to the Christian assembly if they cannot control themselves and wait for the other Christians (11:22, 34). More significantly, he implies that they should do whatever is necessary to avoid shaming the "have-nots" (11:22). They should "discern the body," here probably meaning both the body of the crucified Christ represented by the bread and the communal body of Christ represented by the gathered church, which includes *all* Christians, those of high and low status (11:29).[15] Finally, when they come together to eat, they should "wait on one another" (11:33). Throughout the section, Paul emphasizes that the Lord's Supper is supposed to be the *common* meal of the church and hence that it is the worst time to have divisions surface. And he consistently demands that the "haves" modify their behavior to mitigate status differences in their observance of the common meals. Since this advice flew in the face of accepted practice and common sense of the upper class of Greco-Roman society, Paul's instructions represent a direct challenge to upper-class ideology and required that the higher-status

Corinthians adjust both their expectations and their behavior to accommodate the needs of those of lower status. And that in itself, in Greco-Roman culture, would have meant a reversal of normal status expectations.

In another article, Theissen adopts some of the same methods to address the issue of eating meat offered to idols (1 Cor. 8–10). Here Paul's use of the terms "strong" and "weak" is even more obviously linked to status. Whereas much previous scholarship took these terms to refer to the theological or psychological state of church members (those of "strong conscience" as opposed to those of "weak conscience"), Theissen demonstrates that the terms refer to social status, and specifically class, positions. The Strong were those higher-status Christians who could afford to buy meat in the market, almost all of which would have been sacrificed to some deity or another before sale. They would have found total avoidance of meat difficult, since they would have wanted— indeed, needed—to give and receive dinner invitations from other members of higher society at Corinth. Many such meals might even take place in the dining rooms of the sacred precinct of some god or goddess, these being popular places for private dinner parties hosted by well-to-do Greeks or Romans.[16] Those Corinthian Christians interested in status or social advancement could scarcely avoid such situations; to do so would have amounted to social suicide. Lower-class Christians, on the other hand, like other lower-class inhabitants of Greco-Roman cities, would have had few occasions to eat meat except as part of a public festival in which meat, which of course had been sacrificed to some deity during the festival, was distributed to the "masses" of the city. In that context, eating meat was quite explicitly part of the pagan festival itself, and one could hardly avoid knowing that the animal had been previously offered to a god or goddess. Highlighting the social implications of eating meat in the Greco-Roman city thus enables Theissen to suggest, convincingly, that those Corinthian Christians opposed to eating meat offered to idols were probably of lower status, whereas those who defended the practice, by using arguments and slogans learned from popular moral philosophy, were of higher status.[17]

In this case too, Paul sides with those of lower status. He admits that the Strong are theoretically right to some extent: they *do* have freedom to eat, and eating the idol meat in itself will not harm them—as long, that is, as they do so with proper "knowledge" and a strong conscience.[18] But Paul urges them to give up this right in order to accommodate the Weak, just as he gave up his right to financial support in order to accommodate himself to those of lower status. Just as Paul gave up his own status position as a free man and virtually enslaved himself by practicing a servile, manual trade—becoming a manual laborer to win manual laborers—so the higher-status Corinthians should give up their prerogatives and adjust their behavior to meet the demands and needs of the lower-status Christians who are offended by their practice of eating idol-meat.[19] As was the case with the Lord's Supper, so here Paul pursues a strategy of status reversal, siding with the Weak, directing his criticisms primarily toward the Strong, and overturning the normal expectations of upper-class ideology.

The Strong and the Courts at Corinth

A similar analysis based on status considerations sheds light on the controversy Paul addresses in 1 Corinthians 6:1–11: Christians taking other Christians to court. Until recently, the social status implications of recourse to Greco-Roman courts have not been addressed in interpretations of this passage. But now research by two scholars working independently has opened up possibilities for locating the Corinthian dispute in terms of social status. Bruce W. Winter and Alan C. Mitchell both emphasize the social and class significance of civil litigation in first-century Corinth, and both conclude that it is the Strong at Corinth who are making use of the courts to settle their differences. Mitchell goes further to argue that the higher-status Christians are taking those of less power and influence to court and probably winning their cases.[20]

It is well known, and was well known even in ancient times, that Roman courts were structurally biased towards members of the upper class. Criminal laws, for instance, did not cover most cases of fraud, so if a citizen felt wronged, the only formal legal recourse was civil litigation before a judge or a panel of jurors. But this avenue was not open to everyone. As Winter says, "The right to prosecute was not granted to all. If the defendant was a parent, patron, magistrate, or a person of high rank, then charges could not be brought by children, freedmen, private citizens and men of low rank respectively."[21] Even if a lower-status person were permitted access to the courts, the system, both officially and unofficially, was biased in favor of those of higher status. Judges were almost all from the highest classes, and jurors were chosen from the well-to-do; laws instructed judges to take into account the appearance and status of a person when deciding his or her case.[22] Bribery was always a possibility. And less explicit factors came into play: since the judge, jurors, and lawyers were members of the upper class themselves, they may have shared a rather exclusive social network with other citizens of high standing. Moreover, lack of the funds needed to hire an advocate would have prevented all but a very small percentage of the population from suing someone.[23] It was a commonplace, therefore, that only the rich (or their dependents) could depend on the courts for justice. As the elder Seneca puts into the mouth of the man-on-the-street, "Am I, a poor man, to accuse a rich man?"[24] Or, as a character in Petronius's *Satyricon* complains, "Of what avail are laws where money rules alone, and the poor suitor can never succeed? . . . A lawsuit is nothing more than a public auction, and the knightly juror who sits listening to the case approves, with the record of his vote, something bought."[25]

Building on the work of legal anthropologists, Alan Mitchell argues that the high degree of social stratification in Greco-Roman society suggests that people of higher status were much more likely than those of lower status to initiate litigation—and to do so against people outside their own class. "People of the same rank are more likely to work out a compromise rather than go to court. The further away they are on the social scale the less likely they are to settle out of court. An increase in stratification predicts a decrease in conciliation. One can conclude from these basic principles that people of higher status are favored in the legal process and are more likely to litigate against those of lower status and are less likely to litigate against one another."[26] If these generalizations hold true for Corinthian society, then we would expect that 1 Corinthians 6 is referring to higher-status Christians taking lower-status Christians to court.

Certain aspects of Paul's language in 1 Corinthians 6 support this view. Earlier, in 3:18, Paul pointedly referred to "the wise man among you" with something of an ironic tone, turning the claim of some Corinthians that they were sophoi to his own advantage. He does much the same in 6:5, hinting, with mock incredulity, that there must be *someone* in the church wise enough to settle their disputes. Furthermore, as Mitchell outlines, Paul uses a philosophical topos to convince the Corinthian litigants that it would be better to *suffer* harm than to risk *doing* harm to their fellow Christians. Musonius Rufus, for example, spoke on the subject, "Will the Philosopher Prosecute Anyone for Personal Injury?"[27] Prosecution, according to Rufus, is returning injury for injury, a shameful act for a truly wise man. Furthermore, since a wise man has all important things under his own control (his will, his happiness, and so on), he cannot be injured by someone else. But recourse to litigation is an admission of injury, and therefore a denial of the self-control and self-sufficiency of the wise man. The philosopher should be beneficent in return for insult. As Mitchell concludes, "Thus this element of the *topos* is well established among the philosophers that the truly wise person will never litigate, return injury for injury or concede to having been harmed by involving in that kind of activity."[28] Therefore, when Paul says, "To have lawsuits at all among yourselves is already a loss. Why not rather put up with an injustice? Why not rather let yourself be defrauded? But on the contrary, you yourselves commit injustice and you defraud, and this your own brothers!," he is shaming the Strong at Corinth by means of the very discourse they had prided themselves on: the discourse of the moral-philosophical wise man.[29]

Finally, Paul's *solution* to the litigation problem also suggests that the Strong had been taking advantage of lower-status Christians by means of the courts. As I have argued, throughout 1 Corinthians 1–4 and in regard to both food offered to idols and the Lord's Supper, Paul directs his comments above all to the Strong and proposes solutions that necessitate a change in their behavior to meet the needs of those lower down the social scale. In 1 Corinthians 6:5 he urges the Corinthians to give up any recourse to the courts and, if necessary, to solve disputes by means of private arbitration.[30] Christians, Paul claims, will someday judge the entire cosmos, including the angels. Surely they can find one person among themselves wise enough to settle everyday affairs (*biōtika*).[31] By insisting that disputes be settled within the church, however, Paul has taken away much of the advantage the higher-class Christians would have enjoyed in the courts.

We can only imagine how such private arbitration would have taken place. Presumably the members at odds with one another would have been expected to choose a person or a few persons from the church to settle their dispute. Or the dispute might be played out and decided at a public meeting of the church, the *ekklēsia*. Since it is certain that lower-class Christians outnumbered upper-class Christians in the Corinthian church (see 1:26), the lower-class members would probably have had a better chance of receiving a sympathetic hearing. Furthermore, with several households (and probably more than one house church) represented, the prestige or power of one particular household or patron would have been diminished. In other words, by changing the venue for settling disputes, Paul changes the dynamics of power at work. The house church, with its majority of lower-class members and sometimes an ideology of equality or status disruption, places the lower-class member in a much better position vis-à-vis the higher-class member. Without being explicit about it, Paul has again taken the side of the Christians of lower status and called on the higher-status Christians to give up their prerogatives for the sake of unity within the church.[32]

This issue of unity in the church brings up another of Paul's main concerns: to solidify the boundary between the church and the "world." Whether the Strong are taking lower- or other higher-status members to court, Paul insists that arbitration, if it is necessary at all, take place within the secure boundaries of the body of Christ, the congregation. Paul destabilizes the power of the Strong and, at the same time, underscores the differences between the body of Christ and the cosmos "out there." Paul thus has two goals in 1 Corinthians 6:1–11: first, to deconstruct status difference and reverse normal power and hierarchy, and second, to maintain firm communal boundaries. In the first case, Paul disrupts the expected hierarchy of the body of Christ; in the second, he fixes more firmly the boundary between that body and the corrupt cosmos.[33]

Pauline Economy: The Problem of Money in Paul's Ministry

Another important occasion for status disputes in Paul's dealings with the Corinthian church arises from his financial relations with them. At times, Paul claims that he does not accept financial support from the churches he founded (1 Cor. 9). But at other times, Paul's letters show that he does indeed accept money from his churches, and he provides various explanations for and portrayals of those financial relationships. Scholars have offered many explanations for why Paul refused financial support from some of his churches.[34] The different explanations are so numerous because Paul's letters themselves suggest several different reasons for his attempted financial independence. I will not try to settle that question here but will instead analyze four passages from Paul's letters that highlight the importance of status and power in his financial dealings with his converts.

In what is probably Paul's earliest extant letter, he writes to the recently founded church in Thessalonica, "For you remember, brothers, our labor and toil. Night and day we worked so as not to be a burden to you while we preached to you the gospel of God. You yourselves are witnesses, as is God, how we behaved properly and justly and blamelessly among you who believe. You know how I acted toward each of you like a father with his children, encouraging you and comforting and bearing witness so that you might live in a manner worthy of the God who invites you into his own kingdom and glory" (1 Thess. 2:9–12). Paul reminds the Thessalonians that he and his co-workers supported themselves by manual labor at Thessalonica. He implies that there were several reasons for this. In the first place, they did not want to be a burden to the recent converts. It is apparent from other references in the same letter that most if not all of these converts were themselves manual laborers (4:11; cf. 2 Thess. 3:7–12).[35] Paul is probably being quite realistic, then, when he imagines that financial expenditures for himself would have constituted a hardship for the church. He also implies that his labor had other, pedagogical purposes: his self-support is intended as a sign of his "proper, just, blameless" conduct and intentions. The twentieth century, after all, is not the only century in which religious leaders have turned their ministries to entrepreneurial advantage. Paul wants to make clear that he is not to be lumped among the charlatans of his day who use their preaching to line their pockets. As still another reason for his self-support, Paul hints that his actions are intended as a model for the Thessalonians' own behavior. This becomes more explicit later in the letter when Paul says, "We encourage you, brothers . . . to aspire to live quietly and to mind your own business and to work with your own hands, just as we instructed you, so that you may live in a seemly manner toward those on the outside and that you may need nothing (or no one)" (4:10–12). This is an allusion to Paul's earlier statement already quoted above, and it becomes clear that what Paul means by "living in a seemly manner" (4:12: *peripatein euschēmonōs;* 2:12: *peripatein axiōs*) has to do in part with manual labor. The Thessalonians are urged to work with their hands so that their lives will be acceptable to outsiders and so that they will be independent.[36]

In one sense, Paul shows a strange (though not unknown in the Greco-Roman world) willingness to give up his own opportunities to avoid manual labor, opportunities that were probably his by virtue of his class. He gave up certain prerogatives to demonstrate by example that the Christian life could be lived by manual laborers *as* manual laborers. By contrast, most people of the upper class would avoid manual labor at all costs, even if it meant sponging off friends and family and going monstrously into debt. Paul was able to divorce himself from that value system enough to take on manual labor even when he apparently could have avoided it and even though he himself considers it degrading.

In another sense, though, perhaps one not even intended by Paul, his statements about manual labor in 1 Thessalonians functioned in an anti-revolutionary way to keep Christianity from becoming—or even looking like —the sort of movement that might challenge the class structure of the first century, as did some forms of Cynicism.[37] 1 Thessalonians entertains no vision of a classless society. Paul projects no sympathy for laborers who seek a less laborious life. And his advice here works to keep Christianity as a hierarchy-supporting, rather than a hierarchy-questioning, movement, at least as far as manual laborers are concerned. Paul's instructions to the Thessalonians keep Christianity conservative in both effect and appearance, whether or not this is Paul's intention. It is clear, at any rate, that Paul wants the Thessalonian converts to remain manual laborers, so much so that he is willing to become a manual laborer himself to provide an example.

We find a very different situation in Paul's dealings with the church he founded at Philippi. Writing to that church, he says,

> Nevertheless, you did well becoming partners in my affliction. For indeed you know, Philippians, that in the beginning of the gospel, when I came out from Macedonia, no church entered into partnership with me in an account of giving and receiving except you alone. Because even in Thessalonica, more than once, you sent (funds) toward alleviating my need. Not that I desire the gift, but I desire the interest that accrues to your credit. I have received full payment, and I abound; I have been filled, receiving from Epaphroditus the things from you, a fragrant offering, an acceptable sacrifice, well-pleasing to God. And my God will fill your every need, according to his riches in glory in Christ Jesus. To God our father be glory forever and ever, Amen. [Philippians 4:14–20]

Apparently, in spite of his insistence to the Corinthians that it was not his practice to accept money from his churches (1 Cor. 9), Paul did take money from some churches, and here he writes to thank the Philippians for their support. The different ways in which Paul characterizes the financial situation—the discourses he uses to talk about money—indicate that he recognizes potential problems regarding how his actions may be interpreted. His language shifts from financial terminology and language reflecting the conventions of Greco-Roman "friendship" to cultic-sacrificial language. The Greek for phrases like "partnership," "an account of giving and receiving," "the interest (fruit) that accrues to your credit," "I have received full payment," belongs to the language of the business world.[38] The same language also often occurs in Greco-Roman conventions of friendship, by which people would bind other people to themselves by giving and receiving gifts, including money.[39] Those friendship conventions, however, entailed certain expectations, obligations, and reciprocations. Furthermore, Greco-Roman friendship carried clear status implications in its expectations. To receive a gift from someone without being able to repay the gift could be interpreted as an admission that the receiver was of lower status than the giver. Generally in the Greco-Roman world, money was given downward on the social scale, whereas "honor" was given upward, in return for money.[40] It is important, therefore, to see how Paul's discourse moves from normal business language and the language of friendship to cultic-sacrificial language.

For example, Paul first calls the money a "gift" (v. 16), which is not surprising, given the way people passed around money as gifts and loans disguised as gifts. No one among the higher classes talked about payments in such contexts. But then Paul turns the gift into something spiritual: "I do not care about the gift for myself, of course; I care only about the increase it brings for your spiritual credit." Besides spiritualizing the gift, moreover, Paul transforms his own monetary benefit into a benefit to the givers themselves (v. 17). Next, he turns all this talk about financial support into talk about sacrifice to God. The Philippians have not simply given Paul money; they have actually given God a "fragrant offering," an "acceptable sacrifice" (v. 18). We need not be so cynical as to suggest that Paul is *intentionally* deflecting his own debt to the Philippians by making their gift one to God rather than himself, as if he were merely trying to get off the hook of obligation that accepting the gift would imply. Rhetorically, nonetheless, his discourse has just that effect. What the Philippians gave, they gave to God; the gift accrues to their own benefit, and in the end, it is God, not Paul, who will repay the gift.

Paul's rhetoric takes what would normally be interpreted as a friendship transaction—which, when transacted between persons of unequal status, signals that the recipient is a person of lower status—and transforms it into a three-way transaction in which the naked financial aspect is masked, de-emphasized, and spiritualized. The rhetoric serves to push aside the normal conventions for the giving and receiving of money and its implications for status and substitutes a new set of conventions ruled by a spiritualized "partnership in Christ." Thus, the usual status implications of accepting money— implying that Paul would be a dependent, and even a client, of the Philippians if he did not return the favor—are overturned and replaced by different status implications and obligations. Paul's carefully nuanced shift in discourse indicates how tricky it could be for someone of his social station to accept financial support; it further reveals his own discomfort and insecurity in receiving money, even from a church with which he has a close, trusting relationship, as he obviously does with the Philippian congregation.[41] All this is to be expected, however, if Paul is, after all, someone from a higher-status background whose situation has become a potential embarrassment because of his activity as a manual laborer and his need, at least every once in a while, to accept financial support. As we will see, these problems came to a head in his dealings with the Corinthian church—precisely because problems of status, hierarchy, and power were already besetting the church and manifesting themselves in a variety of ways.

I have dealt at length elsewhere with 1 Corinthians 9, where Paul discusses his reasons for rejecting financial support from the church at Corinth, so will only summarize those conclusions here.[42] In the midst of an argument that the Strong at Corinth should give up their freedom to eat meat sacrificed to idols for the sake of Christians with weaker consciences, Paul digresses to use himself as an example of someone of high status who has given up a right or freedom in order to benefit someone of lower status. Although he had the right as an apostle to receive financial support from his churches, he freely gave up that right, became a manual laborer to earn his own keep, and thus, in a sense "enslaved" himself to the people he was expected to lead. Just as he gave up his right to support in order to reach those of lower status—becoming weak to win the weak, a manual laborer to win manual laborers—so the Strong at Corinth should give up their right to eat meat in order to avoid offending the weak in the Corinthian church.

To make his point, Paul appropriates a political topos that portrays populist leaders as those who enslave themselves to the people they are supposed to lead. They "become all things to all people" and, especially, change their appearance to appeal to the masses. They lower themselves socially in order to appeal to the lower class. Paul's use of this topos suggests that one should interpret his rejection of monetary support and his self-support by manual labor as a self-conscious attempt on his part to lower himself socially in order to identify with the lower class. To people of the upper class, Paul's rhetoric would have looked like flattery and despicable catering to the masses. Lower-class persons themselves, however, would have perceived it positively. They would have interpreted Paul's manual labor as symbolizing an identification with their interests. Furthermore, Paul's rhetoric would have been heard as signifying that he was to be considered patron of the patronless, the populist protector of the common people. In 1 Corinthians 9, moreover, Paul proposes this self-lowering as a model for the behavior he is urging on the Strong. They too, according to Paul, should give up high-status prerogatives—in this case their right to eat whatever they wish—so as to avoid "hindering the gospel" and offending the weak.

In 1 Corinthians Paul himself brings up the issue of his self-support; there is no indication that he is being overtly criticized for rejecting the Corinthians' money. By the time he writes 2 Corinthians 10–13, however, he has been openly attacked for his decision to refuse their money and to support himself by manual labor. Rather than being offended by Paul taking money, some people at Corinth have been offended by his decision *not* to take money from them. This is probably because, as Peter Marshall explains, those Corinthians were people of relatively high status who wanted to support Paul as something like their "household philosopher." They may also have wanted him to give up what they would have considered activity shameful for the leader of their church—that is, manual labor. Several times, therefore, Paul insists that he will take no money from them, which they probably interpret as a refusal on his part to enter into a relationship of friendship with them. Paul's actions seem to them an expression of enmity, or at least a rejection of their offer of friendship, and an implied insult.[43]

One place where this issue comes to a head is in 2 Corinthians 12:14–17, where Paul writes: "Look, this is the third time I am ready to come to you, and I will not be a burden. For I seek not what is yours but you. For children ought not to save up for their parents, but parents for children. I will gladly be spent and completely expended for your lives. If I love you so much more, am I loved less?" Here again, as he had earlier in the same letter (11:9; 12:13), Paul insists that he would be a burden if he accepted money from them. But we must take care not to accept Paul's own, explicit explanation of his actions as all there was to it. The Thessalonian Christians were probably manual laborers, so when Paul tells *them* that he worked with his hands while in Thessalonica in order to avoid burdening them, we may take him at his word. But the Corinthians who urge Paul to take money from them seem to have been quite capable of supporting him.[44] Therefore, his statement that he refuses their money to avoid burdening them is a mask concealing the true significance of his refusal. It may also have been the case that some Corinthians had found out that although Paul told them he refused money from his churches (1 Cor. 9), he had actually been receiving money from other churches, probably even while staying in Corinth (Phil. 4:15–16; 2 Cor. 11:8). We have no way of knowing if Paul was intentionally deceiving the Corinthians on this score, but some of them, not surprisingly, took his actions and words as deceptive. In 2 Corinthians 12:16, for example, he seems to echo Corinthian insinuations that he has taken advantage of them "by guile." In 2:17–18 he insists that his statements to them have *not* been vacillating or deceptive, implying that some at Corinth have claimed that they were. At any rate, Paul's financial relationship with these Corinthians has caused problems. Those problems obviously relate to status issues, and Paul's insistence that he merely wanted to avoid burdening the Corinthians cannot be the whole story. More of the story comes out by analyzing the status implications of his defense of himself here in 2 Corinthians 12:14–17.

Here, as in the letter to the Philippians, Paul puts the problem in terms of personal rather than material currency by insisting, "I seek not what is yours, but you" (cf. Phil. 4:17). Then he attempts a rhetorical maneuver that he has already used with the Corinthians, as examined in the previous chapter (in 1 Cor. 4:14–21). He introduces the discourse of the household, casting himself as the father and the Corinthians as his children. In one sense, this shift allows Paul to decline (gracefully, he hopes) the Corinthians' money by pointing out that parents give money to children, not vice versa. In a more subtle, ideological sense, however, this rhetorical move casts what could be (and had been) taken as low-status behavior—self-support by manual labor—in high-status terms, as the kind of sacrifice that parents (higher status) should make for their children (lower status). Some people at Corinth were clearly implying that Paul was low-class because he would not take their money and instead practiced a craft. By using a different discourse, Paul rejects their evaluation of his activity and interprets it quite differently, as high-status and authoritative. Paul is like the loving father, kind but superior.

Brushing aside his rather disingenuous demurrals, therefore, we can say that the primary reason why Paul refused support from the Corinthian Christians was a hesitance to enter into any financial relationship that might undermine his position of authority with them. Accepting their money might have led them to regard him as something like their household philosopher—indeed, as their client and themselves as his patrons. Given the fact that Paul's status was already a problem at Corinth—due to his questionable rhetorical abilities and his role as a manual laborer—accepting money from these particular people, who, as we have already seen, valued traditional status designations, would have probably undermined his authority. Paul's finances, therefore, directly relate to status issues.

In sum, this examination of Paul's rhetoric about his finances gives rise to a picture of Paul as preoccupied with status problems, especially in his dealings with the Corinthian church. Paul was someone originally of high status whose current status was problematic when seen from an upper-class standpoint. The Corinthians who offered him money were also of high status. In order to retain his position of leadership and independence, Paul, at least in his own mind, had to avoid appearing to be their client or household philosopher. The later reasons (those in 2 Cor.) Paul gives for refusing their support are numerous: he wants to avoid burdening them; he wants to avoid appearing to take advantage of them; he, as their father, should be *their* provider, not vice versa; and so on. In 1 Corinthians, however, his rejection of their support fits his rhetorical strategy of status reversal: it is an example of his up-ending of normal status symbols—an example he calls on the Strong to imitate. Whatever the later complications caused by his self-support, in 1 Corinthians Paul uses it as part of an overall strategy of rejecting the status symbols of upper-class ideology and disrupting the hierarchical assumptions of the Strong.

With regard to four different issues addressed in 1 Corinthians—the divisions evident at the Lord's Supper, eating meat offered to idols, Christians' use of Corinthian courts, and reactions to Paul's means of self-support—the Corinthian church was split along social status lines, high-status members being at odds with lower-status members. In each case Paul pursues the rhetorical strategy introduced in 1 Corinthians 1–4: he addresses primarily the higher-status Christians, urging on them a change in behavior that will support the position of the lower-status Christians. He regularly sides with the lower-status Corinthians. His call for the Strong to alter their behavior also serves to enact what he spoke about mythologically in chapters 1–4: the substitution of the values of the "other realm" for the values and status indicators of "this world" and the consequent reversal of normal status indicators. In each case, the Strong are urged to submit to the Weak and thereby to recognize the alternative value system of the apocalyptic kingdom of God. By the disruptive economics of Paul's rhetoric, the upper-class hierarchical body is repeatedly turned on its head.

4 Tongues of Angels in the Body of Christ

The disruptive hierarchy of the body of Christ, according to Paul, is nowhere more evident than in his discussion of speaking in tongues (1 Cor. 12–14). Paul repeatedly invokes, often subtly, status terms, and his arguments throughout these chapters are built on the assumption that the practice of speaking in tongues has ruptured the Corinthian church precisely because glossolalia carries status implications. Thus in 12:4–11 Paul continually stresses unity in diversity in order to overcome divisiveness owing to different valuations being assigned to different gifts, with tongues as the implied higher-status gift. In 13:4, in the midst of the famous "hymn to love" that has as its purpose a relative devaluing of speaking in tongues by emphasizing the greater value of love, Paul again uses the term "puffed up," suggesting that it is the "wise" or "strong" in Corinth who value—too much, in Paul's opinion—both knowledge and the esoteric language of the angels. He himself normally places a high-status valuation on speaking in tongues. He claims the gift for himself, even going so far as to claim a greater share of it than any of the Corinthians (14:18). In 14:2 Paul says that the person who speaks in tongues speaks not to human beings but to God. "For no one hears, but in the spirit [*pneuma*] he speaks mysteries." Glossolalia is divine discourse; it deals in "mysteries," which for Paul is a highly valued epistemological category. It seems clear that for both Paul and the Strong at Corinth, speaking in tongues is a high-status activity, and its status significance, as we will see, is precisely what, in Paul's opinion, makes it problematic in the Corinthian church.

In most previous research on 1 Corinthians, as surveyed in the last chapter, scholars have not placed glossolalia among the theological issues that divide the Corinthian church along status lines. I believe there are a couple of reasons for this. In the first place, Paul's rhetoric about speaking in tongues addresses issues of status subtly, often using words that are usually translated by English terms that mask the status significance of the original Greek, as will be shown below. In the second place, it seems that many modern scholars have assumed, like most modern intellectuals, that speaking in tongues is an activity of uneducated, marginal people. As a consequence, it is assumed that if glossolalia in the Corinthian church is to be identified with any particular status group, it is probably one of low status; but this assumption does not fit with the force and direction of Paul's argument. I have argued elsewhere, on the contrary, that for many cultures glossolalic-like activity (that is, the practice of esoteric speech acts) was a valued status indicator, unproblematically linked with people in the society who had access to other forms of esoteric but valued knowledge.[1] If we read 1 Corinthians 12–14 with the assumption that the Corinthian speakers in tongues were also the Strong who valued other forms of divine "knowledge," many of Paul's arguments make better sense. Glossolalia—what Paul calls "angelic tongues"—is thus another issue with regard to which Paul's proposed body, the body of Christ, represents the hierarchical reversal of the normal cosmic body of upper-class ideology.

The Social Status of Esoteric Speech

Historians of religion have pointed to several accounts of unusual speech in Greco-Roman society as parallels to early Christian glossolalia, several of which I have rejected as helpful parallels since it seems that the language being spoken, though confusing and in need of interpretation, was after all Greek or Latin or some other language well known to the bystanders. In such cases, the speech activity is esoteric only in that the interpretation of the utterance, not the language itself, is uncertain.[2] But apart from these questionable parallels, we do find several references in Greco-Roman literature to speech acts that look very much like the Corinthian speaking in tongues.

The ancient Jewish text known as the *Testament of Job* is particularly remarkable, in that it portrays glossolalia as a special ability to speak *angelic* languages, possibly a parallel to Paul's use of the term "tongues of angels" to refer, almost certainly, to the Corinthian speaking in tongues.[3] Job's daughters, instead of receiving shares of Job's property as did his sons, are given sashes (or cords) that give them the power to speak and sing in heavenly languages. Although *dialektos* ("dialect") is the term for such speech throughout the account, the rest of the terminology describing the activity varies: "the angelic dialect" (48:2), "the dialect of the archons" (49:2), "her mouth spoke ecstatically in the dialect of those on high" (50:1), "the dialect of the cherubim" (50:2), "each in her own distinctive dialect" (52:7). Although given to Job's daughters as compensation for receiving no property, the language describing the activity clearly demonstrates its perceived high status. This speaking is not gibberish but the rational language of beings superior to humans.[4]

Montanists, a charismatic group of Christians whose history began in the second century C.E., also seem to have considered glossolalia a high-status activity. The main early leaders, Montanus, Priscilla, and Maximilla, probably all spoke in tongues; moreover, we have little evidence of glossolalia among other, lower-status members of the movement.[5] Tertullian, who was of relatively high status and was also doubtless influenced somewhat by Montanism, describes a Christian woman's behavior in ways reminiscent of the *Testament of Job:* "We have now amongst us a sister whose lot it has been to be favored with sundry gifts of revelation, which she experiences in the Spirit by ecstatic vision amidst the sacred rites of the Lord's day in the church: she converses with angels, and sometimes even with the Lord; she both sees and hears mysterious communications; some men's hearts she understands, and to them who are in need she distributes remedies."[6] Tertullian also takes the woman to be granted esoteric, angelic speech.

Jews and Christians, however, were not the only people who assumed that superior, heavenly beings spoke languages different from human language. Dio Chrysostom indicates that the idea was commonplace when he asks rhetorically, "Tell me, do you think Apollo speaks Attic or Doric? Or that men and gods have the same language?" Homer, Dio suggests, seems to know the gods' language: "He talks to us almost as though he were acquainted with their language, tells us that it was not the same as ours, and that they do not apply the same names to the various things as we do."[7] The same idea is found later, in *Poimandres*, which narrates the soul's ascent through the high spheres. When the soul, stripped of the lower elements, finally reaches the eighth heaven, it joins in praise with the other heavenly beings. "And being made like those with whom he dwells, he hears the Powers, who are above the substance of the eight spheres, singing praise to God with a voice that is theirs alone."

The Greek (*phōnē tini idia*) suggests a private language for the sphere of the Ogdoad.[8]

All these references to angelic language or esoteric speech portray it as unequivocally high-status behavior, often connected with leadership roles. This picture is also borne out by Lucian's satirical exposé of Alexander of Abonoteichus, a gentleman who, in the second century C.E., invented and starred in his very own cult. Lucian, unsuccessfully attempting to discredit Alexander, insists that Alexander was originally from a lowly background, from "obscure, humble folk" (*Alexander the False Prophet* 11). According to Lucian, Alexander's fits of prophetic madness, during which he foams at the mouth and raves in typical mantic fashion, considerably raise his stature among the people. As Lucian tells it, Alexander, in a frenzy like that experienced by worshippers of the Great Mother, utters "some insensible sounds, which were probably Hebrew or Phoenician" (13, my trans.). Apparently, Lucian does not know what language Alexander was speaking; he may, in fact, be reporting hearsay. Certainly, the awestruck bystanders do not understand the language, except when Alexander happens to intersperse the names of Apollo and Asclepius. Although it is not altogether clear what Alexander was doing, therefore, it is obvious that he was using esoteric speech—possibly not a human language at all—in a manner not unfamiliar to his audience. In spite of Lucian's slurs, the activity was held in high esteem by a wide range of people who became devotees of the cult. The esoteric speech correlates unproblematically with Alexander's other insignia of a priestly role and high status.[9]

In only one source do we find any indication that glossolalia could possibly have been perceived as low-status activity. I believe it likely that Celsus's description of "several kinds of prophecies" in Phoenicia and Palestine includes an account of glossolalia. After describing the statements of these prophets, Celsus continues: "Having brandished these threats they then go on to add incomprehensible, incoherent, and utterly obscure utterances, the meaning of which no intelligent person could discover: for they are meaningless and nonsensical, and give a chance for any fool or sorcerer to take the words in whatever sense he likes."[10] Of course, Celsus is determined to portray all Christians as gullible, ignorant bumpkins. We should be wary, therefore, of taking his deprecation of this prophetic activity as implying a general societal deprecation of glossolalia as lower-class.

At a time not far removed from Celsus's attack on Christianity, Irenaeus gives a rather glowing, eloquent testimony to the high status attributed to glossolalia:

For this reason does the apostle declare, "We speak wisdom among them that are perfect," terming those persons "perfect" who have received the Spirit of God, and who through the Spirit of God do speak in all languages, as he used Himself to speak. In like manner we do also hear many brethren in the Church, who possess prophetic gifts, and who through the Spirit speak all kinds of languages (*glōssai*), and bring to light for the general benefit the hidden things of men, and declare the mysteries of God, whom also the apostle terms "spiritual," they being spiritual because they partake of the Spirit, and not because their flesh has been stripped off and taken away, and because they have become purely spiritual.[11]

Speaking in tongues is here understood as representing the spiritual perfection of those who partake of the higher realms of reality. Irenaeus reveals neither the slightest embarrassment about speaking in tongues nor any doubt about its status implications: it is clearly a high-status activity. Again—as in the *Testament of Job*, Tertullian, and even Dio Chrysostom—heavenly beings are presumed to use a heavenly language.

A century or so after Irenaeus, a theoretical explanation of the religious use of esoteric language was offered by the Platonist Iamblicus. Prophecy, according to Iamblicus, is divine possession, which "emits words which are not understood by those that utter them; for they pronounce them, as it is said, with an insane mouth (*mainomenō stomati*) and are wholly subservient, and entirely yield themselves to the energy of the predominating God."[12] Later in the same treatise Iamblicus explains that names, terms, and prayers in other languages should be used in rituals even when their meanings are unknown to the participants, because the efficacy of the language lies in the terms, not in human understanding; the gods, after all, understand the language quite well. "And, moreover, though it should be unknown to us, yet this very circumstance is that which is most venerable in it, for it is too excellent to be divided into knowledge" (7. 4–5). Iamblicus, though later than the other authors I have mentioned, shares their common sense that different beings use different languages and that human beings who wish to converse with higher beings may at times speak a higher language. To share that language is to share the status that goes with it.

This brief survey of ancient esoteric speech acts certainly cannot be taken as proof that the Corinthian speakers in tongues were themselves higher-status members of the church there. But it does suggest that they *may* have been, given that people in Greco-Roman society regularly associated esoteric speech with other high-status indicators. Better indications of the status significance of glossolalia in Corinth come from analyzing Paul's rhetoric about the activity, especially that focused on two status-laden images: the church as a body and mind/spirit dualism.

Paul's Use of the Society-as-Body Topos

> Just as the body is one and has many members, and all the members of the body, though many, are one body, so also is Christ. . . . For the body is not one member, but many. Suppose the foot said, "Because I am not a hand, I am not part of the body." That would not mean that it was separate from the body, would it? And if the ear said, "Because I am not an eye, I do not belong to the body," that would not separate it from the body. If the whole body were an eye, where would hearing be? But if the whole body were hearing, where would smell be? In fact, God has arranged each one of the members in the body just as he wished it to be. If all of them were one member, where would the body be? As it is, there are many members, but one body. The eye cannot say to the hand, "I don't need you." Nor can the head say it to the feet. On the contrary, by a great margin the members of the body that appear to be weaker are actually more necessary, and those body parts which seem to be dishonorable we cover with even greater honor, and our ugly parts have greater beauty, while our beautiful parts have no need of this. God has thus put the body together, giving greater honor to the inferior member, in order that there will be no schism in the body but the members may have the same concern for one another. [1 Corinthians 12:12, 14–25]

Use of the human body as an analogy for human society is ancient and widespread.[13] The microcosm of the body was used to explain how unity can exist in diversity within the macrocosm of society. Moreover, the analogy, as I have already shown in Chapter 1 above, usually functioned conservatively to support hierarchy and to argue that inequality is both necessary and salutary.[14] Thus the body analogy usually occurs in Greco-Roman political and philosophical discussions of homonoia, or concord, as can be seen in the writings of Cicero, Seneca, Dio Chrysostom, and many others.[15] But even apart from homonoia speeches, authors use the body analogy to promote social unity by maintaining existing property and social relations and by discouraging conflict.[16] Since upper-class authors naturally want to mitigate conflict lest it disrupt the prevailing modes of production and their own place within them, they invoke the harmony of the body to argue that conflict is ultimately destructive (Xenophon *Memorabilia* 2. 3. 18).

The conservative ideological benefits to be derived from the use of the body analogy are obvious. Conceiving the social group as a body is a strong strategy for establishing the givenness of the current order and hierarchy. Who can imagine a foot becoming a hand—or, even less plausibly, a head? Social revolution is no more a real possibility than is walking on one's hands. Granted, someone may do it temporarily or experimentally, but the given "natural" hierarchy will, in the end, reassert itself. Of course, this is a culturally determined common sense. There is no reason why the verticality of head–foot should automatically lead to construing society as vertical. The etymology of the hierarchy probably works the other way around: the class structure of society prompts those in the position of "heads" to construe the human body as similarly hierarchical. It is the goal of conservative rhetoric to reverse this process in the minds of its hearers and convince them that the physical givenness of the human body mandates the hierarchy of the social body.

Usually the hierarchy is assumed to be a given, neither contested nor even reflected upon in the sources; yet at other times the strong ideological function of the body analogy seems to be evident even to the ancient authors who use it. Livy's famous use of the analogy, for example, occurs on the lips of Menenius, a senator, who attempts to persuade the plebs, who have gone on strike *en masse*, to return to work (*Ab urbe condita* 2. 32. 7–11).[17] Once upon a time, according to the story, the members of the body went on strike against the belly, complaining that they did all the work, only to turn over all the produce to the belly, which simply stuffed itself with the fruits of their labors. Of course, their strike eventually led to the death of all the members. Menenius's story moves the plebs to reconsider their strike, and "concordia" is restored (2. 33. 1). Naturally, everyone lives happily ever after.

Livy's use of the traditional story is blatantly and self-consciously ideological. The belly is explicitly said to represent the governing class (*patres*), while the serving members are the plebs. Interestingly, Livy's analogy does not deny that the ruling class actually produces nothing itself. Instead, it makes the value of that class lie in its circulation, rather than production, of value, as the stomach was considered to supply nourishment to the other parts of the body. Ironically, but not surprisingly, it seems never to have occurred to Livy—or to his docile plebs—that the laborers might use the analogy to demand from the belly a bigger share of the nourishment.[18]

The ideological use of the body analogy is elaborated by the historian Polyaenus in his *Stratagems of War*: "Iphicrates used to resemble an army marshalled for action to the human body. The phalanx he called the breast, the lightarmed troops the hands, the cavalry the feet, and the general the head. If any of the inferior parts were wanting, the army he said was defective: but if it wanted a general, it wanted every thing" (3. 9. 22). Polyaenus's ideological addition to the traditional analogy is his explanation that the ruling part is not only necessary but *more* necessary than any other part of the body, just as Livy's story could be taken to imply that the belly (the ruling, but nonproducing class) is more essential than any other part of the body.[19]

Paul's use of the body analogy in 1 Corinthians 12:12–27 stands squarely in the Greco-Roman rhetorical tradition. In the first place, as I have already hinted in Chapter 2, 1 Corinthians 12–14 contains many elements familiar from homonoia speeches. The theme of mutual benefit is introduced in the first few verses of chapter 12 (*pros to sympheron*, 12:7; cf. 6:12; 7:35; 10:23, 33). The theme of "the different and the same" pervades the first few verses of chapter 12, with a repetition of terms emphasizing both diversity and unity (for example, v. 4: *diaereseis . . . to auto*).[20] In verse 12 Paul emphasizes that the body is one, even though made up of diverse members; he stresses the interdependence of the members (vv. 15 and 21) and repeats the usual assertion that the body would perish—or at least would become a nonfunctioning monstrosity—were it not for the different functions of the different members (vv. 17–20). Finally, Paul is traditional in his claim that the order of the body is a given (v. 18), although, according to him, it is God (not "nature") who has placed each member in its appropriate place.

Whereas traditionally the body analogy is invoked to solidify an unquestioned status hierarchy, Paul's rhetoric questions that hierarchy: "But by much more the members of the body which are judged (supposed) to be weaker (of lower status) are actually necessary, and what we judge (or suppose) to be the less honorable of the body, to these we accord more honor, and our least beautiful (presentable) have more beauty (presentableness), whereas our beautiful parts do not need it. But God arranged the body, giving greater honor to the lesser, in order that there may be no schism in the body, but that the members may be equally concerned for one another" (vv. 22–25).

In these verses Paul uses a variety of terms whose status significance is often lost in translation: *ta dokounta* ("the esteemed"), *asthenestera* ("weaker"), *anagkaia* ("necessary"), *atimotera* ("less honorable"), *timē perissotera* ("abundantly honored"), *hysteroumenos* ("lacking"). The remarkable thing about Paul's imagery is not his use of status terms, which often occur in rhetorical applications of the body analogy to homonoia issues, but his claim that the normally conceived body hierarchy is actually only an apparent, surface hierarchy. The genitals, he says, may *seem* to be the most shameful part of the body; but our very attention to them—our constant care to cover them and shield them from trivializing and vulgarizing public exposure—demonstrates that they are actually the most necessary of the body's members, those with the *highest* status.[21] There is an interesting play on words in verse 22: "the apparently weaker members of the body are actually necessary (*anagkaia*)," the term *anagkaia* being ambiguous. It may imply high status, since homonoia rhetoric was always concerned to demonstrate that the higher-status members of the body, those representing the ruling class, such as the head and the belly, were the most necessary and unexpendable parts of the body. But *anagkaia* may also imply low status, since the penis was euphemistically called the "necessary" member.[22] Hence the ambiguity here: Paul admits that the genitals, the "necessary" members, seem to be the weaker; but, by their very necessariness, they can demand high status.[23] They have a legitimate claim, therefore, to honor and care from the other body members. Through his play on words, Paul both admits and denies the low status of the weaker members of the body.

The same ambiguity of argument is found in verses 23–24. Paul takes with one hand what he has just given with the other. He starts with the assumption that there are "ugly" or "shameful" and "beautiful" or "presentable" members of the body. The different terms carry just such multiple translation possibilities: *aschēmona* means "unpresentable" in the sense that these body members, the "private parts," need privacy; but it also means "ugly" in the sense that these body parts are considered, by Paul at least, as "misshapen" or as possessing no natural beauty. Likewise, *euschēmona* connotes both "beauty" and "presentableness." Furthermore, the terms are, like so many others in this section, clear status terms, given the prevailing upper-class ideology that assumed a necessary connection between physical beauty and nobility—and even divinity.[24]

Initially in verse 23, Paul seems to be saying that *we*, by our own choosing, accede greater honor to the less honorable members. But then, in the second half of the verse, his wording changes: "and our ugly parts *have* greater beauty, while our beautiful parts have no need." It is not our condescension that has attributed more beauty to the less comely; the supposedly ugly parts actually *are* more beautiful than the allegedly beautiful parts. Paul's argument may be confused—it is certainly confusing—but the end result is clear: the conventional attribution of status is more problematic than appears on the surface; the normal connection between status and honor should be questioned; and we must recognize that those who, on the surface, occupy positions of lower status are actually more essential than those of higher status and therefore should be accorded more honor. This is not, then, a compensatory move on Paul's part, by means of which those of lower status are to be compensated for their low position by a benefaction of honor. Rather, his rhetoric pushes for an actual reversal of the normal, "this-worldly" attribution of honor and status. The lower is made higher, and the higher lower.

Paul's argument is a curious twist on the traditional Platonic distinction between the "real" and the "apparent." Whereas Platonism—indeed, practically all upper-class philosophy and ideology—uses the body analogy to exclude any questioning of the prevailing hierarchy by attributing status differentiation to nature and arguing for its necessity, Paul argues on the contrary that the normal status hierarchy is only "apparently" unproblematic and that it is actually the lesser members, those who are weaker and seemingly less honorable, who are "really" the most honored. The dominant Greco-Roman common sense—that honor must accord with status and that status positions are relatively fixed by nature—is completely, albeit confusingly, thrown into question by Paul.

He never explicitly tells us which members of the Corinthian church are the weaker, less presentable ones who ought to be accorded more honor and which are those who already have honor. But, since Paul's ultimate goal in 1 Corinthians 12–14 is to lower the assessment of glossolalia among the Corinthians and to argue that it is less valuable for the assembly than is prophecy, it would appear that the Corinthians themselves accord high status to speakers in tongues.[25] Otherwise, Paul has little to gain in this context from his reversal of status application of the body analogy. Paul first accepts the high status of glossolalia as a given and then questions the expected attribution of honor to those of high status. Greater honor, he says, should be given to those normally considered to be of low status.

The Hierarchy of Pneuma and Nous

Paul's statements about "spirit" (*pneuma*) and "mind" (*nous*) in 1 Corinthians 14:14–17 also demand an ideological analysis with a view to status. Modern readers sometimes assume that Paul's comments about pneuma and nous—that the mind is inactive and fruitless when a person is speaking in tongues—function as an appeal to the use of reason against the argument that speaking in tongues, although irrational, represents a higher source of (esoteric) knowledge. On this reading, Paul would be valuing the rational "speaking with one's mind" over the irrational "speaking in the spirit" or "with a tongue."[26] But a comparison with similar rhetoric in other Greco-Roman sources shows that the rational/irrational dichotomy is not the best way to understand Paul's nous/ pneuma dichotomy. The nous/pneuma distinction is found in other contexts in which philosophers discuss the inspiration that comes to people when under the influence of some divine pneuma. Plato, Philo, and Iamblicus use the same dichotomy when talking about prophecy, rather than when talking about the more particular activity of glossolalia (although there is some possibility that Iamblicus was thinking about normally unintelligible, esoteric speech in some of these contexts). The comparison is apt, however, since what I am considering here are not the phenomena to which Plato, Philo, Iamblicus, and Paul refer but rather the terminology used to conceptualize social behavior; and the rhetoric is similar regardless of whether the phenomena are identical. It should further be noted that the three writers I have chosen, though separated by several centuries from one another, represent a continuous tradition of Platonic interpretation. The theory of inspiration sketched here, though available outside Platonist circles in the first century, originated in Platonic tradition.

One of the most influential ancient theories of the role of mind in prophetic activity comes from Plato himself. In the *Phaedrus* Socrates agrees that madness is usually an evil, unless it is the madness of prophecy. "For prophecy is a madness, and the prophetess at Delphi and the priestesses at Dodona when out of their senses have conferred great benefits on Hellas, both in public and private life, but when in their senses few or none. . . . But it would be tedious to speak of what everyone knows" (244). What everyone knows, according to Socrates, is that these prophetic oracles are sources of esoteric knowledge. The theory that the speakers' minds are inactive when they are possessed by the divine inbreathing, on the other hand, is probably a Platonic scientific explanation rather than simple folk knowledge.

In the *Timaeus* Plato discusses inspiration and says that mantic activity (*mantikē*) cannot take place when a person is *ennous*—that is, in his or her own mind. The nous must be inactive due to sleep, disease, or because it is troubled by "inspiration" (*tina enthousiasmon*, 71E). The interpretation of the messages takes place by means of "reasoning" (*logismos*, 72A), which cannot be engaged in by those under divine influence, precisely because they are not at that time in their sound minds (*sōphrōn*).

In Plato's explanations of inspiration there is no mention of pneuma, but there is the idea that prophecy—discourse with the divine realm—cannot take place in the sphere of normal, human nous. Whereas for Paul the dichotomy is between nous and pneuma, for Plato there is a hierarchical dichotomy between nous and doxa ("opinion"). Many people have access to "true opinion" (*doxa alēthēs*), but only the gods and a few men have access to nous (*Timaeus*

51E). There is a further hierarchy in Plato: prophecy is an ability given to the lower parts of the body (the liver and the lower parts of the soul) rather than to the nous, as if in compensation for the inferiority of those lower parts. This is why the nous, the higher part, remains inactive when a person is under the influence of the mantic force. Since in Plato the hierarchy of body, soul, and mind is unproblematic, the inactivity of the nous in prophecy is also unproblematic. Prophecy occurs when the lower regions of the person receive the communications from the nous of the higher, divine regions. A problem arises only when the superior part of the person, the nous, loses control over the lower parts, such as the liver as the seat of passions. In such cases, the nous must reassert its normal control (71Bff.).

The Platonic hierarchy whereby the nous always retains superiority over the parts of the person that participate in mantic activity is reversed in Philo. In *Who is the Hier?* Philo begins with a Platonic soul/body dualism (later made into a body–soul–mind triad: 286). The soul can be bypassed in the discussion, however, and Philo can speak simply of the nous as residing in and ruling the body (256). The nous is from heaven, and, though it is currently "constrained" in the body, it can, by education, make its way upward again to the high realms of bodiless contemplation (274). Reflecting the traditional upper-class ideology of status and hierarchy, Philo believes that the mind will not allow itself to be pulled down by the passions of the body, though it must momentarily consent to live with the body (see §316 for progress away from the body and mortality). Philo pictures the hierarchy of the body elements in several other ways. The nous is portrayed as the ruling agent over the soul and the body; as the father of the senses, which are its daughters; and as the gentle yet strict father of the soul.[27]

Though the mind will not allow itself to be acted upon by the body, it will allow itself to be acted upon by the divine pneuma. This reflects something of a departure from original Platonic theories, although we need not assume that Philo is the innovator. For Philo "understanding" (*dianoia*) may occur under the influence of the divine in an inspired state. At that time, it is no longer in control of itself (*en heautē*) but is led heavenward by a truth from beyond itself (68). Philo's explanation of inspiration uses several status-laden images: "For when the light of God shines, the human light sets; when the divine light sets, the human dawns and rises. This is what regularly befalls the fellowship of the prophets. The mind [*nous*] is evicted [*exoikizetai*] at the arrival of the divine Spirit [*pneuma*], but when that departs the mind returns to its tenancy. Mortal and immortal may not share the same home. And therefore the setting of reason [*logismos*] and the darkness which surrounds it produce ecstasy and inspired frenzy [*ekstasin kai theophorēton manian*]" (264–265). For Philo—and here he is in agreement with many other theorists of his day—a prophet when under the divine, mantic force is actually keeping silence; his organs of speech are being played by the divine pneuma like a musical instrument (266).

The functional status hierarchy continually places the nous below the pneuma. Whereas nous constitutes mere "human light," prophecy is derived from "divine light" (*Who is the Heir?* 263–266). The nous can be considered mortal, but the pneuma is undoubtably immortal.[28] In *Allegorical Interpretation* Philo's terminology faintly recalls the Greco-Roman preoccupation with active and passive roles in sex: the nous is what receives the input from God, whereas the pneuma is what God puts into or impresses upon the nous (1. 37).[29] In the *Special Laws* Philo uses battle imagery: during prophecy, the *logismos* withdraws and "surrenders the acropolis of the soul," and the divine pneuma takes up residency and "strikes" the speech organs, remaining in control until it freely chooses to leave (4. 49).

In true Platonic fashion, Philo distrusts the body, sense perception, and speech. Speech is misleading because it attempts to reveal "the particulars of underlying realities" (*tas idiotētas tōn hypokeimenōn*) by means of "common language" (*koinotēti tōn onomatōn: Who is the Heir?* 68). This distrust of the common provides the logic for Philo's high appraisal of speech acts that are outside common discourse. But for the logic to work, one must distrust common appearances—and distrust the common in general—and correspondingly trust esoteric epistemology, privileging the private over the public. One must have a hierarchy of special over common, esoteric over exoteric. And for Philo this corresponds to a hierarchy of nous over body (as it did for Plato) and pneuma over nous (as it did not for Plato).

The nous/pneuma dichotomy found in Philo was elaborated a few centuries later by the neo-Platonist Iamblicus, who solidified even further the hierarchy of pneuma over nous. In his book *On the Mysteries* Iamblicus explains that in prophetic inspiration the pneuma, which can be spoken of as fire of the upper realm (cf. Acts 2), comes down upon the weaker entity, the soul, body, and mind of the human being. In fact, the soul and the body must be gotten completely out of the way for the divine power to work its mantic activity effectively. Later, Iamblicus explains that the spirits from the gods cast out our own understanding and willful motion, which is why those possessed do not understand what they are saying. They are "wholly subservient [*hypēretountōn*] and entirely yield themselves to the energy of the predominating god" [*tē tou kratountos energeia*] (3. 8).

For Iamblicus, the function of esoteric language in religious rites is to provide a link between the human and the divine. Language that to us has no sensible significance is nevertheless valuable because it is sensible to the gods and even to the "divine intellect" that is in us. Furthermore, by means of strange, barbaric words the soul is elevated to the gods and joined together with their power (*On the Mysteries* 7. 4). Even if Iamblicus is not talking here about what moderns would call glossolalia, the status implications of his analysis are important for ascertaining the function of esoteric speech in linking the noetic and pneumatic realms. For esoteric speech, precisely in its opacity, provides access to the higher, pneumatic realm, and in so doing the language must necessarily bypass the nous, the realm of normal discourse.[30]

Plato, Philo, and Iamblicus all agree that the mind is somehow displaced or inactive when inspiration occurs.[31] All these theorists, moreover, propose some kind of hierarchy of the human elements that are involved in inspiration and prophecy.[32] Against this background, Paul's argument in 1 Corinthians 14:14–17 may now be read with greater subtlety. First, we must recognize that the very conceptualizing of the nous/pneuma dichotomy and Paul's use of that dichotomy in discussions of divine inspiration are taken over from contemporary theorizing about prophetic activity.[33] Second, Paul agrees with Philo and Iamblicus that in some kinds of inspired speech at least the nous is inactive and the pneuma is the active agent. This is not inconsequential. There is no "natural" reason for this anthropological and epistemological construal of inspired speech. Paul is thinking about glossolalia in terms of the same scientific categories that some of his contemporaries were using to explain prophecy. Third, the comparison of these different accounts suggests that the nous/pneuma dichotomy has nothing to do with a rational/irrational dichotomy. According to modern conceptions, spiritual activity is irrational in that it is not controlled by rules of discourse in the way rationality is; it is arbitrary or chaotic; it lacks a controlling grammar. But, according to all these ancient authors, the pneumatic realm of discourse *is* a language in itself; it has its own form of rationality hidden from the "common." The language of angels is still a language, not an arbitrary jumble of irrational jabberings.[34]

Leaving behind the rational/irrational dichotomy, we must conceive of the nous/pneuma dichotomy as the positing of agents rather than states. The nous represents not abstract rationality but a particular agent that controls the body and soul during normal human activity. The pneuma, either as part of the person or as a force from outside, is also an agent, one that takes over control of the body and soul and displaces the normal "governor," the mind. Understood in this way, Paul probably means "spirit" and "mind" not as abstract categories but as agents that are part of the human person and have particular roles to play in the operation of the person. Furthermore, Paul, like Philo and Iamblicus, appears to be working with an implicit hierarchy, which assumes that the pneuma is the agent of higher status and authority and the nous the lower member of the dichotomy.

Of course, Paul's use of the dichotomy entails several complications. In the first place, Paul speaks not of the divine pneuma that comes upon the speaker in tongues from the outside (although we cannot rule out the possibility that he may have conceived of the phenomenon in something like those terms), but of "my" nous and "my" pneuma. In other words, Paul internalizes the two agents in the individual person rather than making his pneuma/nous dichotomy fit a divine/human dichotomy. This allows him, as we will see below, to make the individual body a microcosm for the social body. Second, perhaps the most interesting difference between Paul and the Platonists is that he finds the inactivity of the nous to be a problem, whereas they do not. For Philo and Iamblicus the inspired speaker is speaking "in the spirit," and therefore the nous *must* be inactive in order to allow full play to the higher, divine element, the pneuma. Why, they would ask Paul, is it any problem that the nous in this instance is inactive? In the view of the Platonists, the pneuma is the higher of the two entities, offering an esoteric but extremely valuable form of discourse, with its own authority, epistemology, and rationality. The Corinthian speakers in tongues may (probably do?) share this view. Paul himself does not deny it. He simply insists that in the church the two entities cooperate, like two politicians who resist acting in their own interests and who, for the good of the polis and the salvation of the whole, agree to work together, giving up selfish claims to priority and hierarchical superiority.[35]

Paul admits (in agreement with the Platonic understanding) that the nous is the realm of common sensibility, as opposed to esoteric knowledge (note v. 16: *ho topos tou idiōtou*); but then, by insisting that all discourse in the assembly be accessible to the nous, the "common," he raises the status of the common over the esoteric. He appeals to what would be the higher member, the pneuma, to submit to an equal partnership with the lower member, the nous. Thus Paul cedes to the lower member, the nous, the privilege of control over the higher member, the pneuma. According to Platonic ideology, it is only right that the nous get out of the way when the pneuma makes its entrance, just as it is only right for clients to give way to patrons, for slaves to give way to owners, and for employees to give way to employers.[36] Paul disrupts these assumptions of higher-class ideology by arguing that the nous and the pneuma must work in tandem.

To us, this sounds like simple, just equality. But to a person of ancient times imbued with upper-class ideology, to say that a slave and a master should work in tandem or that a patron should not expect his client to give way to him would have sounded revolutionary.[37] At the very least, it would have been perceived as overturning traditional status expectations. Conservative ideology portrayed equality as the enslavement of higher-class persons to "the many"— that is, to the lower class.[38] Thus Paul's insistence on an equal partnership of the higher- and lower-status entities would have been heard as a reversal of their statuses. To say that the pneuma should give up its claim to rule un-challenged when it comes upon the scene—that it should join the nous in a mutually cooperative arrangement—is to imply a lowering of the status of the pneuma to the level of or below the nous. It is to disrupt the expected status expectations of the two "politicians" who rule the polis of the human person.

Ironically, the body of Christ presents something of a problem for the tongues of angels. In 1 Corinthians 12–14, as elsewhere in the letter, Paul ar-gues for a version of Christ's body in which status indicators are reversed, with greater honor given to those normally regarded as having lower status and less prestige accorded to those normally accorded badges of honor. Throughout these chapters, supposedly "given" status indicators are rendered problem-atic. Tongues, obviously considered a status indicator by at least one group at Corinth, are repeatedly relativized. Indeed, in the one list in chapters 12– 14 that is explicitly hierarchical, at 12:28, "kinds of tongues" occurs last. At first glance, it may seem that this list does not participate in Paul's status-reversal strategy, since *apostles* occurs first on the list—and clearly both Paul and the Strong at Corinth consider apostleship a high-status category, at least in some sense. Paul does, after all, link *apostolos* (apostle) with *eleutheros* (free man, 9:1). And for their part, the Corinthians are later fascinated by "super-apostles" who seem to possess all the traditional badges of high status such as rhetorical ability, wisdom, ability to work wonders, and freedom from manual labor (2 Cor. 10–13). Is not the hierarchical list of 12:28, then, an instance of Paul affirming the status hierarchy, placing the apostles on top? Actually, once 12:28 is read in its context within Paul's presentation of apostleship in 1 Corin-thians, it is clear that this list also participates in his status-reversal strategy. Paul had earlier elaborately portrayed the apostles, himself especially, as of low status—when judged, that is, by the standards of normal society (those of "this world": 1:20; 2:6; 3:18–19). The apostles are only servants (3:5) and farm laborers (3:6–8). Chapter 4 begins with Paul's insistence that the apostles are simple servants (*hypēretai*) or managerial slaves (*oikonomoi*) of Christ. The apostles are last, in the position of criminals, a spectacle before angels and human beings, foolish, weak, dishonored. They are the hungry, thirsty, naked, reviled, manual laborers of the world, society's "scum" (4:9–12). But immediately after this graphic portrait of the low status of the apostles, Paul uses high-status language to imply that he is actually superior to those at Corinth who consider themselves wise and free: he is a father and they are children (4:14); he is superior to any other teachers they may have, who are called by the servile term "pedagogue." Thus, when Paul calls on the "certain ones" at Corinth, those proud of their positions, to imitate him, what he wants them to imitate is his own voluntary self-abasement (4:16–21).[39] When we come to 12:28, therefore, and find apostles listed first on a list that ends with tongues, the consistency of Paul's rhetoric is clear: the apostles have already been portrayed as those of lowest status in the "world," so they occupy the position of first in the church; that the gift of tongues is last is because it is taken by Paul and the Strong at Corinth to be a high-status indicator by the standards of "this world." As elsewhere in 1 Corinthians, Paul does not deny the status significance of a certain activity or point of view; rather, he switches the venue for status attribution from the world to the church and thereby reverses the normal valuations.

In his uses of the body analogy and the mind/spirit dichotomy Paul pursues the same rhetorical strategy: identifying himself with the position of the Strong and then calling on them to give up their own interests for the sake of the Weak. In 1 Corinthians 12–14 Paul claims that he speaks in tongues more than any of the Corinthians, but then he says that he will give up speaking in tongues in the assembly out of respect for the nonglossolalists (14:18–19). With regard to both the body analogy and the mind/spirit dichotomy Paul advocates the same strategy; and in both instances the human body becomes a microcosm for the macrocosm of the social body. The higher elements of the body are called upon to yield to the lower elements. The spirit is to yield to the mind, the head to the genitals, the Strong to the Weak; and the higher-status Christians to those of lower status. In all cases, what Paul says of the human body, he expects to be applied in the church, the body of Christ, "in order that there be no schism in the body" (12:25; cf. 1:10).

5 *The Resurrected Body*

Few sections of 1 Corinthians illustrate the Corinthian conflict over the nature of the body as explicitly as chapter 15, where Paul goes to great lengths to defend the early Christian belief in the resurrection of the body. Commentators are for the most part agreed that the debate arose because some members of the Corinthian church rejected this belief. But the precise nature of the rejection is unclear: is it that they did not believe in the resurrection of the body or that they did not know what form of afterlife experience, if any, to substitute in its place—and what kind of social and cultural context informed their views of death and the body? Of greater relevance to my own interests, modern interpreters of 1 Corinthians have seldom raised other questions that might inform an ideological analysis of this early Christian debate about the body. For example, do the different views correlate in any way with class or status differences in the church? And how do the differing conceptions of the body relate to broader questions of physiology and cosmology? In this chapter I will offer a historical contextualization of the disagreement about the nature of the afterlife and will suggest that the disagreement was an expression of differing ideologies of the body, ideologies that were linked to differing physiological and cosmological views.

The Position of the Corinthians

Obviously, some people at Corinth, those to whom Paul addresses the bulk of his comments in 1 Corinthians 15, doubted the apocalyptic promise of the resurrection of the body. Biblical scholars have offered various historical explanations for the position taken by Paul's Corinthian critics. For many years, especially in German scholarship, it was held that the Corinthians were influenced by Gnosticism, with its deprecation of the body and "matter" and its teaching that salvation consists in the escape of the soul or spirit from the prison of the flesh and materiality. But, as I have already indicated, Gnosticism as a social movement can be dated to no earlier than the second century, and the kinds of beliefs here called gnostic, such as the deprecation of the body and the emphasis on the salvation of the soul, enjoyed wide circulation in popular philosophy in Greco-Roman culture.

The current consensus among New Testament scholars is that the Corinthian Christians were enamored of "realized eschatology"—which is to say, they had appropriated promises of salvation that, originally in Christian preaching, were seen as reserved for the eschaton (the "end") and the future establishment of the kingdom of God and had transferred those soteriological benefits to the present.[1] On this view, Paul misunderstands the position of the Corinthians. He supposes that they reject any belief in the resurrection, whereas their position is that they have already experienced a "spiritual" resurrection with Christ, perhaps through baptism (see Rom. 6). Thus, when Paul says in 1 Corinthians 4:8, "*Already* you are filled, *already* you are rich, without us you reign," he is sarcastically, but accurately, echoing their own claims to have attained the benefits of eschatological salvation now in the present. Paul's main concern, according to this view, is to refute the Corinthians' "overly-realized eschatology" and urge upon them a "reserved" eschatology, by arguing that the benefits of salvation, status, and glory promised by the Gospel will really be available only at the *parousia* ("coming") of Christ.

The problem with this interpretation is that there is no evidence that the Corinthians claim these benefits as a result of first learning about such eschatological benefits through Christian preaching and then transferring them to present experience. Nowhere in 1 Corinthians does Paul quote anything that could be a Corinthian slogan claiming that they have already been raised. Note, for example, that 1 Corinthians 4:8 does not mention resurrection. As I have noted, the Corinthian Strong believe that they already possess wisdom, freedom, wealth, and status; they already speak with the tongues of angels. But they possess these benefits, they think, due to their status as the wise, a status that they have learned to claim for themselves from popular philosophy. In Paul's eyes, those of an apocalyptic Jew, this might *appear* to be a premature claim of blessings that are supposed to be experienced only in the salvation of the eschaton; but that does not mean that the beliefs of the Strong *came from* Jewish eschatology.[2] Rather, they are simply claiming status symbols that popular philosophy and upper-class ideology attributed to those who were wise. Most important, there is no indication in 1 Corinthians 15 that the reason why the Corinthians reject the resurrection of the body is because they believe they have already experienced a spiritual resurrection. It is much simpler to assume, as Paul's arguments against them indicate, that what they found objectionable about Paul's teaching was not the *future* aspect of the resurrection but that it was to be a *bodily* resurrection.[3] They could have found such teaching objectionable simply because of the influence of popular philosophy, with its despising of the body. A thesis of realized eschatology is actually a more complicated historical reconstruction than the problems of the text require. It is a reading back into Paul's authentic letters of a position that arose only later, first, to some extent, in the Christian communities portrayed in Colossians and Ephesians, and then more fully among the Christians attacked by the author of the Pastoral Epistles (see 2 Tim. 2:18).

Another indication that the debate between Paul and the Corinthians is not one between realized and futuristic eschatologies is that Paul himself assures the Corinthians, when it is to his purpose, that they already have knowledge and, indeed, "all things" (1 Cor. 1:5), an assurance that would be precarious for Paul to give if he were also attacking realized eschatology. What he is emphasizing is that they *all* already have the benefits that higher-class ideology normally reserved for the elite. Paul is not, then, arguing against realized eschatology but against status distinctions and the upper-class ideology of status that saw wisdom as the preserve of the elite. He is arguing not so much for a reservation of eschatological blessings as for a proper distribution and use of those blessings *throughout* the church, in a way that conflicts with the ideology of hierarchy and a particular kind of Greco-Roman elitism.

Other scholars see the Corinthian objection to a resurrection of the *body* as indicating that they are strict dualists who accept an immaterial soul, which can expect immortality, but reject the material body; they object to the resurrection of the body because they believe that matter cannot and should not be saved for eternal existence.[4] But, as I have already argued in Chapter 1, we should be wary of introducing too quickly into this historical situation a matter/nonmatter dichotomy. It is not at all clear that what we moderns mean by "matter" (whatever we *do* mean by the term, which is itself not clear in the latter twentieth century) has much relation to what ancient philosophers meant by *hylē*, which is normally translated as "matter."[5] Furthermore, ancient philosophers, such as the Stoics, Epicureans, and Skeptics, could find the idea of a resurrected body ridiculous without having to posit in its place a belief in an immortal or immaterial soul. As we will see, in the first and second centuries, the body was deprecated by philosophers of many different stripes, even those, like the Stoics, who believed that everything, even the soul, was embodied and material. Thus, as this chapter will make increasingly clear, we should avoid introducing into the Corinthian debate a concern regarding matter and nonmatter. There is no evidence that either Paul or the Corinthians were bothered by the prospect of an eternally existing materiality. The problem for the Corinthians lies in the resurrection of the *body*, not in the existence, in the present or the future, of matter.

Throughout 1 Corinthians 15, Paul assumes that if the Corinthians reject the resurrection of the body, they must be without hope entirely. Many scholars take this to be a misunderstanding on Paul's part and suggest that the Corinthians probably do expect some sort of afterlife, perhaps in the form of an immortal soul freed from the body. But other scholars have recently argued that Paul is accurately reflecting the position of his disputants, who believe, like a great many people in Greco-Roman society, that death means the end of human existence, even for followers of Jesus Christ.[6] This is not a completely implausible suggestion; for it is completely believable that people could be converted to Christianity, allured by benefits other than a promise of eternal life as a continuing, individual consciousness. As Ramsay MacMullen has shown, eternal life seems not to have been one of the things most Greeks and Romans expected from their gods.[7] Yet, Paul mentions that the Corinthians practiced "baptism for the dead" (15:29), and though it is not clear precisely what this practice was, how it was assumed to have efficacy, or even who exactly at Corinth believed in it, the practice itself seems to suggest that the Corinthians believed in some sort of afterlife for their dead loved ones. It is one piece of evidence, albeit a slender one, that even the Corinthians who rejected the resurrection of the body entertained a belief in some kind of existence after death.

My own position, which I will explain and defend in this chapter, is that early Christian preaching about the resurrection of the dead, as about the issues studied in previous chapters, divided the Corinthian church along social status lines. The Strong, influenced by popular philosophy to deprecate the body, opposed the idea of a resurrected body.[8] Indeed, they heard Paul's language about "resurrection of the dead" (*nekros*) as referring to the resuscitation of a "corpse," the normal meaning of the term *nekros*, and they found such a view philosophically ridiculous.[9] This does not necessarily mean that they were strict Platonists or that they believed in some kind of material/immaterial dichotomy.[10] Nor is their position to be interpreted as simply the Greek view, as opposed to Paul's Jewish view. Many Jews of Paul's day did not believe in the resurrection of the body but accepted some notion of the immortality of the soul. More to the point, Jews of the first century seem to have held many different views about death; there was simply no such thing as *the* Jewish view.[11] Moreover, as I will argue, the idea that the dead could be raised, at least temporarily, seems to have been perfectly acceptable to many non-Jewish inhabitants of the Greco-Roman world. As we will see, there were many opportunities for them to hear talk about resurrected bodies, and they could find analogies (though not exact parallels) in their own culture, especially in views apparently held by the masses and generally ridiculed by the philosophically educated. In this context, uneducated persons might readily have accepted early Christian preaching about resurrected bodies, even if they did not understand by such language precisely what Paul intended. To sketch out my scenario, I must survey, at least briefly, various Greco-Roman beliefs about life after death.

Death and Afterlife in Greco-Roman Culture

In *Paganism in the Roman Empire* Ramsay MacMullen makes a strong case for revising our views about the extent to which inhabitants of the early Roman Empire believed in or even cared about life after death. Contrary to earlier accounts, which painted the period as an "age of anxiety" and assumed that Christianity's promise of everlasting life was what won over non-Christians, MacMullen points out how rarely expressions of anxiety about an afterlife occur in inscriptions, and he notes that most people of the Greco-Roman world seem not to have expected such a benefit from their religion. When they appeal to their gods, they ask for more mundane things like health, financial success, protection on the high seas or from bandits, or even information about missing items, such as runaway slaves. "Salvation" [*sōtēria*] in Greek inscriptions, as in the magical papyri (ancient documents containing spells and magical prescriptions), most often refers to health or preservation from some physical illness or danger.[12] When views about death *are* expressed on funerary monuments, they sometimes include clichés about Hades and the underworld, although, just as often, they express skepticism about any afterlife at all. Occasionally, an inscription will have the dead body, so to speak, address random passersby by means of the message on the inscription. Indeed, one of the most common epitaphs occurred so frequently that it was abbreviated in Latin to *n.f.n.s.n.c.*, which stood for *non fui, non sum, non curo;* "I was not, I am not, I care not"; or, in another popular form, "I was not, I was, I am not, I care not."[13] One such inscription, admittedly from a later time, combines the typical "Hail passerby" motif with a short sermon disabusing the reader of popular beliefs: "Wayfarer, do not pass by my epitaph, but stand and listen, and then, when you have learned the truth, proceed. There is no boat in Hades, no ferryman Charon, no Aeacus keeper of the keys, nor any dog called Cerberus. All of us who have died and gone below are bones and ashes: there is nothing else. What I have told you is true. Now withdraw, wayfarer, so that you will not think that, even though dead, I talk too much."[14] Other inscriptions express no such skepticism but merely imply that the person is dead and in the grave. A popular phrase expressing this has the inscription address the dead body, "May the earth lie lightly on you," in Latin sometimes abbreviated: *s. t. t. l. (sit tibi terra levis).*[15] One cannot avoid the impression, therefore, that many people entertained no firm belief in any afterlife experience of personal consciousness; nor did they seem to believe that they could expect such from their gods. We get the impression, rather, of a general lack of interest in an afterlife and a general agnosticism regarding the subject.[16]

We should not overstate the case, however.[17] Other inscriptions do indeed express some kind of belief in an afterlife, some of which sound downright philosophical, positing that death is the separation of the soul from the body: "And your soul has escaped the body, its antagonist."[18] Or, in more elaborate words, "The good and discreet Aelianus was given this tomb by his father in concern for his mortal body; but his heart, which is immortal, has leapt up among the blessed; for the soul lives forever, it is what gives life, and it has come down from God. Stay your tears, my father, and you, mother, stay my brothers from weeping. The body is the soul's tunic; but you must respect the god in me."[19] As these few examples show, there existed no single Greek or Greco-Roman belief about life after death; beliefs could range—to mention only those most commonly encountered—from relatively uninterested agnosticism, to traditional views about the dead dwelling in Hades or under the earth, to expressions of the immortality of the soul.[20]

Popular myths which spoke of an underground region in which the dead lived a shadowy existence probably still held credibility for many people. In three different essays, Lucian, the second-century satirist, ridicules what he claims are traditional views held by the masses (*hoi polloi*) and even, to his mock horror, by some philosophers. One of the "liars" in his dialogue *The Lover of Lies* relates looking through a hole in the ground and seeing the dead in Hades "lying upon the asphodel to while away the time, along with their friends and kinsmen by tribes and clans" (24; see also 25). In *On Funerals* we find out that the popular conception of the dead is that they reside in Hades, a place deep under the earth in which the corpses (*nekroi*) stay. Other dead persons occupy the same region, but without their bodies, "in the form of shadows that vanish like smoke in your fingers. They get their nourishment, naturally, from the libations that are poured in our world and the burnt-offerings at the tomb; so that if anyone has not left a friend or kinsman behind him on earth, he goes about his business there as an unfed corpse, in a state of famine." Lucian takes all the preparations of the corpse in funeral arrangements— putting a coin in the mouth, washing the corpse, anointing it, bestowing it with flowers, and dressing it in fine clothes—to be due to credulous people's beliefs that the body of the dead person really travels down (9). His statements are some indication that these practices were well known; we need not think that everyone who carried them out really believed that the body of the person would actually travel to the realm of the dead, as Lucian implies; but certainly many people, especially those not exposed to the doubts and demythologizations of the philosophers, did indeed hold beliefs that struck Lucian as unsophisticated. In *Menippus, or The Descent into Hades* Lucian describes the popular image of the dead in Hades and sometimes speaks of them as shadows, other times as decomposing bodies, other times as skeletons. The state of the dead under the ground in popular thought was probably just as varied and vague.[21]

Biblical scholars often insist that the resurrection of the body was a Jewish expectation and completely foreign and incomprehensible to Greeks and Romans, and that the corresponding Greek view was a belief in the immortality of the soul.[22] To some extent this is correct, in that the early Christian notion of the resurrection of the body as the primary form of afterlife came from Jewish eschatology, not Greek mythology. But this picture is nonetheless oversimplified and ultimately misleading. As I have already hinted, popular conceptions of the state of the dead were quite capable of portraying them as existing in some kind of embodied state. We are likely to have more success in understanding how Paul's preaching of the resurrection of the body was heard in a Greco-Roman setting if we supplement our use of Greek philosophical sources by attempting a reconstruction of the now less visible popular notions. Moreover, we should ask not where the doctrine of bodily resurrection *came from* but rather, how it would have been heard. What analogies existed whereby Paul's early converts could have made any sense at all of his preaching of resurrection? Approached in this way, the notion is not nearly as foreign to Greco-Roman ideas as we might have supposed initially.

Greek myth and folklore knew many stories of people returning from the dead. The myth of Alcestis, who died in place of her husband and was, as a reward, restored to life, is often mentioned in ancient sources; it provided the subject for Euripides' play *Alcestis*. According to one form of the myth, Persephone sent Alcestis back up to the surface of the earth; according to another, Heracles fought with Hades and raised her back up.[23] Heracles' own return from Hades is spoken of as a resurrection from out of the earth.[24] In his catalogue of mythical subjects and themes, Hyginus lists sixteen people "who, by permission of the Parcae, returned from the lower world."[25]

When Corinthians heard that they would be raised from the dead by the power of Christ, they may also have thought of Asclepius, who was rumored to have restored many persons to life. Pliny the Elder and Lucian both relate the story of Asclepius's revivification of Tyndareus.[26] Pausanias passes on stories of Asclepius's raising of Hippolytus, son of Theseus, who then went on to live in Italy and to become king of the Aricians.[27] Ovid relates the myth that Asclepius restored both Glaucus and Hippolytus to life by using an herb he had seen one snake use on another. It was in punishment for this that Jupiter struck Asclepius with a thunderbolt.[28] The raising of Glaucus is attributed by Apollodorus to Polyeidus, son of Coeranus, rather than to Asclepius. He raised the dead man to life, according to Apollodorus, by rubbing the dead man's body with the herb he had seen the snake use.[29] Elsewhere, however, Apollodorus attributes to Asclepius the raising of several men by application of the blood of the Gorgon.[30] The restorations of the dead accomplished by Asclepius, as the eponymous healer and god of healing, were often portrayed as due to exceptional knowledge of medicine, of course; but for most people that would not have done away with the impression that these were miraculous deeds and expressions of the divine power of Asclepius.

The step from Asclepius to the common magician, while great in terms of status, is phenomenologically perhaps not so far. The magical papyri contain abundant evidence that owners of esoteric knowledge were expected to be able to raise the dead—not to eternal life, perhaps, but to life of some sort. One spell, for example, promises that by using a magical holy name, consisting of 100 letters, the magician will be able to call up anyone, even a "god or dead man."[31] A love spell conjures up "men and women who have died untimely deaths" in order to enlist their help in capturing a desired woman.[32] Some spells are designed to be written on objects (a leaf, for instance) and placed in the mouth of a corpse so that the magician can question it.[33] Lucian, always the mocker, relishes passing on several such "ghost stories." One of his characters tells of a Babylonian (it helps that he is from a country famous for mystical knowledge) who brought a snakebite victim "back to life, driving the poison out of his body by a spell, and also binding upon his foot a fragment which he broke from the tombstone of a dead maiden" (*Lover of Lies* 11). Another man, a "Hyperborean," is also known to perform wonders: "As for the trivial feats, what is the use of telling all that he performed, sending Cupids after people, bringing up *daimones*, calling mouldy corpses to life, making Hecate herself appear in plain sight, and pulling down the moon?"[34] In order to conjure a love spell for a young man, the same Hyperborean called up the man's father, who had been dead seven months (*Lover of Lies* 14). Lucian's rather impressive list of such accounts shows the popularity of stories about men's wives coming back from the grave to visit them, dead bodies walking about above ground, and buried corpses returning to life.[35] A passage in *Leucippe and Clitophon*, the novel by Achilles Tatius, also shows that bringing dead bodies back to life was considered a job for magicians. After seeing his friend Menelaus supposedly bring his betrothed, Leucippe, back to life, Clitophon assumes that Menelaus is a magician (*magos*) or a "servant of the gods" (*diakonos . . . theōn*, 3. 17. 4). This passage in the novel is intended to be humorous: the author is poking fun at people (and there must have been some) who believed that magicians or "servants of the gods" could raise the dead. As we have seen, Lucian scoffs at all such stories; but we should assume that some people believed them, or at least that the notion of bodies being raised again to life was not altogether incomprehensible to *everyone* in the culture. From our perspective, these cases do not look much like Paul's doctrine of the eschatological raising of the body to eternal life, but to a Corinthian the differences we think important may not have been so apparent. He or she may well have thought that what Paul promised was what Alcestis or Heracles had experienced or what Asclepius or various magicians had delivered.[36]

Philosophers and educated persons were expected to be more skeptical. The narrator of Lucian's *Lover of Lies* feigns shock that philosophers could be carried away by telling and retelling such stories. A sophos was supposed to be a doubter of myths about Hades and risen bodies (§§ 2, 5, 29). And the certainty of the corruption of the body was one reason, according to the philosophical view, to doubt such stories. In answer to one of the "liars" who claims to have known a man who came back to life more than twenty days after his burial, the doubting interlocutor asks, "How was it that in twenty days the body neither corrupted nor simply wasted away from inanition?" Of course, Lucian, being something of a skeptic with an admiration for Epicureanism, viewed even the philosophical doctrine of the immortality of the soul as incredible. The one philosopher who is praised by Tychiades, the dialogue's narrator, is Democritus of Abdera, who proved his philosophical character by remaining calm in a graveyard in which boys dressed up as spooks: "So firmly did he believe that souls are nothing after they have gone out of their bodies" (32).

A similar skepticism is found on the lips of other educated men. Herodotus, telling of a man who "proved" his divinity by apparently dying and returning to life three years later, implies that only "simple-minded Thracians" would have been fooled by such a stunt (*History* 4. 95). Sextus Empiricus calls stories about dead men being raised to dwell among the stars "myth and fiction" (*mythos, plasma*); Plutarch calls them "riddles and fabulous tales" (*ainigmata kai mytheumata*).[37] Admitting that the masses readily believe in resurrected bodies, these educated men provide for their readers more scientific explanations of such stories. Philostratus, even in his effusive hagiography of Apollonius of Tyana, cannot resist offering such an explanation for a supposed miracle. Apollonius was said to raise a girl from the dead (as Heracles raised Alcestis). "Now whether he detected some spark of life in her, which those who were nursing her had not noticed, —for it is said that although it was raining at the time, a vapour went up from her face—or whether life was really extinct, and he restored it by the warmth of his touch, is a mysterious problem which neither I myself nor those who were present could decide." In either case, according to Philostratus, Apollonius had awakened the girl from only an "apparent" death (*Life of Apollonius of Tyana* 4. 45, trans. Conybeare).

In his short biography of Romulus, Plutarch relates stories that had circulated among the masses (*hoi polloi*) either that Romulus had not died but had instead been "caught up" to the gods or that he had been restored to life after having been murdered. Though disbelieving them himself, Plutarch passes on such stories, calling them myths (*mythologoumena, Romulus* 28. 4, 6). In Plutarch's view, "to mix heaven and earth is foolish" (28. 6), which is precisely what people do when they claim that any human *body* can participate in immortality or dwell among the gods. What Plutarch objects to here is not what we would call the supernatural aspects of the story but the belief that a body, which is part of the earth, can attain to the realm of the gods. In Plutarch's scientific opinion, only the soul can attain such heights, and then only when "pure, fleshless, and undefiled" (*katharon kai asarkin kai hagnon*, 28. 6). This is a purely physiological issue for Plutarch; the "dry soul," released from the "damp" and "heavy" body, will fly upward. "We must not, therefore, violate nature by sending the bodies of good men with their souls to heaven, but implicitly believe that their virtues and their souls, in accordance with nature and divine justice, ascend from men to heroes, from heroes to demi-gods, and from demi-gods, after they have been made pure and holy, as in the final rites of initiation and have freed themselves from mortality and sense, to gods." Plutarch's universe is a hierarchical spectrum. He is concerned not with a dichotomy of matter and nonmatter but with a physiological hierarchy. The mistake of the masses, according to the philosophical view, is not their belief that men may become gods but their unsophisticated notion that the lower-status aspect of human existence, the body, could possibly attain the high status reserved for the more subtle, purer substances of the self.

Thus the idea of the resurrection of the body would indeed have struck some Greeks as ridiculous or incomprehensible. Specifically, the notion would have offended the educated—those exposed, at least minimally, to philosophical arguments and assumptions. Of course, due to the uniformity of higher education in the Greco-Roman world, all people so educated could be expected to hold similar views, at least on basic points, regardless of which philosophical school commanded their allegiance or lack thereof. And in the early Roman Empire one of those basic points was that, whatever one believed about life after death, promises of resurrected bodies were not to be given any credence. Such gullibility was reserved for the uneducated—that is, the vast majority of the inhabitants of the Empire.[38]

The word used by educated writers to designate the beliefs held by the credulous masses was *deisidaimonia*, meaning "superstition," which the philosophers often attacked when writing about death. What they meant by this term, however, was not belief in the supernatural, as modern discourse might assume. As I have already argued, there was no such thing as the supernatural in the ancient world. Rather, for the philosophers *deisidaimonia* meant "fear of the gods." Views about death that they considered superstitious, therefore, were those that betrayed or evoked fear, whether a belief that the corpse would feel the coldness of the ground and the weight of the earth, that the shadow of the dead person would morosely roam the earth or float in the atmosphere, or that the dead would suffer hunger, thirst, or torment in Hades. The recurring refrain among the philosophers was that death was not to be feared: it meant either the simple absence of sensation, and so would be no more painful than a deep sleep, or the departure of the soul to a better place and the return of the body to the earth, of which it was composed. Cicero, for example, gives the two typical philosophical opinions: either the body and the soul are annihilated at death or the soul separates from the body.[39]

There were many educated persons who believed the former, Epicureans being the most famous in both ancient and modern accounts. Lucian praised Democritus for believing that even souls decompose into scattered atoms. They are "nothing after they have gone out of their bodies" (*Lover of Lies* 32). Others, however, held to the latter of the two main views. Plutarch consoles his wife on the death of their daughter by repeating what she has doubtless heard many times before, that death is no more than the release of the soul from the body; funeral extravagances and superstitious worries are therefore uncalled for.[40] Marcus Aurelius also passes on the cliché: at death the body goes to the earth and the soul to the atmosphere (*Meditations* 4. 21. 59–61). These words are expressed even on tombstones, demonstrating that they enjoyed some circulation outside the scrolls and schoolrooms of the philosophers. An inscription from the fifth century B.C.E. says, "Ether has received their souls, and earth their bodies."[41] Sometimes these sentiments seem to exclude the idea that the soul of the person is an integral, conscious entity, as in this example from Athens: "Earth lifted your body to the light, Siburtius, and earth hides it now, and the air [*aithēr*] has taken again the breath that it gave you."[42] But in other inscriptions the soul seems more personal. The god Apollo, for example, when asked whether the soul is dissolved at death or survives, answers: "The soul, so long as it is subject to its bonds with the destructible body, while being immune to feelings, resembles the pains of that [the body]; but when it finds freedom after the mortal body dies, it is borne entire to the aether, being then forever ageless, and abides entirely untroubled; and this the First-born Divine Providence enjoined."[43]

Belief in body/soul dualism was, therefore, quite widespread in the early Roman Empire, especially in philosophical circles, though also among ordinary folk. But, as I have already argued, this dualism should not be confused with a Cartesian dualism of matter/nonmatter or physical/spiritual. The nature of the soul released from the body was the subject of much speculation and disagreement, but most philosophers speak of the soul as if it were composed of some substance that we would consider "stuff"—even if they would not say that it is composed of *hylē*, which is usually, and rather misleadingly, translated as "matter."[44]

Cicero rejects the Stoic doctrine that the soul is a body but believes that it is probably "fiery or airy." It is swift, hot, and light, like the stars, and therefore ascends to the heavens.[45] Epictetus conceives of the soul as a particle of divine fire (*Discourses* 1. 14. 5–10; 3. 13. 15); whereas Seneca talks of it as "fiery matter" (*flagrante materia*) that will rejoin the essence of the stars.[46] Philo the Jew, taking his lead from Plato, believes that there are different levels of soul, at different points along a spectrum from earthiness to heavenliness. According to one passage, blood is the substance of the "lower" soul (that possessed by both humans and animals), but pneuma (or "ethereal pneuma") is the essence of the rational soul, that which humans share with the divine.[47] Elsewhere, Philo seems to believe that the soul's substance is pneuma and "air," probably reflecting the idea common among philosophers, physicians, and other scientists that pneuma was something like refined or distilled air.[48] Accordingly, if we trust Philostratus, Apollonius of Tyana had taught that upon death the soul "mingles with the unsubstantial air" (*Life of Apollonius of Tyana* 8. 31). A funeral inscription from Sardinia speaks of the *pneuma* (translated by Lattimore appropriately as "soul-breath") that has been released from the body into the atmosphere.[49] And other inscriptions say that the soul has rejoined the "ether."[50] Combining the connection between soul and blood with that between soul and air, Marcus Aurelius calls the soul "an exhalation of blood" (*Meditations* 5. 33; cf. 2. 17; 6. 15). Galen knows of a theory that held that the soul was nourished by vapors from the blood, as stars by vapors from the earth.[51]

At the risk of homogenizing, I suggest that certain beliefs about the body and its elements are held in common by these diverse philosophers. First, they all use, to some extent, a dualism of body and soul, proving that such a dualism was not at all limited to Platonists in the first century. Second, they all seem to assume the deprecation of the body, even those thinkers like the Stoics who, in other contexts, would insist that *all* things that truly exist are embodied in some sense. In other words, when Stoics disparage the body, they are referring to *this* body, the flesh-and-blood body of current human existence. They may elsewhere speak about the "embodiment" of the soul, but that does not seem to affect their tendency to despise the body when talking about what happens to a person at death. Third, all these philosophers assume a hierarchy of elements in the universe. The reason why the normal human body cannot experience immortality is that it occupies a relatively low place on the spectrum of stuff, which ranges from fine, thin, rarified stuff down to gross, thick, heavy stuff.[52] For several theorists, souls may occupy different positions in the hierarchy, with "earthier" souls lower down than purer souls. But in any case, the organizing principle is not an ontological dichotomy between physical and spiritual reality but a gradual hierarchical scale ranging from heaviness to lightness, from inert and lifeless mass to living, eternal divinity.

One embodiment of this homogenized popular philosophy occurs in the person of Epictetus, who is especially well suited to my purposes because he was a teacher of philosophy who lived around the time of Paul and taught in an area not far from Paul's churches. Epictetus assumes a body/soul dualism and portrays death as the separation of the soul from the body (*Discourses* 1. 5.

4–5; 3. 10. 14; 3. 22. 34). He also speaks disdainfully of the body, linking it to the earth and calling it "this my wretched flesh" (1. 1. 9; 1. 3. 5: *ta dystēna mou sarkidia*). The body (*sōma*) is by nature really just a "corpse" (*nekron*, 3. 10. 15; see also 3. 1. 43; 1. 25. 21; 1. 14. 5ff.; 3. 22. 21, 33). Epictetus also speaks of the body as opposed to the pneuma, equating body with "flesh" (*sarx*). Sarx is the location of desires that should be resisted: "For wherever the 'I' and 'mine' occur, there one must speak of the living being; if in the flesh, the ruling agent also will be there; if in the will, it will be there; if in externals, it will be there" (2. 22. 17–19, my trans.; 3. 7. 3, 9; 3. 7. 24). He equates flesh (*ta sarkidia*) with "heavy matter" (*hylē*, 3. 7. 25). But before we take this to mean that he is working with a material/immaterial dichotomy, we should remember that Epictetus was well read in his Stoic predecessors and considered himself a Stoic (3. 7. 17). In other words, although he was not a Platonist, he assumed a body/soul dualism; but, due to his Stoicism, this certainly did not include an assumption that the soul was completely immaterial or lacking in any kind of body. Stoics were famous in the first century for holding that even the gods were, in some sense, embodied. Thus, although Epictetus says that human beings have body in common with the beasts and logos in common with the gods (1. 3. 3), we would be mistaken to take this as reflecting a modern physical/spiritual or material/immaterial dichotomy. Epictetus, like many people of his time, assumed a hierarchy in which the body was despised—but not because it partook of matter. The deprecation of body and the separation at death of soul from body did not imply a rejection of matter in favor of immaterial substance.

Astral Souls and Celestial Bodies

I do not want to give the impression that there were no beliefs held in common by philosophers and "common folk." In fact, there is one proposal regarding what happens to a person at death that seems to have been held by both philosophers and less educated people, if we may take inscriptions as clues to the latter's beliefs. For a number of these texts express the idea that human beings, or perhaps only their souls, become stars or some similar heavenly bodies after death. This subject has received a recent, thorough study by Alan Scott, who has traced the history of the idea from the pre-Socratics to Origen.[53] It proves to be an important idea for my analysis of 1 Corinthians 15, since Paul there argues that the resurrected body, as he conceives it, will be a "heavenly body" as opposed to an "earthly body"; it will have its own substance and "glory," on analogy with the heavenly bodies of the sun, moon, and stars (15:39–49).

The teaching that human souls become heavenly bodies after death precedes Paul by centuries. Pre-socratic Pythagoreans, it seems, believed that the heavens were the origin of the human soul and that it would return to a position among the divine stars after death. In the *Timaeus* Plato proposed that the "body of heaven," like the body of the earth, was composed of the four elements (earth, water, air, fire), but especially of fire, since it is the element of most motion.[54] The precise nature of the heavenly bodies (whether they were composed of fire, ether, pneuma, all four of the primary elements or only one, and so forth) was debated for centuries; Aristotle's own thoughts on the subject are far from clear and gave rise to many different construals (and misconstruals) of his position by later Stoics and Platonists.[55] But eventually the view that the mind or soul was of celestial substance became, in the words of Alan Scott, "part of Hellenistic folklore," and it can be found among the views of several different philosophical schools, as well as in funerary inscriptions. An inscription that may be from the first century, for example, says: "Mother, do not weep for me. What is the use? You ought rather to reverence me, for I have become an evening star, among the gods."[56]

Jews held similar, often identical, beliefs. According to Daniel 12:3, at the resurrection the wise "shall shine like the brightness of the sky, and those who lead many to righteousness, like the stars forever and ever" (NRSV). Further, *2 Baruch* 51:10 promises that the righteous will be "equal to the stars." Repeatedly in Jewish texts the heavens are the future home of the saved, who, whether they occupy resurrected bodies or have resurrected or simply immortal souls, are spoken of as angels or stars.[57] Philo handles the idea with ease, noting that stars are embodied, intelligent souls, or "divine souls." He writes of the patriarchs as stars or constellations. The reward of the righteous soul is immortality and being inscribed "in the records of God, sharing the eternal life of the sun and moon and the whole universe."[58] Although Franz Cumont claimed that beliefs in astral souls or astral immortality came into Jewish and Greco-Roman culture relatively late and under Iranian and Babylonian influences, more recent scholars have rejected this claim, pointing out that such ideas were quite common in Greek as well as Jewish texts from the classical and Hellenistic periods onward.[59]

For many people it made sense that the soul would return to the cosmic region that corresponded to its own nature and substance. It was a Stoic commonplace, found among non-Stoics as well, that the universe was divided into hierarchical regions and that the entities (bodies, forms of existence, living beings) inhabiting each region partook mainly of the substance of the region. Cicero believed that he was passing on Aristotelian doctrine (the passage, according to modern scholars, appears Stoicized) when he explained that each elemental layer of the universe (earth, water, air, fire, and possibly ether) contained bodies of animals appropriate to it. He calls the stars, therefore, "animals," meaning that they are alive and possess sensation and intelligence.[60] The implication is that just as earthly animals are composed of the stuff of earth, so heavenly animals, here referring particularly to the stars, are composed of fire or ether, according to which of these elements the theorist believed constituted the highest region.

Philo, though he certainly did not consider himself a Stoic in the strict sense, assents to the commonplace. He says, "Our name for those which have the power of locomotion is animals [*zōa*]. These took to (i.e., were so made as naturally to belong to) the several main divisions of our universe, land animals to earth, to water those that swim, the winged creatures to air, and to fire the fire-born. . . . The stars found their place in heaven. Those who have made philosophy their study tell us that these too are living creatures, but of a kind composed entirely of mind."[61] Plutarch assumes the same hierarchical arrangement. According to his essay *On the Face on the Moon* the entire cosmos can be spoken of as a "body" (*Moralia* 928A–C). The speaker cites the common Stoic view that even in the heavens there exists a hierarchy of substance that includes a corresponding hierarchy of bodies: "The luminous and tenuous part of the ether by reason of its subtility [sic] became sky [*ouranos*] and the part which was condensed or compressed became stars, and that of these the most sluggish and turbid is the moon" (*Moralia* 928D). This cosmic hierarchy is mirrored in the microcosm of the human body; humans are tripartite: body, soul, and mind. The first death is separation of the body from the soul and the mind; the second is the separation of the soul from the mind. The human parts correspond to the cosmic: body = earth; soul = moon; mind = sun (*Moralia* 943A). Indeed, even the soul is a "mixed and intermediate thing, even as the moon has been created by god a compound and blend of the things above and below and therefore stands to the sun in the relation of earth to moon" (945D). The physiological common sense of this entire system thus underwrites the notion that the human soul after death will ascend to its natural level of cosmic substance and will become either a star or something like a star.

As I have already indicated, there was some disagreement about what precisely constituted the substance of the stars. The most common answer, it seems, was that they (and perhaps all the heavenly bodies) were composed of either fire or ether. Cicero, for example, says that the stars are ether while the sun is fire.[62] Sometimes Philo (never one to be overly concerned about consistency in such matters) speaks of the substance of the soul as ether; in other contexts he says that the "higher soul," or human mind, is composed of pneuma.[63] Various possibilities are mentioned by different authors, but generally the idea is that whatever substance comprises the stars—whether fire, ether, or pneuma—also comprises the soul, and it is to that state that the human soul returns after death.[64]

What is surprising to many of us, and important for Paul's argument in 1 Corinthians 15, is that some philosophers, even those who generally deprecate the body, can speak of these heavenly entities as bodies (*sōmata*). Aristotle, for example, calls the spheres of the heavens "bodies" and the stars "bodies" that exist in these spheres.[65] Plutarch, much later, also speaks of the cosmos as a "body" and the moon as an "eternal body" and "a divine and heavenly body" (*sōma theion kai ouranion*).[66] Following this tradition, Clement of Alexandria calls the stars "pneumatic bodies."[67] In a context in which even philosophers could speak of stars, and by extention human souls, as "heavenly bodies" composed of some sort of stuff like fire, ether, or pneuma, Paul's statements about a resurrected, heavenly body composed of pneuma seem a bit less strange. Precisely because such statements could be interpreted in many different ways, however, Paul faced a daunting task in trying to defend the doctrine of the resurrection against his educated converts. As we will see, the complexities of the ideas apparently generated significant misunderstandings—on both sides.

Misunderstandings at Corinth

It is not surprising that misunderstandings about the resurrection of the body should have arisen within the church at Corinth. As counter-intuitive as it may be to people today—who tend to think of eternal life as one of the primary benefits offered by religions—this particular issue seems not to have been covered extensively in Paul's missionary preaching. We do not know for certain what he initially promised those Greeks considering whether to align themselves with this new apocalyptic, Jewish sect, but judging from what he says about life after death when questions are posed, as in 1 Thessalonians 4 and 5 and 1 Corinthians 15, it appears that he had not made the general resurrection of the body an important part of his initial teaching.

In 1 Thessalonians, possibly his earliest extant letter, Paul addresses the concerns of his recent converts about death (the letter may well have been sent only a few months after the establishment of the congregation). The Thessalonians are not so much concerned about what will happen to themselves after death as worried that other Christians who have died since Paul's departure will not be able to participate in the festivities of the parousia—which they expect to occur quite soon. "Salvation" for them clearly consists in the protection of *living* members of the Christian movement from the eschatological "wrath that is coming" on the rest of the world (1 Thess. 1:9–10). They seem to expect that those still living at the coming of Jesus will escape the apocalyptic wrath and join Christ in his kingdom, whereas those who have died before the coming will miss out on the party.

Paul is thus compelled to explain further the eschatological scenario, only a part of which he had initially told them. Now he explains that when the Lord descends from the sky, "the dead in Christ will rise *first,*" and only then will the living Christians, who remain on earth, "be snatched up together with them for a meeting with the Lord in the air" (4:16–17). The Thessalonians' fears that the community would be split asunder by death are answered by Paul's assurance that their dead loved ones will miss out on nothing but will, in fact, precede the living in their celestial union with Jesus. They should therefore put away their grief.

This passage is remarkable for a variety of reasons, but the point that interests me here is the implication that Paul's converts, just months after the establishment of their church, are relatively ignorant about Paul's beliefs concerning the resurrection of the dead. Paul had obviously stressed the resurrection of *Christ* in his missionary preaching (see 1 Thess. 1:10), but, as other scholars have pointed out, a belief that a god or a hero had been restored to life did not in any way imply that his devotees would share the experience.[68] The Thessalonian Christians appear to have assumed that dead Christians were simply and finally dead. These Christians had been converted by promises of glory or salvation from destruction or perhaps participation in the kingdom of God but apparently not by promises that they would enter into eternal life when they died or be raised from the dead.

The Corinthians seem to have been a bit better informed. Some of them, at least, are baptizing "for the dead," implying that they believe in some kind of afterlife for their loved ones—even, perhaps, those who were not baptized during their lives. Moreover, in 1 Corinthians 15 Paul is battling not just ignorance about the resurrection but skepticism toward it and, as I will explain further below, misunderstandings of his own position about the nature of the resurrected body. Yet the misunderstandings of the Corinthians should not surprise us when we realize how little they may have had to go on. Teaching about the resurrection of Christ and the future eschaton, both of which were certainly part of Paul's usual missionary message, did not necessarily include teaching about the general resurrection or the state of the dead. Paul had apparently not spent much time at Corinth talking about life after death or about his own views of the resurrection of the dead. And, as we will see, what the Corinthians rejected was not exactly what Paul believed anyway.

Contrary to what some scholars maintain, Paul does *not* mistake a Corinthian belief in a realized, spiritual resurrection for a denial of resurrection entirely. There is no evidence that the Corinthians are talking about a present, spiritual resurrection. Paul does, however, misconstrue their position in another way. He insists that if they reject the resurrection of the body, they must also reject the resurrection of Christ and any possibility of an afterlife—neither of which need be the case. The Corinthians do believe in the resurrection and glorification of Christ, and, if we may take their practice of baptizing for the dead as any indication, they probably believe in some kind of afterlife. What they question is the idea that human *bodies* can survive after death and be raised to immortality. Theirs would be a natural response if, as I have proposed, they have been influenced by popular philosophy and its ideology of the body. It is thus, in my opinion, the Strong at Corinth who object to Paul's teaching about the body. Paul, for his part, either misunderstands or rhetorically misrepresents their position because he himself cannot imagine an afterlife totally divorced from some form of embodiment.

The Strong, for their part, misunderstand Paul—partly because he has not explained his views to any extent and partly because of the vocabulary he has used to describe the resurrection. When upper-class writers speak of popular beliefs about restorations of dead persons to life, they sometimes use the term *anastasis* (or something similar from the same word group). Pausanias, for example, uses the verb *anistēmi* for Asclepius's restoration of dead corpses (2. 26. 5; 2. 27. 4). Apollonius uses it when speaking of the raising of Glaucus's body by application of a herb (*Library* 3. 3. 1–2). Heracles' resurrection from Hades is called a "raising" by Euripides (*Hercules* 719).[69] LIkewise, Paul's use of *egeirein nekron* would probably be heard as a crude form of "wake the dead," also referring to a corpse, as in an example from the magical papyri.[70] Thus when Paul uses the phrase *anastasis nekrōn* or the like (15:21, 42), it would be natural for the Corinthians to imagine a bringing to life of human corpses along lines familiar from popular myth and folklore.

The term Paul uses for "the dead" would also evoke the primary connotation of "corpse." The bodies raised out of graveyards by magicians are called by Lucian "corpses" (*nekroi, Lover of Lies* 13), as are the emaciated, unfed, dead bodies that credulous people believe occupy the region below the earth (*On Funerals* 9; see *Menippus* 17, 18). The most natural way in which a Greek speaker would have heard Paul's language in 1 Corinthians 15 would have been as a reference to what we would call resuscitation of corpses. As we will see, Paul himself rejects such an interpretation; but it is easy to see how his Greek audience might take his language in this way. For lower-class Christians, not educated in the assumptions of philosophers, such language would perhaps not be off-putting; they may indeed have believed that magicians and gods could bring corpses back to life and endow them with immortality as in the case of Heracles. But for the educated such beliefs would have appeared vulgar and naive at best and ridiculous at worst. It is against such skepticism that Paul must show his position to be more sophisticated than would appear on the surface, and do so without giving up his apocalyptic belief in the resurrection of the body and without alienating those lower-class Christians who may very well want their bodies redeemed.

The Nature of Paul's Resurrected Body

It is no wonder that the Corinthians understood Paul's language about the res-urrection of the body to refer to the crass resuscitation of a corpse. For one thing, as I have shown above, that would be the most obvious interpretation of the terms he employs. Moreover, that is apparently just what many Jews and Christians thought when they considered the resurrection of the body. The author of Daniel apparently combined a belief in the resurrection of the body (at least of some people) with an assumption that at least the wise would attain astral immortality (12:2–3, 13), suggesting that his view of the resurrection was more sophisticated than the simple revivification of a corpse (although we should not, in this as in most cases, attempt to impose rigid consistency on the author). By contrast, 2 Maccabees 7:10–11 assumes a more literal resurrection of the very flesh and blood: one of the seven brothers, before being killed, stretches out his hands toward the king and says, "I got these from Heaven, and because of his laws I disdain them, and from him I hope to get them back again."[71] The two houses of Hillel and Shammai are said to have debated the resurrection of the body, both accepting resurrection but disagreeing on the precise form. The followers of Shammai argued that the resurrected body would be exactly the same body as the present one, the Hillel faction that it would be differently formed.[72]

In the first century there was no general agreement among early Christians about the nature of the resurrected body. While the New Testament does not speak explicitly of a "resurrection of the flesh," a conscious rejection of this term can be shown only for Paul. The author of Luke and Acts presents Jesus' resurrection as one of the "flesh" (Luke 24:39; Acts 2:31). In John, Jesus' death and resurrection are emphasized as physical (19:33–34; 20:27), but the nature of Jesus' resurrected body is not at all clear. For example, both Luke and John narrate scenes in which the disciples do not recognize Jesus after the resurrection, implying that his resurrected body was different from his previous body (Luke 24:16; John 21:4–12). In Matthew, a simple resuscitation of the fleshly body of Jesus may not be envisioned, given that there is no need to roll back the stone before the body of Jesus can exist (Matt. 28:2–6; contrast the resurrection scene in *The Gospel of Peter*). There seems to have been, in sum, no fixed tradition as to the exact nature of the resurrected body of Jesus. And, since beliefs concerning the general resurrection were firmly linked in early Christian thought with the perception of Christ's resurrection,[73] we may suppose that there was no fixed belief among Christians about the expected nature of their resurrected bodies.

In the second century, however, the resurrection of the body is adamantly defended by Christian leaders against skepticism (both from outside the churches and from within, from some Gnostics, for instance), and it is in this period that early Christian authors insist explicitly on a resurrection of the actual flesh and blood of the dead body. For many of them the resurrection of the body is synonymous with that of the flesh.[74] The expressions are interchangeable. Many of these second-century authors admit that some change will affect the body, in the words of Athenagoras, "for the better of what still remains in existence at that time." The soul, on the other hand, will need no alteration to survive into eternity.[75] Tertullian, however, will have none of this sophistication—or, as he would probably put it, sophistry. He insists that "body" is "none other than all that structure of the flesh, of whatever sort of materials it is composed and diversified, that which is seen, is handled, that in short which is slain by men."[76] *That* is what will rise again, "all of it indeed, itself, entire."[77]

Of course, these were educated writers, and we can only speculate as to what most ordinary Christians might have believed. My guess is that they seldom thought about the resurrection systematically but simply assumed that the resurrection of the body meant the resurrection, completely, wholly, and crassly, of the flesh-and-blood body. This proposal may find some support in the fact that non-Christians often deprived Christian martyrs of burial, burning their remains and scattering their ashes, intending thereby to foil the martyrs' hope of resurrection and to ridicule the Christians' beliefs. Although in the case of martyrs, other Christians believed that they had already departed to God and did not have to await the resurrection, it is clear that deprivation of burial was seen as a sore blow, certainly due in part to a rather literalistic conception of the resurrection of the corpse.[78] I assume that many Christians and Jews of Paul's day held similar beliefs about the nature of the resurrected body.

Against such a background, Paul's more nuanced position is striking. In the first half of chapter 15 Paul concentrates on arguing for the necessity of the resurrection of the body. It is part of the basic gospel message (15:1–11); questioning the possibility of a bodily resurrection undermines the possibility that Christ has been raised, and if Christ has not been raised, then Christians have received none of the benefits promised by the Gospel (15:12–19). On the other hand, if Christ has been raised, then the rest of the apocalyptic scenario follows, including the final resurrection of believers (15:20–28). Finally, if there is no resurrection of the body, then there is nothing to look forward to but the problems of this life, and the Corinthians' own practice of baptizing for the dead is futile (15:29–34).[79]

In verse 35 Paul finally turns his attention to defense of his doctrine of the resurrection of the body and does so by quoting what may well be an explicit objection by the Strong at Corinth: "How are the dead raised? With what sort of body do they come?" As these questions and Paul's defense from here to the end of the chapter show, the objection to the resurrection of the body centered on the question of the nature of that body, the assumption being that no body could be so constructed that it *could* be raised and made immortal.

At first, Paul does not answer the question: he merely argues that the resurrected body will be very different from the pre-resurrected body, like a flower compared to its seed (15:36–38). He then sketches a hierarchy of bodies. Initially, he uses the term "flesh" (*sarx*) to refer to these different kinds of bodies. In what is probably a descending hierarchy, Paul says that there is a different kind of flesh for human beings, beasts, birds, and fish (v. 39). One is here reminded of the philosophical commonplace sketched above whereby different kinds of creatures exist in different cosmic realms, each occupying a body appropriate to its own realm and composed of substances derived from that realm. Thus Paul's argument here would strike the philosophically educated as familiar and completely acceptable. We should also notice that Paul uses the term *sarx* only for these "lower" beings: humans, animals, birds, and fish.

He then extends the argument to show that a similar hierarchy exists for heavenly bodies. Here Paul switches terminology and substitutes the term *sōma* ("body") for *sarx* ("flesh"). This is necessary because he will later insist that the resurrected human body is analogous to the heavenly "bodies," which are not composed of "flesh." Paul himself believes that the resurrected body will not be composed of flesh (see v. 50). In verse 40, however, he is speaking of both heavenly bodies (for which the term *sarx* would not be appropriate) and earthly bodies (for which it would be). The switch in terminology is the first clue as to how important a physiological hierarchy is for Paul's own conception of the resurrected body.

In 15:41 he speaks of the differing "glory" (*doxa*) of various heavenly bodies. Although he has again switched terminology and now speaks of the glory of the sun, moon, and stars rather than of their bodies, we must keep in mind that he believes all these heavenly entities to be bodies, and that it is by analogy with their bodies that he will argue for a resurrected human body. His listing of the sun, moon, and stars and his reminder that even different stars have different "glories" evoke the cosmology of popular philosophy, as well as popular assumptions among the masses. The resurrected human body will partake of a nature similar to that of heavenly bodies and will be as much higher than the current earthly body in the physiological hierarchy as the heavenly bodies are in comparison to earthly bodies.

Paul next defines the resurrected body by several contrasts with the current body (15:42–44): it will be immortal rather than mortal, glorified rather than dishonored, powerful rather than weak, and pneumatic rather than psychic. Whereas the current body is "dirt from the earth" (*ek gēs choïkos*), the resurrected body will be "celestial" (*ex ouranou*, 15:47–49), again recalling popular beliefs about the composition and hiearchy of heavenly bodies. Finally, to close his account of the substance and composition of the resurrected body, Paul admits, as if finally to put the minds of his philosophical critics to rest, that he himself does not believe that a resurrection of a "flesh-and-blood" body is possible, because "flesh and blood *cannot* inherit the kingdom of God" (15:50, emphasis added).

One cannot help being impressed by how similar Paul's arguments are to the assumptions underwriting "astral soul" theory in popular philosophy. Paul, like the philosophers, assumes a physiological hierarchy of the cosmos, a scale of stuff along which the stuff (or more precisely, the various stuffs) of the human self can be placed. Unlike most Greek philosophers, Paul does not speak of the *psychē* ("soul"), but rather of the pneuma as the entity held in common by human beings and stars; and whereas they seldom use the term *sōma* ("body") for the heavenly entities, Paul readily speaks of the "bodies" of the sun, moon, and stars while rejecting the term *psychē* ("soul") for the heavenly entities. What human beings have in common with heavenly bodies is, in Paul's system, incorporation as a "pneumatic body"—that is, a body composed only of pneuma with sarx and psyche having been sloughed off along the way.

The philosophers, nevertheless, would have had little objection to speaking of a celestial entity as a pneumatic body, as long as it was understood that the term "body" in that phrase did not refer to an entity composed of the heavier matter of the earth. They did, after all, use the term *sōma* to refer to the stars and the heavenly spheres, and at least some of them considered pneuma to be the substance of the stars.

Modern commentators on 1 Corinthians 15 tend to be preoccupied with arguing that Paul's resurrected body is not a "physical" body. They take Paul's term "pneumatic" to be equivalent to the modern English term "spiritual," which usually designates something that is not "physical" or "natural." The entire chapter, therefore, is read as built on a Cartesian dichotomy of physical versus spiritual or natural versus supernatural. As should by now be apparent, I believe that the contrasts in the chapter are not between physical and spiritual (in spite of the misleading translation in the Revised Standard Version) or between matter and nonmatter. Neither Paul nor most of the philosophers of his day considered celestial bodies as "immaterial" in our sense of the term. Rather, the contrasts in the chapter are those of hierarchy and status, not ontology, as is clear when the various terms are juxtaposed:

sōmata epigeia (earthly body)	*sōmata epourania* (heavenly body)
en phthora (in corruption)	*en aphtharsia* (in incorruption)
atimia (in dishonor)	*doxa* (in glory/fame)
astheneia (weakness)	*dynamis* (power)
sōma psychikon (a psychic body)	*sōma pneumatikon* (a pneumatic body)
psychē zōsa (living soul)	*pneuma zōopoioun* (life-giving spirit)
ho choïkos (the dusty/earthy)	*ho epouranios* (the heavenly)
sarx kai haima (flesh and blood)	————
to phtharton (the destructible)	*aphtharsia* (the indestructible)
to thnēton (the mortal)	*athanasia* (the immortal)

Modern commentators usually work with a modern duality between body and spirit, in which the body equals "flesh and blood." But as the above juxtaposition of categories shows, "body" occurs in both columns, "flesh and blood" in only one. What contrasts with pneuma, moreover, is not matter or the physical but some form of psyche. Therefore, Paul's use of "flesh and blood" in 1 Corinthians 15 cannot be taken to refer to the whole body in any sense (that is, not even to what we today would call the physical body); rather, it refers to certain elements that, along with others such as psyche and pneuma, make up most bodies. Some commentators attempt to explain Paul's concept of the resurrection by speaking of a nonmaterial or nonphysical body, leading to the impossibly difficult concept of a "noncorporeal body."[80] The impossibility of the concept is clear when one tries to translate such language back into Greek and imagine how Paul could have conceived, in Greek, of a "nonbody body."

As I showed in Chapter 1, according to many ancient philosophical and medical theories, flesh and blood constitute only part of the body, which is also made up of various humors and substances such as pneuma in different forms. Flesh, blood, and pneuma are all parts of the body—or rather, different forms of substance that together make up a body. When Paul says that the resurrected body will be a pneumatic body rather than simply a psychic body or a flesh-and-blood body, he is saying that the immortal and incorruptible part of the human body will be resurrected—or, to put it more accurately, that the body will be raised, constituted (due to divine transformation) only by its immortal and incorruptible aspects, without its corruptible and corrupting aspects such as sarx.[81] No physical/spiritual dichotomy is involved here, much less a material/immaterial one. Rather, Paul has a hierarchy of essences, probably all assumed to be stuff, but of varying degrees of density or "stuffness." Paul would have thought of *all* of it as "material"—if, that is, he had been able to think in such a category without a material/immaterial dichotomy. At any rate, all the "stuff" here talked about is indeed stuff.[82]

For Paul, the current human body is made up of sarx, psyche, and pneuma. The resurrected body will shed the first two of these entities—like so much detritus—and retain the third, a stuff of a thinner, higher nature. This means that Paul has had to redefine "body" so that it can refer to something his hearers would not have thought of when they heard early Christian preaching about the "resurrection of the dead (corpses)." Even so, in 1 Corinthians 15, Paul, using shared assumptions about a hierarchical scale of substances ranging from lower earthly levels to higher celestial levels, is arguing for the resurrection of a body composed of an element that even many educated persons would have agreed *could* be immortal. Paul thus redefines *sōma* as something that the philosophically educated would not automatically think of, even though it was possible within philosophical circles, especially those influenced by Stoicism. But even Platonists could speak of astral bodies and believe that they were composed of fire, ether, or pneuma. Paul's redefined position, therefore, is much closer to that of the Strong than either they or most modern interpreters suppose.

Cosmology, Physiology, and Mythology

The disagreement between Paul and the Strong at Corinth over the resurrection of the body was due to their different constructions of the body. I have argued that everything we know about the position of the Strong can be accounted for by recourse to popular philosophy. We need not propose specifically religious precursors to the views of Paul's opponents. The Corinthians need not have been influenced by any nascent Gnosticism, Jewish mysticism, realized eschatology (whether from the implications of Paul's own preaching or from some other source), or "spiritualism." Their rejection of the resurrection of the body probably indicates that they disparaged the body generally; but this need not mean a deprecation of materiality or the physical. They could have learned to despise the body from the general popular philosophy of the time; that is, they need not have been Platonists or Cynics or Stoics or Epicureans or adherents of any particular school. I would guess that they, like other higher-status persons, had been exposed to a smattering of philosophical truisms and topoi and would have resisted an overly enthusiastic allegiance to any one philosophical school. It seems that a sort of genteel and amateur eclecticism was fashionable in the period, and this is what I take to be the source of the views of these Corinthian Christians.

We can go deeper into Paul's views than those of the Strong because we have his own words. Paul defends the Jewish apocalyptic idea of the resurrection of the body, but he does so by redefining *sōma* to such an extent that it would probably have made the doctrine unrecognizable to many, less educated Christians. According to Paul, the resurrected body is stripped of flesh, blood, and soul (*psychē*); it has nothing of the earth in it at all, being composed entirely of the celestial substance of pneuma. Far from rejecting the physiological and cosmological hierarchy of his disputants, Paul assumes it and redefines the term "body" in order to allow it a place higher in the hierarchy and hence the possibility of immortality. This, however, is only a bare sketch of Paul's view; by analyzing the controlling logic of his arguments, we can dig further and expose his broader assumptions about the cosmos and the body. I will do so by analyzing three themes around which 1 Corinthians 15 is composed: hierarchy, participation, and cosmic myth.

Hierarchy

I have already insisted that the framework important for Paul's views of the body and its resurrection is not a dichotomy between physical and spiritual entities but rather an assumption of a hierarchy of essence and a belief that all entities of the cosmos occupy positions within that hierarchy. Paul agrees with the Strong that whatever about a person is to be immortal must be of a higher nature than the current earthly body. What initially sets the Strong apart from Paul is that they interpret "resurrection of *nekrōn*" as "resurrection of corpses" (which would be a natural interpretation) and "resurrection of *sōma*" as equivalent to "resurrection of flesh and blood." Neither position would be acceptable to them—or, in fact, to Paul: the Strong place soma in a lower-status position in the hierarchy of essences, and Paul, for his part, rejects the notion of a resurrection of corpses or of flesh and blood. Rather, he defines *sōma* as a possible form for all kinds of stuff, even heavenly essences that make up the nature of heavenly bodies. As I have suggested, it is quite possible that the Strong would have been able to accept this kind of resurrected body, since they could probably accept the idea that the sun, moon, and stars were heavenly "bodies."

It is important for my reading of Paul's rhetorical strategy throughout 1 Corinthians to recognize that he does not completely carry out his agenda of status reversal in 1 Corinthians 15. On the one hand, he raises the status of soma, rendering it capable of the high status of heavenly participation. On the other hand, he makes no attempt to argue for the resurrection of the flesh or the psyche; he instead admits their lower natures. This constitutes an accommodation to Christians of both high and low status. Along with the (probably) less educated Christians, Paul reaffirms the resurrection of their *bodies;* but to convince Christians influenced by philosophy, he admits that he himself does not believe in a resurrection of *this* body. Rather, he redefines "body" so as to make it an acceptable category for immortality according to philosophical physiology.

I do not want to imply that Paul makes these rhetorical moves merely for reasons of expediency: there is no reason to doubt Paul's sincere acceptance of a cosmic and physiological hierarchy that leads him to *deny* that flesh and blood can inherit the Kingdom of God. Constrained by the physiology of those corporeal elements, Paul modifies the tendency manifested elsewhere in 1 Corinthians to overturn the status hierarchy of upper-class ideology. He sides with the uneducated by reaffirming the resurrection of the body in the face of educated criticisms, and he tries to convince his cultured converts that they should accept the traditional apocalyptic belief. Thus he here rehearses the rhetorical strategy he has employed elsewhere in 1 Corinthians: he sides with the lower-status members of the church and attempts to modify the behavior of those of higher status. But in order to do so, he has had to strip the resurrected body of its lower-status elements and define it as an entity that may appropriately claim and attain for itself a high physiological status. According to Paul, the creation will be redeemed (and not destroyed or abandoned; see Rom. 8); but this is possible only because the lower elements of that creation are capable of experiencing a transformation—an alchemy of the universe—that will enable bodies and creation to participate in higher realms of reality. Paul's apocalyptic revolution is constrained by his physiology. And that physiology is unalterably hierarchical.

Participation

A second theme of 1 Corinthians 15 is Paul's assumption (manifested elsewhere in 1 Corinthians, as we will see in the following chapters) that individual bodies have reality only insofar as they are identified with some greater cosmic reality. In 15:12–24 Paul insists that the resurrection of Christ necessarily entails the future resurrection of Christians. Christian bodies have no integral individuality about them. Due to their existence "in Christ," they *must* experience the resurrection. To deny the resurrection of their bodies is to deny the resurrection of Christ; to deny the resurrection of Christ is to render any future hope void. The Christian body has no meaning apart from its participation in the body of Christ.[83]

Paul so firmly assumes that identity is constructed upon participation that he can refer without demurral to the practice of baptism for the dead. As I conceded above, we do not know precisely who was baptizing for the dead or their intentions in doing so. Some scholars, pointing out that Paul himself does not advocate the practice, try to distance Paul's own theology from it, or at least to interpret it in a way that minimizes its "magical" aspect for modern readers. But their attempts to explain away this bizarre belief—that actions performed on the bodies of the living can affect the bodies of the dead—are only special pleadings.[84] Paul mentions the practice as proof of an afterlife for the dead, and his argument depends on certain assumptions: that the baptism of a human body incorporates it into the body of Christ, thus demonstrating a connection between the Christian's body and Christ's body, and that the baptism of a living body can affect the state of a dead body, incorporating the dead body into the body of Christ, thus demonstrating the connection between a person's body and the bodies of his or her dead loved ones. The sensibility of the logic underwriting baptism for the dead is thoroughly consistent with Paul's assumption that identity is established by participation in a larger entity.[85]

Existence in the body of Christ is not, however, the only reality. Indeed, insofar as human bodies are subject to death at all, it is due to their incorporation in the body of Adam (15:21–22). The body of Adam is the location of death, and it is human participation in that body, even after baptism, that makes possible a Christian's experience of death at all. Christians, although incorporated into the body of Christ through baptism, are still burdened, at least until the resurrection or transformation of their bodies in the eschaton, by their participation in the body of Adam. Just as the "first human being, Adam" is (not "was"; since human beings currently share this existence by participation in Adam's body, it is misleading to speak of Adam purely in the past tense) a "living psyche" (15:45), so are Christians; as his body is "dirt from the earth," so are the bodies of Christians (15:47–48). The current image (*eikōn*) of the earthly and earthy human body is due to its participation in the body of Adam (15:49).

Paul's argument comparing the resurrected body to the bodies of the sun, moon, and stars is also built on assumptions about identity through participation. Just as philosophers taught that living beings were composed of the elements constituting the region of their existence, so Paul teaches that the different forms of the human body are composed of the elements appropriate to the realm in which they participate at any particular time. Thus, resurrected bodies will partake of the same nature as heavenly bodies like the sun, moon, and stars. Christians currently partake of two natures: because they possess pneuma, they share something with the heavenly natures; because they are also made up of sarx and psyche, they share something with the earth, Adam, animals, birds, fish, and even dirt (15:39–40, 47–48). The transformation expected at the eschaton will cause the Christian body to shed the lower parts of its current nature and be left with the purer, transformed part of the pneuma. Christians will have bodies without flesh, blood, or soul—composed solely of pneumatic substance—light, airy, luminous bodies. The presupposition underwriting Paul's argument here is that the nature of any body is due to its participation in some particular sphere of existence. It gets its identity only through participation. It is difficult to imagine how any kind of individuality as we conceive it today could exist in such a world view. The individual human body is envisaged as a coagulation of the essences surrounding it.

Cosmic Myth

Paul, to be sure, was no ancient philosopher or scientist, and it is not my intention to represent him as such. He shares certain physiological and cosmological assumptions with other ancient thinkers; but when push comes to shove, he slips into a discourse of Jewish apocalypticism that would have struck Greek and Roman intellectuals as bizarre in the extreme. Biblical scholars have for years indulged in a misguided and fruitless debate over whether the background of Paul's thought and language is "really" Jewish or Greco-Roman. That this futile battle has been so long-lived is partly because both sides have had plenty of ammunition: Paul's language and arguments shift quickly back and forth between Jewish scripture and Greek rhetorical commonplaces, between Jewish apocalyptic and Greco-Roman popular philosophical topoi. He seems as comfortable with the myths of Jewish apocalyptic as with the moral exhortations current in urban Mediterranean culture. His letters are wonderful examples of what Mikhail Bakhtin calls "heteroglossia"—that is, the capacity of language to reflect several different discourses. According to Bakhtin, every linguistic event is composed of utterances and speech codes derived from a variety of social settings. The different "voices" of a text have their own different cultural histories, locations, and realms of meaning, complete with different mechanisms for the exercise of power through discourse. Moreover, the multi-voiced character of language is not merely a potential or occasional quality of a particular speech act but is inevitable because the inherent essence of language is social—and therefore multiple.[86] In 1 Corinthians 15 one of the strands of Paul's argument comes from a social location quite different from the cosmological presuppositions of Greco-Roman intellectuals: the cosmic myth provided by early Christian apocalypticism.

The belief in the resurrection is itself a Jewish apocalyptic belief, and as such it forms part of a scenario about the entire cosmos, its current state of embattlement and the final victory of God over the evil powers of "this world." Even when Paul says, in 15:19, that Christians (whom I take to be the referent of the "we") are most pitiable if they can hope only in "this life," he is referring to the eschatological dualism that poses "this world" as the evil counterpart of the kingdom of God, as in 1 Corinthians 1–4. The resurrection of Christ is interpreted as the harbinger—the "first fruits"—of the general resurrection predicted by apocalyptic preaching (15:20). In 15:23–24 Paul evokes the apocalyptic theme of cosmic revolution, as he has already in 1 Corinthians: after the general resurrection, the "end" will come "when he [Christ] will deliver the kingdom to God the Father, when every rule and every authority and power is destroyed." The universal experience of death is for Paul not simply an expression of neutral "nature," as it is for Greek and Roman philosophers, but is the last and greatest of the hypostatized "enemies" of God. Last of all the beasts that fight against God and his people, death will be destroyed (15:25–26).

After his more "scientific"-sounding explanation of the nature of the resurrected body (15:35–50), Paul again returns to the familiar ground of the cosmic myth provided by Jewish apocalypticism.

> Look, I'm relating to you a mystery. We will not all die; but we will all be changed, in a moment, in a wink, in the last trumpet. For the trumpet will blare, and the dead will be raised incorruptible, and we will be changed. For it is necessary that this corruptible thing be endowed with incorruptibility and this mortal thing with immortality. When the corruptible puts on incorruptibility, and the mortal puts on immortality, then will occur the word which has been written, "Death has been swallowed into victory. Where, Death, is your victory? Where, Death, is your sting?"

Paul's views are informed by a myth that encompasses the entire cosmos within its explanatory frame. Christians are not free selves exercising their wills in their individual bodies; they are pieces in a cosmic conflict, who occupy places on a cosmic map of battle. The parousia (the final coming of Christ) will effect a defeat not just of physical reality in an inanimate sense but of personal forces of evil, rulers and powers. Furthermore, resurrection constitutes not just a resuscitation of the same old bodies but a military rout of death itself.

Paul here introduces the cosmic agent that is more central to his thoughts in his other letters: the Law. He says, "The sting of Death is Sin; and the Law is Sin's power" (15:56). Resurrection means the defeat of sin and even of the Law. Paul's introduction of the Law in this context seems perplexing initially. In his other letters, especially Romans and Galatians, Paul struggles to fit the Law into his cosmological-mythological drama. Is it good or bad? Does it prohibit sin or promote it? Has it taught people or entrapped them? Has it been a positive force for humanity or a negative one? Paul elsewhere has so many problems defining and defending his views of the role of the Law in the cosmic myth that one would expect him to omit reference to it wherever possible. Yet he appears to introduce the Law in this context not because there are Judaizers at Corinth (as there are in Galatia) but because *nomos* (law) for Paul is (at least by this time in his life, if not before) a mythological, hypostatized, cosmological force that has heretofore succeeded in keeping humanity (all of it, not just Jews) separated from God. According to Paul's apocalyptic drama in 1 Corinthians 15, the Law can be lumped together with death and sin; it is at best an ambivalent cosmic agent that must be put in its place by the victory of Christ.[87]

Paul's apocalypticism perceives enemy agents everywhere in the cosmos as presently constituted. Death and sin are not abstract states but demonized beings. Even the Law is not an abstract concept or a list of rules but an agent of a dangerous nature, good in its basic intent but responsible for a disastrous state of affairs. Because humans are enslaved to sin, the Law is functionally an enemy of humanity. It is Paul's odd combination of a physiological hierarchy with a cosmological mythology that gives his rhetoric about the resurrection of the body its peculiar structure.

For both Paul and his ideological opponents at Corinth, the body is a microcosm structured as a continuous physiological hierarchy. Unlike his disputants, Paul does not accept the dominant hierarchy as an unproblematic given but rather struggles to disrupt the hierarchy of "this world" and restructure both it and the body to reflect the topsy-turvy status system of apocalyptic eschatology and faith in a crucified Messiah. In loyalty to that apocalypticism, he insists on the future resurrection of the body, thereby denying the lowly status attributed to the body by Greco-Roman elite culture. At the same time he admits that the resurrected body will have to be thoroughly reconstituted so as to be able to rise from the earth to a new luminous home in the heavens. The eschatological body must be one without earth, flesh, blood, or even psyche (soul). The tendency towards cosmic revolution inherent in Paul's apocalypticism must bow to some aspects of cosmological hierarchy. Paul's theology is constrained by his physiology.

By analyzing various of the issues that divide the Corinthian church—the role of wisdom, philosophy, and rhetoric, the Lord's Supper, the use of non-Christian courts, eating meat sacrificed toidols, speaking in tongues, and the resurrection of the body—I have argued that Paul sharply disagrees with one segment of the church and its acceptance of the conservative ideology of benevolent patriarchalism. To this point, perhaps, Paul has seemed more innovative, or even radical, than much modern popular opinion has taken him to be, and many readers may find that a comfort. But before we settle down comfortably in liberal and egalitarian camaraderie with Paul, we must consider another question that recurs in several of the disputes in 1 Corinthians, one that also divides Paul from his educated converts: the role of pollution in their different conceptions of the body. The last half of the book may well render Paul less acceptable to a modern audience, or at least make him appear more foreign, or even bizarre. Paul's anxieties about the boundaries of the body—both the social and the individual body—and his fears about pollution resulting from dangerous eating, sexual intercourse, desire, or unveiled women separate Paul not only from the Strong at Corinth but also from us as modern readers unfamiliar with the universe inhabited by Paul. Thus far I have insisted that Paul differentiates himself from the Strong—even while conceding some points to them—in his challenge to their conservative hierarchical ideology; henceforth I will argue that he also differentiates himself from them with regard to views about pollution and the boundaries of the body. Concerns about hierarchy give way to concerns about pollution. In each case, Paul's hopes of winning the theological battle depend on his ability to succeed in the struggle for the right to construct the body.

II Pollution

6 *The Body, Disease, and Pollution*

To the man or woman today for whom pollution in the religious sense is not an everyday concern, it sometimes seems that the inhabitants of the ancient world, especially Jews but also Greeks and Romans, were paranoid about pollution. Indeed, in almost every part of the ancient Mediterranean one can find notions of ritual pollutions, purifications, and cleansings.[1] But precisely what the ancients meant by "pollution" is not always clear, and scholars do not always notice that there were degrees of concern about pollution among the ancients and that there existed a diversity of opinion about the susceptibility of the individual and the social body to contamination. That diversity depended to a great extent on differing ideologies of the body.[2]

In the ancient world, notions of the body and pollution were related to concepts of disease. Although disease and pollution do not automatically go together in the modern mind, the logics of the discourses surrounding them are interconnected and mutually informative—possibly in modern culture, certainly in ancient. One way to assess the level of concern about pollution in ancient culture, for example, is to analyze the way in which disease was thought to threaten the body. Is disease a result of pollution, contamination, or infection? Or does it operate by different mechanisms and procedures? In this chapter I will attempt to further our understanding of ancient ideologies of the body by concentrating on the role pollution played in the ancient understanding of disease. I will argue that the differing roles assigned to pollution in disease etiologies are directly related to differing ideologies of the body, and that different ideologies of the body were linked, at least in Greco-Roman antiquity, to different social status positions.

Disease Etiology in Comparative Anthropology

Just as different cultures construe the body differently, so they experience disease differently. In fact, how a society constructs disease tells us a great deal about the nature of the body in that society. What kinds of language are used to talk about disease? How does disease interact with the body? What is the constitution of a healthy body, and how does it differ from the body when it is ill? How does one heal the diseased body? Until the latter part of the nineteenth century, the conventional wisdom of Western culture held to a modified Hippocratic doctrine that disease was caused by a breakdown in the harmony between the human body and its environment or by the disruption of the balance among various substances (bile, phlegm, blood, pneuma, and water) or states (hot–cold, dry–moist) of the body. During the nineteenth century, however, a shift took place, as scientists like Louis Pasteur and Robert Koch convinced the medical world that disease often results from the invasion of the body by "virulent microorganisms." There occurred what René Dubos calls "the discovery of agents of disease."[3] Although the process of dissemination was gradual, this scientific knowledge eventually became part of the common sense of inhabitants of the modern world. Almost all of us educated in North America or Western Europe in the twentieth century, for example, carry some form of germ theory as part of our conceptual baggage: disease is caused—for most of us in spite of scientific criticisms of simplistic germ theory—by hostile, living agents that attack and invade our bodies and that must be expelled or killed by defensive actions. Although none of us would hold that *all* illness is caused in this way (gradually scientists, physicians, and now lay persons are adopting more holistic notions of health that de-emphasize the importance of germ theory for disease etiology), this particular disease etiology is part of the common sense of our culture.

To encourage a fresh approach to ancient concepts of disease, I will briefly introduce various ways in which anthropologists present the disease etiologies of different cultures. My purpose in introducing comparative anthropology here is not to underwrite a universalistic or essentialist notion that particular models of disease or structures of knowledge are really the same, regardless of divergent cultural trappings. Nor shall I assume that so-called primitive medical ideas necessarily match ancient ideas, as if we could fill in the gaps in our knowledge of ancient experience by culling data from "primitive" cultures of our own day. Rather, my purpose is to note various cultural constructions of disease in order to decenter assumptions about the supposed naturalness of our or anyone's categories of knowledge. By first thinking about others' forms of knowledge, we may be able to perceive ancient language about the body in a new light. Comparative material helps us to critically recognize, in the words of Judith Farquhar, a "certain lumpy, taken-for-grantedness that still clings to our concept of body."[4]

The problem of characterizing and categorizing disease etiologies has exercised medical anthropologists. Too many have fallen into the easy, unreflective modern discourse that simply opposes "primitive" medicine, with its beliefs in supernatural causation and magico-religious therapeutics, to "rational" medicine, with its emphasis on so-called natural cause and effect.[5] Thus, almost all disease etiologies except those of European science of the twentieth century are sometimes lumped together as "primitive," and "natural" is simply opposed to "supernatural."[6] If, as I have already argued, the category of the supernatural is itself an invention of modern rationalism (since, let us say, the time of Descartes), we should hardly expect to find skepticism of it in cultures not influenced by that particular form of rationality. My approach will reject the natural/supernatural dichotomy (as well as the rational/primitive) and attempt to compare disease etiologies by analyzing not what particular causative agents they ascribe disease to, but the internal logic of the systems viewed processually. This, I believe, will enable a more thorough cross-cultural comparison.

Even a cursory look at medical anthropology reveals a wide diversity of ways in which different cultures speak of disease,[7] and no typology will do complete justice to the variety. Systematic grouping of some etiologies, however, may be useful for heuristic purposes. In a study of *East Asian Medicine in Urban Japan* Margaret M. Lock appropriates terminology from René Dubos that categorizes disease etiologies as either "ontological" or "physiological." The ontological view holds that disease is a specific "entity separate from oneself and caused by an agent external to the body but capable of getting into it and thereby causing damage." On this conception, disease is theoretically unrelated to the human being's personality, bodily constitution, or mode of life; that is, it has its own ontological status separate from the functioning of the host's body. According to the physiological model, on the other hand, "disease is seen simply as an abnormal state that is due to imbalance experienced by the individual organism at a given time." Health is regarded as a harmonious relationship between the human body and its environment.[8]

According to Lock, early Japanese medicine (ca. 700 C.E.) reflected the ontological logic, portraying disease as evil that attacked the body from outside; the aim of therapy was to "drive out the offending material." Disease was implicated in systems of pollution and cleansing, "avoidance taboos," and concerns about contagion.[9] Similarly, Chinese medicine before its classical period (which began about 200 B.C.E.) attributed disease to the anger of unsatisfied ancestors or evil spirits. But classical Chinese medicine effected a shift in etiology. After 200 B.C.E., fears of attacks from (what we would call) the spirit world become rare in Chinese medical texts, and the emphasis is instead placed on the proper controls to be put upon living in order to maintain or restore the natural harmony of the body and its relationship to its environment. "It is man's duty to keep healthy, and he does this by living according to the rules of society and by taking care of his body in a highly practical way. Through poor diet, lack of sleep, lack of exercise, and so on, or by being in a state of disharmony with one's family or society, the body can get out of balance, and it is at times like this that diseases occur."[10] Or stated a bit differently, "Diseases become manifest when the body gets out of balance and the *ch'i* [the stuff of life-force] does not circulate properly."[11] While internal or external forces may affect this balance or the state of *ch'i*, the causative factor is a disruption of balance due to influence from climatic change or other environmental factors, not to hostile, personalized agents that attack the body and seek to invade it. With the advent of modern, Western forms of medicine (what Lock calls "cosmopolitan medicine"), segments of Japanese and Chinese culture have once again experienced a shift, now toward a different manifestation of the ontological theory. In modern Western thinking, the mechanistic influences of (among others) Descartes and Newton combined with the arguments of Pasteur and Koch (along with, undoubtedly, other ideological factors) rendered the ontological etiology more dominant, and it is embodied in modern concerns about contagion, infection, and bacteriological microorganisms.

I am not suggesting that these different logics of disease alternate *seriatim* through history or that a given culture can be placed unproblematically in one or other category at any given time. Indeed, classical Chinese medicine based on the physiological model seems to have been the dominant court medicine without displacing ideas among the general populace about demonic or ancestral causation of disease.[12] Different segments of society may hold different etiologies of disease within the same era. For example, Lock sees the two etiologies reflected in classical East Asian medicine and Shintô medicine as currently practiced in Japan. "In East Asian medicine, therapy is mild, designed to help the body itself restore equilibrium; the patient is considered in relation to his total environment, and the healing process involves social participation. In contrast, Shintô therapy is strong, designed to purge; the patient is isolated from his group until such time as he should recover."[13] Thus different logics of disease may each find their own space in a society, and seldom will we find a culture that holds "purely" to one or another theory. The different models or logics of disease are recognizable by their relative emphases rather than by any consistency in explanatory rhetoric.

Building on the studies of Lock and Dubos, I will speak of two main disease etiologies: one of imbalance and one of invasion.[14] According to the first (similar to the physiological system described above), the body is normally a balanced ecosystem whose elements or forces are all necessary: good health results when none of those elements or forces oversteps its natural bounds or becomes too dominant. By contrast, disease results when there is imbalance, whether due to internal processes (such as, among many other possibilities, faulty digestion, putrefaction of bodily substances, or movement of a bodily organ or substance away from its normal position) or external factors (such as change in temperature, ingestion or inhalation of harmful materials, or contact with unhealthy "winds"). According to this imbalance etiology, the important element in the causation of disease is not invasion by a hostile, foreign element but the influence of outside forces (which are usually composed of the same basic materials as the internal elements of the body) on the composition and balance of the internal elements. Health is restored by reestablishing the natural equilibrium of the body's elements and forces, either by altering the external factors (heat and cold, for example) or by purging the body of putrefied or excessive elements (food that has not been digested properly or an overabundance of a certain material like bile or water). Thus, although expelling harmful material from the body is a factor in "balance" therapeutics, the emphasis is on restoring the equilibrium of the body rather than on a fear of the invasive agent itself; likewise, the material that needs to be expelled is construed not as ontologically alien and hostile but simply as a natural force or material (food, heat, air, and so forth), the processing of which has gone awry. Health regimens in this etiology tend toward moderation; the natural state of the body is considered good and may be maintained by nonradical control mechanisms. Fears of pollution or infection (if they exist at all) are not as paramount as fears of disruption.

According to the invasion etiology (comparable to Dubos's ontological etiology), the body is construed as a closed but penetrable entity that remains healthy by fending off hostile forces and protecting its boundaries. Disease is caused by alien forces, either personal agents (for example, demons or gods) or impersonal but harmful materials (for example, germs, pollutants, or "tiny animals"), that invade the body. Disruption of the normal state of the body is, of course, also a factor here, but the emphasis in health regimens is on protecting the body from invasion and, in cases of disease, expelling the harmful agent from the body. Concerns about pollution, contagion, and infection (though the last of these should not necessarily be taken in the modern sense) tend to be more important than a mere concern to maintain an equilibrium of bodily elements. Purgation procedures, for example, may be radical and even violent. Health regimens according to the invasion etiology concentrate on solidifying the boundaries of the body, assuring purity and avoidance of pollutions or infectious agents, and quarantining polluted or infected persons.

The usefulness of this taxonomy is demonstrated by its ability to group disease etiologies from widely separated cultural locations and compare them according to the logic of each system regardless of whether they appear to us as superstitious or as invoking supernatural explanations for disease, for instance. Many different cultures use some form of invasion etiology. In addition to the above-mentioned Chinese and Japanese construals of disease, which speak of angry ancestors or hostile demonic forces as the culprits, the Gimi of New Guinea depict disease as due to attacks from superhuman forces, and Tuareg notions (Muslims in northeastern Niger) attribute disease to polluting spirits that must be exorcised but can be relatively kept at bay by veiling the face to block entry through facial orifices.[15] These etiologies should not simply be dismissed as "primitive," since, after all, they operate by a logic quite similar to modern germ theory. Although most people today would not think of viruses as personal agents, the discourse surrounding our diseases makes it sound as if we do: even in cases of disease not caused by virulent microorganisms, such as cancer, our medical discourse portrays the disease as a hostile enemy that attacks and invades the body and must be either killed, defeated, or expelled.[16] The discourses of these etiologies are similar in spite of the fact that some are considered supernatural and others scientific.

Otherwise divergent disease systems may also be grouped together as reflecting the imbalance etiology. In classical Chinese medicine, as already noted, disease is normally construed as the dysfunction of the normally balanced ecosystem of the body. As Shigehisa Kuriyama explains, "The failings of the body, therefore, were inseparable from failures of self-mastery. Sickness in this view had little to do with ancestral ire or demonic cruelty. It arose principally from within, from immoderation and carelessness, from gluttony and overexertion, from protracted grief and explosive anger, and sometimes also from the mere imagination of dangers." [17] In the move from preclassical to classical Chinese medicine, "the earlier rhetoric of defense and attack was giving way to the new logic of balance and compensation; fears of threatening outsiders were being supplemented, and to an extent supplanted, by a conception of disease as unequal distribution." [18] As Kuriyama explains and I will demonstrate below, classical Greek and Roman medicine operates with a similar disease etiology. [19]

Some cultural contexts combine the two etiologies in interesting ways; that is to say, the two are not mutually exclusive. According to Carol Laderman, "rural east coast Malays" divide diseases into "usual" and "unusual." Ordinary ailments are attributed to a humoral imbalance and are treated accordingly, with adjustments to diet, herbal remedies, massage, or some such everyday therapy. Diseases unresponsive to such remedies, however, are attributed to disembodied spirits that have invaded the body, destroyed its balance, and must be forcibly ejected through a seance conducted by a *minduk*, a special therapist. [20]

As is already clear from these examples, disease etiologies correlate with distributions of social power and other social constructions of knowledge. Kuriyama notes, "The cosmic dimensions of Han medical thought mirrored the expansive ambitions of the first great age of universal empire. In the same way that the political vision of universal empire would survive the rise and fall of subsequent dynasties, so the vision of the body as a seasonal microcosm would continue, along with the *yangsheng* ideals of somatic integrity, to define medical orthodoxy for nearly two millennia." [21] René Dubos notes that much modern drug therapy operates through a certain "cowboy philosophy" of American populism: "In the crime-ridden frontier town, the hero singlehandedly blasts out the desperadoes who were running rampant through the settlement." [22] Another example comes from a completely different environment: in an intricate and fascinating study, Brad Weiss has shown how a new disease called "plastic teeth" by its sufferers, an African people of northwest Tanzania, expresses the ambivalent social role played by imported commodities, such as plastic, that the people experience as both foreign and indispensable. The disease is caused by the growth of plastic teeth in the mouths of Haya infants, the body being threatened and destroyed from within by a commodity over which the people have no control. "Used in the daily course of domestic affairs, plastic is a part of every person's intimate experience. At the same time, plastic carries the symbolic weight of commoditized practices that render transient and dislocate forms of well-being that should characterize such experience." [23]

All this is not to say that social structures or economic systems simplistically or straightforwardly produce a particular disease etiology, as if we could extrapolate or predict a logic of disease by categorizing the system of production. But forms of the social exercise of power recur in dominant symbol systems— and vice versa. Particular ways of exercising social power are echoed (and perpetuate themselves) in particular linguistic matrices. We can learn a great deal about a culture's ideology of the body by connecting its disease etiologies with other social structures, class systems, and means of production. I will argue that such a connection is important for locating different disease etiologies in Greco-Roman society.

Disease Etiology in Classical Greco-Roman Medicine

The classical Greek theory of disease as expressed in medical and philosophical writings from the time of Alcmaeon (about 500 B.C.E.) and Hippocrates (fifth century B.C.E.) consistently evokes the imbalance etiology. At the very beginning of the Hippocratic treatise *On Affections* (*Peri Pathōn*) the writer explains the theory of disease that will rule Hippocratic doctrine for centuries:

> All human diseases arise from bile and phlegm; the bile and phlegm produce diseases when, inside the body, one of them becomes too moist, too dry, too hot, or too cold; they become this way from foods and drinks, from exertions and wounds, from smell, sound, sight, and sexual intercourse, and from heat and cold; this happens when any of the things mentioned are applied to the body at the wrong times, against custom, in too great amount and too strong, or in insufficient amount and too weak. All diseases in human beings, then, arise from these things.[24]

Whereas this text stresses the role of bile and phlegm in disturbing the balance of the body, other writers pay attention to other bodily substances (water, blood, and pneuma, for example); but the emphasis is always on the balance or harmonious constitution of the body and disruptions to it. Disruptions may be caused, it is admitted, by either internal or external factors, but the external factors are composed of the same basic elements and forces (air, water, heat, cold, and so on) as those inside the body. That is, they have no ontologically independent status. As Alcmaeon said even before Hippocrates, "Disease occurs sometimes from an internal cause such as excess of heat or cold, sometimes from an external cause such as excess or deficiency of food. It may occur in a certain part, such as blood, marrow, or brain; but these parts also are sometimes affected by external causes, such as waters, or a particular site, or fatigue, or constraint, or similar reasons. Health is the harmonious mixture of the qualities."[25]

My claim that all Greek professional medicine reflects the imbalance etiology constitutes an etic rather than emic analysis. When Greek and Roman writers themselves talk about disease causation, they point to differences among writers and schools. The first-century Latin compendium by Celsus, for example, lists what he considers very different explanations for disease. Some theorists argue, he notes, that an excess or deficiency among the four elements (fire, water, air, and earth) causes illness; others follow Herophilus in laying the blame on the humors (usually bile, phlegm, blood, and water). Celsus cites Hippocrates as pointing to breath (*spiritus*, the Latin translation of *pneuma*) as the most important factor in illness. Erasistratus, however, taught that "blood is transfused into those vessels [*venas*: veins] which are fitted for *pneuma*, and excites inflammation which the Greeks term *phlegmone*, and that inflammation effects such a disturbance as there is in fever." Asclepiades, on the other hand, taught that "little bodies" that usually passed through the pores of the body without incident occasionally blocked those passages, resulting in illness.[26]

Later in the same work, Celsus categorizes diseases as those resulting from "hidden causes" on the one hand and "evident causes" on the other. The hidden causes are those given above. The evident causes are factors like heat and cold or hunger and surfeit. In still another context, Celsus describes the views of the "Methodists," a school of medical theorists and physicians active in the first and second centuries. They hold that there are three classes of disease, "one a constriction [*strictum*], another a flux [*laxum*], the third a mixture [*mixtum*]. For the sick at one time excrete too little, at another time too much; again from one part too little, from another too much; and these classes of diseases are sometimes acute, sometimes chronic, at times on the increase, at times constant, at times diminishing."[27] Thus the terms which Celsus uses to describe disease are quite different from mine, employing distinctions that reflect the interests and debates of first-century scientists.

However varied the descriptive terms of these systems, they all fit my category of imbalance etiology. They may attribute the cause of the imbalance of the body to different factors, but they all depend upon the logic of balance and imbalance to conceptualize health and illness. According to Hippocratic tradition, disease is the result of an imbalance or disruption of the elements of the body or the humors caused by, among other things, excess of heat or cold or dryness or moisture. According to the Methodists, on the other hand, disease results from a disruption of the normal tension of the body or a part of the body; it is either too constricted or too lax or some mixture of the two. Thus the Methodists teach that "if the body is constricted, it has to be relaxed; if suffering from a flux, that has to be controlled; if a mixed lesion, the more severe malady must be countered first."[28] As Galen says, "Health is some kind of balance (*symmetria*) for all the sects; for us it is a balance of wet and dry, hot and cold, but for others a balance of corpuscles and pores, for others of atoms, or *anarma*, or partless bodies, or homoiomeries."[29] What the ancient theorists disagree on is not the necessity of balance but what precisely is to be kept in balance and what causes the balance to be disrupted.

In spite of the occasional success of Asclepiades or the Methodists, the Hippocratic doctrine of humors was the most influential theory in antiquity, pervading the writings of physicians and philosophers. Disease resulted when one of the humors became dislocated from its normal place in the body or if a particular humor became too dominant in some particular part of the body. For example, since bile was usually the hot humor and phlegm the cold, a displacement of either would upset the balance of temperature in the body. The offending humor had to be removed from the body in some way or coaxed back to its accustomed location. In the Hippocratic *On Affections*, for instance, an inflamed and swollen uvula results when the head has become overheated, and phlegm moves downward toward the throat, swelling the uvula. The text first recommends gargling, but if that does not work, "shave the back of the head, apply two [suction] cups, and remove as much blood as possible, in order to draw the flux of phlegm back up again." The treatment is designed to force the phlegm back up toward the top and back of the head, or failing that, the uvula is incised to allow egress for the excessive phlegm.[30] For the ancient physicians, a person had a "cold" and experienced a flow of what we would call mucus because of an overabundance of phlegm, which was a cold humor.[31]

According to the ancient theorists, the environment of the body was important for health, but usually not because of concerns about infection or contagion. Rather, the body's surroundings were expected to have an impact on the balance of temperature or moisture in the body or on the constitution of the humors. As Galen, who wrote a century after Celsus, notes: "Health is a sort of harmony. . . . For in every instance, health in us is a due proportion of moist, dry, warm, and cold, sometimes of molecules and pores, sometimes of atoms or items or minims or isotopes, or of each of the primary elements; but always we function in our parts through their due proportion."[32] It is important, therefore, to attend to environmental factors: "Now the surrounding atmosphere harms us by making us unduly warm or cold, dry or moist; but the other agents by bruising, straining, wounding, or dislocating." [33]

Besides this concern to maintain a moderate environment, notions of balance and moderation ruled therapeutics. The governing principle of prescription for almost all physicians was *contraria contrariis curantur*, "opposites are cured by opposites." [34] Warm drugs or baths treat cold diseases, moist remedies treat dry diseases. [35] Even different body types should be manipulated to conform to an ideological mean. As Celsus says, "A thin man ought to fatten himself up, a stout one to thin himself down; a hot man to cool himself, a cold man to make himself warmer; the moist to dry himself, the dry to moisten himself; he should render firmer his motions if loose, relax them if costive; treatment is to be always directed to the part which is mostly in trouble." [36] The main danger to the body is disruption of its normal balance and equilibrium; concerns about environment and treatment therefore revolve not around worries about invasion but around fears of instability.

This is not to imply that concerns about pollution are entirely absent in these classical medical writings. One does encounter notions of corruption and purification and the language of "cleanliness" and "uncleanliness" in prescriptions, demonstrating that although abstract statements about disease etiology seldom refer to pollution issues, ideas of purity and impurity nonetheless play some role in the medical construction of the body. For example, according to a Hippocratic text, swelling may be due to "white phlegm" and excessive moisture in parts of the body, but impurity is also a factor: "This disease arises because of phlegm, when a person that is phlegmatic after chronic fevers becomes unclean (*akathartos*), and the phlegm turns into his tissues (*sarx*)." [37] Several treatments speak of cleansing patients, which seems to mean forcing evacuation through the bowels (if the prescription recommends "cleaning downwards") or inducing vomiting or expectoration (if "cleaning upwards" is advised). Cleansing treatments can be tricky, however, because one must force evacuation of some elements without violently affecting others. The diagnosis and treatment of dropsy provides an interesting case in point:

> Dropsy arises, in most cases, when a person continues for a considerable time after a lengthy illness in an unclean state; for the tissues [*hai sarkes*] become corrupted [*phtheirontai*], melt, and turn to water. . . . If dropsy arises from uncleanness, the belly becomes filled with water, the feet and the legs below the knees swell up, and the shoulders, regions about the collar-bones, chest and thighs melt away. If you take on this patient at the

beginning, before he becomes very dropsical, have him drink a medication that will clean water and phlegm downwards, but not set bile in motion; prescribe a regimen of foods, drinks, exercises, and walks from which he will become lean and dry and his tissues will be strengthened as much as possible.[38]

In these cases the uncleanness is attributed not to an alien, infectious agent but to the putrefaction or corruption of the normal elements of a body which for some reason has been prevented from fulfilling its natural self-cleaning activities (such as proper evacuation). The cleansing is spoken of not as the expulsion of an alien, hostile force but as the encouragement or inducement of the normal mechanisms of the body.

In many of these treatments, "evacuating the cavity" is important, suggesting that purity issues have little to do with anything comparable to "infection"; the body is to be cleansed to allow it to return to its normal balance. Blood, to take one instance, can be "corrupted"; but it is corrupted by being mixed with bile or phlegm, normal elements of the body, not by external agents that are biologically different from the materials of the body.[39] According to Celsus, corruption results not from contamination but from the natural rotting process of materials; food, for example, that is not properly digested will putrefy in the body and thereby cause disease.[40] The healing principle when dealing even with "corruption," therefore, is implicated more in the logic of balance than of infection or invasion, and the rhetoric of cleansing in these contexts imitates the rhetoric of healing by opposites: "In cleaning, employ medications according to the following principle: when patients are bilious, give medications that clean out bile; when they are phlegmatic, give medications that clean out phlegm. . . . Medicinal drinks that are not given to clean out bile or phlegm must, when they enter the body, exercise their faculty by cooling, warming, drying, moistening, collecting or dispersing."[41] The mechanics of purification here operate by the logic of balance, not invasion.

Did classical medical theory have any concept of "infection"? Ancient theorists acknowledge that the plague spreads through the population due to something like contamination; that is, they note that geographical proximity puts one in danger of contracting it. Aelius Aristides tells of a summer plague that spread throughout a town, including his household and even his livestock. "First two or three of my servants grew sick, then one after another. Then all were in bed, both the younger and the older. I was the last to be attacked. . . . The livestock too became sick. . . . Then the disease increased and I was attacked by the terrible burning of a bilious mixture, which troubled me continuously day and night."[42] A mechanism that at least somewhat resembles our notions of infection seems here to be acknowledged.

Most of the time, though, the mechanism by which the plague was seen to affect different people in one locality operated by a completely different logic from our modern notion of infection or the etiological logic of invasion. Doctors attributed plagues to *miasmata* (bad or polluted air) or some other environmental factor like heat. The Pseudo-Aristotelian work *Problems* explains that people who visit a feverish person themselves get sick because the heat radiating from the fever heats up their bodies.[43] Alternatively, the plague spreads because the sun's heat combined with a marshy locale produces bad air, which is then breathed by all the people in the area. Sextus Empiricus notes that astronomers can forecast plagues by observing changes in the "surrounding vault"—that is, the sky.[44] Philo and Galen also attribute the plague to an unhealthy atmosphere or water.[45] Galen believes that one should be careful that the "psychic *pneuma*" in the body does not become affected by "nasty vapors."[46] And Celsus advises people who expect to be in "sickly localities and seasons" to rest often so that their bodies can better deal with cold, heat, surfeit, fatigue, and sexual desire.[47] The underlying logic of all these views has more in common with the imbalance than the invasion etiology. Environmental factors that affect the balance of one person's body, whether heat, unclean water, or air that is too dense and oppressive, naturally affect the bodies of other people in the same area. The disease is still not thought of as being ontologically independent of the body or as attacking or invading the body like a hostile agent.

The one ancient writer to offer a theory of the plague that uses an actual concept of contagion is Thucydides. Thucydides' account of the plague of Athens in 430 B.C.E. is remarkable in that he notes how the plague spread from one person to another due to bodily contagion and not simply to a shared environmental influence.[48] He says, for example, that the disease was carried by soldiers traveling from one place to another. What is also remarkable, however, is how little Thucydides' account affected later thoughts concerning the plague. As J. C. F. Poole and A. J. Holladay write:

> Thucydides' conclusions seem to have had next to no influence on his contemporaries or on those who came after. . . . After Thucydides there are references to epidemics by various historians, for example Diodorus 14. 70 (of 396 B.C.) and Livy 25. 26 (of 211 B.C.). Diodorus attributed his epidemic to bad weather and miasma, as did Livy. Thus both conformed with orthodox medical theory, but both went on to say that subsequently

the disease was spread by coming in contact with the sick. So it is clear that common observation noted the occurrence of contagion. But the odd thing is that the idea of contagion made little appearance in medical literature.[49]

Observing that ideas of contagion are absent from the entire Hippocratic corpus, Poole and Holladay suggest that intellectuals in the classical Greek world simply could not fit such notions into their concepts of disease and the body. "It almost seems as if professional medical men were the victims of their own *a priori* theorizing about the causes of illnesses and epidemics, which assigned overriding importance to climate, air, breath, and miasma, so that both Hippocrates in the *Nature of Man* 9 and Celsus in *De Medicina* 1.10 recommended that in time of pestilence one should seek a different climate and, if this cannot be done, rest as much as possible so as to breathe in less miasma."[50] The reason for this situation is that, although our modern notion of contagion operates by the logic of invasion, classical Greek medicine was overwhelmingly implicated in the logic of balance and imbalance.

I should be clear that when I speak of "classical Greek medicine" I am referring to professional physicians and medical theorists who wrote books. Yet, we find plenty of evidence that other educated people, though not themselves doctors, held much the same views. In Platonic thought, pains result from the sudden imbalance of the particles or organs in the body; pleasure from the restoration of balance. Fevers are caused by an excess of fire in the body and cured by the return of a balanced temperature.[51] Epictetus knows that doctors prescribe a change of environment to cure many diseases.[52] Artemidorus's *Dream Handbook* speaks of disease as a "lack" in the body or as a "crisis" in the normal constitution of the body; diseased blood in a dream signifies "discord" (the opposite of "harmony") with the members of one's household; and vomiting bile or phlegm in a dream indicates "a release from present ills. For all such things, once they have been rejected, no longer trouble a person."[53]

Aelius Aristides' account of his many bouts with illness provides an interesting case. He occasionally thinks of disease as something that invades a person. He relates a dream in which "some Parthians had got me in their power, and one of them approached me and made as if to brand me. Next he inserted a finger in my throat and poured in something, according to some native custom, and named it 'indigestion.'"[54] The images of penetration, especially by a foreigner, and the imagination of disease as invasion show that on some level (even if not the level of conscious theorizing) Aristides imagines disease as caused by the invasion of an alien agent. When he describes his treatments, though, they always fit the logic of balance and imbalance. He applies a hot drug to remedy a cold ailment; he attributes health to an equilibrium of proper warmth in his body, brought about, ironically, by a cold bath.[55] Even after appearing to recognize that the plague is passed around by contagion, or at least by geographical proximity, he heeds the goddess Athena's prescriptions to rid himself of the fever, which he says was caused by a bad "bilious mixture," by purgations of the offending humor (bad bile).[56] Thus even an upper-class person who is as convinced of the constant activity of the gods as is Aristides will tend to conceptualize disease along the lines of the imbalance etiology rather than as caused by the invasion of a hostile agent. By the early Roman period, physicians had succeeded in solidifying a relatively new common sense that portrayed disease as imbalance rather than invasion, at least among the educated class.[57]

Disease and Superstition in the Greco-Roman World

I call this common sense "new" because it seems to have displaced older ideas about disease constructed more along the lines of invasion etiology. But it was never common in Greco-Roman society as a whole. Though thoroughly marginalized in professional writings, the opposing etiology of invasion continued to hold sway in popular thought, although unearthing instances of it is difficult due to the fact that only the theorizing of the educated elite has, for the most part, survived in the literature.

Though they rejected the idea themselves, medical writers admit that "in the old days" people believed that disease was the result of attack by the gods or *daimones*. Celsus, for example, writing probably in the reign of Tiberius (first half of the first century C.E.), begins his medical textbook by noting that long ago diseases were attributed to the anger of the gods. He, of course, rejects this view.[58]

The idea that disease results from attacks by gods or daimons occurs regularly in pre-Socratic Greek texts. In the *Odyssey* disease is the result of attack by an "evil [or base] daimon" (*kakos daimōn*, 10. 64, 5. 396).[59] In the famous story of "Pandora's Jar" from Hesiod, diseases are personified evils released by Pandora that wander the earth and attack humans: "Countless plagues [*nousoi*] wander amongst men; for earth is full of evils and the sea is full. Of themselves diseases come upon men continually by day and by night, bringing mischief to mortals silently; for wise Zeus took away speech from them."[60] The notion that disease is due to divine anger, jealousy, or caprice furnishes much of the plot of Greek tragedy, leading Plinio Prioreschi, citing works of Euripides, Aeschylus, Sophocles, and even the comedian Aristophanes, to observe, "The concept of the divine origin of disease . . . is typical of the tragedy."[61] The belief that disease was due to divine displeasure or attack was thus quite common in pre-Hippocratic Greece and continued in classical Greek literature and thought.[62]

The popularity of the idea was one reason why the Hippocratic author of *The Sacred Disease* had to work so hard to refute—or at least modify—it. This author, referring to some form of madness and perhaps to what we would identify as epilepsy, notes that the masses believe it to be caused by divine attacks, hence its label "the sacred disease." In arguing against this belief, he does not so much refute it outright and attribute the disease to other, "natural" sources, as argue that all diseases are divine in the sense that all disease is part of nature, which is imbued with divinity (or divinities). Diseases are all part of natural processes, which include divine processes. It is therefore correct *in one sense* to ascribe disease to divinities but wrong to think simplistically that a person's body is "defiled by a god."[63]

The Hippocratic author has no intention of completely excluding divine activity from the mechanisms of disease and healing. He is not, in other words, arguing for a natural cause-and-effect mechanism unaffected by supernatural beings.[64] Indeed, he believes that the gods can assume benevolent roles in healing diseases. "The gods are the real physicians, though people do not think so. But the truth of this statement is shown by the phenomenon of disease."[65] What the author objects to is assigning to a particular disease the epithet "sacred," as if divinities were uninvolved in disease and healing in other cases. As the author of *Airs, Waters, Places* says, rejecting the naive beliefs of the "Sythians" who attribute sexual impotence to the gods, "I too think that these diseases are divine, and so are all others, no one being more divine or more human than any other; all are alike, and all divine."[66] He then proceeds to explain that impotence is due to the particular way in which Sythians attempt to cure lameness (caused by too much horseback riding) by cutting and bleeding the veins beside the ear, thereby unwittingly destroying the seed, which cannot then travel through those veins from the brain to the genitals. He provides what looks to us like a purely natural etiology of a disease yet without claiming that the gods are not involved. He objects not to divine causality but to attributing only particular diseases to the gods and portraying those diseases as due to personal attacks by divinities.[67] Other educated authors also allow the gods a role in the treatment of disease: Pliny the Elder attributes the healing power of drugs to the gods; Herophilus calls drugs "the hands of the gods"; and Galen considers himself a "servant of Asclepius" (*therapeutēs Asklēpiou*) and composes a medical text as, in his words, "a true hymn of the god who has created us."[68] Hippocratic authors object to rites of "purifications and incantations" that, though approved by the masses, they believe to be ineffectual.[69] Thus they reject specific therapeutic rites of purification and magic first by implicating divinity in *all* of nature and then by arguing for a treatment of disease that will manipulate the different forces of nature rather than seek to appease a personal, and thus potentially capricious, being.

Hippocratic medicine was never completely successful in its attempts to turn popular thought away from an etiology of invasion to one of the balance of nature. It is true that members of the educated class came more and more to reject the invasion etiology, but their writings reveal that other, less educated people never made the epistemological shift. Lucian's *Lover of Lies* offers portraits of both views existing contemporaneously. Gullible people, according to our skeptical narrator, believe that a statue is capable of sending fevers "upon whomsoever he will"; it can also send diseases away. In another case, illness is attributed to a daimon that has entered a person's body and must be exorcised. One speaker claims to have seen a man healed when the infecting daimon, "black smoky in colour," was expelled from the body.[70] The educated narrator objects to the use of magic and the application of magical materials to effect healing, since he believes that disease arises from forces within the body, not from without: "Do you really think," he asks, "that certain incantations put a stop to this sort of thing, or external applications, when the trouble has its seat within?" One should not, therefore, try to "frighten away" a fever by use of a holy name or foreign phrase but should treat it "according to nature."[71]

Again, this last statement does not mean that the narrator is offering natural explanations for processes understood by others in the dialogue as supernatural. When accused of atheism, the narrator says, "For my part, I revere the gods and I see their cures and all the good that they do by restoring the sick to health with drugs and doctoring. In fact, Asclepius himself and his sons ministered to the sick by laying on healing drugs, not by fastening on lions' skins and weasels."[72] The author rejects not the idea that the gods may heal but the idea that they will make someone sick. And the treatments he rejects are rejected not because they are supernatural but because they are the practices of the unlettered and the unprofessional—that is, the masses. The line is drawn not between those who believe in supernatural causation and those who believe in "nature" but between those who fear the gods and those who do not, between those who look to magicians and old women for healing and those who put their faith in the knowledge of the professionally educated class.

The philosophically educated referred to the beliefs they despised as "superstition" (*deisidaimonia*). But, as noted earlier, in ancient texts "superstition" does not refer to a belief in supernatural beings or supernatural causation; it means simply "an unreasonable fear of the gods," a "dread of divinities." (Of course, that leaves open the important question "Unreasonable to whom?" But it is precisely that nice ambiguity that allows the charge to be leveled so effectively and discriminately.) Plutarch, in an essay on superstition, juxtaposes atheism and superstition. The atheist is bad enough for denying the existence of the gods, but the superstitious person is worse for believing that the gods are malicious beings who harm people. Superstition is "an emotional idea and an assumption productive of a fear which utterly humbles and crushes a man, for he thinks that there are gods, but that they are the cause of pain and injury."[73] Uncouth self-prostrations and humiliations are superstitious, as are fears of punishment after death in the nether world and beliefs in "judges and torturers and yawning gulfs and deep recesses teeming with unnumbered woes."[74] The problem with superstition, for Plutarch, is that it robs human beings of their pride, their "love of honor" (*philotimia*), that good valued most by upper-class Greeks or Romans. Superstition keeps the free citizen from standing before his gods with his head held high in the confidence and self-assurance appropriate to his class.

Superstitious people attribute disease to attacks by the gods or invasions by daimons.[75] Hence they attempt to keep themselves healthy by avoiding pollutions and attending to purifications.[76] Theophrastus, in his book on various *Characters* (fourth to third century B.C.E.), portrays the "Superstitious Man" as the one fearful of the divine (*to daimonion*). He washes his hands a great deal; he is always cleaning his house; and he is careful to avoid pollution (*to mē miainesthai*).[77] Reflecting the very fears of contagion that the Hippocratic writer attacks, Theophrastus's "Superstitious Man" is afraid of contamination when in the presence of a madman.[78] Although some notions of purity and pollution existed even among upper-class, educated writers, too much attention to matters of purity and anxieties about pollution were considered marks of superstition, the fear of the gods.

Of course, to call someone superstitious was to render a status judgment, even if the person so called was actually a member of the higher class. Plutarch speaks of a Spartan citizen who ended up going to "cleansers" (*kathartai*) and "seers" (*manteis*) for healing of a disease even though he had disdained them before.[79] The statement shows that upper-class men might avail themselves of such therapists, but that they thereby ran the risk of losing face as educated men. Women and the masses (*ochlos, hoi polloi*) are assumed to be especially superstitious.[80]

Plutarch reveals the disinclination of the educated to ascribe much credence to fears of pollution when he, ironically, explains and praises the purification rituals of the Egyptian Isis and Osiris cult but does so by reinterpreting them according to the imbalance etiology of disease. In his treatise *On Isis and Osiris* (*Moralia* 351E–384C) Plutarch interprets the purification rituals in terms of Greek medical discourse on healthy environments. He explains that the Egyptians burn resin on their altars in the morning because the air during the night "becomes dense and oppresses the body and brings the soul into depression and solicitude, as if it had become befogged and heavy." The burning of resin "revivifies" and "purifies" (*kathairontes*) the air and "fans into fresh life the languished *pneuma* innate in the body." They burn myrrh on the altars at midday because "the sun is forcibly attracting a copious and heavy exhalation from the earth and is combining this with the air . . . for the heat dissolves and scatters the murky and turgid concretions in the surrounding atmosphere. In fact," he continues, "physicians seem to bring relief to pestilential affections [*ta loimika pathē*] by making a large blazing fire, for this rarifies the air."[81]

Plutarch claims to be following Aristotelian medical theory. He says that according to Aristotle the vapors given off by perfumes and flowers are healthy, because they are warm and light; "they gently relax the brain, which is by nature cold and frigid." Plutarch proceeds to note that the Egyptian word for myrrh is *bal*, which he glosses as "the dissipation of repletion."[82] Throughout this section, then, Plutarch reinterprets what are probably rituals of cultic purification so that they make sense in terms of the humoral theories of contemporary medicine, with its logic of balance of temperatures, tensions, and liquids. More popular ideas of pollution, contamination, and ritual purity are not mentioned.[83]

Thus we see that those most disposed to reject an etiology of pollution belong to the classes most apt to have some familiarity with popular philosophy. We could also mention the stories about Diogenes, who scorned popular fears of pollution when he ate fruit from a tree on which a man had been hanged and claimed that he could enter polluted areas since the sun also shone on cesspools without itself being polluted.[84] These are stories of the philosophers and those under their influence. Not everyone in Greco-Roman society considered fears of contamination and invasion by disease-daimons something to be sneezed at, however.

One interesting source of evidence of the invasion etiology of disease in Greco-Roman culture is provided by the magical papyri. Intellectuals like Plutarch and Lucian might mock people who held superstitious notions about capricious and potentially hostile gods surrounding them, but the papyri provide abundant evidence that such beliefs existed. Like the philosophers, the people who used this magic also believed in the gods. "But," as Hans Dieter Betz writes, "Zeus, Hermes, Apollo, Artemis, Aphrodite, and others are portrayed not as Hellenic and aristocratic, as in literature, but as capricious, demonic, and even dangerous, as in Greek folklore."[85]

Concerns about dangerous pollutions recur throughout the magical instructions. There are many injunctions against sexual intercourse before and during the practice of magic.[86] Many spells portray disease as the attack by a daimon prompted by the magic force of the spell. A bilingual curse tablet calls on a "demon of impurity" (*demon im[m]unditi[a]e*) to pursue someone.[87] Another spell, which compels a disease-daimon to attack someone's body, contains a prophylaxis meant to guard the magician performing the spell from any evil daimon.[88] People could also obtain charms, including magical names, designed to protect the wearer against daimons.

Much of the invasion logic found in the magical papyri occurs in love spells, which speak of passion as a disease sent into the body of the person desired. One love charm sounds to us quite sadistic in its call for the "infernal gods and daimons" to infect the different parts of a woman's body with love-pain and sickness. Another speaks of desire as burning in the guts, breast, liver, breath, bones, and marrow. The daimon, addressed as "Flesh-eater" and "Inflamer of the heart," is commanded to enter the woman's body and produce disease.[89]

This sort of language was not limited to the esoteric realm of the professional magician's spell scroll. A poem by Theocritus (third century B.C.E.) portrays a woman, racked by jealousy concerning her lover, addressing Love as a hypostatized disease: "[Thou] hast clung to me thus, thou muddy leech, and drained my flesh of the red blood every drop." Love is a "parching fever" described as a hostile invader, storming, sacking, and destroying the city of the body. (The Greek is *exalapazō*, evoking military imagery.)[90] The woman's spells in turn send an attack of burning (a "fire-spell") upon her neglectful lover (2. 160–164). The logic of love magic depends upon a disease etiology of invasion and contagion.

Anxieties about pollution and the accompanying logic of attack and invasion occasionally surface in other texts. It seems to have been accepted by many people, philosophers included, that dog-bites were responsible for the spread of rabies, which could be spread further by the bites of human beings; but often the idea is that the dog-bite is poisonous, like that of a snake.[91] In popular thought, madness was spread by contact with persons themselves polluted with the disease, leading Aeschines to portray his enemy Demosthenes as a threat to the city of Athens by his very presence. Whatever Demosthenes touches is implicated in misfortune; he is a source of pollution for the entire city; a daimon that possesses Demosthenes threatens the whole body politic.[92] Demosthenes, never outdone in insults, also calls Aeschines an *aleitērion* (a "plague, avenging spirit, pollutant") threatening not just "all of Greece," but "all the human beings, all the regions, all the cities that have perished." Reflecting the popular practice of averting one's gaze when encountering a madman in order to avoid catching the madness oneself, Demosthenes says, "I marvel that you [the citizens of Athens] did not avert your faces the moment you set eyes on him!"[93] Even Plato, though his own concepts of the body and disease are ruled by the imbalance etiology, uses such popular images. In one dialogue, Socrates plays with the idea that inspiration is an invasion of the body by an alien agent; it "fills the ear" and "takes possession" by means of "daimonic wisdom." Afterwards, the body must be "purified" from the invasion and made normal and clean again. Socrates is, of course, here speaking playfully—as Aeschines and Demosthenes invoke popular fears of pollution without necessarily believing in an invasion etiology themselves—but the language reflects popular concepts of the invasive activities of divine agents that render the body impure by their presence in it.[94]

The Ideology of Etiology

It does not take much imagination to see the social and political overtones of language about disease in these two etiologies. In the imbalance etiology the healthy body imitates the stability of the polis when there is no strife between the classes; disease occurs only when that stability is disturbed. This equilibrium model should not be understood to imply that all members of the polis should be politically or economically equal. As explained in the chapter on homonoia speeches, in the dominant, conservative political theory of Greco-Roman antiquity, concord was maintained not by an equality of members but by all members occupying their rightful places in the social hierarchy. Equilibrium, not equality, is the ruling mechanism. In medical texts the balanced body is also expected to maintain an equilibrium within a hierarchy. In the Hippocratic treatise *Disease IV*, for example, the various humors have different natural densities in the body: bile is lightest, then blood, then phlegm, with water the heaviest. Any humor may, during agitation, mix with the others and go anywhere in the body; the result is illness or at least discomfort, since the "hostile humor" affects the other, healthy humors, as they are "used up and consumed by the disease." A humor unsatisfied with its normal allotment of the body's fuel, for example, may take more than its normal share, use up all the body's nourishment, and proceed to consume the other humors. "For the healthy humour is used up in addition when the disease no longer has sufficient fuel, but all that fuel has been consumed by the humour in the affected place."[95] The diseased body is one instance of what happens when people and things rebel against their assigned positions in the hierarchy of the cosmos.

Moreover, according to the imbalance etiology, corruption and putrefaction lead to disruption in the normal balance of production and consumption within the society of the body. Putrefaction increases in one part of the body until it uses up all the nutriment in that area; it then spreads to other parts of the body, seeking nourishment. "So too the disease, when there is insufficient nutriment left in the place where it begins, advances further, beginning from the nearest part; and when it has advanced over the whole body, its nutriment is consumed, and there is no sound humour left to prevail over it. When this happens, the man dies."[96] The unruly humor, like an antisocial citizen, must be kept in check by healthy humors, alias sound, upstanding members of the body; disease results from the demand of one part of the body for more than its alloted share of space and nutriment. Thus the body is an economy of limited goods and a site of conflict over goods and real estate. Words used in these medical contexts (like *isonomia* for the balance of powers or *monarchia* for the state in which one power becomes too predominant) come from political theory and from speeches on homonoia. For the ancient hearer, such language would have evoked the conservative ideology of moderation advocated by benevolent patriarchalism.

The etiology of balance, moreover, reflects a sense of control over one's body and the environment. Fears of invasion and loss of power over one's self are not paramount. The gods are relatively benign beings with whom any sensible person can get along, and disease-daimons exist only in the imaginations of the uneducated. Therapeutics for the medicine of balance is a matter of reasserting control and reestablishing the proper hierarchy of the "natural" body. The sick man, like a sensible paterfamilias, must set his house in order, discipline unruly members, and, if need be, expel those who will not respond to discipline. His physician is his advisor in the political science of the body.

The invasion etiology, on the other hand, evinces a social position of helplessness in the face of outside powers. The world is a much more precarious place, with threats on every side. As Hans Dieter Betz writes, referring specifically to the world view reflected by the magical papyri,

> The people whose religion is reflected in the papyri agree that humanity is inescapably at the whim of the forces of the universe. Religion is nothing but taking seriously this dependency on the forces of the universe. Whether the gods are old or new, whether they come from Egyptian, Greek, Jewish, or Christian traditions, religion is regarded as nothing but the awareness of and reaction against our dependency on the unfathomable scramble of energies coming out of the universe. . . . Individuals seem to be nothing but marionettes at the end of power lines, pulled here and there without their knowledge by invisible forces.[97]

The potential for invasion is an important issue in this world view, because the body is not a secure microcosm of the balanced universe but a site of cosmic battles between good and evil. For both etiologies, the body is continually pervaded by cosmic forces and is even constituted by those forces; it is a vacillating moment in an energy field. For those convinced by the logic of balance, this is not necessarily bad: the body is simply a microcosm of the balanced universe and is naturally constituted of the same substances. Others perceive the penetrability of the body as threatening, however, necessitating protection against invasion, manipulation, and disintegration. This view may reflect the position of someone further down in the structure of patron–client society, someone who must depend on a powerful patron for protection against outside aggression. Thus, it is only in this system that we encounter concerns for firm boundaries and protection by the patron (the god) and recognition that one is a member of a household or social group and dependent upon one's position in the household or group for safety (*sōtēria*). To us, this latter position may appear to emphasize the communal aspects of life, whereas the balance ideology seems more individualistic. But that is a modern misconstrual. Both positions are communal in that they see the body as a form of society and one's identity as dependent on one's place in that society. Yet the former point of view, which sees the body as a balanced ecosystem, is that of a person with a greater sense of empowerment, probably due to his or her position in the higher levels of society.

These are only musings about the possible dispositions of the people who hold these different disease etiologies. We can say with more confidence that the writings of upper-class intellectuals advocate the logic of balance and imbalance, and that those same writings despise fears of invasion and pollution, portraying them as superstition worthy only of the uneducated masses. That is, the two different disease etiologies occupy recognized status positions in society. Ancient epistemologies of disease thus reflect the conflict evident in so many other discourses of Greco-Roman culture, the conflict between those higher and lower in the highly stratified society.

7 Sex, Food, and the Pollution of the Corinthian Body

The ideology of the body presupposed by most early Christian literature, though not by any means all, reflects the invasion etiology of disease. We should expect, however, that a church like that at Corinth, which included persons from different social levels, would contain within it differing assumptions about disease and pollution. In this chapter I will analyze four particular issues in 1 Corinthians that involve questions of pollution, disease, and the boundaries of the body: the case of the man having sexual relations with his stepmother (1 Cor. 5); Paul's concerns about Christian men visiting prostitutes (6:12–20); the debate about eating meat sacrificed to idols (chaps. 8–10); and Paul's claim that some Corinthians have become sick or have died owing to improper eating of the Lord's Supper (11:17–34). Biblical scholars usually treat these issues as separate questions that are addressed seriatim by Paul. It is my belief, however, that they are particular instances of what is essentially a single conflict regarding the boundaries of the body. Paul and the Strong are at odds on each of these questions because of their different ideologies of the body, and the two disease etiologies sketched in the preceding chapter lie at the heart of the difference. The concern of the higher-status Corinthians for stability, hierarchy, and moderation is countered by Paul's concern for purity and avoidance of pollution. The Strong operate by a logic of balance, with its relative lack of concern about pollution or invasion; Paul operates by a logic of invasion, with its anxieties about purity and firm boundaries. The theological and ethical disagreements between Paul and the Strong over issues related to eating and sex can be understood by sketching their respective assumptions about the body, its boundaries, and its susceptibility to pollution. Before addressing 1 Corinthians, however, I will briefly survey concepts of disease causation in early Christianity as evident from other parts of the New Testament.

Disease in the New Testament

Early Christians seem generally to have believed that disease was caused by the invasion of hostile, cosmic, personal agents. The Synoptic Gospels are full of such assumptions. In Mark 9:17–27 a man asks Jesus to heal his son, who has been deprived of speech by a pneuma. The boy also suffers epileptic-like seizures, being thrown into water and fire by the "spirit." In 9:25 the disease is explicitly called an "unclean pneuma" (*akathartos*), expressing the common link between the invasion etiology and pollution anxieties.[1] In order to cure the boy, Jesus commands the spirit, "Come out from him, and no longer enter into him!" (*exelthe ex autou kai mēketi eiselthēs eis auton*, 9:25). The mechanics of this healing would have been self-evident to Mark's audience, who would assume that disease is caused by a hostile, alien agent invading the body and rendering it unclean, an agent that can only be expelled by a superior power. The healing is implicitly a cleansing.

The disease-spirits are often spoken of as "unclean," demonstrating the assumed connection between disease and pollution. Jesus cures people of "unclean *pneumata*" (Luke 6:18), and in Matthew's Gospel Jesus gives authority (*exousia*) to the twelve to cast out "unclean *pneumata*" and heal disease and illness (*noson kai malakian*, 10:1).[2] Leprosy in particular is considered an unclean disease. According to Luke 5:12–14 Jesus tells the man healed of leprosy to show himself to the priest to have his cleanliness confirmed. Whereas today we think of ritualistic purity as different from physiological cleanliness, no such dichotomy existed for Luke's original readers. In their world view, cleanliness was not *next* to godliness; godliness *was* cleanliness.[3]

At the same time, there are contexts in which the Gospels do not explicitly link disease to invading daimons or spirits. Peter's mother-in-law is healed of a fever that is not ascribed to a daimon or spirit (Mark 1:29–31; Matt. 8:14–15; note, however, that Luke, unlike Mark or Matthew, says that Jesus "rebuked" the fever and forced it to leave: Luke 4:38–39). Matthew sometimes speaks of Jesus' healings of diseases (*nosoi* and *malakiai*) without mentioning possession by spirits (Matt. 9:35; see also 8:17, which is a quotation of Isa. 53:4). In

Acts 4:9 Peter and John heal a lame man whose disease is not attributed to a spirit or daimon. In still other contexts the Gospel-writers mention diseases and daimonic possession in the same context without explicitly attributing the former to the latter (e.g., Mark 1:34; 4:24; Luke 6:18; 7:21; 9:1–2; Matt. 10:1). Other texts, however, make the causal connection explicit. In Matthew's version of the healing recounted above from Mark 9:17–27, the boy is initially said to be "moon-struck" (*selēniazetai*) and then simply to "be ill" (*kakōs paschei*, Matt. 17:15); yet Jesus heals the boy by commanding the *daimonion* to leave the boy's body (17:18; cf. Luke 9:37–42). Luke narrates the healing of a woman crippled by a "spirit of disease" (*pneuma . . . astheneias*); later in the story Jesus explicitly attributes the woman's illness to Satan (Luke 13:10–17). These texts suggest that the connection between diseases and daimons is closer than mere juxtaposition would imply. In most cases the daimon or spirit is the cause of the sickness or is the disease itself.[4]

But this is not the only New Testament view of disease. The Gospel of John nowhere attributes disease to daimonic activity. In John, Jesus never performs an exorcism; indeed, the only mention of daimons in the fourth Gospel occurs in the accusations and denials that Jesus himself is daimon-possessed (John 7:20; 8:48–52; 10:20–21). Jesus does heal people in John's Gospel (5:2–9; 11:1–16), but in no case is a daimon or spirit said to be the cause of the illness. In one case a "fever" is said to "leave" a boy (4:46–54), but this may be simply a figure of speech and in itself hardly suggests an etiology of invasion. Indeed, in the one case in which the cause of disease becomes an issue in John, Jesus insists to his disciples that a man's blindness is not attributable to sin but exists simply as an opportunity for God's good work (John 9:2–3; a Hippocratic writer might have said the same). Mention should also be made of 1 Timothy 5:23, where Paul is made (by the pseudepigrapher) to suggest that Timothy treat his "frequent illnesses" by drinking wine. The prescription would have been quite at home in professional medical circles of the period.

Despite these voices to the contrary, the overriding etiology of disease in early Christian texts is that of invasion. Christianity's background in apocalyptic Judaism is, of course, one reason why it construed the activity of daimons and angels as it did.[5] But the difference in disease etiologies and concerns about pollution should not be simplistically portrayed as a difference between Jewish and Greco-Roman world views. As I outlined in the previous chapter, many Greeks and Romans, probably most of those outside the circles of the philosophically educated, never hesitated to ascribe disease to invading non-human agents. Furthermore, we have some evidence that many Jews, those more influenced by the Hellenistic education mandatory for any upper-class inhabitant of the ancient Mediterranean, were party to the medical institutions and traditions of Hellenistic culture and thus probably assumed a disease etiology of imbalance.

The educated Jewish writer known as Ben Sira, or, in the Greek form, Sirach, writing perhaps around 200 B.C.E., praises physicians who diagnose and treat disease by means of drug therapy as well as health regimens (Sirach 38:3–15; note the reference to pharmacists in 38:8).[6] Some of those health regimens have to do with moderation of food and rest (31:19–22), much like the regimens of Greek doctors already examined. Moving closer to Paul's time, we would expect Philo to have many of the same ideas as educated Greeks in Alexandria, and thus it is no surprise to find him assuming pneumatic theories like those common among medical writers, as already mentioned in Chapter 1. Philo also subscribes to the humoral pathology of Greek medicine in his belief that fevers may be caused by *miasma* ("bad air").[7] Greek and Roman writers sometimes mention Jewish physicians, from which we should probably infer that the latter practiced much like their non-Jewish colleagues. Celsus (first century C.E.) mentions with approval a plaster developed by a Jewish doctor whom he calls simply "Judaeus," which could be either the man's name or merely a designation of his ethnicity. Galen knows of a medical compiler named Rufus of Samaria, whom he calls a Jew. And from a fifth-century philosopher, Damascius of Damascus, we hear of Domnus the Jew, a teacher of medicine.[8]

Even in Palestine, and even in the sectarian Jewish community at Qumran, we find evidence of a disease etiology quite similar to Greek theories of humoral pathology. Joseph M. Baumgarten has reconstructed a portion of the "Damascus Document" from the Dead Sea Scrolls that deals with skin disease and, in part, offers an etiology for the disease. The disease is linked to the presence of *ru'ah*, a Hebrew word normally translated as "spirit" that appears to be equivalent to the Greek *pneuma*. In Qumran texts *ru'ah* is sometimes linked to the punishment of sinners by disease, leading Baumgarten to admit, "It is thus possible to take the attribution of scale disease to the *ru'ah* in our text as involving the intrusion of evil or demonic influences."[9] Baumgarten notes, however, the similarity between this etiological explanation and the humoral balance theories in Greek medicine: "It (*ru'ah*) causes the blood in the arteries to recede upwards and downwards and makes the hair turn yellow. Conversely, the spirit of life is associated with the return of normal blood flow to the arteries."[10] Baumgarten concludes that even these sectarian Jews adopted a disease etiology of humoral balance (here between the blood and pneuma) similar to that current among the Greeks.

Similar hints of humoral theories occur even later in Rabbinic texts. Whereas the Talmud speaks about disease-demons, there are Rabbinic references to bloodletting and to diseases due to ru'ah (air, wind, or pneuma), bile (*mara'*), or a plethora of blood. According to *Leviticus Rabba* 15.2, health involves a balance between blood and water; in other texts, disease is due to change (a recurrent theme in Greco-Roman medicine).[11] In the Midrashim, dropsy is explained as a disruption in the blood–water balance.[12] Such texts lead Stephen Neumyer to argue against previous scholars who maintained that the Rabbis completely rejected humoral pathologies; Neumyer insists that "vestiges" of Greek theories, such as concepts of health involving humoral balance and the importance of climatology for the prevention and cure of disease, survive in Rabbinic texts.[13] Although it is much later than the period here under review, the earliest Jewish medical text we have, attributed at least in part to the sixth-century Jewish physician Asaph, reflects a total embeddedness in Greek medical theories, showing knowledge of the major Greco-Roman theorists and basing its treatment on the four humors pathology and balance therapies of Hippocratic medicine.[14]

Given these different possibilities for construing disease causation in Paul's culture, it is significant that his own assumptions are ruled by the invasion etiology. Paul does not mention disease or even pollution very often in his letters, but the few references found therein are revealing. I will devote much attention to pollution and disease in 1 Corinthians later in the chapter but will here explore other texts as an introduction to Paul's views.[15] In 2 Corinthians 12:7–9, for example, Paul tells us the cause of his "thorn in the flesh." As already discussed in Chapter 2, there has been much debate among New Testament commentators about the precise nature of this, with some scholars suggesting that it is not a physical ailment at all. Most scholars, however, believe that Paul is referring to some bodily disease or disfigurement that was a source of humiliation to him.[16] In my view, it does not matter whether what Paul is referring to is something we would call physical or psychological, since this modern dichotomy had little, if any, place in ancient conceptions of the body. Ancient writers do, of course, speak of afflictions of the body and those of the mind, but those categories do not match our dichotomy of physical versus psychological. I will, in any case, take Paul's thorn in the flesh to be a reference to a physiological ailment, at least according to the way Paul and others in his culture construed physis (nature).

Paul calls his disease an *aggelos satana*, a "messenger" or "angel" of Satan. He believes it has been given to him—and that God allows it to afflict him—to keep him from becoming proud. The expected remedy is prayer, which Paul attempts three times, asking that the disease be "taken away" from him (*apostē*). His request is denied, and he is told that God's grace should be sufficient for him: "For strength is completed (made perfect) in disease/weakness" (*astheneia*, 2 Cor. 12:9). This is a good place to point out that the Greek word *astheneia* meant both "weakness" and "disease" or "illness." The English speaker's inclination to force a decision as to which meaning should be assigned the word is misguided. For Greek speakers the word meant both at the same time, indicating an essential connection in ancient ideology between health and status. Illness is a problematic status indicator, calling into question the strength of the sufferer. Paul realizes the normal status significance of his suffering; he also believes that the disease is the result of an attack by Satan and is itself an invading agent of Satan.

Paul, therefore, along with what was probably the majority of early Christians, presupposes an invasion etiology of disease. The body, rather than being a balanced ecosystem or microcosm of an equilibrated nature, is a permeable entity susceptible to attack by daimonic agents. Protection from attack is possible only by means of the powerful action of God. Cures are obtained by appeals to God that the hostile, alien attacker be expelled or by recourse to charismatically endowed healers who function as conduits for the purifying power of God (see 1 Cor. 12:28). As the rest of this chapter will show, this logic of the body underwrites Paul's ethical arguments against the Strong at Corinth, educated believers who appear to subscribe to the *other* etiology of disease.

The Health of the Pneuma

The first place in which Paul's concerns about pollution become obvious is in 1 Corinthians 5, where he addresses the issue of the man who has been sleeping with his stepmother. Paul demands that the church expel the man and turn him over to Satan "for the destruction of the flesh [*sarx*] in order that the pneuma may be saved in the day/court of the Lord" (1 Cor. 5:5).[17] Paul's primary concern in this passage is the purity of the church, the body of Christ, and his anxieties center on the man as a potentially polluting agent within Christ's body, an agent whose presence threatens to pollute the entire body. Indeed, although many commentators have focused on the individual man—

what is expected to happen to him? what is meant by the "destruction of the flesh"? does Paul expect him to die physically or merely spiritually? how is the destruction of the flesh expected to save the spirit?—Paul's main concern is with the health of Christ's body; the man's individual fate is secondary, at best.[18] Paul does not say that the *man*'s flesh must be destroyed so that *his* spirit will be saved. He simply speaks of *the* flesh and the spirit. And though the man's fate is somewhat at issue (it is not until v. 6–8 that Paul's concerns about communal pollution become evident to the reader, who may therefore rightly assume up to that point that Paul is concerned with the fate of the man himself), Paul's primary worry is that the pneuma of Christ's body will become polluted by the corrupting presence of the sinful sarx represented by the body of the immoral man.[19]

For many Jews of Paul's day, *porneia* could refer to sexual immorality of a number of types; it was used to denote Gentile culture and idolatry in general and, often, prostitution in particular. The condemnation of porneia in Jewish circles was a way of solidifying the boundary between the chosen people and everyone else with their idols and loose morals: porneia was something "they" did.[20] Therefore, when Paul categorizes the issue of 1 Corinthians 5 as one of porneia, and of a particularly egregious sort, he already invokes issues of boundaries, self-identity, and pollution.

Moreover, immediately after his instruction to turn the offender over to Satan for the destruction of the sarx to insure the "health" (*sōtēria*, of course, meant health and wholeness as well as eschatological salvation) of the pneuma, Paul proceeds to speak of "cleansing" the lump. "Do you not know that a little yeast leavens the whole lump? Clean out the old yeast so that you may be a new lump, as you are indeed unleavened; for Christ our passover lamb has been sacrificed for us" (5:6–7). Paul is recalling the Jewish rite of Passover, with its ritual of ridding the house of yeast and eating only unleavened bread along with the Passover lamb. But the reference to yeast or leaven would have had currency outside Jewish circles; "leaven" in early Christianity and much of the ancient world was conceived as rotten matter that might pollute surrounding foodstuffs, its effect spreading like an infection.[21] By equating Christ's body with a lump of dough and the offender's body with leaven, Paul's language reveals his anxiety about the permeability of Christ's body and its susceptibility to infection from without.

Just as early Christian healers cured diseases by casting out daimons and cleansing the body, so Paul demands that the Corinthians cleanse the body of Christ by expelling the source of pollution, the offending Christian. His concerns about firm social boundaries have caused some confusion in Corinth, it seems, because he then feels compelled to explain that he does not intend that the Corinthian Christians have no social relations at all with non-Christians:

> I wrote to you in my letter not to associate with those who are sexually immoral, not meaning at all the sexually immoral of this cosmos or the greedy and rapacious or idolators, since in that case you would have to leave the cosmos entirely. But now I am writing to you that you should not associate with someone who is called a brother but who is sexually immoral or greedy or an idolator or a slanderer or a drunkard or rapacious; do not even eat with such a man. For what business of mine is it to judge those outside? But shouldn't you judge those inside? [1 Cor. 5:9–12]

Paul exhibits a modified sectarianism.[22] Although he insists on maintaining firm boundaries between those inside and outside the church, socially those boundaries are permeable. Paul is not afraid that social contact between a Christian and a non-Christian will pollute the church; but he does think that the disguised presence within the church of a representative from the outside, from the cosmos that *should* be "out there," threatens the whole body. The body of Christ is not polluted by mere contact with the cosmos or by the body's presence in the midst of the corrupt cosmos, but it may be polluted if its boundaries are permeated and an element of the cosmos gains entry into the body. In that case, the only remedy is violent expulsion of the polluting agent, which will result in the return of the body to a clean, healthy state.[23]

In 1 Corinthians 5 the fear of pollution centers on the purity, or healthy state, of the pneuma. As shown in Chapter 1, medical writers also knew that illness could result from the corruption of the bodily pneuma. If one happened to breath miasma ("bad air"), the dirty or putrefied pneuma within that air would enter the body and corrupt its inner pneuma and even, perhaps, other humors of the body with which the pneuma might mingle.[24] Texts speak of fever as causing the body's pneuma (and blood) to condense and flow like water, upsetting the humoral balance of the body.[25] According to Galen, epileptic seizures occur when moisture seeps into the origins of the nerves, affecting the pneuma within them; a seizure is caused "by a thick humor obstructing the outlets of the pneuma in the cerebral cavities, since the origin of the nerves is agitated during extrusion of this noxious substance." Aretaeus, a medical writer probably contemporary with Galen, writes that diseased pneuma is the cause of angina (*synagchē*).[26] In all these cases, pneuma may either be diseased or be the cause of disease. The pneuma may become polluted and need cleansing. Paul's concerns about the "salvation of the spirit" or, alternatively

put, the "health of the pneuma" may indeed have been shared by even educated members of Greco-Roman society (although it must be admitted that the
medical doctors are much less concerned about pollutions and cleansings than
was popular thought, according to which disease was construed as invasion).

We now have a glimpse into the logic underlying Paul's claim that the
destruction of the sarx will entail the health/salvation of the pneuma. The
pneuma is affected by the destruction of the flesh because of the continuity,
or perhaps contiguity, of the elements that make up the human being. It is
impossible to know, and difficult to imagine, what Paul had in mind for the
unfortunate man who had been sleeping with his stepmother. In consigning
him to the clutches of Satan, did Paul expect the man to burst into flames
in the midst of the church service? Did he foresee a long, agonizing period
of torture? Did he leave open the possibility that the man would continue to
live, at least for the present time, a trouble-free existence? From this distance,
we have no answers to such questions. But it is not difficult to see that Paul
views the man's anticipated suffering as inevitably efficacious. And why not?
The suffering will bring about the destruction of that corrupting stuff of the
body, the sarx. It will purify the life-giving essence that alone can survive into
eternity, the pneuma (recall, from Chap. 5, that the resurrected body will be
a purely pneumatic body). Furthermore, on the level of the individual man,
his self will undergo inevitable changes to the extent that the very material
that constitutes it will be changed. Purified from corrupting sarx, the pneuma
body will be able to become truly "healthy" (possess *sōtēria*) in the final court
of the Lord.

At this point we see how much Paul's views about the purity of the pneuma
differ from those that higher-class, educated members of his church would
have found acceptable. In the first place, in speaking of sarx as "corrupting,"
I have introduced an important point on which Paul differs from the medical
writers. Throughout their writings, *sarx* is used for the most part to refer to
muscle or any fleshy part of the anatomy (the "meat" of the body), as opposed to
the bones, blood, humors, and internal organs. The flesh may itself be a location of disease or a source of disease for other parts of the body. For example,
unclean phlegm may seep into the flesh and thus spread disease throughout the
body; alternatively, bodily tissue (*sarx*) may become corrupted, melt, and turn
into water, thereby saturating the body with excessive moisture and causing
dropsy.[27] Likewise, the sarx may itself become polluted; Plutarch calls even digestion a "pollution of the flesh" [*miasma tēs sarkos*], one that happens when the
internal weather of "frightful streams and winds [*pneuma*]" buffets the body
while breaking up the food.[28] But in these cases the sarx is no more corrupting

or corruptible than any other part of the body. Given the interconnectedness of the whole person, a disease manifesting itself in the sarx may affect other parts of the body, and the doctor may need to administer certain regimens (diet, exercise, massage, evacuations) in order to keep the sarx healthy, so that the rest of the body may also be healthy. But the notion that the sarx is an especially corrupting and corruptible element would have struck the medical writers as odd, and they would not have entertained fears that the sarx would automatically (that is, by "nature") pollute the pneuma.

This is where Paul's apocalyptic view of the cosmos again plays an important role. Sarx and pneuma constitute a radical dualism in Paul's ethical cosmos. In spite of the way Paul can sometimes speak of sarx as an apparently neutral agent or substance (see Rom. 9:3–5; 2 Cor. 4:11; Gal. 2:20), the overwhelming bulk of his references to sarx place it in the category of "this world" in its opposition to the plan of God. "To set the mind on the flesh is death, but to set the mind on the Spirit is life and peace" (Rom. 8:6, NRSV; see the entire chapter for the cosmic opposition of pneuma and sarx; see also Gal. 3:3; 4:29; 5:16–26; 6:8). And although Paul may sometimes use the term *pneuma* to refer to something that is morally ambiguous (1 Cor. 2:12; 12:10; 2 Cor. 7:1; 11:4), it usually occupies a position on God's side in the battle between God and "this world." It is this apocalyptic dualism and demonizing of sarx that makes Paul's world view so different from that of the upper-class ideology of the Greco-Roman Mediterranean. Paul's mythological-cosmological notion of flesh as a corrupt element, that element of the cosmos in opposition to God and the Spirit, assumes an agency for sarx that would have appeared odd and superstitious to medical writers.

Paul can speak of the interaction between sarx and pneuma in something like mechanical or anthropomorphic terms. In the former case, he speaks of the pneuma as the element that comes from God and enlivens the church. It extends throughout the church, giving life to it and functioning as the stuff of divine epistemology (1 Cor. 2:10–3:3; recall that the Greek theorists also considered pneuma the material of perception and thought). Sarx likewise pervades "this cosmos." Human beings are flesh insofar as they partake of the fleshiness that is part of all present humanity. Both pneuma and sarx are essences that move in and out of human bodies; indeed, they are cosmological essences that constitute, along with other materials of reality, human beings. Thus they may act upon one another, and each is susceptible to influences from the other.

On the other hand, Paul also speaks of Pneuma and Sarx as anthropomorphic or hypostatized powers of the cosmos.[29] Pneuma is the power that enables Sarx to live, although it is also in continual battle with it. Pneuma and Sarx have their own values, their own goals, and their own spheres of power. They wage constant warfare in the cosmos at large, a war that is fought out on a small scale in the bodies of women and men. The battle being waged in the body of the sexual offender in 1 Corinthians 5 is a microcosm of the battle between Pneuma and Sarx being fought throughout the world. Moreover, the church is dangerously susceptible to becoming yet another battleground for the attacks of Sarx on Pneuma, which is why the expulsion of the offender is so important: Sarx must be prohibited from establishing a beachhead within the social body of the church by means of the corrupting body of the offender.

Whether we think of the interaction between pneuma and sarx mechanically or anthropomorphically, we should avoid introducing a dichotomy between the individual and the social body into the picture. Although I have some-times spoken of the individual body of the offender and the social body of the church, the terms should be taken not as references to "real things" but simply as heuristic and momentary tropes. No ontological dichotomy between the individual and the social can be located in Paul's logic in 1 Corinthians 5. One may argue that the modern concept of the individual is simply unavail-able to Paul. In any case, the logic underlying 1 Corinthians 5 depends on the breaking down of any possible boundary between the individual body and the social body. The destruction of the flesh that endangers the whole church and the preservation of the spirit that gives life to the whole church constitute the battleground. The individual offender is merely the breach in the wall that Paul so desperately attempts to build to keep the cosmos out of the church and sarx from contaminating pneuma.

Paul differs from the medical writers not only in demonizing sarx and ren-dering it a polluting element but also in his emphasis on notions of invasion and contagion. Even if they were willing to grant that sarx might somehow pollute pneuma within someone's body, Paul's cultured despisers would have scoffed at the idea that the mere presence of a "polluted" man within the social group could lead to infection of the pneuma of other people in the group. We need not, therefore, attribute any libertarian attitude to the Strong at Corinth to explain their failure to excommunicate the offender. They may easily have shared some amount of disapproval of sexual offences without sharing Paul's fear about the wider polluting effects of the offender's presence.[30] The differ-ence between Paul and the Strong, I would argue, lies not in moral strictness on the one hand and laxity on the other but in degree of concern about pollution and boundaries. Because Paul fears pollution, he is anxious to maintain firm boundaries; because the strong do not share his fears, they are less concerned with boundaries.[31]

In the end, Paul is in an ironic position. He has set out to reinforce the boundary dividing the church from the world, but his very concerns demonstrate how permeable that boundary really is in his own world view.[32] Since no secure boundary separates the offender's body from the church's body, the offender's presence in the church represents an invasion of sarx into the church itself. The pneuma that needs to be saved is both the pneuma of the man and that of the church; the sarx that must be destroyed is both that of the man and that of the church. The presence of Paul's pneuma, though Paul himself is distant, is also necessary for the pneumatic cleansing of the church's body (5:3).[33] Sarx is everywhere—or, at least, there is the ever-present danger that it *may* be everywhere. Pneuma is everywhere, giving life to all but always under threat from the death-dealing of sarx. All boundaries dissolve in the cosmological soup of competing and combatting forces of sarx, pneuma, death, life, impurities, and cleansings.

For Paul, firm boundaries must be drawn between the church and the world precisely because firm boundaries do not exist between flesh and spirit, body and spirit, divine spirit and human spirit. For the Strong at Corinth, Paul's anxieties about possible pollution of the pneuma and therefore of the whole church and his desire to solidify boundaries between sarx and pneuma and between the world and the church probably appeared unreasonable—something like compulsive hand-washing.[34] Or to put it, perhaps, in their own terms, like superstition.

Intertextual Intercourse

The connections between the various sections of 1 Corinthians 5–6 may not be immediately obvious. Paul moves from speaking about the man sleeping with his stepmother, to demands for excommunication and talk about the purity of the church, to an argument against Christians' use of law courts, to a list of "sins" (or, more precisely, kinds of people who will not "inherit the kingdom of God"), to a rebuke of Christian men who are visiting prostitutes. In the midst of all this, Paul suddenly interjects the subject of food, albeit by quoting a slogan of some of the Corinthians: "Food is for the belly and the belly for food, and God will destroy both" (1 Cor. 6:13). What underlies and connects all these issues is Paul's anxiety about the boundaries of the body. This is clear for 1 Corinthians 5, as I have demonstrated in the preceding section, but even with regard to Christian recourse to the courts, Paul's primary concern is to maintain the boundaries separating the church from the cosmos; he considers it inappropriate for internal arguments to be settled by outsiders.[35] At the end of that section, after giving a list of those stereotypically pagan character-types who will not "inherit the kingdom of God," Paul stresses the difference between such people and the Corinthian Christians: "Some of you were those kinds of people; but you were thoroughly washed, you were made holy, you were made innocent by the name of the Lord Jesus Christ and by the pneuma of our God" (1 Cor. 6:11). The name of Christ and the pneuma of God are the cleansing agents; they set the boundary separating the Corinthian believers from the immoral cosmos. This boundary-setting statement by Paul is an appropriate point of departure for the discussion that follows in 6:12–20, in which Paul deals with the threat to that secure boundary that occurs when Christians engage in sexual intercourse with persons outside the body of Christ.

As we will see later in this chapter, eating food sacrificed to idols presents a problem for Paul because it may lead, first, to pollution of the person who eats without proper "knowledge" and, ultimately, to the joining in commensality of Christ and daimons, an unthinkable possibility for Paul. The same danger is presented by sexual intercourse between Christian men and prostitutes: a Christian's copulation with a prostitute constitutes Christ's copulation with her—also unthinkable for Paul. Here we see connections that are often unnoted and unexplained by New Testament commentators: between issues of food and sex and between the boundaries of the individual Christian's body and the boundaries of Christ's body. The connection between food and sex in 6:13 does not entail a conjunction of actual events—as if the people who are eating idol-meat are doing so in idol temples that employ sacred prostitutes. Rather, it is due to an underlying logic about the body and its boundaries: potentially, both eating and sexual intercourse are boundary-transgressing activities.

I noted above that Paul is probably quoting the Strong at Corinth when he says "Everything is permitted to me," and "Food is for the belly and the belly for food, and God will destroy both" (6:12–13). Scholars have pointed to Cynic and Stoic moral philosophy as possible sources for these slogans; but, as I have attempted to show, such sentiments and slogans were in no way limited to Cynic and Stoic philosophical circles. A general deprecation of the body enjoyed wide currency among the educated elite of Greco-Roman society. It is to this, more general milieu that we should look for the source of the Strong's views concerning the body. They may not themselves actually condone visiting prostitutes, but they certainly place such activities in the realm of misdemeanor. From their point of view, probably, one should not be a slave to either food or sex, and perhaps the truly strong person will exercise strict personal discipline with regard to both eating and sexual activity; but indiscretions of the body, whether centered on the belly or those unruly organs just below it, merit attention, not anxiety.

Paul, by contrast, rejects a hierarchical notion of the body according to which relative importance is attached to the actions of the different levels of the human self, as if the body and food are lower on a hierarchical scale of meaningfulness than the human mind or will and therefore simply do not matter very much. In place of such a hierarchical view, Paul posits an ethical-cosmological dualism in which Christ is opposed to "this cosmos." He responds to the Corinthians' belief that food and the belly will both be destroyed with "The body is not for *porneia* but for the Lord, and the Lord for the body; and God raised the Lord and will raise us through his power" (6:13b–14). He constructs a dichotomy; but instead of placing the human will or soul on one side and food and the body on the other, he opposes porneia, as representative of the estranged cosmos, and God, Jesus Christ, and believers as fully embodied beings. The prostitute (*pornē*, vv. 15–16), therefore, is not a person in her own right (as if such a thing were imaginable for Paul) but a representative of the cosmos that is estranged and opposed to God and Christ. As in 1 Corinthians 1–4, Paul's argument depends on the radical separation of Christ's body from the cosmos, in an apocalyptic, ethical dualism.

Also at work here is Paul's assumption, seen above in the discussion of 1 Corinthians 15 and the resurrection of the body, that the individual body has no independent ontological status. The prostitute's being is defined by her status as a representative of the cosmos; the Christian man's being is defined by his participation in the body of Christ.[36] "Do you not know that your bodies are members of Christ? Will I therefore take the members of Christ and make them members of a prostitute? Absolutely not!" (6:15). The pneumatic union between the body of the Christian man and the body of Christ (6:17) is what identifies the Christian man. The man's body and Christ's body share the same pneuma; the man's body is therefore an appendage of Christ's body, totally dependent on the pneumatic life-force of the larger body for its existence.

The man who has sex with a prostitute is, in Paul's construction, Christ's "member" entering the body of the prostitute. Since her body is also only part of a larger whole, the cosmos, the simple act of copulation between a man and a woman becomes for Paul copulation between Christ and the cosmos. Furthermore, as we saw in Chapter 2, Paul has already set up a radical opposition between the cosmos, with its value system, epistemology, and power structures, and the kingdom of God, with its very different values, revealed knowledge, and revolutionary challenge to the power hierarchy of "this world." The two realms represented by the body of Christ and the cosmos constitute two different worlds of meaning, contrary axiological systems of signification, different "texts." Copulation between representatives of these two cosmic bodies enacts a collision of worlds of meaning: intertextual intercourse. The Christian man penetrating a prostitute constitutes coitus between two beings of such different ontological status that Paul can hardly contemplate the consequences.

Paul argues for his point of view by quoting the Jewish Bible, interpreting Genesis 2:24, which spoke of the primordial union in marriage between the first man and woman, to refer to any act of coitus: "Do you not know that the one who is joined together with a prostitute is one body (with her)? For it says, 'The two shall be one flesh'" (6:16). Not only marriage, according to Paul's view, but any sexual intercourse effects a blending of the man's and the woman's body into one body. The idea that intercourse effected a union of the two partners would probably have struck Paul's auditors as odd, though not completely unfamiliar. The Greek word commonly used for coitus, after all, was *synousia*, "being" (*ousia*) together "with" (*syn*) someone else. But the more common way of conceptualizing sexual intercourse was not as a mutual joining together but as an action done to someone by someone else, a penetration perpetrated by a sexual actor on a passive recipient. As John Winkler, for example, has shown in a study of Artemidorus's *Dream Handbook*, "The privileged terms for sexual activity . . . are *perainein* and *perainesthai*, to penetrate and to be penetrated."[37] Greek language seems almost always to have constructed sexual intercourse as a one-way street; the pleasure was assumed to belong naturally to the penetrator, and the penetrated was expected to submit without enjoyment. Whoever enjoyed being penetrated was considered weak, unnatural, or at least suspect—or (to sum up all three terms into one body) a woman.[38] Paul's emphasis on the joining of the two into one body would probably have struck his more educated converts as bordering on unnatural fears. But it is this "becoming one" that threatens the body of the male penetrator and, by extension, the body of Christ.

Paul himself is not above invoking notions of penetration to discourage intertextual intercourse. Immediately after hinting that the man's penetration of the prostitute makes Christ a penetrator of the prostitute also, Paul says, "Flee porneia. Every sin that a human being commits is outside the body; but the one who commits porneia sins into his own body" (6:18). The usual English translation of this last phrase (*eis to idion sōma*) is "against his own body," and that is certainly correct to the extent that *eis* in some contexts means something more like the English "against" than "into." But the primary meaning of the preposition denotes motion from outside into something. Even when it is translated "against" (as in "the soldiers came against the city"), it tends to retain its connotations of penetration and invasion ("the soldiers are attempting to break through the walls and invade the city"). Aeschines, for example, uses a phrase quite similar to this one of Paul when he mentions certain men notorious for "sinning against themselves" (*eis heautous exhamartanontas*).[39] In this case the phrase is well chosen to say something without saying it: Aeschines is disparaging certain men who, he insinuates, give up the traditional position of male honor and allow themselves to be sexually penetrated for profit. They are sinning "against" their bodies by allowing entry "into" their bodies.

In Paul's Greek this essential ambiguity is preserved. Porneia quintessentially represents the invasion of the body. The man, by penetrating the prostitute, is himself penetrated by the sinful cosmos. He penetrates himself with sin. Thus, whereas in 6:16–17 Paul's rhetoric implied that sexual intercourse between the Christian man and the prostitute enacted sexual intercourse between Christ and the prostitute—in which case, Christ is sexually penetrating the evil cosmos—in 6:18 the roles are reversed: the man is fucked by sin, so Christ is fucked by the cosmos.

In the face of such cosmic consequences of coitus, Paul insists on limiting the freedom of the Christian man. Again, as in 1 Corinthians 5, what is at stake is the pneuma of God: "Or do you not know that your body is the sanctuary of the holy pneuma in you, which you have from God" (6:19). Although Paul does not explicitly spell it out here, he is again concerned about possible pollution of the pneuma through the boundary-breaking activity of sexual intercourse with outsiders. Thus he must insist that the Christian really does not have absolute freedom over his own body. His body has been "bought"; Christ was the buyer, something like a *sōmatemporos*, a slave-dealer, a dealer in "bodies" (6:19–20). The individual Christian body, like that of a slave in Roman law, has no ontological status of its own.

The way Paul deals with porneia is soaked in the logic of pollution and invasion. This is sexual immorality that involves a member of the church and an outsider. How Paul would have dealt with fornication (that is, sexual intercourse between unmarried persons not involving adultery on either side) within the church is unknown, since he nowhere addresses the subject in his letters. Doubtless he would have disapproved, but he appears not to have considered it a very real possibility. It seems clear, at any rate, that if he had wished to argue against it, he would not have done so by invoking the logic used in 1 Corinthians 6; that is, he would not have seen the sexual union as monstrously conjoining the body of Christ to the body of the cosmos or as entailing any kind of invasive pollution, since both the man and the woman in such a case would be in the body of Christ. Rather, he would probably have dealt with "internal" fornication by invoking the property relations disrupted by such intercourse outside marriage, as in 1 Thessalonians 4:3–8. In that context Paul uses the language of uncleanness (4:3, 7)—porneia is always for Paul a matter of pollution to some extent. But the real objection to inappropriate sex within the church is put in economic terms: don't defraud your brother! "Let each man know how to possess his own vessel in holiness and honor, not in the passion of desire like the Gentiles who do not know God. Do not step on or take advantage of your brother in this matter."[40] Paul here argues against adultery in the church by citing the Christian man's property rights over his wife. In the case of an unmarried woman, the property rights would presumably belong to the woman's betrothed (as I argue in the next chapter is the case in 1 Cor. 7) or to her father or guardian. The logic of invasion, therefore, applies to sexual intercourse only when one partner is outside the body of Christ. When two Christians commit fornication, there seems to be little danger that the body of Christ is implicated in copulation with the world. Copulation that crosses the boundary of the body of Christ, on the other hand, implicates Christ's body in coitus with the cosmos and makes the entire body dangerously susceptible to pollution and dissolution.

Prophylactic Gnosis

I have already dealt, in Chapter 3, with 1 Corinthians 8–10 and the issue of eating meat sacrificed to idols. There I argued, following many other scholars, that the issue divided the Corinthian church along social status lines and that Paul, while agreeing with the Strong that such eating should not be categorically forbidden, urges them to give up their prerogative, based on superior knowledge, to eat idol-meat so that they may avoid influencing the weak—that is, those of lower status—to do so against the strictures of their conscience. The subject of conscience, however, brings up an issue that could not be addressed until the groundwork had been laid on the subject of pollution. I refer to the question of what Paul means by "corrupting (or polluting) the *syneidēsis* (usually, but as we will see, misleadingly translated "conscience") in 1 Corinthians 8:7, and how he conceives *gnōsis* (knowledge) to work in protecting the stronger "consciences" of other Christians from being similarly polluted. In order to understand Paul's logic of pollution and protection in this section, we must critically examine what he means by the words *syneidēsis* and *gnōsis;* for his views were probably quite different from those of his ideological opponents at Corinth.

For us today, the conscience is that part of the self, whether implanted by nature or inculcated by society, that knows the difference between right and wrong. Taught from childhood to "let your conscience be your guide," we assume that behavior contrary to the dictates of our conscience will probably be wrong; even if we possess overly scrupulous consciences and the behavior we feel to be wrong is not actually wrong, we are wary of performing actions condemned by our consciences because the result will be a conflict within the personality, due to guilt feelings that arise when we do something we believe to be wrong, even if it is not actually wrong. Conscience, then, is the site of the values that constitute the integrated self and hence a site for the potential destruction of a normally coherent personality.

As several scholars have pointed out, *syneidēsis* in ancient texts does not correspond very well to this modern conception. In particular, C. A. Pierce has argued that syneidesis is not an internal guide to future behavior, informing a person as to the rightness or wrongness of a prospective action contemplated in the abstract. Rather, it is a knowledge within the self of past action performed by the subject, a conviction of past misdeeds; and as such it is portrayed as a pain, a disease, or an agent that punishes and inflicts pain. It may also refer to the organ or faculty of the body or self in which such pain is felt. In Pierce's words, "The fundamental connotation of the *syneidēsis* group of words is that man is by nature so constituted that, if he overstep the moral limits of his nature he will normally feel pain—the pain called *syneidēsis.*"[41] In the absence of syneidesis or, alternatively put, unconvicted by one's syneidesis, one may assume that no wrong—or at least no intentional wrong—has been committed.

Scholars have rightly suggested that the term *syneidēsis* has been introduced into the discussion of idol-meat not by Paul but by the Corinthians.[42] Paul is here responding to questions raised in a letter from the Corinthians, and he thus takes up the discussion using more or less their language. When he himself introduces the subject of idol-meat in Romans 14, syneidesis makes no appearance at all. Paul speaks there of the person who is weak in *pistis* ("faith"), rather than of the person weak in syneidesis (Rom. 14:1). It is, moreover, not hard to see how the Strong at Corinth may have appealed to syneidesis to justify their practice of eating food sacrificed to idols. First, they point out, in a philosophical-sounding argument, that there is only one God and that the daimons feared by the masses to be lurking within and behind every rock (or piece of meat!) do not actually exist at all—or that if they do exist, they are "nothings," hence powerless. Food is just food, the body is just the body, and idols are nothing. The Strong then point to the fact that their syneidesis does not convict them of any wrongdoing in eating idol-meat. They appeal to their syneidesis, informed by superior knowledge (*gnōsis*), for confirmation that their behavior and their beliefs about that behavior are correct. In the absence of a pained syneidesis, they must be innocent.

Paul himself has no firm theory of syneidesis, any more than he has a consistent theory of other aspects of the human self, like *kardia* (heart), *pneuma* (spirit), or *psychē* (soul).[43] In undermining the position of the Strong, though, he appropriates their term *syneidēsis* but uses it in a way that would probably have seemed strange to them. To understand his response, we must first recognize that Paul has no concept of conscience in the modern sense of an internal and dependable guide to right and wrong for future behavior. Second, Paul has already in this letter insisted that self-knowledge is not a reliable guide for judging one's behavior (even one's past behavior).[44] The fact that his syneidesis has not convicted him does not mean, Paul insists, that he is thereby innocent; only the Lord can judge (1 Cor. 4:4). Furthermore, Paul's use of "strong" and "weak" is contrary to philosophical notions of a strong or weak syneidesis. As Richard Horsley explains, "According to Philo this convicting consciousness is part of the nature of the soul as created by God (see *Dec.* 87). Its function is to prevent the soul from wrong and/or to accuse and 'convict' the soul of having acted unjustly."[45] Logically, therefore, a strong syneidesis is one that successfully convicts a person and correctly influences behavior and recognition of past misdeeds. For Paul, on the contrary, it is a weak syneidesis that convicts and a strong syneidesis that has no scruples. The sign of a weak syneidesis in the Corinthian church is its ability to convict its possessor. Thus for Paul the function of syneidesis has nothing to do with moral guidance or reliable self-knowledge. Syneidesis may very well be a false guide: a weak syneidesis may be mistaken about the existence and power of idolatrous gods, but it can still be polluted by eating their food!

In the end, the only significant aspect of syneidesis in Paul's view is that it can be polluted. Paul, probably unlike the Strong, gives no functional role to syneidesis as something independent of the person as a whole. Everything that Paul says about syneidesis in 1 Corinthians 8 and 10 could also be said about the body as a whole: it may be weak or strong (8:9–10); it may be "built up" (*oikodomeō*) to do something (8:10; cf. 14:4, 17); it may be "wounded" (*typtō*, 8:12; this term is functionally parallel to *molynō* in 8:7); and Paul can alternately speak of doing something (or avoiding something) for the sake of the person or for the sake of his or her syneidesis (10:28–29). As C. Maurer puts it, "The attitude to one's *syneidēsis* is the attitude to oneself, and the attitude to the neighbour's *syneidēsis* is the attitude to the neighbour himself."[46] We should not make too much out of Paul's use of the term, therefore. For him, syneidesis is in a synecdochic relationship with the body: it simply stands in for the body of the Christian. For the weak Christian (the Christian who possesses a weak syneidesis) unprotected by gnosis, idol-meat pollutes the syneidesis—that is, the body.

Indeed, the only difference between a strong consciousness and a weak consciousness, or between a strong and a weak Christian, is the presence of gnosis. Gnosis is the prophylaxis against the pollution that would otherwise result from ingestion of idol-meat. Paul's argument in chapters 8–10 is rather confusing. At times he appears to agree with the Strong that idols are "nothing"—that is, nonexistent or absolutely powerless (8:4)—and that food has nothing to do with our relationship with God (8:8); that "the earth and all its fulness are the Lord's," and so all food is edible (10:26); and that a Christian may without scruples eat whatever is sold in the marketplace or served at a dinner, even a dinner hosted by an idolator (10:25, 27). In chapter 10, however, Paul seems to be saying something different, admitting that idol-meat has been sacrificed not to figments of someone's imagination but to daimons—his actual word is *daimonion*, the diminutive, which a Greek speaker would understand as a god or some divine being quite near to a god (10:19).[47] Thus, eating the sacrificial food might constitute commensality between the Christian and the daimons, rendering the Christian a "partner" (*koinōnos*) with the daimons and disrupting the firm boundary between the realm of Christ and the cosmos of daimons (10:20–22). As was the case with sex in 1 Corinthians 5 and 6, the body of the erring Christian becomes the site of permeation between the two separate, opposed realms of meaning.

Some scholars have proposed that this seeming self-contradiction by Paul is a result of his attempt to address two different situations in which food sacrificed to idols would be consumed. They claim that in chapter 8 and in 10:23–33 Paul is talking about ordinary, noncultic meals, meals that are not explicitly part of an idolatrous cultic activity, whereas in 10:14–22 he is assuming a situation in which sacrificial food is consumed in a temple as part of a cultic ceremony, which is why, in their view, he introduces his comments with the admonition "Flee from idolatry!" (10:14). It is only participation in idolatrous worship that constitutes "sharing the table of daimons."[48]

I do not find this proposal persuasive, for several reasons. In the first place, Paul himself does not make any such shift explicit. The only place where the location of the eating is mentioned is 8:10, where Paul suggests in passing that a weaker Christian might see a stronger Christian eating in a sanctuary. The supposed alternative, eating in a private home, is nowhere mentioned. (The invitation in 10:27 could just as easily be to a meal in a temple area.) Throughout these chapters the focus of Paul's attention is the food that is eaten and its effect on the Christian, not the environment in which the eating takes place. Second, Paul's admission in chapter 8 that the Strong are not adversely affected by eating idol-meat recognizes that they may be doing so in the temple of an idol (8:10); and although there were what we might call "private" dining rooms in temple sanctuaries, in which people hosted what would look to us like "private" dinner parties, the Greeks and Romans would have construed such dinners as implicated in the worship of the god or goddess honored in the sanctuary.[49] Finally, as my placement of the term *private* in quotation marks suggests, the proposal that Paul is assuming a difference between "cultic" eating and "private" eating seems to me to invoke a differentiation between religious, or sacred, activity as opposed to the same activity construed as secular, a dichotomy that is strikingly modern. In the ancient world, all eating (and practically all activity) was construed as an aspect of interaction with unseen powers; libations to the gods, for example, might be poured out on any drinking occasion, regardless of whether the event was thought to be an "official" observance of a god's cult. To suggest that Paul is here advising one kind of behavior in a private setting and another in a cultic setting goes beyond Paul's own words and introduces a modern conception of the secular.

Thus the differentiation Paul makes is not between two different settings but between two different states of people. The same action performed by the Strong without ill effect, eating idol-meat in a cultic setting (8:10), is dangerous when performed by the Weak. The only difference between "protected" consumption and "polluting" consumption is that the former is done with gnosis, the latter without. Thus, the only difference between a strong and a weak syneidesis is the possession of gnosis by the former. We must examine precisely what gnosis means for Paul, therefore, to determine how it functions as prophylaxis against pollution and destruction from idol-meat.

Gnosis for Paul obviously does not mean the simple possession of information. One does not "get" gnosis by "learning" something. This is clear if we imagine how the Strong at Corinth might answer Paul. "Well," they might say, "if the weak Christians are harmed by a lack of knowledge, mistakenly believing that they can be harmed by these nonexistent or, at most, frail daimons, we will teach them otherwise. We will tell them that the idols are just rock or wood or metal but nothing more. We will show them by our own actions that they have nothing to fear. Once they have this information, their fears will be seen to be groundless." The Strong in Corinth, moreover, seem not to hold any "Gnostic" belief in esoteric knowledge that is the presence of only a few. Their slogan "We *all* have knowledge" (8:1, emphasis added) is probably quite sincere: they are convinced that true notions about the nature of the gods are available to anyone in the church regardless of status. They themselves may have come to their beliefs through education in a philosophy that attempted to free people from irrational fears of pollutions and daimons, but they are probably quite prepared to pass along this liberating information. From their point of view, the solution is no more arduous than informing the less educated of the truth and demonstrating the irrationality of their fears by the superior, heuristic activity of the Strong themselves. "If the Weak need knowledge," they might respond to Paul, "we will give it to them!"[50]

Why is this apparently simple solution not entertained by Paul? Because for him gnosis is not a matter of possessing information; nor is it procured by education. But why is the possession of information not enough to protect the Weak from pollution? From a certain modern perspective, we might imagine that Paul is concerned that the Weak might "know" the truth about idols on one level, say the conscious level, but not have "worked through" the problem enough to "know" the truth on a subconscious or unconscious level. This modern perspective would posit guilt feelings due to a previous inculcation of values still held by the person at a deep, hidden level of the mind, even though the person has rejected the older beliefs at the level of consciousness. I would suggest, however, that this perspective reflects modern assumptions about human psychology not available to Paul. I am suspicious of positing different levels of the mind—whether in terms of ego, superego, and subconscious or in other, non-Freudian, but equally modern, psychological categories—to explain Paul's views here. What Paul appears to believe is that a person either has or does not have gnosis; it is not a matter of integrating information throughout the subconscious realms of the person's self. Furthermore, Paul is not concerned with guilt feelings but with pollution. We must resist the temptation to modernize Paul too quickly.[51]

The position of the Strong is not hard to imagine. Moral philosophers had long taught, and had harangued the uneducated masses on the subject, that knowledge could set people free. Superstitious or uneducated people lacked knowledge about what they should rightly fear and what they should despise. Epictetus, for example, berates those who spend their lives in slavery to fears because they are ignorant of the true facts of the case. They do not recognize what is truly good and what is truly evil, foolishly fearing death, for example, even though it is really no evil at all but only the separation of the soul from the body (*Discourse* 3. 22. 32). Epictetus would have laughed at those who feared attacks by daimons; and being the civic-minded teacher that he is, he would have attempted to inform them that their fears are groundless because the things they are afraid of either do not exist or cannot harm them. He might recall the actions of Diogenes, who ate fruit from a tree on which a man had hanged himself in order to demonstrate that fears of pollution are unfounded.[52]

Similarly, Plutarch advises a groom that some education is suitable for his bride because knowledge is an antidote to superstition.

> Studies of this sort, in the first place, divert women from all untoward conduct; for a woman studying geometry will be ashamed to be a dancer, and she will not swallow any beliefs in magic charms while she is under the charm of Plato's or Xenophon's words. And if anybody professes power to pull down the moon from the sky, she will laugh at the ignorance and stupidity of women who believe these things, inasmuch as she herself is not unschooled in astronomy, and has read in the books about Aglao-nice, the daughter of Hegetor of Thessaly, and how she, through being thoroughly acquainted with the periods of the full moon when it is subject to eclipse, and knowing beforehand the time when the moon was due to be overtaken by the earth's shadow, imposed upon the women, and made them all believe that she was drawing down the moon.[53]

Plutarch is speaking quaintly, portraying knowledge as an antidote to the disease of superstition. Galen does much the same in his "Diagnosis and Cure of the Soul's Passions." The disease of passion arises "from an irrational power within us which refuses to obey reason."[54] Knowledge, gained through education, works like a drug to cure the body of harmful emotions and unnecessary anxieties.

In the view of the philosophers, knowledge sets one free from fear and superstition—that is, from needless anxiety. The emphasis here is on "needless": the anxiety is lamentable because it is unnecessary; knowledge protects people from anxieties about pollution. Daimons do not pollute people—even people who do not *know* that daimons do not pollute them. Gnosis does not protect people from pollution, therefore; it simply informs them that pollution does not occur.

This is quite unlike the function of gnosis for Paul. For him, gnosis protects its possessor from pollution by daimons: the person who "has" gnosis is not polluted, whereas the person who does not "have" it is polluted. Whereas for the philosophers the function of gnosis is to show that daimons do not pollute, for Paul it serves as a prophylactic talisman to protect the possessor from the very real danger of daimonic pollution. The fear, in Paul's view, is justified. Whereas the Strong probably believe that the Weak have nothing to be afraid of and simply need to be educated about the facts of the case, Paul believes that their fears are well-founded and that they should avoid idol-meat as long as they lack the prophylactic protection of gnosis.[55]

Paul's view of gnosis is quite unlike that known from moral philosophy, but it has much in common with the view found in the magical papyri. Describing the meaning of gnosis in Gnosticism, Bultmann wrote, "It is an esoteric knowledge, and the instruction is more like the teaching of initiates than philosophical instruction." Gnosis is "a mysterious quality of the soul which is regarded as a substance, not as knowledge which in the act of comprehension controls the content of what is comprehended."[56] Although referring to Gnosticism, Bultmann's statement describes the function of gnosis in many magical papyri as well. As Betz remarks, the magician was a "knower," one who possessed a special commodity called gnosis: "He knew the code words needed to communicate with the gods, the daimons, and the dead. He could tap, regulate, and manipulate the invisible energies."[57] Many of the papyri contain spells in which the magician asks for some kind of revelation, information, or knowledge that will then be used as an instrument or prophylaxis (for example, *PGM* IV. 1323–30). The content of the knowledge often has to do with the god or daimon addressed, the assumption being that knowledge is, quite literally, power; in this case, knowledge of the daimon constitutes some power over him or her. In a spell that asks for power, including protection against daimon possession, "Lord Hermes" is addressed thus: "I also know what your forms are . . . I also know your wood: ebony. I know you, Hermes, who you are and where you come from and what your city is: Hermopolis. Come to me, lord Hermes, many-named one, who know the things hidden beneath heaven and earth . . . I also know your foreign names." Furthermore, possession of gnosis is implicated in the union between the magician and the god or daimon: gnosis is a result of and also effects a union between the human and the divine. "For you are I, and I am you; your name is mine, and mine is yours . . . I know you, Hermes, and you know me. I am you, and you are I. And so, do everything for me, and may you turn to me with Good Fortune and Good Daimon, immediately, immediately; quickly, quickly."[58] This search for powerful gnosis leads the magician to enter the precarious and frightening world of interaction with gods and daimons, even inviting them into his own body: "Come into my mind and my intelligence for the whole time of my life, and accomplish for me all the wishes of my soul. For you are I and I am you."[59] In order to procure the protection of gnosis, the magician must go to its source, just as a physician or herbalist must procure prophylactic drugs from the pharmacy of nature.

In Greek, drugs used to "ward off noxious effects" or to avert the effects of other drugs or witchcraft were called *alexipharmaka*. Squill, hung up over the door of a house, is able to ward off mischief.[60] The line between the "magical" pharmacology reflected in the papyri and the "scientific" pharmacology of the more philosophical-medical texts is a blurry one. Dioscorides, for example, in his pharmacological text *De materia medica* observes that Greco-Roman doctors used "hellebore-wine" as a drastic purgative; but he also notes that it was commonly sprinkled around houses to protect them from hostile spiritual forces.[61] Many charms survive, some using drugs, others not, that were used as phylacteries against daimons who might enter the body and cause disease.[62]

According to the more popular assumptions—the "folk medicine," one could say—reflected in the magical papyri, the state and status of the user of the drug was important, both as regards avoiding harm while handling the drug and assuring the drug's potency. One papyrus states that "Among the Egyptians herbs are always obtained like this: the herbalist first purifies his own body, then sprinkles with natron and fumigates the herb with resin from a pine tree after carrying it around the place three times. Then after burning *kyphi* [a prescribed mixture of materials] and pouring the libation of milk as he prays, he pulls up the plant while invoking by name the daimon to whom the herb is being dedicated and calling upon him to be more effective for the use for which it is being acquired."[63] The combination of proper gnosis, proper use of the drug, and proper state of the practitioner is notable: all are necessary for the effective functioning of the prophylaxis.

Paul's view of gnosis in 1 Corinthians 8–10 reflects the logic of prophylaxis revealed in the magical papyri far more than that taught by the philosophers. Knowledge of certain facts is not what will free weak Christians from the dangers of pollution, but only the possession of gnosis, which they, as the Weak, cannot, by definition, possess. The Strong cannot simply hand over their gnosis to the Weak, as if it could be taught; rather, in Paul's rhetoric, people either have it or do not have it. Possession of gnosis is a matter of state or status, not education. But its possession, just like a charm, a talisman, or an *alexipharmakon*, protects the Strong from pollution even when they engage in the very behavior that would pollute the Weak.

The way Paul poses the danger of eating food associated with idols also reflects the logical structure assigned to eating in the magical papyri. The philosophically educated would mock the idea that eating sacrificed food involved potential invasion of the human body by the daimon or god to whom the food had been offered. The magical papyri, on the other hand, assume a world in which commensality with daimons and gods and even the ingesting of the divinity are both fearful and necessary. By drinking the milk in which a falcon, for example, has been "divinized" (that is, drowned), the magician takes into his body "something divine." In another text, eating "with" the god is enacted as part of the spell. Commensality with daimons implicates the practitioner in the realm of their power.[64] We do not know exactly how Paul thought that pollution of idol-meat took place, but the danger he makes explicit centers on commensality with daimons: eating food sacrificed to daimons without the protection of gnosis effects a koinonia (partnership, commonality, sharing in essence) with those daimons, and this is intolerable because the Christian is already a *koinōnos* (sharer) with Christ (1 Cor. 10:20–22). Again, the boundary between the body of Christ and the cosmos is at issue. Although Paul nowhere explicitly states that he believes that ingesting food sacrificed to idols constitutes ingesting the daimons themselves, it is altogether likely that some of the more fearful converts in Corinth, who had only recently turned their backs on the worship of gods and daimons, assumed that it did. Other aspects of Paul's logic of pollution in 1 Corinthians 8–10 would certainly not discourage such assumptions: sharing the cup of Christ means sharing in his blood, and eating the bread means sharing in Christ's body (10:16). This eating and drinking renders the participants one body with Christ (10:17). Paul appears to have assumed, then, along with the more superstitious Christians (as seen, that is, from a more educated point of view), that eating idol-meat meant ingestion of the daimon into the body of the weak Christian.

Studies of 1 Corinthians have commonly pointed to Paul's theological opponents in Corinth as those who emphasize gnosis as a status symbol, much as the Gnostics of the second century reserved the possession of gnosis for the spiritual elite of the church.[65] It should by now be clear that my reconstruction of the situation is quite different. In 1 Corinthians 8–10, it is Paul, not the Strong, who assumes that gnosis is a possession not available to just anyone. The Strong say, "We all have knowledge!" Paul responds, "Gnosis is *not* in everyone" (8:7). The Strong probably attribute their superior knowledge to philosophical education, which should be relatively transferable to the less educated, an idea that seems not to have occurred to Paul, who treats gnosis not as information that sets one free from fear but as a talisman that protects the holder from pollution. Paul's view of gnosis makes it much less transferable; it is linked securely to the status or state of the possessor. The Weak simply do not have it, and no means for acquiring it are entertained. It is Paul, not the Strong, who makes gnosis into a prophylaxis possessed by only an elite within the church.

Another way to describe Paul's view of gnosis is in terms of commodification. Gnosis (and hence a strong syneidesis) for Paul is a commodity. Here, however, we must be careful to note the difference in commodification between ancient Mediterranean culture and modern, capitalist culture. According to modern, liberal, capitalist ideology, anyone who can buy a good or procure it through "legitimate" means may possess it. A (false) economic democraticism assures dwellers in a modern commodity culture that goods are there for the taking by anyone, regardless of their state or status. In Paul's world, on the contrary, goods were possessed by virtue of status. Even if a person could afford them, certain gold rings were prohibited to all but members of certain orders. Not just anyone could buy and possess a purple-striped toga but only those whose status merited it. A slave might be able to afford a freedman's cap but could not possess it due to his servile status. Paul's view of gnosis fits this ancient ideology of commodification: gnosis could not be freely bought and sold but could only be "owned" by people of a certain status.

By commodifying gnosis in 1 Corinthians 8–10, Paul ironically raises its status while simultaneously denying its use by the Strong as a defense of their actions. Paul's logic, however, depends on portraying gnosis as a prophylaxis against pollution. Because the Weak do not possess the commodity or phylactery of gnosis, they are endangered by an activity, eating idol-meat, that does not harm the Strong. Paul's solution is not for the Strong (those with knowledge) to teach the Weak (those without knowledge). Rather, he insists that the Strong recognize that the Weak do not possess gnosis and modify their behavior so that the Weak will not be encouraged to behave in a way that will endanger their bodies through pollution from daimon-food. Without prophylactic gnosis, the weak members of the body of Christ endanger themselves when they ingest the food of daimons. Furthermore, not only are they themselves endangered, but their actions may also constitute joining the table of Christ to the table of cosmic daimons. To make sure nothing of this sort takes place, Paul urges the Strong to follow his own example and give up eating idol-meat entirely (8:13; 10:32–33).

Consuming Your Own Condemnation

If Paul's view of gnosis follows a logic of prophylaxis—in Greek, an *alexiphar-makon*—his language about the consumed eucharist in 1 Corinthians 11:17–34 follows the logic of the more general term *pharmakon*, which refers to a drug that may function as either curative or a poison. In this section Paul deals with problems surrounding the Lord's Supper, during which, apparently, the church has become divided along social class lines, with the richer members enjoying a fine meal and even, if Paul is not exaggerating, "getting drunk," while the poorer members are being left out and going hungry (11:21). Other scholars have adequately reconstructed the probable situation, noting that the primary problem addressed by Paul has little to do with a proper "sacramental" attitude towards the elements of the Lord's Supper but is instead one of schism within the congregation based on social status differences. Paul's solution is to urge the richer members, the Strong, to wait for the poorer members, the Weak, so that a more equal sharing of the common meal may take place and no member will be embarrassed due to obvious economic inequalities manifested during the meal.[66]

Along the way to this more general solution, however, Paul introduces some rather curious language. He insists that those who eat the bread and drink the wine of the Lord "unworthily"—that is, without "discerning the body" (the meaning of which will be pursued below)—eat and drink their own condemnation (or judgment; the two terms here mean the same thing). The phrase is often translated "eat and drink judgment against themselves," but the dative case of *heautos* carries many different nuances and more generally means "with regard to oneself." Here again, the Greek is conveniently ambiguous. In any case, the image Paul invokes is one of persons consuming their own condemnation, ingesting the material of self-destruction.[67]

Unlike other early Christian writers, Paul nowhere explicitly speaks of the eucharistic elements as curative, as the "medicine of immortality" (*pharmakon athanasias*) of Ignatius and later Christian theology (Ignatius *Ephesians* 20:2). On the other hand, Paul clearly believes that something "real" happens to the body of the Christian through partaking in the Eucharistic meal. It is anachronistic to attribute to Paul the notion that the Eucharist had a "merely" metaphorical or, in the modern sense of the term, "spiritual" effect on the Christian. As Jean Héring observes, "Descartes' distinction between 'res cogitans' and 'res extensa' was . . . unknown in the apostle's times. It is always the whole human reality which preoccupies him."[68] This is why Paul was so concerned, as we have seen, about the "weak" Christians' consumption of idol-meat: without the prophylaxis of gnosis, their eating constituted a sharing in the table of dai-mons; they became, to some extent, integrated into the very being of those daimons. Conversely, when they share in the table of the Lord, the Eucharist, they are integrated into the being of Christ (10:14–22). The bodily ingestion of idol-meat could mean the dangerous ingestion of the daimonic realm; the parallel with the Eucharist is simply assumed by Paul: normally it would con-stitute the ingestion of the body of Christ, which would of course be positive, even soteriological.[69]

This is why it is so shocking when Paul suggests that the ingestion of the Eucharist, Christ's body, might under certain circumstances have a toxic effect on the Christian's body. When they eat unworthily, they eat and drink their own condemnation, with the result that "many" of them "are feeble or ill and quite a few have died" (11:30). What should have had a positive effect on the Christian's body has had a negative effect, since it was taken without the proper precautions or in an improper state. These Corinthians are being poisoned by what should heal them.

The Greek word *pharmaka* denoted both curative drugs and poisons. As Hugh Parry explains, *pharmakon* refers to "any drug or plant able . . . to trans-form the condition of the human body, for better or worse."[70] In Greek myth, tragedy, and poetry, gods and goddesses were known to possess pharmaka that could either help or harm human beings, and the agents of divinities, whether magicians or doctors, were people with knowledge to manipulate the ambiguous power of these materials to bring either disease or health, death or salvation.[71] Love philters especially were known to contain poisonous sub-stances intended to arouse erotic desires in the victim. In Sophocles' *Women of Trachis*, the love charm contains snake venom and the toxic blood of a dead centaur.[72] This explains why people so often got sick or died from love potions. Juvenal wonders if Caligula was poisoned by his wife's love philters (6.610–626). In a mock trial scene, composed as a rhetorical exercise for students, a woman is made to insist that she administered a love potion, not a poison, to the now dead victim; but of course, it could have been both.[73] As one of the prostitutes in Alciphron's *Letters of Courtesans* puts it, "Love-philters tend to be uncertain and can hurl one into disaster" (*eis olethron*, 4. 10. 5, trans. Parry, 263). A slip-up in their use could produce a corpse instead of a lover.[74]

Love potions aside, pharmaka in general were recognized as ambivalent agents; the word embraced what seem to us opposite things, leading John Riddle to translate it as "medicine-poison."[75] Learned writers—that is, the higher-status, educated persons who wrote the scientific treatises on medicine and pharmaceuticals that survive—offered their own explanations for the dual function of pharmaka. A drug that should heal a person might kill or drive someone mad if administered in too large a dose. Dioscorides, who composed a pharmaceutical manual in the first century, cites coriander (*korion*) as a drug for worms and as an aphrodisiac but warns that given in large doses it leads to madness.[76] Furthermore, if a patient's condition is not amenable to a particular drug therapy, disaster can result. Thus Theophrastus notes in his *Enquiry into Plants* that some people's bodies, by repeated exposure to incremental amounts, are immune to the ill effects of some poisons (9. 17). A knowledge of the bodily condition of the patient is therefore necessary for the proper prescription of drugs, which were always seen as potentially dangerous.

Popular culture, as exemplified in folk medicine and magic, attached even greater importance to the state of the body to which the drug was to be administered. We have no firsthand accounts of folk beliefs, but many such beliefs are passed on by upper-class writers, who sometimes express their disdain for them. Theophrastus, for example, lists precautions that are usually taken when people cut, dig, or gather dangerous plants, some of which he considers reasonable. When cutting *thapsia* (and certain other plants), one should stand windward and anoint the body with oil to keep from swelling up. Some plants should be gathered only at night, others only during the day, and still others just before the sun strikes them. When digging hellebore, one should take frequent breaks to keep the head from growing heavy. Hellebore-diggers, according to Theophrastus, also eat garlic and drink unmixed wine before digging, to offset the effects of the poison (*Enquiry into Plants* 9. 8. 5).[77] But Theophrastus considers other notions farfetched, such as the belief that if one digs peony during the day and is seen by a woodpecker, one will become blind (by having one's eyes pecked out by the bird), and one's anus will fall out (*ekpiptein tēn hedran*, ibid. 9. 8. 6). He concedes that it may be a good idea to pray while cutting some roots and plants, but he rejects other precautions as unnecessary—for instance, that when cutting *panacea* ("all-heal") "one should put in the ground in its place an offering made of all kinds of fruits and a cake; and that, when one is cutting gladwyn, one should put in its place to pay for it cakes of meal from spring-sown wheat, and that one should cut it with a two-edged sword, first making a circle round it three times, and that the piece first cut must be held up in the air while the rest is being cut" (ibid. 9. 8. 7, trans. Hort). Although he rejects such ideas, he passes them on as popular beliefs. They reflect a combination of prayers, poses, and protections designed to render the body of the root-cutter impervious to the dangers of the plant and to insure the full potency of the drug. "One should also, it is said, draw a circle round the black hellebore and cut it standing towards the east and saying prayers, and one should look out for an eagle both on the right and on the left; for that there is danger to those that cut, if your eagle should come near, that they may die within the year" (9. 8. 8, trans. Hort). Theophrastus calls these notions superfluous (*epithetos;* not, it should be noted, superstitious). Thus the dividing line between good and bad precautions is not a matter of natural versus supernatural considerations, since he admits that prayer may be efficacious in root cutting. The sorts of things that Theophrastus rejects are the need for a state of purity on the part of the cutter, fears concerning the possibility of anger on the part of gods or beasts or the earth (any of which may be understood to be the "owner" or "protector" of the power of the drug), and the belief that some kind of atonement or propitiation is necessary in exchange for the drug.

Other writers were not as judgmental about such beliefs as Theophrastus. Pliny the Elder mentions many of these same precautions without rejecting them. He records, without disdain, the belief that one should, as a "religious observation" (*religio*), fill in the hole of dug-up panacea with "various cereals as an atonement to the earth."[78] And he cites, without condemnation or discrimination, the various precautions for gathering hellebore, including drawing circles with swords, prayers, watching for eagles, eating garlic, and drinking wine.[79] As we have already seen, the magical papyri show similar concerns: some spells emphasize that purity with regard to sexual intercourse (or rather abstinence) on the part of the magician is necessary for the proper handling of the *materia magica*.[80] It should be noted that Pliny was a rather traditional Roman gentleman with a traditional disdain for Greek professional medicine. Thus he ridicules a practice that Theophrastus, Dioscorides, and other Greek doctors took for granted: using poisonous drugs as curatives. Pliny attributes such nonsense to a perverse fascination with experimentation, which again sounds like a traditional Roman criticism of Greek ways.[81] This would explain Pliny's more lax acceptance of "folk" remedies and beliefs as opposed to Greek professional doctrines. At any rate, both Theophrastus and Pliny, though with different evaluations, pass along popular beliefs that the constitution, even the "religious" state, of the human body affects whether or not a particular drug harms or helps the body.

Both folk and professional medicine, then, assumed the concept of the pharmakon as an ambiguous, dual-functioning agent; it could either kill you or cure you. Furthermore, they both held that the state of the person could determine the outcome. Professional medical opinion emphasized aspects of dosage, timing, and the level of strength of the person taking the drug and advocated precautions like anointing with oil, drinking wine, or taking breaks while cutting particularly dangerous plants. More popular beliefs focused on purity issues and played on fears of divine, personal (even bestial!) agency in judging the person who used the drug without taking the proper precautions. It is this latter point of view, with its emphasis on divine punishment effected through disease and death, that provides the conceptual context for Paul's suggestion that some of the Corinthians are eating themselves to death.

Paul says that the person who eats the bread or drinks the cup of the Lord unworthily is liable for the body and blood of the Lord; that is, he or she is indictable for the death of Christ. Contrary to traditional sacramental interpretations of this passage, Paul is not concerned that the Corinthians are not exercising a proper attitude of piety toward the sacramental elements or that they are disputing a certain doctrinal position on the nature of the elements.[82] But, contrary to other Protestant interpretations, Paul's assertion that certain Corinthians are getting feeble or sick or dying is not merely a metaphorical statement about some spiritual malaise or a reference to judgment that is causally unconnected with the eating.[83] The overall context indicates that Paul is very much concerned about the Corinthians' bodily state. And what he means by eating and drinking unworthily is related to the body— in this case, the body of Christ. Paul focuses his argument on the fracturing of the church, the body of Christ. His solution to the problems surrounding the Lord's Supper is a social one: heal the fragmented body and restore unity. Thus, what Paul means by "unworthily" has to do with fracturing the body of Christ. Unworthiness consists in participation in the destruction of the integrity of Christ's body. The Strong at Corinth, by reinforcing social distinctions in the church, divide the church. They are quite literally, in Paul's view, "killing" Christ by tearing apart his body. They pervert the meal of unity, the "common meal," by making it an occasion for schism and difference. And in Paul's logic, one puts one's own body in a state of vulnerability to disease by dissecting the body of Christ. By opening Christ's body to schism, they open their own bodies to disease and death.

The multiple meanings of "body" throughout this passage are brought out by the initially confusing phrase "discerning the body" in 11:29. Much ink has been spilt over this phrase. Does *sōma* here point to (a) the eucharistic substances ("discerning the body" thereby meaning handling the elements properly and recognizing their true nature), (b) the body of Christ (meaning that one should fully recognize the Eucharist as a memorial of the death of Christ), (c) the Church as the body of Christ ("discerning the body" thereby meaning understanding the significance of a united church and treating that social entity properly), or (d) the body of the Christian (either one's own body, about which care must be taken, or the body of one's Christian neighbor, which one must be careful not to offend or mistreat)? I want to take *sōma* in 11:29 as referring to all these things.

(a) *Sōma* undoubtedly evokes the bread as a eucharistic element. Rehearsing the traditional eucharistic words that he had apparently already passed on to the Corinthians (11:23), Paul says, "and giving thanks, he broke [the bread] and said, 'This is my body for you'" (11:24). In 11:27 he uses a parallel construction in which "the bread or the cup of the Lord" is juxtaposed with "the body and blood of the Lord." The Corinthians at this point might even recall Paul's earlier language in 5:6–7 in which unleavened bread and a lump of dough were equated with the body of Christ. When Paul's converts heard the statement about "discerning the body" in 11:29, therefore, they could scarcely have excluded the bread of the Eucharist as a referent.

(b) When Paul says that those who eat unworthily are "liable" (*enochos*) for the body and blood of the Lord, the term would evoke legal images: being liable for Christ's body means being indictable for his death. "Discerning the body," therefore, reminds the hearer of the crucified body of Christ.

(c) Throughout 1 Corinthians, the church is equated with Christ's body. Moreover, the argument of 1 Corinthians 11:17–34, as has been repeatedly demonstrated in recent literature, centers on the unity of the church. Since "not discerning the body" is the primary problem in this section, it must relate to the unity of Christ's body, the church.

(d) It also refers, however, to the body of the Christian. It is not hard to see how it refers to the body of one's fellow Christian. Paul is, after all, complaining about the mistreatment of the poorer Christians by the richer Christians. The higher-status members of the church eat their fill while the lower-status members go hungry and are humiliated. "Discerning the body," therefore, certainly has something to do with paying attention to the bodily needs of other Christians. I want to argue, however, that the phrase also refers to one's own body; that "discerning the body" means giving proper attention to one's own body so as to keep it from the judgment of disease and possibly even death.

There is a little recognized parallel construction in verses 29 and 31, which forms an ABBA chiastic structure:

verse 29   A: *The one who eats and drinks judgment* (krima) *in (against) himself*

B: *eats and drinks not discerning* (diakrinō) *the body.*

> *verse 31   B: If we discerned* (diakrinō) *ourselves*
>
> *A: we would not be judged* (krinō).

In verse 31, the way to avoid judgment (*krinō*) by the Lord is to "discern" (*diakrinō*) oneself. In verse 29, the way to avoid judgment (*krima*) is to "discern the body" (*diakrinō to sōma*). The parallel construction suggests the possibility that "discerning the body" means taking proper account of one's own bodily state, realizing one's contingent status as a member of the larger body of Christ, and recognizing one's vulnerability to dissolution and destruction. As we know from other references to judgment in Paul, destruction was sometimes pictured as a sudden apocalyptic event. According to 1 Corinthians 11:17–34, however, it could also manifest itself as the slow dissolution of the body experienced in disease and death.

As we have already seen in Chapter 2, philosophers and rhetoricians portrayed discord within the social body as disease. In most of those contexts the rhetorical commonplace served to prop up the conservative ideology of benevolent patriarchalism. Ironically, Paul, who has for the most part in 1 Corinthians opposed the ideology of benevolent patriarchalism and who even here in 11:17–34 is attacking the conservative behavior of the richer Christians, plays with the topos linking disharmony with disease. But what for the philosophers and the rhetoricians was a political metaphor is for Paul a physiological fact: discord causes disease.

The philosophers and rhetoricians would have been uncomfortable with Paul's realism. That is to say, they would have seen it as superstitious to use their political metaphor as an etiology for actual bodily disease, especially since Paul here links the causation of disease so closely to "judgment" by the divine. Yet Paul has not altogether traded in his normal invasion etiology for an imbalance etiology. By portraying the consumed body of Christ as a pharmakon that brings disease and death to the one who eats it unworthily, Paul bizarrely makes the body of Christ the invading agent of disease.[84] The logic of invasion is still at work: one eats one's sickness. But ironically the thing that should be the most "inside," the body of Christ, is made into the external agent of infection and disease due to the perverted state of the schismatic Christian's body. By promoting the dissolution of Christ's body (the church), the Strong at Corinth render their own bodies vulnerable to the pharmakon of Christ's body (the bread). Their schismatic actions alienate them from the true body of Christ by tearing apart that body. The body of Christ that they consume is now an alien agent that brings disease and death rather than health and salvation to their own bodies. By eating the Eucharist while destroying the body of Christ, they make the inner outer and the outer inner. And they consume their own condemnation.

In the first half of the book, I argued that Paul's position differs from that of the Strong in that he challenges the conservative hierarchical ideology that they take as "natural." Paul repeatedly questions the givenness of hierarchy and calls on the higher-status Christians to become weak, to give up their superior positions, to accept the status-disrupting consequences of loyalty to a crucified Messiah.

In this chapter I have argued that Paul also differs from the Strong in that his concept of the body includes anxieties about pollution. Whether addressing issues of sex with outsiders or eating food sacrificed to idols, Paul's rhetoric reveals concerns about firm corporal and social boundaries, fears of pollution, and assumptions that disease is caused by the invasion of the body by hostile, daimonic agents. Even in his remarks about the Eucharist, which utilize the classical notion that disease arises from discord and disruption of the body, Paul makes the ingested body of Christ resemble under certain circumstances a hostile, polluting, invading agent that can cause disease. These differences between Paul and the Strong are to be expected, however, if they are working with essentially conflicting ideologies of the body—ideologies that are linked, I would argue, to different social positions in the Greco-Roman world.

8 *The Dangers of Desire*

As the first part of this book has shown, Paul's rhetorical strategy of status reversal repeats itself throughout 1 Corinthians: Paul urges the Strong to yield to the Weak in his treatment of idol-meat and the Lord's Supper; he lowers the status of speaking in tongues and raises the status of common discourse; he spurns the exalted "wisdom of this world" in order to exalt the despised wisdom of God manifested in the cross of Christ. Moreover, in 1 Corinthians 7:22–23, as I have argued elsewhere, Paul applies much the same strategy in addressing slaves and free people within the church.[1] By insisting that the Christian slave is "really" a freed person of Christ and that the free man is "really" a slave of Christ, Paul reverses the normal hierarchy, assigning to Christian slaves higher status "in Christ" than even their free owners. By this point in my discussion, Paul's rhetoric of status reversal should not surprise the reader: it has been at work throughout the letter and is clearly a primary goal of his message to the Corinthians.

Yet Paul does surprise us after all; for he suddenly drops his strategy of status reversal when dealing with one group within the Corinthian church: women. One would expect that Paul's theology of the weak and strong would lead him to undermine, at least theoretically, the male–female hierarchy that was so important for the maintenance of Greco-Roman patriarchal society. As the discussion of body hierarchy has shown, both individual and societal bodies were assumed to be structured so as to maintain the hierarchy of male over female, masculine matter over feminine matter, men over women. If my analysis of Paul's theology in 1 Corinthians is correct, we should expect him to attempt just such a reversal with regard to the roles of women in early Christianity.

Much recent interpretation portrays Paul as egalitarian with regard to gender. But in fact, his writings confirm the Greco-Roman gender hierarchy. It is true that Paul assigns women a larger role and more respect in his churches and in his theology than they would have enjoyed in many other areas of Greco-Roman society. He believes, at least eschatologically and ideally, that in Christ there is no male and female (Gal. 3:28). Women occupy leadership roles in his churches; he calls one woman a deacon and another an apostle (Rom. 16:1, 7). In 1 Corinthians 7:4 Paul allows wives the same authority and power over the bodies of their husbands as their husbands hold over them. And, in spite of 1 Corinthians 14:34–35, Paul has no desire to silence women in the church or keep them from praying and prophesying publicly.[2] Yet he never makes the claim that the female is equal to, much less superior to, the male; he never attempts to accomplish for women the kind of ideological undermining of hierarchy that he has assayed with regard to socioeconomic status, educational privilege, or freedom and slavery. In these other instances I have argued that Paul, while allowing the social structure of hierarchy to stand, undermines its ideological supports. In the case of women, on the other hand, Paul bases several of his arguments, as this and the following chapter will show, on an assumption of a strong–weak hierarchy that must not be undermined.

The reason for Paul's inconsistency, I will argue, is the physiology of gender dominant in Greco-Roman society, which is taken over by Paul as an unquestionable given. Paul does not seem to think that a slave's body is a different kind of body from that of a free person, or a manual laborer's from that of a man of leisure, or that a Jew's is different from a Gentile's—hence his repeated arguments that circumcision does not make any difference. Yet Paul does not use the same arguments (or draw the same conclusions) when addressing issues concerned with women because he believes, unquestioningly, that women's bodies are different from men's bodies. The physiological differences between male and female mean that women (and, incidentally, feminized men) are at much greater risk from a variety of threats, of pollution, invasion, and corruption. A look at this physiology of gender will clarify why Paul mounts arguments in 1 Corinthians 7 and 11 that seem surprising given the rhetoric of status reversal evident elsewhere in the letter.

The Dangers of Sex

Christianity has sometimes been considered the originator of sexual asceticism, as playing the role of the oppressive mother superior to the gay and
sexually liberated pagan culture of Greece and Rome. Most recent works on
sexuality in the ancient world, however, have shown this to be an oversimpli-
fication, if not totally inaccurate.[3] As several scholars have pointed out, before
the inception of Christianity, sex was already seen as a problem. From several theoretical positions and for a variety of reasons, intellectuals urged either
severe controls on sexual activity or complete abstinence.

A rich source for the debate about sexual control can be found in the medical writers of the early Empire. In his *Gynecology*, written around the end of
the first century C.E., the physician Soranus rehearses the debate regarding
whether sex hurts or helps the body. Those maintaining the former say that
"desire" (*epithymia*) makes the body ill. Anyone can see, he says, that lovers are
always pale, weak, and thin.[4] Soranus furnishes evidence from animals proving
that the avoidance of desire and sex renders the body healthier, as shown by
the greater usefulness and health of neutered animals. The same empirical evidence is available for humans: "Since men who remain chaste are stronger and
bigger than the others and pass their lives in better health, correspondingly it
follows that for women too virginity in general is healthful."[5] Fair gentleman
that he is, Soranus presents the other side of the debate. Some scholars, he admits, claim that desire exists even if a person has had no sexual experience. As
I will explain more fully below, these medical writers taught that the craving
and passion of some virgins could be abated only by their submitting to sexual
intercourse.[6]

In spite of these differences in interpretation, all writers seem to agree that
sexual intercourse should be limited and controlled; complete abstinence may
harm most people but too much sex definitely harms anyone. This belief was
due in part to the common opinion about the vital (literally) importance of
sperm to both men and women.[7] In the first and second centuries C.E. most
theorists, and probably most people in general, believed that both male and
female bodies had testicles and that both men and women produced sperm.
Sperm or semen was concocted from other bodily fluids, mainly blood, due
to the heat of desire or friction.[8] The body's fluid becomes hot and foams, and
that foam is carried from all parts of the body to the genitals. Since sperm
is something like the boiled-out distillation of the most powerful part of the
bodily fluids, any loss of sperm constitutes a loss of power. As the Hippocratic *On Generation* puts it, "The sperm of the human male comes from all the

humour in the body; it consists of the most potent part of this fluid, which is secreted from the rest" (1. 1).[9] The author proceeds to explain that humans are thus weakened by the emission of sperm, even in very small amounts. Soranus, for example, says that both men and women may suffer from a "flux of semen," an illness in which their bodies discharge "seed without desire or erection," and that in such cases the body, as a result of even a small, involuntary discharge of sperm, "becomes pale, loses strength, and is consumed" (*Gynecology* 3. 12, trans. Temkin).

Part of the danger of sex, therefore, lay in the depletion of sperm, which, as a foamy concoction of blood (or other bodily fluids) and pneuma, was the most powerful material of the body. Another reason why the emission of sperm was dangerous, at least if indulged in immoderately, was that the discharge of sperm from the testicles caused those depleted organs to drain more of this precious fluid from other organs of the body, thus upsetting the delicate equilibrium of exploitation that normally existed in the body. Quoting Galen, Oribasius, a late antique compiler of medical opinions from previous centuries, explains the phenomenon in a passage rife with ideological significance:

> When, as a result of continual sexual excess, all the sperm has been lost, the testicles draw seminal liquid from the veins immediately above them. These veins contain only a small quantity of this condensed liquid; so when they are suddenly deprived of it by the testicles, which are stronger than they are, they in turn drain the veins above them and so on. This draining process does not stop until it has involved every part of the body, so if it is constantly repeated and if all the vessels and all the parts of the body are forced to give up their supplies until the strongest part is finally satisfied, the result will be that all the parts of the animal (of the living creature) are drained not just of seminal fluid but also of their vital spirit [*pneuma*], for this is taken from the arteries along with the seminal fluid. It is hardly surprising, therefore, that those who lead a debauched life become weak, since the purest part of both substances is removed from their body. As well as this, pleasure itself can dissolve vital tension to such an extent that people have died from an excess of pleasure. We should therefore not be surprised if those who indulge [im]moderately in the pleasures of love become weak.[10]

Sex reflects the economy of the body, with the weaker members in danger of being overly exploited by the stronger members. Oribasius's theory assumes, it should be noted, that some exploitation will take place naturally, but it must be moderated so that the weaker members are not totally dissipated. Although ejaculation entails a precarious loss of pneuma, the vital spirit of the body, the balance of the body may be maintained by control of both emission of sperm and experience of passion.

Rufus (late first to early second century) and Galen (second century) were among the physicians who believed that moderate sexual activity, carefully controlled, would not harm the normal body. Indeed, they cautioned against refraining from all sexual intercourse too suddenly and without proper training. It must be remembered that our word "asceticism" is derived from the Greek *askesis*, which referred to all sorts of self-control and regimens but particularly recalled the exercise and training undergone by athletes. In the view of doctors, every free man (and woman by extension, since the female was understood as an imperfect male) was an athlete whose good health could be assured only by observing a professionally planned regimen of diet, proper rest, exercise, bathing, and massage. Although control of sperm and desire was an important element in the regimen, a too sudden continence could be as harmful as over-exertion in weight lifting or introducing a youth too quickly to his first cold bath.[11]

Galen notes that certain people may succumb to illness due to the avoidance of sex and that "retention of semen" does great harm to the body, especially "in persons who have an abundance of poorly conditioned humors, who lead a lazy life, and who initially had indulged quite frequently in sexual relations but suddenly stopped their previous habit." Galen believes that "all people of this type must ejaculate their abundant semen." He cites a case in which a widower, grieving for his wife, avoided sex though he had previously indulged regularly. The man became nauseated, vomited frequently, and became melancholic for no apparent reason. As soon as he resumed sexual activity, the symptoms subsided, furnishing Galen with empirical proof that retention of sperm in a man unaccustomed to such self-control could be as harmful to him as retention of menses could be to a woman.[12] If the accustomed economy of the body is to be altered, it must be done gradually, with training and control. According to these doctors, therefore, the untrained and inexperienced should not attempt continence too quickly. The doctors, however, could prescribe regimens that would reduce desire and sperm by drying and cooling the body while at the same time maintaining the proper strength of sperm necessary for energetic living.[13]

The same concern with control that preoccupied medical writers also occurs in moral-philosophical notions about sex. There are indications that even as far back as the Pythagoreans some philosophers advocated abstinence from sex, at least at certain seasons. If Pythagoras taught his disciples sexual continence, this was probably connected with issues of ritual purity related to the Pythagorean concern with cultic practices. Tradition held that Epicurus had discouraged marriage, substituting the philosophical community of the Garden for traditional family and social structures.[14]

In the first century, Cynic traditions and influences were very much alive, some of which counseled the avoidance of marriage. Antisthenes supposedly held marriage in low esteem. Diogenes rejected marriage and family as burdens that would distract the Cynic from the free pursuit of virtue, and a pseudepigraphic letter that may date from or just before the first century c.e. has Diogenes argue against marriage.[15] Yet Cynics were famous for avoiding not sex itself but just the social conventions surrounding it. Indeed, they were reputed to be sexually promiscuous, copulating in public (the "doggey" way) and openly masturbating when there was no other relief in sight.[16] Cynicism, however, was far from a monolithic or even a philosophical system; it is possible that some Cynics taught that complete mastery over the body (one of their constant themes) necessitated mastery over one's sexual desires, a control that might manifest itself in sexual continence—not for the sake of some abstract moral principle in itself, of course, but to demonstrate and exercise the complete freedom from desire that should characterize the truly "free" man.

Epictetus's lecture on the ideal Cynic provides one instance of a "Stoicized" version of the Cynic view of marriage.[17] Epictetus makes no claim to be a Cynic himself, but he gives a portrait of one that borrows heavily from traditional Cynic motifs. According to Epictetus, the true Cynic would consider marriage and children only if he lived in a city of people like himself, all wise men (*sophoi*); for then all his social contacts—his wife, father-in-law, everyone—would be like himself. But as it is, the Cynic, who is the only free, wise, noble, royal man, cannot afford such luxuries because he is on hostile terrain. He must be free from distraction (*aperispastos*), committed solely to the service of God (*diakonia tou theou*). Were he tied to the cares of normal social responsibilities, he would not be able to fulfil his special role as "messenger, scout, and herald of the gods" (3. 22. 67–70). According to Epictetus, the Cynic must be the loving father of all his fellow human beings, which precludes special attention to his own children. Marriage and family necessarily bring distraction (*perispasmos*), which would keep this true "king"—Epictetus's repeated designation for the wise man or true Cynic—from looking after the common good (*ta koina*, 3. 22. 72).

Throughout this discussion, Epictetus denies that the Cynic, the "servant of God," will marry and have children, but he does not explicitly condemn all sexual intercourse. Indeed, there were some Cynics, it seems, who disdained family life but thought nothing of sexual liaisons with prostitutes, boys, or whoever else might be available. Epictetus emphasizes even more than those Cynics the control over both desires and actions that the sophos is to demonstrate. He repeatedly castigates men who fall in love with "lovely girls" or "pretty little slave boys" (as at 4. 1. 15, 22, 143). He claims that the one seeking to become a Cynic must "utterly wipe out desire." The word for "desire" here, *orexis*, refers to all kinds of longings, including sexual longings (3. 22. 13). Just after this statement, Epictetus says, "No little girl will appear beautiful to you, no paltry fame, no boy, no dainty pastry" (3. 22. 13, my trans.). Although he does not explicitly promote abstinence, therefore, it appears that engaging in sex, for Epictetus, represents a lack of self-control. Indulgence, though not a major error, shows weakness and puts the person in even greater danger of desire.

Such advice forms part of Epictetus's hierarchy of strength and weakness. The weak man or the man not divinely chosen should not attempt the strenuous life of a Cynic. Only some men can be leaders, like Agamemnon, or noble warriors, like Achilles. If a Thersites (traditionally the ugly, ignoble, lower-class fool) attempts such noble roles, he will simply disgrace himself (3. 22. 2–8). The true Cynic is superior to the common crowd, just as his will is far superior to his paltry body. In each case, it is only just that the strong be superior and rule over the weak (3. 22. 101). For Epictetus, desire and sex occupy a place on the hierarchical scale of strength and weakness. Those lower on the scale are expected to indulge and will not be particularly harmed thereby, though they will probably never attain complete freedom and virtue. Those higher on the scale will exercise more restraint, controlling their passions, but perhaps indulging moderately and with appropriate controls. But the man at the pinnacle of the hierarchy, the true Cynic, will forgo sexual activity entirely, thus demonstrating his complete self-mastery, his absolute freedom and virtue, the control of his body.

The devaluing of sexual intercourse by some medical writers and Epictetus was, of course, not the only attitude current in the first century. If we take into account others besides the upper classes, and perhaps even if we do not, it was probably no more than a minority opinion. Even Musonius Rufus, Epictetus's teacher, praised marriage and family.[18] But the arguments for continence were well enough known to infiltrate other social contexts besides those of medicine and moral philosophy. We know, for example, that athletes refrained from sex in order to retain their sperm and thereby their strength, even going so far as to weight their testicles down with cold metal while they slept to avoid the genital heat that led to nocturnal emissions.[19] Certainly throughout the literate culture of Greco-Roman society, and doubtless among other social strata to some extent as well, sex was taken to be an arena of the battle between strength and weakness. Sex had to be controlled and manipulated, if not completely avoided, if someone was to maintain a strong, healthy body, free from disease, dissipation, and weakness.

The Asceticism of the Strong

It is commonly agreed among scholars that 1 Corinthians 7:1, "It is good for a man not to touch a woman," is another of the slogans of the Strong quoted by Paul, probably from their letter to him.[20] But it is not immediately clear why these Corinthians advocate abstinence from sex. What kind of theoretical or ideological position on their part would explain this ascetic element? For long enough, as I noted in Chapter 3, the tendency among scholars was to read back into the Corinthian situation a kind of Gnosticism known to us only from texts of the second through fourth centuries, with its deprecation of the body, matter, and thus desires, passions, and the needs of the body. In an age before the advent of reliable methods of birth control, moreover, any hetero-sexual intercourse might result in conception, and why would good Gnostics ally themselves with the ignoble, lower powers in the propagation of the fallen human species, bringing more and more lost souls into this present darkness? As much as this Gnostic reconstruction makes sense of certain aspects of the Corinthian situation, there are too many problems with reading later forms of Gnosticism back into the time Paul was writing, as I have already indicated.

Other scholars use the hypothesis of overly realized eschatology to explain Corinthian asceticism. Since these Christians believe, according to this re-construction, that they have already experienced a spiritual resurrection, they have therefore already overcome the male–female division in a spiritual an-drogyne. If "in Christ there is no male and female" (Gal. 3:28), there is no longer any need for enslavement to sexual desire, and any concession to desire would constitute a lapse back into materiality and the bondage of the spirit that characterized their pre-Christian existence.[21] The problem with this ex-planation, as I have pointed out in previous chapters, is that there is no direct evidence that realized eschatology is a *cause* of the beliefs held by the Strong at Corinth. Their primary objection to Paul's doctrine of resurrection is not that the body has *already* been raised but that a resurrected *body* is not necessary—indeed, not acceptable—at all. It is true that several aspects of a realized eschatology would have been readily welcomed by the Strong—emphasis on a present spiritual state of being, possession of heavenly wisdom, the ability to speak angelic languages, the consequences of eschatological androgyny—but only because those beliefs were amenable to a belief structure whose roots lay elsewhere. Otherwise, one must assume that these Corinthian Christians took over Paul's certainly apocalyptic gospel and rather imaginatively and quickly transformed it into a present experience.

Does Judaism provide any assistance in understanding the sexual renunciation apparently advocated by some Corinthian Christians? David Balch has demonstrated the existence of precursors to Corinthian asceticism in Judaism, represented particularly by Philo.[22] Philo presents Noah, for example, as a man who conquered his "lower passions" and Moses as the divine man *par excellence* who completely controls his body, maintaining his purity in soul and body by avoiding "passions."[23] Indeed, as Balch points out, Moses was required to avoid sexual intercourse in order to be ready "to receive the oracular messages." Noting that 2 Corinthians 3 provides evidence that Moses was an important figure in the theology of the Corinthians, Balch concludes, "Since the interpretation of Exodus xxxiv which appears in this passage [from Philo] was a central part of the Corinthians' theology, I suggest that the ascetic ideas which also appear here were also a part of their practice." Like Moses, the Corinthian Christian avoids sex as training "for revelations from or a vision of God, or in still other words, to become a 'perfect,' 'wise,' 'strong' 'prophet.' "[24]

Balch's reconstruction has much to be said for it, especially as an example of the way Judaism in the Roman period partook of ascetic tendencies that were gaining strength throughout the Empire, at least among those of a certain social and educational level.[25] As a proposal regarding the theoretical underpinning of the Corinthians' own position, however, it founders on an important issue: the connection between food and sex. In the texts Balch cites from Philo, Moses' self-control and cleanliness are attributed to both factors: "purifying himself from all the calls of mortal nature, food and drink and intercourse with women."[26] The Strong at Corinth, on the other hand, are not in the least concerned about pollution from food, or even about eating in the temple of an idol or, possibly, participating in some Greek or Roman cult.[27] It is difficult to imagine Philo approving of the kind of disregard concerning idol-meat that characterizes the position of the Strong. Admittedly, those at Corinth who opposed sexual intercourse may represent a different group from those who advocated liberty regarding diet; but, given the way Paul deals with their slogans, it is more likely that the same group is being addressed. We must seek some theoretical context for the position of the Strong that will take into account both their sexual asceticism and their dietary freedom.

I propose that there is no need to seek a particularly Jewish source for the asceticism of the Strong. They, like an increasing number of higher-class, educated people of their time, assume that sex is a dangerous site of possible disruption; it must be controlled and if possible avoided in order to maintain the proper strength and hierarchy of the body. Diet, of course, is also very important for the medical writers. Regimens are carefully constructed and advocated for food as for sex, and moral philosophers stress the importance of control over eating so as to maintain the proper bodily hierarchy and virtue. The Strong may well have believed that one should eat certain kinds of foods rather than others, avoid liquids that were too cold or too hot for the season or for one's bodily constitution, or combine a rigid schedule of eating with a regimen of emetics and enemas; but their concerns about diet would have had little in common with Paul's.[28] They entertained no fears about pollution from eating meat offered to idols or from associating with others who do so. The source of the asceticism of the Strong is therefore probably not Philo or Jewish theology, but a more general upper-class, Greco-Roman ideology of the body.[29]

Furthermore, in order to make sense of the Corinthian situation, one must explain how the Corinthians could seem so unconcerned (at least judging from Paul's accusations) about the sexual activity described in 1 Corinthians 5 and 6 and yet be advocates of sexual asceticism in 1 Corinthians 7. Here again, it may be that Paul is addressing two unrelated groups in Corinth, one libertine, the other ascetic.[30] But his rhetorical tone is consistent throughout, portraying his interlocutors as people who take pride in their high status but who ought to be humbled: "And you are puffed up!" (5:2); "Your boasting is not good" (5:6). Furthermore, in 6:12–20 the slogans quoted by Paul are the same as those used by the Strong in 10:23, and the position of disdain for the deeds of the body is consistent throughout. It is reasonable, therefore, to assume that both 7:1 ("Now concerning what you wrote") and 8:1 ("Now concerning idol-food") address issues raised by a single group at Corinth. Although the Corinthians' letter did not itself raise the issue of sexual immorality addressed by Paul in chapter 6, Paul there uses the same slogans and attacks the same theoretical position as is reflected in 1 Corinthians 8–10, indicating that 6:12–20, in which Paul's supposed interlocutors defend their lack of concern about certain sexual activities, contains a believable representation of the position held by the group that is reflected in the letter quoted in 7:1 and 8:1. That group is the Strong.

How, then, can these people look to asceticism as an ideal while simultaneously showing little concern for the sexual conduct of members of their community? Given the hierarchy of strength and its relation to sexual continence as portrayed by the medical writers and Epictetus, it would be understandable if the Strong were to value sexual abstinence for themselves while at the same time showing little anxiety about the sexual misdemeanors of "weaker" persons at Corinth. The Strong value sexual asceticism not out of some fear of pollution from the body of a prostitute or one's spouse but because of a concern for the continued strength, and therefore health, of the body when it is properly controlled and its hierarchy maintained. Thus, they have no fear of pollution entering the communal body through the genitals of a wayward Christian brother. Continence is, naturally, an ideal for all; but it is recognized that the further down one goes in the human hierarchy, the less likely it is that one will find strength, control, and therefore complete sexual continence. The weaker must be given an example of strength, but their sexual activity simply demonstrates their lower status and weakness; in itself it constitutes no threat to the Strong—according to the view of the Strong, that is.

It is important to realize that the position of the Strong cannot be simplistically characterized as individualistic, as opposed to Paul's concerns for the whole community.[31] Epictetus, who appears individualistic to many modern readers, advocates celibacy for his ideal Cynic not merely out of a concern for private benefit but for the sake of the common good, *ta koina* (*Discourse* 3. 22. 72). In the same way, the Strong may have viewed their own abstinence as the appropriate exercise of strength necessary for their continued leadership of the whole body. Their own sexual control would be a result, as well as a badge, of their higher status and spirituality, a status that those lower down should aspire to. Moreover, their theology and example should teach the weaker members of the church first to recognize the relative unimportance of the body and then to bring the body into submission to the higher elements of the self, the spiritual and mental elements. Thus the difference between Paul and the Strong is not a matter of individualism but of different constructions of the body— in particular, how they conceive the susceptibility of that body to pollution. Unlike Paul, the Strong do not believe that the social body as a whole will be polluted by the sexual peccadilloes of its weaker members.

The Asceticism of Paul

Since the inception of Protestantism, there has been a broad, concerted attempt to package Paul as a promoter of sex and marriage, in spite of (and in reaction to) most of Christian history, which has taken Paul to be an advocate of sexual asceticism, allowing marriage only for those too weak for celibacy. Particularly in recent times, biblical scholars (most of them Protestant, male, and married) have argued that Paul does not advocate celibacy in 1 Corinthians 7 but rather endorses the goodness of human sexuality, at least within the confines of the marriage bed. Reflecting contemporary sexual ideology derived mainly from modern psychology and psychotherapy (including acceptance of the modern category of "sexuality"), many biblical scholars go so far as to rejoice that "Paul has a robust sense of the fittingness of sexuality in the Christian life."[32] There have also been voices on the other side, claiming that Paul's view of sex is "pathological" or a "morbid aberration."[33]

Both positions are incorrect. As to the first, nowhere in Paul's genuine letters does he unreservedly endorse marriage or family. Particularly in 1 Corinthians 7, Paul's statements repeatedly reveal that he advocates celibacy while allowing marriage only as a necessary option for the weak. In 7:2 Paul grants that, though the Strong are correct in principle, that "it is noble for a man not to touch a woman," marriage is sometimes necessary "because of the fornications (*porneiai*)."[34] Of those already married, Paul says that they owe one another a "duty" or "debt" (*opheilē*) of sexual accessibility (7:3; this "debt," of course, need never be paid if both partners exercised adequate self-control and never demanded payment from the other). Thus, in 7:5 Paul advises married couples to avoid forced and prolonged abstinence "in order that Satan may not test you because of your lack of control" (*akrasia*). None of these instructions says anything about human sexuality being good or about realizing one's divinely ordained sexuality or living up to some human psychological potential as a "sexual being." Rather, in 7:2 marriage is merely a prophylaxis against *porneia*; in 7:3 it is a duty or debt owed by spouses to one another; and in 7:5 it is a prophylaxis against Satanic testing.

Some scholars have interpreted 7:6 ("This I say by way of concession, not command") to mean that Paul here concedes (rather than commands) moments of abstinence; that is, Paul, though preferring that married couples be sexually active, is willing to concede to the ascetics periods of abstinence for purposes of prayer.[35] But the next verse reveals Paul's commitment to abstinence as the highest goal: "I want all persons to be as I myself am" (7:7). Those who are unattached he urges to remain as he is—that is, celibate. It is more likely, therefore, and more in keeping with his general statements on the subject in verses 7 and 8, that in verse 6 Paul is conceding not abstinence but indulgence in sex at all. In 7:6 he makes it clear that he is not *commanding* married persons to have sex but only *allowing* them to do so if they are weak. Paul would prefer that they all be like him, continent (cf. 7:8), but he concedes that some Christians are unable to be so due to a lack of self-control (*akrasia*, 7:5). In 7:8–9 he counsels celibacy "to the unmarried and widows"[36] unless they are "out of control" (note the present tense of *egkrateuontai*). Therefore, when Paul says that "it is better to marry than to burn," one understands that there is another option that is better than both: continence (see also 7:39–40, where Paul insists that the widow will be better off remaining single; more on the question of "burning" below). True, Paul calls the ability to control oneself sexually a charisma, a "gift" (7:7); but the issue of control and a hierarchy of strong and weak constitute the frame in which possession of this gift is understood. Indeed, in verses 6–9 we see Paul using the same strategy as elsewhere in 1 Corinthians: he claims for himself the position of greater strength then notes that he is willing to be more flexible for the sake of weaker members. The construction assumes that celibacy is the practice of higher status and greater strength.

In 7:28–35 Paul uses the argument for celibacy that we have already noted in Epictetus's speech on the ideal Cynic.[37] Married persons have "affliction in the flesh," and Paul would spare them that by urging them to remain unmarried. Verses 29–35 unpack and explain Paul's statement in verse 28. He urges celibacy not in order to "cast a snare" for people or "enmesh them in bonds" (possible translations of *brochon epibalein*) but for their "benefit" (*sympheros*). Celibacy allows the Christian to be completely devoted to the Lord (note the parallel with Epictetus's notion that the unmarried Cynic is the only one who will be completely devoted to the "service of God"). Paul goes to some lengths to explain why marriage—not celibacy—is the restrictive lifestyle. To be sure, his argument seems counter-intuitive to many people today, convinced as we are that renunciation of all sexual activity is the heaviest of burdens. Its presence here, however, indicates that, whereas *some* people at Corinth were advocating continence, *others* (like most people today) needed some explanation for Paul's denigration of marriage and sex.

In 7:36–37 Paul ends his discussion of "virgins" (which will be discussed more fully below) by setting up an axiological hierarchy in parallel constructions.

Verse 36   A: The one who, due to compulsion, marries his virgin

            B: does not sin.

Verse 37   A: The one who, due to self-control, does not marry

            B: does well.

"Doing well," of course, is preferable to "not sinning." In verse 38 the same hierarchy occurs, but with different words:

        A: The one who marries

        B: does well (kalōs).

        A: The one who does not marry

        B: does better (kreisson).

Paul's hierarchy of virtue could not be clearer. Since he had just said that the celibate man did "well" (*kalōs*) in verse 37, his statement in verse 38 that the man who marries his virgin does "well" could have been taken as implying no difference between the virtue of the one as compared with the other. Paul therefore revises what he has just said, now insisting that the celibate man does not simply "do well" but does "better" (*kreisson*). The words are clear status terms in Greek culture, *kalōs* describing the noble, aristocratic, beautiful man. Paul's rhetoric carefully manipulates the status implications of the terms. No equality of status is allowed to slip in as a result of Paul's initial imprecision of language.

As all Paul's arguments show, modern Protestant attempts to enlist Paul as an advocate of marriage, family, and heterosexual intercourse entail, from a historical point of view, ideological misconstruals. Even more misleading are claims that Paul supports a healthy view of human sexuality. As recent theorists of the history of sexuality have argued, the category itself—whether one is speaking of homosexuality, heterosexuality, or human sexuality in general—is a modern one, heavily indebted to psychology, psychotherapy, and the medicalization of the self so important to modern culture, especially since the nineteenth century.[38] Paul does not speak of sexuality but of sexual actions and desires. And whenever the subject arises, Paul treats sex as potentially dangerous. If it cannot be completely avoided, it must be carefully controlled and regulated so as to avoid pollution and cosmic invasion. On the other hand, modern pronouncements of Paul's "pathological" abhorrence of sex or his "morbid" compulsion to asceticism are also misleading and anachronistic, since they introduce the modern view that any strong opposition to sex must be a symptom of mental illness. We cannot expect someone of the first century to think about sex in the categories of psychological health and illness that frame practically every discussion of the subject today. Instead of declaring Paul to have been in healthy support or pathological denial of human sexuality, we must look at how sex and desire functioned in his economy of the body. This does not entail a demedicalization of desire for Paul; for, as we have already seen, sex and desire were heavily medicalized in Greco-Roman culture. But it is the role of sex in those *ancient* discourses of control rather than in *modern* ones that needs to be analyzed.

Porneia as Pollution and the Dangers of Desire

We have already seen that Paul's anxieties about porneia in 1 Corinthians 5 and 6 are linked to concerns about the boundaries of the body (see 5:1; 6:13, 18). In both those case, Paul is worried that the integrity of the body—both the individual Christian's body and the body of Christ—will be compromised by the breach in the wall occasioned by dangerous sexual intercourse. The mention of porneia again in 1 Corinthians 7:2 reveals that Paul is not introducing a completely new subject in this chapter. All these issues—the man sleeping with his stepmother, men visiting prostitutes, and desire—fall under the heading of porneia and pollution. For Paul, then, marriage in the church serves as a mechanism for protecting the boundaries of the church's body from external contamination through sex with those outside.

A careful analysis of 1 Corinthians 7, however, reveals that Paul is concerned more about desire than about sexual intercourse itself. An important clue occurs in his statement that it is "better to marry than to burn" (7:9). Whereas some interpreters have taken Paul's "burn" to refer to eschatological judgment, the great majority rightly understand it to refer to passion and desire.[39] This certainly fits the context better, since throughout chapter 7 Paul is concerned with the compulsion and control of desire (see 7:2, 5, 9, 36). Moreover, regardless of Paul's intention at the time of writing, given the usual way of speaking of sexual desire as "burning" in Greco-Roman culture, it is hard to imagine any Greek speaker taking Paul's use of the term in any other way. It was part of the common sense of Greco-Roman culture that desire constituted an internal burning, the smoldering of the inner body's fire. Thus a lover in Alciphron's *Letters of Courtesans* says, "I'm on fire for him" (*kaiomenēn ep' autō*, 4. 10. 5). Love spells found in the magical papyri repeatedly send desire into the body of the beloved as a burning in the "guts, breast, liver, breath, bones, and marrow." The disease-daimon of desire is called "Flesh-eater" and "Inflamer of the heart."[40] Since desire was fire, intercourse led, by sensible consequence, to a heating of the body. For the medical writers this could be health-enhancing, the Hippocratic writer noting that intercourse "warms" the blood of a woman and thus makes it more fluid and easier to evacuate in menstruation.[41] But in most cases the fire of desire was portrayed as a danger and a disease.

Although the disease of desire could occur in moral-philosophical writings in ways that initially appear to be metaphorical, in all sorts of texts it was continually portrayed as frankly physiological.[42] Plato provides such an explanation: "The truth is that sexual incontinence [*hē peri ta aphrodisia akolasia*] is generally a mental disease caused by a single substance (the marrow) which overflows and floods the body because of the porousness of the bones" (*Timaeus* 86D). Archilochus speaks of desire as breaking one's limbs, taking away one's breath, causing pain, and piercing the bones. Sappho lists the symptoms: a melting heart, aphasia, fire burning under the skin, misty eyes, ringing ears, sweating, shuddering, turning green, and feeling like dying.[43] A lovesick woman in Theocritus's poem "The Spell" complains about the disease of love that clings to her, sapping the blood from her flesh; it is a "parching fever" that put her to bed for ten days and nights; she seeks relief(!) by sending an attack of "burning," a "fire-spell" upon her neglectful ex-lover (2. 55, 85, 160–64; see also 2. 40).[44] As Ruth Padel writes, "Disease is a staple Greek image for erotic obsession, and it pulls into erotic discourse resonances of battle and pollution. Illness in the Greek thought-world is inseparable from passion or pollution. Together they make an interlocking set of dangerous intrusions on life and self."[45]

In ancient sources it is more than as metaphor that desire is disease, as is proved by the medical writers' concern to control and contain the disease of desire. In order to keep young virgins from suffering from the passion (that is, sickness) of desire, and thus hastening too quickly into marriage even before puberty, Rufus advises that they not be allowed to drink wine because of the "burning nature" that is within them.[46] Soranus passes on the common medical opinion that the "body is made ill by desire," with which he agrees, though he believes that other doctors are wrong to prescribe early sexual intercourse (before puberty for girls) as a cure. The burning of desire, according to some theorists, may even exceed the amount of heat required for impregnation; the "darkening" and "change" caused by excessive passion may burn up the deposited seed entirely.[47] From Galen's point of view, desire is disease because it causes radical changes: passions and desires alter the body, and diseases of the body alter the mind; and change in Galen's system of healthy stability and balance is the very definition of disease.[48] These varied texts demonstrate the pervasive notion, among educated and uneducated alike, that desire is a potentially dangerous burning that threatens the body with disease.

Recognizing that Paul's reference to burning is a reference to sexual desire, however, introduces fresh problems. Although the notion is completely counter-intuitive to us today, Paul seems to be suggesting that marriage functions not as a legitimate avenue for the expression of desire but as what will preclude it altogether. Paul does not say that persons should marry so that they will burn only moderately (as if it were acceptable for them to "simmer"). He presents a clear either/or: marriage is the prophylaxis against "burning"; that is, marriage guards against the experience of desire. Can this be possible? Can Paul have conceived of sexual intercourse as void of passion and desire?

The medical writers would have found such a position incomprehensible. The heat of passion was physiologically necessary for the concoction of sperm from blood or humors. The compulsion to have sex sprang from the internal combustion accompanying the burning of desire. Furthermore, a proper level of burning was necessary for impregnation, that all-important goal of the male doctors who wrote the medical treatises and the male heads of households who read them.[49] Of course, one must be careful to choose a daughter-in-law with the proper level of body heat; if she is too hot, which a careful observer can tell from her coloration and similar bodily signs, her body will burn up the sperm after it is deposited in her womb and before it has had time to gestate.[50] The medical writers recognized, that is, that desire posed many dangers to the body, especially to weak bodies, and that too much desire could lead to all sorts of illnesses. But, in spite of these dangers, doctors were concerned to *control* the fire of desire, not quench it. The exclusion of such burning would condemn their upper-class households to infertility.

But Paul, it must be remembered—especially in light of a long Christian tradition insisting that the purpose of sex is procreation—never shows any concern about fertility or the "propagation of the race," at least not by means of childbirth. As far as we can tell, he is not concerned in the least with the fertility of his flock. And why should he be? With the time being so short, why would anyone want to bring children into this "present distress" (7:26)? Since Paul, unlike most Christian teachers after him, does not believe that the goal of sex is procreation, an objection by those more educated in the science of his day that some burning was necessary for procreation would carry no weight with him.

As I have noted, the ideal of sex without desire is inconceivable to most people today. But before we dismiss the concept too quickly, we should recognize that certain Church Fathers, closer to Paul's world than we are, viewed it as admittedly rare but possible, especially for those of superior virtue and strength. Clement of Alexandria argued that desire itself, not merely illicit sexual intercourse, was evil. Christians, he said, should have sex with their wives only for the sake of having children and not as an outlet for desire: "The man who marries for child-bearing purposes must exercise self-control so as to have no desire (*epithymia*) even for his own wife, whom he ought rather to love (*agapan*), producing children with an honorable and controlled will."[51] The divorce here between love and desire sounds odd to modern readers, convinced that sex (properly oriented and controlled) is an expression of love, but for Clement's ethic of virtue, strength, and control, the separation of the two is indispensable. As he says, "Our ideal is not to experience desire at all."[52] Thus intercourse with a pregnant wife is condemned, since it is clear in such a case that the motive is pleasure rather than procreation. Ambrose, using the regular topos that animals furnish clues about virtue "according to nature," says that human beings should learn from animals, who indulge in sex out of an impulse for generation, not a desire for sex, and Jerome expresses similar sentiments.[53] Augustine, as is well known, taught that the prelapsarian Adam and Eve had been capable of sexual intercourse without desire. He believed that this is impossible now, given the radically fallen state of all human will. But it must be remembered that Augustine's doctrine of the corruption of the will was new and unusual; other Christians of his time and before had not given up on the possibility that the Christianized will could master—and exclude—desire, even within sexual intercourse.[54]

Though Paul is in a very different philosophical environment from these Church Fathers, he too believes that sexual intercourse without desire is possible in marriage. Modern persons, to whom sex without desire seems bizarre and certainly anything but preferable, read Paul's comments about burning in 1 Corinthians 7 to condemn not sexual desire in general but only uncontrolled or illicit desire. But this is based on the mistaken notion that Paul must have had in mind different *kinds* of desire. Paul does not disdain, on this modern reading, good ("healthy") desire properly oriented and channeled. A careful study of what Paul actually says about desire and passion (*epithymia, pathos*), however, shows that he never refers to sexual desire in anything but negative terms. (He does sometimes use the term *epithymia* in a neutral or positive sense, but never when speaking of sexual desire.) Indeed, the other place in the letters known to be by Paul that explicitly addresses the issue is 1 Thessalonians 4:3: "For this is the will of God, your holiness, that you abstain from porneia, that each of you know how to possess (or hold, maintain) his own vessel, in holiness and honor, not in the passion of desire as do the Gentiles who do not know God." Desire and passion are the characteristic sins of the Gentile world "out there" and are linked to porneia and idolatry. Christians are to avoid desire completely, and to do so by marrying if necessary. Several of the concerns found in 1 Corinthians 7 thus also occur in 1 Thessalonians 4:3: the role of porneia as the polluting element that enters the church from the Gentile world, the function of marriage as a guard against porneia, the absence of any concern for procreation, and the assumption that sexual intercourse (for this is probably the meaning of the euphemistic Greek terms) within marriage is to be experienced without passion and desire ("not in the passion of desire, as do the Gentiles"). We must take Paul at his word and not attempt to make him say that he is opposing not desire but *inordinate* desire.

Perhaps this is another occasion on which our modern categories, indeed our language itself, simply fails us—by failing to bridge the categorical chasms of cultural difference. Although he rejected desire or passion as a proper motivation for sexual intercourse, Paul must have assumed that some kind of inclination or urge could arise without causing pollution. Why have sex at all if *nothing* like what we experience as desire is present? Maybe we need to invent or appropriate some other term to convey this necessary urge for sex without invoking Paul's rejected category of desire. Perhaps, that is, we might legitimately speak of a sexual "inclination" that is not taken in Paul's system to carry the same kind of polluting agency that Paul assumes for "desire." At any rate, I would insist that Paul's language is quite clear, even if it refers to something that remains for us almost incomprehensible. For Paul, sexual desire and passion are out of the question for Christians, something indulged in only by "Gentiles" outside the body of Christ, the people of Israel. Surprising as this may be from a modern point of view, the function of marriage for Paul is to quench desire.[55]

As I noted above, the medical writers would have found this position puzzling. In their view, desire is the impulse for sexual intercourse and a necessary component for conception. For most of them, sexual intercourse within marriage functions to domesticate passion, but it cannot—indeed, should not—eliminate it entirely.[56] Desire is to be controlled, not killed. Significantly, this point of view corresponds to the ideology of the body and the disease etiology of imbalance assumed by educated society. For that ideology, desire is a feature of the normal, natural body. Like all the various aspects of the body, it must be kept in balance with the other elements and forces; desire is dangerous and must be controlled, but it should not, and probably cannot, be eliminated entirely, any more than can cold or heat. The healthy body is a balanced ecosystem whose different factors must be kept in equilibrium. Thus the medical writers' solution to the dangers of desire is control combined with some sort of pressure valve that may be employed when desire gets dangerously intense.

Paul's solution to the problem of desire is quite different, precisely because it fits *his* ideology of the body and *his* etiology of disease as pollution and invasion. In Paul's ethical and cosmic dualism, desire, like any other disease, is pictured as a foreign, utterly hostile, polluting agent that threatens the body. And, like any other disease, it must be cast out of the body entirely. In Paul's conception, there can be no truce, no meeting the enemy half-way. Desire is the burning disease that threatens to corrupt the body from within; therefore it must be completely avoided.

For the most part, the Strong at Corinth share the body ideology of the medical writers. They probably also share the idea that desire is necessary for sexual intercourse. Therefore, Paul's instruction that persons unable to control themselves should get married—and even that they should have sex frequently (*palin epi to auto*, 7:5)!—would have been unacceptable to them. And with good reason. In their minds, submission of a person to sexual intercourse signifies that the person has already submitted to desire. Sex constitutes for them a yielding to desire, not a prophylaxis against it. Therefore, Paul's either/or, "It is better to marry than to burn," would have seemed uninformed and naive. The man who marries and indulges in frequent sexual intercourse, even with his wife, proves by that action that he already burns. His sexual activity is a consummation of the burning, not its avoidance. Paul's view is different, not because he is less convinced of the need for control and strength, nor because he is less an advocate of sexual asceticism; on those points Paul is in agreement with the Strong. His view differs in that he is concerned more about desire than about sex itself and therefore is willing to permit sexual intercourse under certain conditions in order to preclude desire. Furthermore, he is concerned about sex because it represents a dangerous channel for pollution, both to the individual body and the church's body.

Insider-Outsider Marriages

If Paul, as I have argued, is so concerned about avenues of pollution from the outside world into the church and if he believes that sexual intercourse between insiders and outsiders constitutes such an avenue, how can he allow marriages between Christians and non-Christians? We would expect Paul's rather mechanistic view of pollution to preclude sexual intercourse even between Christian and non-Christian mates. As 7:12–16 demonstrates, the question does arise, and the situation provokes a rather unusual (and to us today, somewhat inscrutable) logic of pollution and cleanliness on Paul's part. Paul recommends that the believing man not divorce his unbelieving wife and that the believing wife not divorce her unbelieving husband. But why? According to Paul's logic of pollution outlined in Chapter 6, we would expect him to think that the believing partner runs a risk of incurring pollution and thereby of polluting the entire body of Christ. Yet this is not the position we find him espousing.

Paul's answer reveals to an even greater extent his concerns about pollution and boundaries. He answers that the unbelieving partner is made holy "in" the believing partner (7:14). That is why their children, who would otherwise be "unclean" (*akatharta*), are now "holy" (*hagia*). In Greek, "holiness" language does not always function in opposition to "uncleanness" or pollution; but here it obviously does, as indicated by Paul's opposition of *hagia* and *akatharta* in verse 14 (*hagiotēs* is the solution to the problem of *akatharsia*). Paul extends the boundaries of purity to include even the unbelieving partner and the children in a marriage. Whereas we often think about contamination as resulting from proximity, Paul here allows that the opposite of contamination, cleansing, may also work by proximity. He insists that the purity of Christ holds such power that it may, in certain situations, purify even nonbelievers.[57] The Christian is purified by his or her location "in" Christ; by extension, the unbelieving spouse is purified by his or her location "in" the believing spouse. Paul's own logic forces him to this conclusion, so his very real fears of pollution do not necessitate the separation of "mixed" couples. As so often, Paul shows himself here to be something of a pragmatist, adjusting to the necessities of the social situation. His final statement to this couple, however, indicates the extent to which his concerns in their regard are with purity. He allows that the unbelieving partner may decide to separate, in which case the Christian should not resist. "For how do you know, woman, if you will save your husband? Or how do you know, man, if you will save your wife?" (7:16). In other words, Paul admits that the unbelieving spouse may not, in the end, be saved—*in spite of the fact that he or she has been "sanctified."* How Paul conceives of sanctification

that does not include salvation is unclear, but his rhetorical questions demonstrate that in this passage he is concerned with pollution, not so much with
final judgment.

The Problem of Virgins

The understanding of Paul's physiology of desire that has underwritten much
of my discussion of 1 Corinthians 7 also sheds light on 7:36–38, where Paul
addresses the man who is as yet unmarried and is uncertain whether to proceed
with the marriage or to "keep his virgin," presumably meaning that he would
continue to maintain her but without marriage or sexual relations.[58] There are
several exegetical conundrums in this short passage, but I will address only a
few. What is the meaning of the Greek in the phrase "if he/she is *hyperakmos*"
in 7:36? Most commentators note that there are at least two ambiguities: first,
the subject could be either the man or the woman, and second, the meaning of *hyperakmos* is unclear, most commentators taking it to refer either to
chronological age (someone who is past his or her prime) or to sexual passion
(someone who is overly passionate). There are thus four possibilities: (1) the
man is too passionate; (2) the man is past his prime; (3) the virgin is too passionate; or (4) the virgin is past her prime. But modern interpreters offer only
two. They assume, without acknowledgment, that if the subject of the phrase
is the man, *hyperakmos* must refer to his passions, whereas if the subject is
the virgin, it must refer to her age. Modern interpreters appear to be reading
the text through the sexual ideology dominant since the nineteenth century
that construes women as relatively passionless and sexually passive and men as
driven by sexual "needs" and desires that are controlled only with great difficulty. The relevant factor in women's sexuality, according to this ideology, is
not their desire (if they have any) but their age and what it has to do with their
availability and desirability.[59] But just as modern sexual ideology has ruled the
way in which contemporary interpreters read Paul's ambiguous Greek, so ancient sexual ideology would have ruled ancient readers' perceptions. Indeed,
I will argue that in his own day Paul's statement would have been taken to
refer to the virgin and the dangers her desire posed to her own body and, by
extension, to the body of the church.

There are few occurrences of *hyperakmos* in ancient Greek, even fewer that
are relevant to our investigation, and none that is absolutely decisive for the interpretation of the term in 1 Corinthians 7:36.[60] Interestingly, however, a near
contemporary of Paul, the physician Soranus, uses the term when speaking

of virgins in his *Gynecology*. In a significant passage, Soranus discusses the fact that the amount of menstrual flow will vary according to "nature, age, season, physique, habits, and mode of life" (1. 4. 22). In the part on age (*hēlikia*), Soranus explains, "For in women about to cease menstruating and in those just beginning, less blood is excreted. In such women, indeed, often only the area close to the uterus is moistened" (trans. Temkin). His next sentence is more ambiguous: "For in a very few women, and these being *hyperakmoi*, before their first sexual intercourse a concentrated flow appears—however, as I said, it only stains the region" (Temkin's translation modified). Temkin takes *hyperakmos* to refer to chronology, and translates it as "women past puberty"; that is, as referring to women who are just past puberty but not yet married. Caelius Aurelianus, a fifth-century translator of Soranus, gives the same interpretation: "sed excedentibus pubertatem, quamquam manete virginitate congestum appareat, sola tamen polluit loca."[61] Thus, Soranus may provide evidence for the chronological interpretation of the term. On the other hand, Soranus's usage could also refer to the passions, since he is speaking of the flows of young women who are soon to experience their first sexual intercourse, and it was the widespread opinion at the time that young women at this point in life were especially passionate and eager for copulation.[62]

Even if we take Soranus to be referring to age, it should be noted that his use of *hyperakmos* includes only girls from the age of about fourteen (which is when Soranus claims menstruation typically begins) to seventeen or eighteen (which is when almost all girls of any concern to Soranus—that is, girls of the higher class—would have been married).[63] The "acme" that these girls are "past," therefore, is the point of puberty itself, which Soranus considers the best time for marriage, the "natural" time for "defloration" (*Gynecology* 1. 8. 33). We should not take Paul's use of the term, therefore, to refer to women who are "past their prime" in the modern sense, meaning something like past child-bearing age or past the age of marriageability. Paul is not referring to "old maids" or to the danger that these virgins will miss out on a chance for marriage and family. If the term is taken as referring to age at all, it is probably the time immediately after the onset of puberty, considered by many to be the prime time for marriage.

But in thinking that *hyperakmos* must be interpreted as *either* a reference to age *or* a reference to desire, we may be introducing a dichotomy that would have been confusing to ancient readers. As I mentioned above, it was assumed that young women were filled with dangerous desire and that the longer sexual intercourse was postponed the more desperate and endangered virgins became. Thus, even if *hyperakmos* is taken to refer to the girl's age, it carries with it connotations of desire: the reason one should be concerned about a virgin getting older is because the more her first intercourse is delayed, the more her body will be inwardly ravaged by the fire of passion. This, indeed, is the way some early Christian writers took Paul's language. Epiphanius, commenting on the text of 1 Corinthians 7, explains that Paul here is speaking to fathers who, because of a dearth of eligible Christian men and a desire not to marry their daughters to non-Christians, had been keeping their daughters virgins.[64] "But they [the virgins], *being past the height* (*hyperakmazousai*), fell into porneia because of natural compulsion" (*dia tēn kata physin anagkēn, Panarion* 61. 5. 5, my trans.). Likewise, an anonymous commentator on the same verse, calls a virgin a "wanton daughter" (*luxuriosam filiam*) and an "incontinent daughter" (*filiae incontinenti*), indicating that he understands the term to include a reference to her female tendency to passion.[65]

One of the reasons why these Church Fathers read the text this way is certainly because they are taking the man addressed to be the father, because of their wish to preclude any possible reference here to spiritual marriage. It would make little sense to take the father as the one who is *hyperakmos*. But another reason why they read the text this way was their assumption, which they shared with a great many people of their culture, that women, more than men, were especially susceptible to the dangers of desire. Anne Carson gives a remarkable catalogue of such expressions, which merits a long quotation:

> Women are assumed to be markedly more open to erotic emotion than men and sexually insatiable once aroused. A long tradition concerning female lewdness derives from this assumption, of which a few examples may be mentioned. Aiskhylos warns against the "blazing eye" of a woman who has once "tasted man" (. . . fr. 243 Nauck) and deprecates female license as "ready to dare anything" for love (. . . *Ch.* 594). Sophokles observes that even women who have sworn to avoid the pain of childbirth cannot resist sexual desire (fr. 932P). The lust of women is a frequent joke in Aristophanes (e.g., *Thesm.* 504ff.; *Ekkl.* 468–70; 616–20; . . . *Lys.* 553ff.). Alkiphron characterizes female sexual voracity as a "Kharybdis" (1. 6. 2), warning another man that his *hetaira* will swallow him whole (3. 33). Both Hippokrates (*de Morb. Mul.* 1) and Plato (*Tim.* 91c) promote the theory of the "wandering womb," an explanation of feminine hysteria which is predicated on women's uncontrollable longing for sex. Aristotle takes female incontinence for granted as a consequence of feminine weakness (*EN* 7. 7. 1150b6) and a reason for marrying girls off not later than the age of eighteen (*Pol.* 7. 14. 1335a29). In the Greek historians, whenever

mention is made of a society or state of affairs managed by women, it is assumed that such situations would feature total female promiscuity. For example, Philo of Byblos, accounting for traditions of matrilinear descent in antiquity, explains: "They traced their descent on the mother's side because women at that time had intercourse casually with any man they ran into." Philo takes it for granted that, unrestrained by an alternate system, women would incline to complete wantonness.[66]

As Carson makes clear, this attitude pervaded Greco-Roman culture for several centuries. The medical writers expressed it by pointing out that female physiology was to blame.

As I have shown above, the medical writers, especially those of the Roman period, encouraged their patients to control their desire and moderate their sexual activity, and some advised those capable of it to abstain completely. They were writing, however, for men—in fact, upper-class, free, educated heads of households.[67] When discussing sexual regimens for women, their comments are rather different. They agree that the desires of women are problematic, and this seems to be due to the fact that women are implicated in a physiology of excess.

For example, a Hippocratic document well known in the first and second centuries C.E. explains that female flesh is softer and more porous than a man's, like a sponge that retains moisture. It has a tendency, therefore, to become filled with blood and not allow that blood to be sloughed off as it should be. The fullness causes the woman's body to heat up, which causes pain. Men are not subject to this problem because their flesh is different: "Because a man has more solid flesh than a woman, he is never so totally overfilled with blood that pain results if some of his blood does not exit each month. He draws whatever quantity of blood is needed for his body's nourishment; since his body is not soft, it does not become overstrained nor is it heated up by fullness, as in the case of a woman. The fact that a man works harder than a woman contributes greatly to this; for hard work draws off some of the fluid."[68] Reasoning in what appears to us today a somewhat circular manner, the writer proceeds to explain that female heat may cause the womb to dry up. (This would seem to take care of the problem of too much moisture, which had caused the heat in the first place, but the author does not mention this possibility.) When the womb dries up, it becomes displaced from its normal position and moves about the body, seeking moisture. The desiccated, sex-deprived womb "hits the liver and they go together and strike against the abdomen—for the womb rushes and goes upward toward the moisture, because it has been unduly heated by hard work, and the liver is, after all, moist. When the womb hits the liver, it produces sudden suffocation as it occupies the breathing passage around the belly."[69] The author's solution to the problem is coitus, for "if her womb is damp from coitus and her belly is not empty, her womb is not easily displaced."[70]

Besides the dangers of a "wandering womb," dryness of the uterus may also cause the mouth of the womb to close, leading to a cessation of menstruation, the dangerous "fullness" already described above, and a host of dire results. In the third month of such a condition a woman will experience suffocation and fever "accompanied by intermittent chills and pains in the lower back." In the fourth month the symptoms may become acute and then subside, or additional symptoms may manifest themselves: thick urine, an "unyielding" stomach, teeth grinding, lack of appetite, and insomnia. In the sixth month the symptoms become grotesque, and the woman, stuffed with her own putrid blood and suffocating from internal excess, eventually dies, all from a malady that copulation could have prevented.[71] No wonder, then, that the Hippocratic texts hold that "if women have intercourse, they are more healthy; if they don't, they are less healthy. . . . While intercourse is warming the blood and making it more fluid, it also furnishes an easier path for menstruation. When the menses do not flow, the woman's body becomes sickly."[72]

By the second century some physicians had given up the notion of the "wandering womb," having become convinced that the uterus was fairly well fastened down. Galen argues that people should stop thinking of the womb as a raging animal, roaming about seeking whom it may devour in search of moisture, and he calls the idea that a dried-up womb might seek moisture from the viscera "totally absurd."[73] (Galen did not win the day in this debate; as is well known, the "wandering womb" remained an important concept through-out Western history until relatively modern times.) He agrees, however, that "suffocation" and "hysteria" in women may result from an unnatural retention of menstrual blood. He points out that the condition usually affects widows, "particularly those who previously menstruated regularly, had been pregnant and were eager to have intercourse, but were now deprived of this."[74] But he knows that some women have experienced the same symptoms even though menstruating regularly. He explains that in these cases the harmful agent that has been retained is semen, not menstrual blood: "The female semen is a burden to them." Men, Galen says, are different. Some men are made weak by intercourse; others, who are used to regular sexual relations, become ill from the retention of their semen if they suddenly abstain from sex. Just as the retention of menstrual blood will suffocate a woman, so the retention of semen will cause illness in men *and* women. In other words, women seem to be in somewhat more danger than men, due, in the first place, to their weaker constitutions, and secondly, to the fact that they may suffer retention of both menstrual fluid and semen if they are suddenly and totally continent. Fortunately for women, relief can be had by submitting to penetration. Galen even knows of one widow who found relief through administration of a drug that heated up the sexual organs and simulated the "pleasure and pain" of intercourse: "As result the woman secreted a large quantity of heavy semen and thus lost the bothersome complaints."[75]

As we might expect, the care and keeping of virgins constituted a subcategory of debate within these concerns about passionate women. Soranus provides a valuable source, because he relates not only his own views but also those he opposes. A young man's first sexual intercourse is not a problem for him, Soranus says, because he only discharges semen. The young woman, on the other hand, both discharges semen and receives it—and may become pregnant. The timing and control of her sexual experience is therefore a matter of great concern. Soranus relates that some people advocate sex for a girl as soon as she experiences sexual desire, marrying off their daughters even before their first period. Such people are concerned, as we saw above, that virgins will suffer more the longer their first copulation is delayed, "for the only abatement of the craving is found in the use of intercourse not in its avoidance." These people claim that loss of semen in itself is not harmful except in excess. The body is actually rendered more healthy by occasional and moderate emission of semen, just as the occasional discharge of menstrual blood is necessary for health. Intercourse, according to their view, relaxes the female body, opens an egress for menstrual blood and boiling semen, and gives a virgin some relief. The release of the pressures of the fluids provides relief from the heat of desire.[76]

As already noted, Soranus knows of these opinions but himself advocates complete abstinence, even for women. Other hygienic controls, in his opinion, can take care of the abundance of blood and semen in the female body, without resorting to sexual intercourse. He allows intercourse, however, for the purposes of procreation. Thus he insists that one should wait until puberty, until after the first period, and ignore a girl's early licentious inclinations. "Since virgins who have not been brought up wisely and lack education arouse in themselves premature desires; one must, therefore, not trust the appetites. It is good to preserve the state of virginity until menstruation begins by itself" (1. 8. 33, trans. Temkin).

This concern to control the dangerous desires of young girls prompted Rufus, a medical writer who flourished at the end of the first and beginning of the second century, to prescribe an entire "Regimen for Virgins." He begins by noting that it is dangerous for young girls to remain virgins too long, since the repletion of blood in their bodies, due to the fact that no penetration has opened an egress for menstruation, will cause many passions and diseases. Once a girl arrives at marriageable age (usually twelve for Rufus), she desires sexual intercourse immediately, which is why custom has ordained that younger women marry old men, "because they [the virgins] are surging (with desire)."[77] Rufus recognizes that early sexual intercourse will ease the internal pressure and aid menstruation (see also 18. 25); but he also notes that it may lead to early pregnancy, which he believes is not healthy for either the girl or the fetus. Since he wants to delay first intercourse, yet knows that it is dangerous for virgins to be filled with blood, heat, and passion for too long, he prescribes a regimen that will keep girls from arriving at their "peak" too soon.[78] The regimen should not be enforced on girls from infancy but only when they are approaching puberty, the "precarious" time (*sphaleros*, 18. 9). At that time, girls should be introduced to the regimen gradually and moderately. They are to avoid meat or any strong food; they should exercise moderately, walking about, then running through sand and exercising by "dust-rolling" (an exercise used by wrestlers). They may also practice singing and dancing and sometimes even play with a ball. In general, they must avoid leisure; by proper activities, they should moderately raise the temperature of the body—but not to the extent that they become "masculinized" (18. 15). Although as younger girls they were allowed to drink wine, they should now drink only water, or perhaps water mixed with a little wine, since the "boiling nature" that is within virgins will ally itself with the heat of the wine, with dire results. Furthermore, as Rufus sensibly notes, "Water-drinking (regimens?) conduce toward self-control [*sōphrosynē*], but wine makes them more licentious" (*akolastoterai*, 18. 17).

Rufus's regimen is an exemplary model of ancient medical manipulation. He even points out how one can tell when virgins will arrive at their peak (puberty). Those with colder, moister natures arrive later, those with warmer natures sooner. Those who are large-veined, with ruddy complexions and good flesh around the loins and hips, are "better" (he doesn't say for what) than those who are pale and skinny—or fat but flat-hipped (18. 21–23). All these prescriptions and suggestions illustrate the concerns that physicians—who were simply reflecting the upper-class assumptions and sexual ideology of their culture—had about the dangers of desire to women in general and virgins in particular. Given the hierarchy of strength and physiology also assumed by that culture, it is only reasonable that Greco-Roman authors should have considered women, and especially young, inexperienced women, especially susceptible to the dangers of desire. And most of them believed that those dangers became more threatening the longer the virgin went without sexual intercourse.[79]

I am not suggesting that Paul had read any of these medical writers, or that he would have subscribed to such sophisticated physiological theories. I do suggest, however, that he shared with them a "common sense" current in his day that desire was dangerous. As I have argued above, Paul's major concern as expressed in 1 Corinthians 7:9 was not sexual intercourse itself but the burning of desire. Paul also shared with his contemporaries the assumption that women are more susceptible to the dangers of desire and pollution than men, and that young girls, weak virgins, were in the most precarious position of all.

Given the assumptions about women and desire that pervaded Greco-Roman culture, Paul's readers would probably have understood his statements about marriage and virgins as expressing a concern about the danger of desire for virgins. If we may take a guess as to Paul's intentions, his statement about "over the limit" (*hyperakmos*) was probably meant to refer to a virgin's precarious situation, either due to her having passed the point of puberty or simply because her desire was about to get out of control. But my concern is less with authorial intention than with sketching the believable historical connotations of his language and the ideological context it evoked. Within that context Paul's rhetoric functioned to urge celibacy but allow marriage where abstinence would endanger the frail physiology (body *and* soul) of the weaker members of the church, young virginal girls.

Of course, certainty of interpretation when dealing with such ambiguous language is never possible, and Paul may have intended his remarks to describe the age or passions of the young man. But the logic of Paul's position still holds: virtue commendable for the Strong will be forced upon the weak at their peril. A man who is unable to control himself thereby "feminizes" himself on the hierarchical scale of bodily control and strength. In Greco-Roman moral philosophy, as well as popular culture, the "effeminate" man (*malakos*) was not the one who preferred male partners but any man who was too given to sex, even sex exclusively with women. The effeminate man is the "ladies' man," the one who becomes soft because of his addiction to sexual intercourse with women, the "softer" sex.[80] Hence, when Paul ends with a hierarchy of virtue (the one who marries does not sin, but the one who abstains does well; the one who marries does well, but the one who abstains does better), he is simply reflecting the ideology of sexual hierarchy of his time, which assumed that at the masculine end of the scale stood strength and control, at the feminine end weakness and vulnerability.

In spite of this possibility, however, I believe it more likely that Paul had virgins in mind when expressing his concerns about being "over the limit." That is why Paul addresses the man alone in 1 Corinthians 7:25–38. The patristic interpretation that Paul is here speaking to a father about his daughter has been, in my opinion, rightly rejected by modern interpreters. There is no mention of a father in the text, and to find a father here, one must interject into Paul's discussion a character not thus far encountered. Taking the man to be the fiancé of the virgin, on the other hand, leaves us with the problem of explaining why Paul, who has generally been careful in this chapter to address men and women alternately in each instruction, here addresses the man alone, as if the virgin were simply a passive object about which a decision must be made. From 7:25 on, virgins are spoken *about*, not *to:* "Are you bound to a wife? Do not seek release. Have you been released from a wife? Do not seek a wife. If you marry, you do not sin. And if the virgin marries, she has not sinned" (note the shift from second to third person in 7:27–28). Verse 37 leaves the entire decision in the hands of the man: "Whoever [masc.] has established in his heart steadfastly, not having any compulsion, and he has authority over his own will and this he has decided in his own heart, to keep his virgin [that is, not marry her], he will do well." The woman is excluded from taking part in the decision, just as we would expect given the assumptions that a strong–weak hierarchy corresponds to a male–female hierarchy in Greco-Roman sexual ideology. If Paul were concerned about weaker people in general in 7:36–38—that is, both women and men who were unable to control their desires—he would have addressed both the man and the woman as he has elsewhere in the chapter. Paul's exclusive address to the young man thus reveals his assumption of the male–female hierarchy of strength. He addresses the one who has power, the man, and delegates to him the responsibility for doing what needs to be done in the woman's best interest (at least according to Paul's point of view). The weaker of the two, the woman, cannot be relied upon to make a decision for herself. Paul is here following the same rhetorical strategy pursued so many times elsewhere in 1 Corinthians: he addresses the one presumed to be the stronger—here, the man—and urges him to modify his behavior for the benefit of the weaker, the woman.

This last point reveals that Paul has *not* done something he has done elsewhere in 1 Corinthians: he has not undercut the ideological assumptions of the body hierarchy assumed by the Strong. That Paul has attempted no such undermining of the hierarchical ideology here is because he cannot. The very physiology of women makes them more vulnerable than men to the dangers of desire and pollution. Furthermore, weak men, who by that designation are placed closer to the female end of the physiological scale and hence to the weaker end of the scale of virtue, are also more endangered by porneia and desire than are strong, masculine men. Virgins, as young, inexperienced girls whose very physiology makes them more susceptible to desire and its destructive powers than all the others, are in the most precarious position of all, and thus special consideration must be given their situation before they are hastily assigned to what may be a too arduous celibacy.

The Strong and Paul both view sexual intercourse negatively, as a threat to the health of the body and a sign of weakness. In this they simply reflect a growing consensus among, at the very least, a significant minority of Greco-Roman society who believe that sex and desire weaken and harm the individual—or at least the man. But, as we have noted, what Paul really fears is not so much sexual intercourse as the burning of desire, reflecting his concerns about boundaries and pollutions; by contrast, the Strong are concerned more with self-control and power over one's body—the maintenance of equilibrium (not, however, equality).

The main problem addressed in 1 Corinthians 7 is the danger of desire to the weak. Paul's solutions depend on whom he is addressing. To married couples, he says: avoid sex if possible, but if you are too weak, don't attempt abstinence, for weakness must be accommodated. To the betrothed Paul has a slightly different solution, albeit one based on an identical logic and goal. In this situation his concern is more for the woman, the weaker of the two partners: if she is in danger, they should marry; if not, it seems almost assumed that the male will, in this case, be able to control himself. After all, Paul here addresses a man who would prefer to remain celibate but who must keep in mind someone else who is weaker. The logic is the same as before: the weakness must be accommodated. The difference between Paul and the Strong at Corinth, therefore, is not that he is *for* marriage and they are *against* it, or that they affirm a hierarchy that Paul wishes to challenge. Rather, the two positions differ with regard to their constructions of the body. The Strong wish to place sex under careful control so as to maintain the proper hierarchy of strength over weakness, the power of the will and the spirit over the weakness of the body. Paul shares with the Strong their assumptions about the danger of sexual intercourse and the male–female hierarchy, but, unlike them, he also wants to guard against the pollutions that threaten the body of Christ, both porneia that corrupts from without and desire that corrupts from within.

9 *Prophylactic Veils*

In 1 Corinthians 11:2–16, Paul insists that women who pray and prophesy in the Christian assembly wear veils. The passage has been a source of perennial debate: besides the obvious problem of the veils themselves—why are they necessary? what do they signify? what does Paul mean by "because of the angels" in verse 10? and so on—Paul seems to be condoning, indeed encouraging, the subordination of women (vv. 3, 7–10) while simultaneously acknowledging the equality of men and women, at least "in the Lord" (vv. 11–12). He elsewhere quotes the baptismal formula that in Christ there is no "male and female" (Gal. 3:27–28), invoking the ancient notion that the eschatological human being will be androgynous, having overcome the oppositions of the male/female dichotomy. According to many biblical scholars, the implication is that Paul's true ideal is one of equality between the sexes but that he yields to cultural commonplaces and conventions because of practical concerns or a desire not to force eschatological hopes onto a pre-resurrection body.

Actually, Paul's statements about women in 1 Corinthians 11 are not as problematic as seems the case on first blush. The mistake made by most modern interpreters stems from their assumption that ancient notions of androgyny implied equality between the sexes. In a ground-breaking article, Wayne Meeks traces the ancient "image of the androgyne" and its influence on early Christianity.[1] He notes that the unification of the sexes does not always function predictably in ancient texts and that androgyny does not always connote equality. For example, the gnostic *Gospel of Thomas* speaks of male and female becoming one without challenging the assumption that the female is inferior; as Meeks says, "Rather, if the female is to become a 'living spirit' and thus be saved, she must become male (logion 114)."[2] In his discussion of Pauline Christianity, however, Meeks assumes that early Christian ideas about androgyny functioned to promote equality within the early church. He interprets 1 Corinthians 11:11–12, which states that the male and the female are mutually interdependent, in an egalitarian light: "the order of creation has been replaced by reciprocity."[3] The veils, according to Meeks, are only a "symbolic" vestige of the old order. "Paul accepts and even insists upon the equality of role of man and woman in this community which is formed already by the Spirit that belongs to the end of days."[4]

Unequal Androgyny

More recent studies, informed by feminist theory, have demonstrated that for the ancient world androgyny does not imply equality. Ancient texts portraying women becoming "male" (they rarely if ever show men becoming "female") teach the interdependence of the sexes but not their equality. This was due in large part to a common presupposition that females were simply imperfect males. As explained in Chapter 1, when ancient writers talk about the difference between female nature and male nature, they are referring not to deep ontological differences but to a difference in degree or position on a spectrum. In such a system, obviously, any androgyny that is taken to be salvific must be oriented toward the higher end of the spectrum, the male. In Thomas Laqueur's words, "In a public world that was overwhelmingly male, the one-sex model displayed what was already massively evident in culture more generally: *man* is the measure of all things, and woman does not exist as an ontologically distinct category. Not all males are masculine, potent, honorable, or hold power, and some women exceed some men in each of these categories. But the standard of the human body and its representations is the male body."[5]

The advice of the medical writers bears out Laqueur's observations. Soranus at the beginning of the second century can speak of the imperfection of female nature in a way that shows its common currency from Aristotle to his own day: "The female is by nature different from the male, so much so that Aristotle and Zenon the Epicurean say that the female is imperfect, the male, however, perfect."[6] Such writers had physiological explanations for the male–

female hierarchy. Some pointed out that women were closer to the irrational than men due in part to "having more blood in their breasts than men," the breast being understood by some scientists as the seat of rationality.[7] Others argued that women's bodies were cooler than men's, or alternatively, hotter. As Lesley Dean-Jones explains, "The hot–cold issue continued to be debated throughout antiquity. The Hippocratic gynecologists tended to view woman as hot, Aristotle and the author of *Regimen* i as cold. . . . Whether the women were considered hotter or colder than men, it was always they rather than the men who were considered *too* hot or *too* cold."[8]

Androgyny was invariably defined in male terms. Not surprisingly, therefore, even religious texts interested in the androgynous nature of divine beings, such as Gnostic texts, always view femaleness negatively. In the *Apocryphon of John*, for example, the female is linked with sexuality, procreation, and material hindrances to the divine light. Masculinity and androgyny are both linked to "knowledge." Repeatedly in these texts, women must become male in order to be saved, but nowhere is it claimed that men must become female. According to Ingvild Saelid Gilhus, "The impression is given that androgynousness is a characteristic which is important in connection with female entities because femaleness implies imperfection, but not with male entities because the male form represents perfection."[9] Gilhus concludes, "[F]emaleness and sexuality are interconnected and condemned, whereas maleness and androgynousness are interconnected with knowledge and are vehicles of salvation."[10] Thus androgyny did not dispense with hierarchy but embodied it.

This maintenance of hierarchy within androgyny was not, of course, limited to the Gnostics. Tertullian, at about the same time, could say to women, "For you too (women as you are) have the self-same angelic nature promised as your reward, the self-same sex as man."[11] Later, Jerome, advocating asceticism, proclaimed, "As long as a woman is for birth and children, she is different from man as body is from soul. But if she wishes to serve Christ more than the world, then she will cease to be a woman and will be called man."[12] Dennis MacDonald reads Paul's statements in a similar way, noting that in Galatians 3:28 "Paul claims that believers are no longer male or female inasmuch as they have become one male person—the masculine *heis* [one], not the neuter *hen*." MacDonald concludes: "Contrary to the opinion of many interpreters, the androgyne myth is not antiquity's answer to androcentrism; it is but one manifestation of it."[13] In sum, neither Paul's androgynous statement in Galatians 3:28 nor his admission of women to important positions within his churches demonstrates that he was a gender egalitarian. He can subscribe to eschatological androgynous statements without believing that Christian women are equal to Christian men ontologically—or that female will equal male eschatologically.

The Unequal Female in Paul's Theology

Paul clearly does not believe that women are equal. In verse 7 he says that man is the "reflection" (or "glory"—the term *doxa* is ambiguous) of God, whereas woman is the "reflection" (or "glory") of man. The implication of hierarchy that is obvious in the first pair (God–man) cannot be denied to the second pair (man–woman). In verse 8 Paul explains: "for man is not of woman, but woman of man." Here the priority of origin, as is usual in ancient ideology of status and hierarchy, supports Paul's statement of hierarchy in verse 7.[14] As further support, Paul continues, "And man was not created because of woman but woman because of man" (v. 9). Again, to the ancient reader this would clearly imply hierarchy, since only those of lower status are said to exist for the sake of someone else; slaves, for example, exist for the sake of their owners, to "please" (*areskein*) them.[15]

Some scholars have attempted to defuse hierarchical readings of Paul's statements in verse 3 ("The head of every man is Christ, the head of woman is man, the head of Christ is God") by claiming that the term for "head" here, *kephalē*, carries connotations of "source" or "origin" but not of hierarchy or rulership.[16] But the preceding analysis of verses 7–9 mandates that verse 3 also be interpreted to imply hierarchy, and it is difficult to see how such interpreters, presumably wishing to save the text for contemporary, egalitarian theology, can insist that Paul is here not teaching the subordination of women.[17] Even leaving out the problematic term "head," one comes up with the structure:

A: Christ is to man as

B: man is to woman as

C: God is to Christ.

Since two of these parallels (A and C) are clearly in a hierarchical relationship in Paul's thought, so the remaining parallel (B) can hardly be taken to mean something else.[18] The subordination of women could hardly be clearer.

In the previous chapter I noted that Paul does not do for women in the church what he has, to some extent, attempted for slaves, Gentiles, and people of low economic status. Whereas Paul does, at least ideologically, disrupt the status hierarchies that keep masters unquestioningly over slaves, the "strong" over the "weak," and Jews and Gentiles separated by the barrier of circumcision and Torah, he does not question the ideology of hierarchy implicit in the subordination of woman. I have also suggested that the reason for this has to do with physiology. The lower hierarchical position of women cannot be challenged until the resurrection of the body, because the bodies of women before the resurrection are constituted differently from men's bodies and are weaker. Women are in particular danger due to the nature of their bodies. They are more vulnerable than men to desire, danger, and pollution. Furthermore, the precarious nature of female physiology renders them a potential locus of danger to the church's body. In the words of the medical writers, their bodies are "porous" and therefore more susceptible to penetration and invasion. Paul never discusses these concepts explicitly, but I will show in this chapter that he assumes them and that the ideology of the female body exemplified in those concepts underwrites his statements about the need for women to veil themselves when they pray and prophesy in church.

Greco-Roman Veiling

A few scholars have suggested that the issue in 1 Corinthians 11:2–16 is one of hairstyles rather than veils. Corinthian women, it is thought, are letting their hair down, thereby uncovering the top of the head, when prophesying, much like the devotees of Dionysus or other gods and goddesses who inspired prophetic frenzy.[19] It is better, however, to side with the majority of interpreters and take Paul's words about uncovering to refer to the removal of veils. For one thing, although hairstyles constituted an important symbol system in Greco-Roman society, veiling was a much more common way of indicating the covering of women important for the honor–shame culture of the ancient Mediterranean.[20] Furthermore, we should give some weight to the evidence of ancient interpreters, who almost unanimously take Paul's words here to refer to veiling and unveiling.[21] But why is veiling an issue at Corinth? How do we explain the logic of Paul's statements about the importance of veiling women when they are prophesying?

A good place to begin an analysis of the various ancient meanings of veiling is the classical Greek wedding. Literary evidence for the Greek wedding is sparse, but recent scholars have made progress reconstructing certain aspects of the wedding ceremony on the basis of other kinds of evidence, such as that provided by vases that depict various moments in the ceremony. An important part of the ceremony was the *anakalyptēria*, the unveiling of the bride. According to one reconstruction, the bride unveiled herself before the groom in the bridal chamber.[22] Other scholars place the unveiling (or perhaps an additional unveiling) in the context of a larger wedding party, at which time the bride faced her groom (and possibly his relatives as well) and lifted her veil, thereby exposing herself to his gaze. The groom responded by giving the bride gifts, called, appropriately enough, *anakalyptēria*, "things given at the time of, or to celebrate, the unveiling of the bride." According to Cynthia Patterson, these gifts were also called *prosphthenktēria*, referring to the "address" or "salute," and *optēria*, referring to the seeing that then took place.[23] Each of these actions and the words used to describe them symbolize the breaking down of boundaries. The bride unveils herself before the groom; she thus submits to his penetrating gaze; he and his family cross the household boundary by giving her gifts, thus making her a dependent of their household as she leaves that of her family.[24]

The usual term for "veil" is *krēdemnon*, the ambiguity of which is important for the multivalent significations of veiling. In Homeric texts *krēdemnon* can refer to the stopper, seal, or cover of a wine jug. Since both medical writers and, it seems, popular opinion conceived of the uterus as an upside-down jug, *krēdemnon* could also connote the "closed" (in common opinion) uterus of a virgin; "to loose the *krēdemnon*" could refer to either the breaking of the seal and unstopping of a wine jug or the defloration of a virgin.[25] Moreover, as Michael N. Nagler has shown, *krēdemnon* in the Homeric corpus was also used for the battlements or protections of a city. In this case to "loose [or destroy, since the Greek term could mean both] the *krēdemnon*" of a city meant to breach its battlements and penetrate its walls.[26] As Ann Hanson puts it, "With virgins and city walls, a thrust through a closed and protective gate lays the innermost parts within easy reach of an outsider to appropriate as he chooses."[27] For ancient Greeks, then, the veil (*krēdemnon*) not only symbolized but actually effected a protective barrier guarding the woman's head and, by metanymic transfer, her genitals. For the upper-class, Homeric heroine, the veil functioned like her attendants, shielding her from touch, reproach, and even the gaze of anyone but her husband and immediate family members. To tear off the veil was to invite or symbolize sexual violation.[28]

The sexual significance of unveiling pervades Greco-Roman culture, even though the actual practices of veiling vary according to time and place.[29] It was also closely linked with the function of veiling to symbolize order over potential chaos; in ancient myth it connoted civilization. As Anne Carson explains, "According to one ancient cosmology, the cosmos was first assembled out of chaos when Zeus threw a veil over the head of the goddess of the underworld and married her. So Pherekydes tells us . . . , and he goes on to describe the veil, on which were embroidered earth, ocean, and the houses of ocean—that is to say, the contours of the civilized world. Once veiled by her bridegroom, the dark and formless chthonic goddess was transformed and renamed *Gē*, goddess of the visible world, decorous and productive wife of Zeus."[30] To veil a woman, therefore, meant not only to protect her but also to civilize her; to guard her from invasion and penetration but also to protect society from the dangers and chaos represented by her femaleness. It meant to keep her intact, but also to keep her in place.

The relation of veiling to social order, hierarchy, control, and sexuality, all at the same time, can be better understood by glancing at various anthropological studies of modern societies in which women are veiled and analyzing the multiple meanings of veiling found in them. Although no one should *assume* that veiling in modern societies carries the same meanings as veiling in Greco-Roman society, a brief survey of studies of those modern societies proves suggestive for ancient veiling practices as well. Many cultures, for example, include veiling rituals as part of wedding ceremonies, one scholar noting such practices in Egypt, Morocco, the Zulus, Melanesia, Alaska, Korea, Manchuria, Russia, China, and Burma.[31] Almost all modern interpreters of such practices point out that the covering of a woman's head or face functions to cover her sexuality. The veil usually limits the movements of the woman, at least symbolically, since she is expected to veil herself whenever in public or, in some cases, whenever in the presence of someone besides her husband. In a study of South Asia, for example, Hanna Papanek concludes that the veil symbolizes "what is already seen as feminine in the culture: sexuality, a special sense of vulnerability, and an inability to move freely in public."[32] The connection between a woman's head and her sexuality is found in many diverse cultures, leading some scholars to posit some phenomenological explanation for what they see as a universal link between the head/hair and the genitals or between the mouth and the womb.[33] Other scholars rightly demure from such universalistic explanations but nevertheless note that, especially in veiling societies, the head and hair are symbolically linked to sexuality and often specifically to the genitals. As E. R. Leach puts it, "Even the most sceptical anthropologist must admit that head hair is rather frequently employed as a public symbol with an explicitly sexual significance."[34] In veiling societies, then, the covering of a woman's head and hair emphasizes the covering of her most vulnerable organs, her genitals. The woman is seen as particularly penetrable, and a veil as providing her with protection.

Although these societies see women as particularly vulnerable, they also see female sexuality as particularly dangerous and threatening to men and the social order. According to a study of a group in Libya, for instance, Arab Muslim men view women as possessing "animalistic sexual appetites."[35] The veil controls the chaos that might be unleashed if female sexuality were allowed free reign. In some cases, this is due to the assumption that men, by nature, cannot control their sexual urges if confronted with irresistible female lures.[36] Thus John Mason says, "Protection is provided . . . not simply to guard the Arab Muslim female's virtue, for there is an equally critical matter at stake here: male honor."[37] In other cases, it seems that the veil functions simply to contain the unpredictable sexual drives of the woman herself.[38] But in all these cases, the female is seen as both threatened and threatening. Female sexuality, as either an active or a passive force, constantly threatens to disrupt the order of society, its proper hierarchy, its ability to maintain control. Fatima Mernissi explains the concept of *fitna*, probably in this case best rendered "social disorder," for some modern Muslim societies: "The woman is *fitna*, the epitome of the uncontrollable, a living representative of the dangers of sexuality and its rampant disruptive potential."[39] Because of the double threat symbolized by uncovered women, the veil does a double duty of protection. In the words of Carla Makhlouf, "The veil is a double shield, protecting the woman against external offences of society and protecting society against the inherent evil of woman."[40]

In some social contexts, moreover, the protection provided for women and for society against the danger of women has something to do with what we might call the realm of the sacred. In a study of veiling in Afghanistan, for example, Jon Anderson notes that women are considered more susceptible than men to malicious supernatural beings who incite sexual desire in both men and women.[41] Makhlouf makes much the same point for North Yemen: "Perhaps the veil should be seen as a symbolic reminder of woman's liminal, and hence equivocal, dangerous and sacred status in society, as well as an attempt to neutralise the anxiety arising from contact with the sacred."[42]

As mentioned earlier, we should not expect veiling to mean the same thing in societies as disparate as modern Muslim societies and ancient Greco-Roman culture. Nevertheless, several elements noted in this brief survey are paralleled in Greco-Roman society: the assumption that women are more sexually driven and insatiable than men (rather than less, as is often assumed by modern, Western ideology); the belief that women are both dangerous and endangered; the perception of the female as a location of danger both to men and to society; and the ensuing need for seclusion and covering of women in certain social contexts, including those in which a fear of invasion or disapproval from sacred beings is present.

I mentioned above the agreement among anthropologists that connections exist in many societies between the head/hair and the genitals. Speaking of certain Buddhist and Hindu assumptions, E. R. Leach goes so far as to say, "Ritual impurity is not a concept invented by the subtle minds of anthropologists but a matter of fundamental importance in ordinary everyday life; everyone knows that impurity attaches indiscriminately both to the genital–anal region and to the head. The most typically impure things are faeces, urine, semen, menstrual blood, spittle, and hair. The first requirements of a person who wishes to achieve a state of purity is that he must bathe and shave and avoid sexual relations."[43] There is much evidence that the same connection was made, perhaps not consciously but certainly symbolically and ideologically, in ancient Greco-Roman culture. It is well known, for example, that loosened or wild hair was a sign both of bacchants and prostitutes.[44] There is also a joke from the second century c.e. that depends on an assumed cultural connection between the anus and the mouth.[45] But some of the most interesting evidence comes from the medical writers.

In the first place, it is not without significance that the terminology for women's genitalia in the ancient texts, as is still reflected in modern terminology, appropriates terms that refer to the head region. The womb is called a "mouth"; the labia are, of course, "lips"; the cervix is spoken of as the "lower neck."[46] Beyond the parallels in terminology, however, a physiological connection was believed to exist, so that activities of the "upper head" would affect activities of the "lower head," or vice versa. For example, women singers expended so much energy in their demanding profession that their menses were said to be affected. As Thomas Laqueur explains, "[W]hat we would take to be only metaphoric connections between organs were viewed as having causal consequences in the body as being real. Here the association is one between the throat or neck through which air flows and the neck of the womb through which the menses passes; activity in one detracts from activity in the other."[47] In ancient writers this connection is usually made unselfconsciously. Aristotle, for instance, notes that a woman's womb should become moist during intercourse in the same way that the mouth is lubricated by saliva when eating.[48] Soranus makes a similar link when insisting that intercourse should take place when the woman is desirous: just as a woman who eats without appetite will have trouble digesting her food, so a woman who receives seed without desire will not be able to retain the seed in the womb.[49] In one interesting, if rather confusing, passage a Hippocratic author suggests that in order to retain the seed after intercourse a woman should avoid baths, and especially avoid getting her head wet. No reason is given for the fear that a wet head might bring about the rejection of the seed by the womb, but perhaps no explanation was needed because of this assumed, causal connection between the two regions of the body.[50]

Certain diseases or medical problems of the genitalia could be diagnosed by concentrating on the patient's head. According to Aristotle, seminal discharge originates in the diaphragm and normally descends to the genitals. It may, however, ascend to the eyes as, in the words of Lesley Dean-Jones, "the most 'seminal' part of the head." In a related note, Dean-Jones explains, "Thus if a person overindulged in sexual intercourse, the first part of his body to show it would be the eyes, which become hollow and sunken."[51] Reflecting a related common sense, Hippocratic texts taught that the uterus could expel excess menses upward; the cause of some nosebleeds in women, therefore, was superfluous menstrual blood exiting through the nose.[52]

One medical phenomenon that regularly highlights the ancient head–womb connection is that of the "wandering womb," already discussed to some extent in the previous chapter. Although Soranus and Galen, in the second century, rejected the theory that female hysteria and suffocation were caused by the actual displacement and movement of the womb, they did not succeed in overturning traditional Hippocratic therapeutics that taught that the womb wandered around the body and could be manipulated by various techniques to return to its rightful position. In Hippocratic gynecology the most common method for coaxing the womb back to the genital region was to place objects emitting sweet odors in or near the vagina and those emitting foul odors near the nose, mouth, or ears. The womb, sensitive to such things, would flee the offending smell of, say, burnt hair, squashed bedbugs, or castor oil rubbed on the nose and ears and retreat back toward the vagina, lured by the smell of spikenard and storax suppositories. (Women doubtless recovered as quickly as they possibly could.) Soranus seems to be in the minority, however, when he censures physicians like Asclepiades, who "applies a sternutative [something to provoke sneezing], constricts the hypochondriac region with bandages and strings of gut, shouts loudly, blows vinegar into the nose, allows sexual intercourse during remissions, drinking of water and pouring cold water over the head."[53]

These physiological connections between the womb and the head are so important for Hippocratic therapeutics that one modern scholar has hypothesized that the authors must have believed that an actual tube connected the "upper mouth" with the "lower mouth" in women's bodies.[54] The belief in a specific "tube" is not certain, however; many of the therapeutics recommended by the medical texts could be explained simply on the assumption that various passageways existed in the body through which humors, odors, and vapors could travel between the mouth and the anus or vagina. At any rate, the various therapies demonstrate the physiological connection assumed to exist between the head and the genitals. It is a rather small step to recognizing how that connection may have expressed itself through veiling procedures.

The Dangers of Prophecy

That Paul's concerns about veiling should come out in the context of prophecy is natural, given many of the common conceptions in his time about what transpired in prophecy. Greco-Roman culture often pictured prophecy as taking place when a god or goddess placed something into, inhabited, or allowed some force, usually described as some sort of stuff, to enter a human being.[55] Plutarch himself rejects the idea that a god enters the bodies of prophets to "prompt their utterances," calling the idea "simple-minded and childish"; but his remarks indicate that the notion was popularly held, in spite of his more "scientific" views.[56] Even Plutarch, however, speaks approvingly of the explanation that prophecy is due to some material force acting on the body of the prophet or prophetess. Indeed, ancient theorists spoke of the physiology of prophecy in the same way that they explained the onset of illness due to vapors and other physical forces. One speaker in the dialogue *On the Obsolescence of the Oracles* notes that the earth is the source of many "potencies": some cause disease, death, or madness; others provide the "prophetic current." As he continues, "But the prophetic current and breath (*rheuma kai pneuma*) is most divine and holy, whether it issue by itself through the air or come in the company of running waters; for when it is instilled into the body, it creates in souls an unaccustomed and unusual temperament, the peculiarity of which it is hard to describe with exactness, but analogy offers many comparisons" (*Moralia* 432D–E). Sounding like the medical writers of his own day, the speaker proceeds to compare the "prophetic current" to the way fumes from wine rise into the head, affecting thought and perception.

From this (as we moderns, but not the ancients, would call it) "materialist" conception of prophecy, it is easy to understand how prophecy could be conceived in terms redolent of sexual intercourse. The analogy is seldom explicit (though it sometimes is, as I will shortly note); but one can hardly read accounts of the physiology of prophecy, especially descriptions of prophecy enacted by a male god on a female seer, without detecting the sexual connotations of the language. Plutarch says that the mortal body is unable to remain still when it "yields" (*parechein*) itself to "the one that moves it," but "as though tossed amid billows and enmeshed in the stirrings and emotions [*pathesin*, "passions"] within itself, it makes itself more and more restless" (*Moralia* 404E). He also speaks of the prophetic virgin as one would speak of the innocent bride of a respectable groom:

> Even so the maiden who now serves the god here was born of as lawful and honourable wedlock as anyone, and her life has been in all respects proper; but having been brought up in the home of poor peasants, she brings nothing with her as the result of technical skill or of any other expertness or faculty, as she goes down into the shrine. On the contrary, just as Xenophon believes that a bride should have seen as little and heard as little as possible before she proceeds to her husband's house, so this girl, inexperienced and uninformed about practically everything, a pure, virgin soul, becomes the associate of the god. [*Moralia* 405C]

It is no coincidence that Plutarch, describing prophetic activity, recalls Xenophon's treatise on "Household Management" (*Oikonomikos*), in which a gentleman explains to Socrates how he "possesses" and trains his young bride, and that Plutarch's terminology about "associating" with the god, in spite of the rather prudish English translation quoted here, means "to have sexual intercourse" (*syneimi*). Pausanius also informs us that the early Sybil traditionally called herself the "wedded wife" of Apollo (*gynē gametē*, 10. 12. 2).

The "prophecy as penetration" theme expresses itself in the literary commonplace that prophecy is divine rape. Aeschylus, in *Agamemnon*, describes Cassandra's prophecy as the (overly?) strong seduction of her by the god; her insights into the future were a result of Apollo's desire for her:

Cas. It was the seer Apollo who appointed me to this office.

Chorus Can it be that he, a god, was smitten with desire?

Cas. Oh, but he struggled to win me, breathing ardent love for me.

Chorus Came ye in due course to wedlock's rite?

[*Agamemnon* 1202–1207]

Centuries later, in Virgil's *Aeneid*, the prophecy of the Sybil is pictured as the taming of a horse, but with rather ambiguous imagery that also recalls a god's rape of a young girl: "But the prophetess, not yet brooking the sway of Phoebus, storms wildly in the cavern, if so she may shake the mighty god from off her breast; so much the more he tires her raving mouth, tames her wild heart, and moulds her by constraint" (6. 77–82). After gaining control over her, the god plunges toward the act of penetration: "so does Apollo shake the reins as she rages, and ply the spur beneath her breast" (6. 98–101). Then, as if simulating post-coital relaxation, the poet describes the end of the prophesying as a subsiding of "frenzy" (*furor*).[57]

Just as medical writers give advice about the proper conditions for successful coitus, so theorists discussing prophecy describe the proper conditions for the reception of the divine influx. Soranus, for example, explains that the woman's uterus must be neither too dry nor too moist, neither too lax nor too constricted, in order for retention of the seed to occur.[58] Plutarch's intellectuals in *On the Obsolescence of Oracles* mention that dryness or moisture in the body may affect the ability to discern and receive true prophecy. The priestess must be kept "holy and clean" throughout her life (*hagnē . . . kathareuousa*). Any number of bodily states could inhibit reception of the inspiring spirit. "For many annoyances and disturbances of which she is conscious, and many more unperceived, lay hold upon her body and filter into her soul; and whenever she is replete with these, it is better that she should not go there and surrender herself to the control of the god, when she is not completely unhampered [Greek: "clean," *kathara*] (as if she were a musical instrument, well strung and well tuned), but in a state of emotion and instability" (*Moralia* 437D). Furthermore, just as medical writers insist that a woman must be desirous and willing in order for coitus to be successful, since if she lacks desire she will not produce the requisite seed or will not retain the seed implanted in her womb,[59] so Plutarch notes that a prophetess who went down into the oracle unwillingly not only failed to prophesy properly but even injured herself fatally: "she was like a labouring ship and was filled with a mighty and baleful spirit" (*Moralia* 438B). She screamed, rushed from the oracle, collapsed, and expired a few days later. Plutarch concludes that it is essential to observe a woman's body and even to take omens from the oracle before submitting her to the god's penetration, so that one can be sure "when she has the temperament and disposition suitable to submit to the inspiration without harm to herself" (*Moralia* 438C). Plutarch's language recalls the medicalization of sexual intercourse by the physicians of his day. The physiology of prophecy could be analyzed by analogy with the physiology of sex, because prophecy was thought of as the penetration of the body of the priestess by the god or some other, perhaps inanimate, invading force. The moment of prophecy was the moment of invasion. Thus people were especially vulnerable and endangered when open to the forces of prophetic inspiration.

Moreover, according to the dominant Greco-Roman ideology, women were generally more vulnerable than men. The penetration of heterosexual inter-course furnished the paradigm for constructing female physiology itself. The medical writers, Hippocratics especially, expressed this by noting that female flesh was different from male flesh in that it was moister, more absorbent, and more porous.[60] This connection with moisture was taken to explain why women were more susceptible to pollution and disease than men: water, and moisture in general, does not respect boundaries; it is difficult to contain or keep out. Anne Carson demonstrates how Aristotle's views on female nature (which influenced culture after him even when later theorists disagreed with particular points in his system) linked women's moist porousness to their vul-nerability to seepage and pollution. Femaleness, like "wetness" (*to hygron*), has no boundary of its own, and thus must be contained by artificial procedures. As Carson continues, "If we consider the ancient conception of gender in the light of this distinction, we see that woman is to be differentiated from man, in the ancient view, not only as wet from dry but as content from form, as the unbounded from the bounded, as polluted from pure, and that these qualities are necessarily related to one another."[61] The assumption that women were more endangered by surrounding forces, therefore, was not simply a meta-phor for feminine weakness or dependence on masculine protection; rather, it was a physiological fact, anchored in the very nature of female flesh. We can now see why women would have been perceived as both more "penetrable" by prophetic forces and more open to whatever potential perils might accompany prophetic invasion. Their natural precariousness would be heightened when their bodies were exposed and open to inspiration.

The Function of Veiling in 1 Corinthians 11:2-16

The material presented to this point leads naturally to the question, if veil-ing was understood in ancient culture to protect vulnerable women from the penetrating gaze and from dangerous invasion, who or what were those forces thought to threaten the Corinthian women prophets? The answer is twofold. In the first place, we must recognize that throughout 11:2–16 Paul is anxious about the maintenance of order—in this case, the natural order of gender hier-archy. In the second place, his statement that women should cover themselves "because of the angels" suggests that angels constitute the force that threat-ens the exposed prophetesses. My treatment of the passage, therefore, will attempt to hold together two issues that are often separated by modern biblical commentators on this passage: order and sexuality.

Paul is clearly drawing on notions of shame and sexuality in his advice about veiling. In verses 4–6 he appeals to the "natural" fact that women whose heads are shaved are thereby exposed as "shameful" women. The removal of their hair symbolizes the shameful uncovering of their genitals that has transpired in some socially unacceptable transgression.[62] Paul's theological arguments from hierarchy that follow (in vv. 7–9) should not make us forget the issue of sexuality and exposure that has already been broached in verses 4–6.

Paul's confusing statement in verse 10 has prompted many interpretations. He states: "Because of this [that is, because of the place of woman in the hierarchy God–man–woman] a woman ought to have authority upon her head, because of the angels."[63] The two principal explanations of the final phrase have been either that the angels represent a sexual threat to the women because they would be tempted by seeing the women uncovered or that they are the defenders of order and would thus be offended by the hubris of women prophesying with uncovered heads.[64] Joseph Fitzmyer has proposed an explanation related to the latter. By comparing the function of angels in Qumran texts, Fitzmyer argues that the angels would have perceived an unveiled female head as a "bodily defect" inappropriate in a "sacred assembly." He concludes, "We are invited by the evidence from Qumrân to understand that the unveiled head of a woman is like a bodily defect which should be excluded from such an assembly, 'because holy angels are present in their congregation.'"[65]

Historically, the most common interpretation of the passage has been that Paul fears that angels will be sexually tempted by the exposed women and may try to have relations with them.[66] It was quite common in Paul's day for Jews to interpret Genesis 6, which narrates how the sons of God mated with the daughters of men, as a reference to a primordial event in which angels, "watchers," or some other kind of heavenly being lusted after human women and mated with them. As the tradition occurs in 1 *Enoch* 7:

> And they took wives unto themselves, and everyone (respectively) chose one woman for himself, and they began to go unto them. And they taught them magical medicine, incantations, the cutting of roots, and taught them about plants. And the women became pregnant and gave birth to great giants whose heights were three hundred cubits. These (giants) consumed the produce of all the people until the people detested feeding them. So the giants turned against (the people) in order to eat them. And they began to sin against birds, wild beasts, reptiles, and fish. And their flesh was devoured the one by the other, and they drank blood.[67]

According to this and other versions of the myth, the angels caused all kinds of havoc in human history, teaching women mysterious and forbidden arts, like magic and makeup, and introducing disastrous mechanisms, like warfare, into the world. Thus, in spite of some indications that Jewish theology held angels to be sexless (see, for example, Matthew 22:30 and parallels), there were those who evidently believed that angels were sexual beings indeed and that previously in history they had sexually attacked humans. These themes were later developed in ascetic Gnosticism, with its portrayal of "archontic angels," taken to be those who mated with women aboriginally, as the paradigm of a condemned sexuality.[68]

It is therefore not at all unlikely, despite modern sensibilities to the contrary, that Paul, as an apocalyptic Jew, viewed angelic beings as a potential threat to the purity of women.[69] Angels in Paul's theology are never unambiguously benign or positive characters. Their moral characters and roles in God's salvific scheme are highly ambivalent. In 1 Corinthians 6:2–3 Paul says that Christians will be the eschatological judges of angels, revealing his supposition that they are quite fallible. In 2 Corinthians 12:7 Paul speaks of an "angel of Satan" whose purpose is to torment Paul (with divine permission, of course). And in Romans 8:38 angels are listed along with other persons and forces that may try to separate Christians "from the love of God in Christ Jesus our Lord." As Gerhard Kittel correctly notes, "What are in view are the elemental or natural angels which were widely accepted in Judaism and which might in isolation become ungodly and demonic powers. Also in view are the earlier pagan gods, which in part came to be identified with the guardian angels under which God placed the nations."[70] We must also bear in mind just how prominent the "sexual angels" reading of Genesis 6 was during Paul's day.[71] All these factors suggest that the angels in 1 Corinthians 11:10 represent some kind of threat to the female prophets, and that one aspect of this threat is sexual. As Gail Paterson Corrington has suggested, by unveiling their heads during the particularly vulnerable activity of prophesying, the women would in effect "open" another "orifice"—their *heads*—to potential invasion by cosmic forces—in this case, cosmic angels.[72]

This is not to say that Paul, while writing, is actively and consciously imagining some sexual act perpetrated on these women by angels with masculine bodies. Indeed, throughout my interpretation of this passage, as throughout this book, I want to insist that ascertaining Paul's authorial intention is not an adequate goal for interpretation, even if it were possible. What I am attempting here is a reconstruction not of Paul's conscious intentions but of the ideological matrix in which the veiling of women could be thought necessary during the act of prophecy. Given the ambivalent role played by angels (and similar beings) in Greco-Roman culture, the physiology of prophecy, and the sexual significance of veiling outlined above, the meaning of Paul's reference to angels, regardless of his conscious intentions, must include a sexual threat.[73]

Moreover, the attempt by other scholars to defuse the sexual reading of this passage by emphasizing the role of angels as protectors of order or policemen of proper worship is misguided. Any modern insistence that Paul's statement about the angels refers *either* to Paul's concerns about the sexual vulnerability of the women *or* to his concerns about order, stability, and propriety is a false either/or. Paul is anxious that women be veiled for three reasons: first, because his society (and he himself) worries about their sexual vulnerability; second, because a woman's unveiled head (at least in public) constitutes a bodily defect; and third, because female sexuality endangers the social order. As the anthropological and Greco-Roman accounts of veiling have shown, issues of female sexuality and social order cannot be separated in veiling cultures.

We must therefore take Paul's "because of the angels" as a pregnant ambiguity. Whether he intended the phrase to be ambiguous (he certainly made no attempt to make it clear), its multivalent possibilities serve Paul's purpose well. Whether Paul is concerned that the angels will be offended by a breach of the natural hierarchy or that they will lust after the women, or both, what he wants to accomplish is accomplished by his rhetoric: the women are threatened into submission. Furthermore, the threat of authoritative action against them can scarcely exclude the implied threat of aggressive penetration to enforce their submission. They will be "put in their place" by means of a super-male symbol of power: the angelic phallus. None of this need be explicit in Paul's language or in his mind in order for his threats to the women to include it implicitly.

I should point out that the women are not expected (or even allowed) to be completely passive: they must participate in their own covering. As previous research on veiling has shown, in Greco-Roman culture, as in many modern veiling cultures, the veil a woman places upon her head functions as the proper "authority" over her person—an authority that she herself, to some extent, controls. The veil is her own way (as an act that is within her power) of encasing her body within confines (both restrictive and protective) mandated by the culture. *She* places the veil over her head, thereby situating herself in her proper position in the ordered hierarchy of society. Paul's language urging veiling reflects the same power configuration. He says, "A woman ought to have authority (*exousia*) over her head" (11:10). As mentioned before, some scholars even want to translate *exousia* here as "veil."[74] To my mind, such a translation is unnecessarily specific, once it is recognized that in these veiling cultures the veil is both the sign of the woman's own authority and power as well as the sign of her weakness and relative powerlessness (relative, that is, to men). On the one hand, she retains the power to veil her head: she veils herself. On the other hand, this cannot be allowed to mask the ideological significance of the veiling (at least in ancient culture) as symbolizing and effecting the subordination of the female. By veiling herself, she (willingly?) implicates herself in the discourse that justifies her seclusion and control as both weak and dangerous.[75]

Lest my interpretation of the significance of veils in 1 Corinthians 11 seem too bizarre, I should note that Tertullian's interpretation of this passage and his statements on veiling contain all the elements of the ideological matrix sketched here. In "On the Apparel of Women" and "On the Veiling of Virgins" Tertullian argues for veiling. He takes it to be common throughout the Mediterranean world and notes that even the veiling of virgins, which seems not to have been so common in the West, was practiced "throughout Greece and certain of its barbaric provinces" and to some extent in Africa. He takes it as a matter of course that God commands women to be veiled.[76] Tertullian interprets Paul's words "because of the angels" (1 Cor. 11:10) as referring to Genesis 6 and the possibility that lustful angels would be tempted by unveiled women ("Apparel," 1. 2; 2. 10; "Virgins," 1. 7). Although one might think that the androgynous nature of angels would preclude the possibility of them lusting after women and mating with them (if angels are androgynous, according to the *modern* notion of androgyny, they have overcome the difference between male and female and therefore should be incapable of lust—in the traditional heterosexual way), Tertullian believes that angels present a sexual threat to unveiled women. Thus he simultaneously holds two views that seem to us contradictory.

Veiling is important, according to Tertullian, as protection against the penetrating gaze. He notes that Rebecca veiled herself (Gen. 24:64–65) even before she was married to Jacob. "For she showed that marriage likewise, as fornication is, is transacted by gaze and mind" ("Virgins," 1. 11). Veiling shields not only the virgin's face from the world but also the lures of the world from the virgin's gaze: "Seeing and being seen belong to the self-same lust" (1. 2). The covering of a woman's head, moreover, symbolizes—and in some way actually seems to enact—the covering of her genitals. Thus Tertullian can reason, "Let her whose lower parts are not bare have her upper likewise covered" (1. 12).

In one remarkable passage in which he urges virgins to remain veiled in church, Tertullian, excellent rhetorician that he is, allows his language to reflect the titillation, crescendo, climax, and post-coital relaxation of sexual intercourse, in a rhythm that comes out even in English translation: "Let her strive as much as you please with an honest mind; she must necessarily be imperilled by the public exhibition of herself, while she is penetrated by the gaze of untrustworthy and multitudinous eyes, while she is tickled by pointing fingers, while she is too well loved, while she feels a warmth creep over her amid assiduous embraces and kisses. Thus the forehead hardens; thus the sense of shame wears away; thus it relaxes; thus is learned the desire of pleasing in another way!" ("Virgins," 1. 14). The only protection against such penetration lies in the veil, which Tertullian advocates in language recalling Ephesians 6:13–17: "It [true virginity] betakes itself for refuge to the veil of the head as to a helmet, as to a shield, to protect its glory against the blows of temptations, against the darts of scandals, against suspicions and whispers and emulation; (against) envy also itself" ("Virgins," 1. 15). Like other Greco-Roman authors noted above, Tertullian portrays unveiling as rape. "Every public exposure of an honourable virgin is (to her) a suffering of rape. . . . You have denuded a maiden in regard of her head, and forthwith she wholly ceases to be a virgin to herself; she has undergone a change" ("Virgins," 1. 3).

As in other cultural constructions of veiling, however, the danger to the woman is only part of the problem for Tertullian. Women endanger society as much as they are endangered. Their uncontainable sexuality must be contained as far as possible by means of the veil, so that the boundaries and order of the community may be maintained against the onslaught of evil forces. In a section in which he takes Paul's reference to angels in 1 Corinthians 11:10 to refer to the lust of the angels in Genesis, Tertullian explains, "So perilous a face, then, ought to be shaded, which has cast stumbling-stones even so far as heaven" ("Virgins," 1. 7). Again evoking military language, though this time with a view to the protection of the virgin's society rather than her own person, Tertullian urges women, "Veil your head: if a mother, for your sons' sakes; if a sister, for your brethren's sakes; if a daughter, for your fathers' sakes. [Note that in each case it is *men* who are endangered by a woman's unveiled head!] All ages are perilled in your person. Put on the panoply of modesty, surround yourself with the stockade of bashfulness; rear a rampart for your sex, which must neither allow your own eyes egress nor ingress to other people's" ("Virgins," 1. 16). The danger of unveiled women threatens not just the women but the entire social body. Women are the weakest chink in the communal armor. Their bodies constitute the locus for invasion of the church by evil forces. In Tertullian's unforgettable words to the women of his church, "You are the devil's gateway: you are the unsealer of that (forbidden) tree" ("Apparel," 1. 1).

Tertullian's texts are important for my purposes because they make explicit a concern that is implicit in Paul's statements about veiling in 1 Corinthians 11.

I have argued in previous chapters that Paul is much more anxious about pollutions invading the body of Christ, the Christian community, than many of his modern commentators are willing to admit. Once we understand the ideological functions of veiling in Greco-Roman society, we see that 1 Corinthians 11:2–16 addresses not an individualistic issue of piety, respect, or subordination. Rather, the issue is a communal one, affecting each member of the body. As is so often the case in ancient ideology, the female represents the primary locus of possible invasion of the social body.[77] The medical writers expressed this by noting the more porous nature of female physiology. The practice of veiling served several functions: it made visible the ideological notion that the female was a possible locus of dangerous invasion; the veil itself provided protection against invasion and penetration, both for the woman and by extension for the social body; the veil therefore protected the woman's body from dangers posed by external forces and protected the social body from dangers posed by the female body itself. We can thus see that the veiling of women in church, especially when they were in an extra exposed state of inspiration, functioned as prophylaxis against external penetration and pollution for the community, the church, the body of Christ. The pollution of the body is thus the underlying issue of 1 Corinthians 11:2–16, both the pollution of the female body and the pollution of the communal body through that of the female.

Finally, this passage is also important for demonstrating the intersection of pollution and hierarchy in 1 Corinthians. Throughout this study I have dealt with the theological issues raised in 1 Corinthians by tying them to Paul's concerns about either the hierarchy of the body or the pollution of the body. In Paul's statements about veiling, we find these issues conjoined as nowhere else in 1 Corinthians, and that conjunction is understandable given the importance of physiology for Paul. Throughout 1 Corinthians Paul attempts to undermine the hierarchical ideology of the body prevalent in Greco-Roman culture. He attempts to make the strong weak and the weak strong. He calls on Christians of higher status to please those of lower status. He insists that those who see themselves as spiritual ones modify their behavior, such as speaking in tongues in the assembly, to accommodate those they consider spiritual inferiors. Paul even implies that higher-status Christians should follow his example and lower themselves socially in order to identify themselves with those of lower status. But when it comes to the male–female hierarchy, Paul abruptly renounces any status-questioning stance, accepting and even ideologically reinforcing a hierarchy of the body in which female is subordinated to male. The reason for this seeming inconsistency, I have argued, has to do with physiology. The "stuff" of female nature is differently constituted from that of male nature. Women's bodies are different from men's—not just in the way we today think of them as different, in that they have different "parts," but in that the very substance, the matter that makes up their bodies, is constitutionally different. Until the resurrection, women's bodies will be different from men's, more porous, penetrable, weak, and defenseless. Even after the resurrection femininity will not be any less inferior; it will simply be subsumed into the superior strength and density of masculinity. Because of the ancient definitions of masculine and feminine, therefore, "female" can never be equal to "male"—in spite of the fact (in Paul's language) that in the kingdom of God people who are now women will then be equal to people who are now men. Those who were formerly female will be equal, however, because their femininity will be swallowed up by masculinity. The inferior nature of their female stuff will be transcended as their bodies are raised to a higher level on the spectrum extending from higher male to lower female. Strange though it may seem to modern Christians, Paul cannot consider the female equal to the male, and for the present he cannot consider women equal to men, due to the hierarchy of physiology. Until the resurrection, the way to protect the church's body from invasive pollutions through the heads/genitals of women is for them to remain veiled, especially when participating in the boundary-breaking activities of praying and prophesying.

Postscript

The word (or in general any sign) is interindividual. Everything that is said, expressed, is located outside the "soul" of the speaker and does not belong to him. The word cannot be assigned to a single speaker. The author (speaker) has his own inalienable right to the word, but the listener also has his rights, and those whose voices are heard in the word before the author comes upon it also have their rights (after all, there are no words that belong to no one). The word is a drama in which three characters participate (it is not a duet, but a trio). It is performed outside the author, and it cannot be introjected into the author.
—*Mikhail Bakhtin, "From Notes Made in 1970–71"*

What did Paul's first letter to the Corinthians accomplish? Were the Strong at Corinth persuaded by Paul's arguments? Did they change their minds about the body and its hierarchy or its boundaries? Or did they simply become convinced that Paul was hopelessly naive, uneducated, and superstitious? If they did, did they remain in the church founded by Paul? Or did they give up? Or did they leave to form their own groups, their own house churches, their own "bodies of Christ"? We have no way of knowing. True, we have the writings that now make up 2 Corinthians, but they hardly tell the end of the story.

When reading most scholarship on Paul, it is easy to get the impression that he always won the argument, or at least that he deserved to. Paul's perspective is often taken to be the only perspective, or perhaps the only correct one. I am not so convinced. I believe it quite possible—indeed, probable—that with respect to several of the issues discussed in this book, Paul did not win the day. In some cases, after all, he was arguing a rather weak case. For example, it is hard to see how Paul can insist that sexual intercourse between a Christian man and a prostitute pollutes the pneuma of Christ (Chapter 7 above) and simultaneously argue that the holiness of Christ's body works the other way in the case of mixed marriages: that the unbelieving spouse, rather than polluting the Christian partner, experiences a sort of "reverse contagion," being made holy by contact with the sanctified body of the believing spouse (Chapter 8). It would not surprise me at all if Paul's disputants at Corinth found his arguments here unpersuasive. In the end, Paul's rhetoric, powerful and brilliant though it sometimes is, may not have succeeded.[1]

As should be clear, I have not attempted an apologia for Paul. Not only do I doubt that he won all his arguments, but in some cases I hope he did not. It would be nice to believe, for instance, that some women refused to accept his and their society's characterization of them as inferior. But all such hopes remain in the netherworld of historical speculation; we simply have no way of knowing.

Doubtless, for some people Paul will remain an unquestionable authority, for others a convenient whipping boy. Though harboring no fantasies that this book will radically change anyone's overall stance, I hope it has demonstrated that the situation is more complex than either position allows. On a deeper level, one goal of this study has been to argue that religious language must be analyzed ideologically. How does it intersect, challenge, or protect the structures of power in a given society? Whom does it help? Whom does it hurt? Finally, and perhaps most important, are we—whether Jews, Christians, nonbelievers, or whatever—willing to own the (even unintended) ethical ramifications and political consequences of the things we say we believe? If this study has led us to examine the often unrecognized implications of our own constructions of the bodies of ourselves and others, then some purpose will have been served by our attempt to enter the Corinthian body.

Notes

The editions used in this book are from the Loeb Classical Library unless otherwise indicated. Translations of Greek and Latin texts, as also of Scripture, are my own unless otherwise indicated in the notes.

Preface

1. See Kümmel, *New Testament*, 206–324; for a placement of the history-of-religions school in relation to recent social-scientific methods of biblical study, see my "Social-Scientific Criticism."

2. For more on this, see my *Slavery as Salvation*, xvii, xx, and 148–149, and my review of Hamerton-Kelly, *Sacred Violence*.

3. Griffin, "*Urbs Roma, Plebs*, and *Princeps*," 23.

4. See J. B. Thompson, *Ideology and Modern Culture*, 7; Giddens, "Four Theses on Ideology," 19. I am grateful to Elizabeth Clark for these references and for suggestions on different uses of *ideology*.

5. D. B. Martin, *Slavery as Salvation*, 123; see also Malherbe, *Paul and the Thessalonians*, 55.

6. See Meeks, *First Urban Christians*, 53–55; Holmberg, *Sociology and the New Testament*, 21–24, 63.

7. Ste. Croix, *Class Struggle in the Ancient Greek World*, 41.

8. Ibid., 59.

9. On the importance of class for analysis of early Christianity (with a critique of how Ste. Croix uses it), see further my "Ancient Slavery, Class, and Early Christianity."

10. See Stambaugh, "Social Relations in the City." See also Stambaugh and Balch, *New Testament in its Social Environment*. This is, of course, a simplistic sketch, but in relation to my point here, it is both accurate and sufficient.

Chapter 1: The Body in Greco-Roman Culture

1. See, e.g., the survey by Koyré, *Closed World to Infinite Universe*.

2. Kenny, *Anatomy of the Soul*, 113; see also Wilkie, "Body and Soul in Aristotelian Tradition," 19–20. In the ancient world one popular dichotomy in philosophy was between "nature" and "culture" or "convention." I would argue that even in this case the nature/culture dichotomy functioned quite differently in ancient culture from how it does in modern culture (and therefore meant something quite different). For one treatment of the problematics of the distinction in ancient texts, see Winkler, *Constraints of Desire*, 17–44.

3. See Beck, *Metaphysics of Descartes*, 6.

4. Descartes, *Meditation* VI; see *idem*, *Discourse on Method*, 152. The bracketed words indicate changes made by Descartes to the second French edition of the *Meditations*.

5. Descartes, *Discourse on Method*, pt. 4; see Lindsay, Introduction to *Discourse on Method*, xx.

6. Descartes, *Discourse on Method*, 96.

7. Descartes, *Second Meditation*, 95–96 (brackets in the edition).

8. Descartes, *Sixth Meditation*, 154.

9. Descartes, *Discourse on Method*, 5.

10. Descartes, *Second Meditation*, 97.

11. Descartes, *Sixth Meditation*, 151, my emphasis; cf. 156. See Riese, "Descartes' Ideas of Brain Function," 132: "The first affirmation of the Cartesian system is that man is essentially a thinking being and that the unity between mind and body is merely a unity of composition (*unitas compositionis*), but not a unity of nature (*unitas naturae*)."

12. For one argument that Descartes's categories were quite different from ancient philosophical ones, see Burnyeat, "Idealism and Greek Philosophy." M. E. Dahl (*Resurrection of the Body*, 48–50) also objects to using "supernatural" as a gloss for "spiritual" (as in "spiritual body") or as opposed to "material." He observes that the term "supernatural" "is practically a coinage of St Thomas Aquinas," but that Thomas could still speak of a "supernatural material body." As Dahl concludes, "The term

'supernatural' was almost unknown before the thirteenth century and is unknown in the New Testament, indeed in the whole Bible. It is begging the question to say that 'spiritual' means the same thing" (50).

13. Perhaps the most famous example of this widespread view is Robinson, *The Body*, esp. 11–16; see also Bottomley, *Attitudes to the Body*, 1–30; Cullman, "Immortality of the Soul," 24–25. Despite passing concessions that Paul's world cannot be cleanly divided into a Greek half and a Jewish half (25), Stacey's treatment of *The Pauline View of Man* reveals by its very organization that tendency. The organization of the *TDNT* articles also reflects and has encouraged this view.

14. Lucretius *De rerum natura* 1. 419–444. For many of the texts of Greek philosophy I have used the translation of A. A. Long and D. N. Sedley, followed by *HP* and the section number and letter from their anthology *The Hellenistic Philosophers;* this passage from Lucretius, e.g., is *HP* 5B.

15. Lucretius 4. 877–891 (*HP* 14E); see also 3. 136–176 (*HP* 14B); Epicurus *Letter to Herodotus* 63–67 (*HP* 14A).

16. Seneca *Epistle* 58. 13–15 (*HP* 27A).

17. See also Alexander *On Aristotle's Topics* 301. 19–25 (*HP* 27B).

18. Diogenes Laertius *Lives of Philosophers* 7. 134 (*HP* 44B).

19. Galen *On Bodily Mass* 7. 525. 9–14; trans. Long and Sedley (*SVF* 2. 439; *HP* 47F).

20. Plutarch *On Stoic Self-Contradictions* 1053F–1054B (*HP* 47M).

21. Hierocles *Elements of Ethics* 1. 5–33, 4. 38–53 (*HP* 53B).

22. Plato *Phaedo* 83D, trans. Fowler.

23. "The monism which comes most naturally to a Greek philosopher is materialism, as in the Stoics, or, very differently and provided that an infinite void does not count as an extra item in one's ontology, Democritean and Epicurean atomism" (Burnyeat, "Idealism and Greek Philosophy," 19–20).

24. Lynch, *Aristotle's School*, 177–189; Glucker, *Antiochus and the Late Academy*; Dillon, "'Orthodoxy' and 'Eclecticism.'"

25. Berchman, *From Philo to Origen*, 27.

26. On the revival of Platonism, see ibid., 9. On Stoicism as especially popular in the early Empire, see Malherbe, *Moral Exhortation*, 12; Stowers, *Letter Writing in Greco-Roman Antiquity*, 40.

27. On Philo's Stoicism, see Mansfeld, "Philosophy in the Service of Scripture."

28. Philo *Questions on Genesis* 2. 59; on the "material soul" in Philo, see Maddalena, "L'ENNOIA e l'EPISTEME THEOU." For Plato's three parts of the soul, see *Republic* 434E–444D, *Phaedrus* 246B–249D, *Timaeus* 69C–71A.

29. Philo *On the Unchangeableness of God* 45–46; *idem, Who is the Heir?* 283. Philo's use of the term *ousia* ("substance") is also somewhat confusing. According to Berchman, Philo uses it in the Stoic sense, thereby implying that it is material; God (although not necessarily "the divinities"), for Philo, is therefore not "substance" (Berchman, *From Philo to Origen*, 38). We must also keep in mind that the *sōma* ("corporeal") is not for Philo equivalent to the *hylē* ("material"); see ibid., 47–48.

30. Dillon, *Middle Platonists*, 129. Dillon points out that Crantor may have influenced Eudorus (an Alexandrian Platonist who preceded Philo) to accept that the soul was constructed of elements of both the "intelligible" world and the "physical," since it had to relate to both (131). John Rist claims, "The doctrine that we have in the *Quod Deus* looks like a blend of the Stoic thesis that both the human mind and the heavenly bodies are composed of fire and the Aristotelian thesis (vouchsafed in the *De caelo*) that the heavenly bodies are composed of a 'first body'" (*Use of Stoic Terminology*, 8). To which Dillon responds, "Admittedly, in this passage it remains quite ambiguous whether Philo means the soul to be composed of pure fire, like the heavenly bodies, or of immaterial *pneuma*. It is possible that he was not quite clear himself" (19).

31. For a historical survey of theories of *pneuma*, see Verbeke, *L'Évolution de la doctrine du pneuma du Stoïcisme à S. Augustin*.

32. Philo *Questions on Genesis* 2. 59 ("breath" here is *pneuma*). See Runia, *Philo of Alexandria*, 270, 299, 318. Runia points out that Philo's account of "hearing" is closer to Stoic theory than to Plato's *Timaeus* but that there existed other parallels to Philo's position in Middle Platonism.

33. Plutarch, *Whether the Affections of the Soul are Worse than Those of the Body* (*Moralia* 500B–502A). See similar treatments by Cicero (*Tusculan Disputations* 3) and Maximus of Tyre (*Oration* 7: *Dissertation* 41, in *Dissertations of Maximus Tyrius*).

34. Donini, "Science and Metaphysics," 140–142. See also Plutarch *Moralia* 943C. In 944F Plutarch speaks of the *physis* of the soul, his use of the term reminding us again that "nature" for the ancients had a completely different meaning from what it has had since Descartes, precluding any possibility of a realm called "supernatural" in the ancient world.

35. Ptolemy, "On the *Kriterion* and *Hegemonikon*," 3. 1 and 3; text and trans. in *Criterion of Truth*, ed. Huby and Neal, 179–230.

36. Ibid., 223, note to 7. 2. 4; see Phillip de Lacy, "Galen's Platonism."

37. Note Cicero's list of different views of the nature of the "soul." He claims that "the Romans" generally identify "soul" with "breath"—both philosophically and popularly. He says that other views that render the soul immaterial (like a relationship or harmony or number) are not widespread but are "peculiar to individual thinkers" (*Tusculan Disputations* 1. 9. 18–1. 10. 20).

38. Barkan, *Nature's Work of Art*, 8.

39. Padel, *In and Out of Mind*, 43. According to Hippocrates *Breaths* 3. 7, *physa* is

pneuma inside the body, and *aēr* is pneuma outside the body.

40. Padel, *In and Out of Mind*, 48.

41. Hippocrates *Nature of Man*.

42. Hippocrates *Breaths* 3 and 13; see Padel, *In and Out of Mind*, 51.

43. Padel, *In and Out of Mind*, 51; see Hippocrates *Humors* 13–16 for an interesting discussion of the link between disturbances in the weather and resulting disturbances (diseases) in the body. For a later depiction of the internal weather of the body, see Plutarch, "Advice about Keeping Well" (*Moralia* 129A–B).

44. Note the philosophical precursors to the function of microcosmic theory in medical sciences: see, e.g., Longrigg, *Greek Rational Medicine*, 46.

45. *PGM* I. 1–42; IV. 94–153 (and see p. 40, n. 43, in Betz's edition); IV. 475–829.

46. Padel, *In and Out of Mind*, 42, see reference at n. 100.

47. Ibid., 58, citing Hippocrates *Regimen* 1. 36, *Breaths* 8. 30, 12, and Lonie, "Medical Theory in Heraclides of Pontus," 128. See also Padel, *In and Out of Mind*, 86.

48. Sextus Empiricus *Outlines of Pyrrhonism* 1. 79–91 (trans. *HP* 72C).

49. Evans, *Physiognomics*, 23.

50. Galen *Ars Medica* 10 (in *Opera Omnia*, ed. Kühn, 1. 332; trans. Evans, 24).

51. *hoti ta tēs psychēs ēthē tais tou sōmatos krasesin epetai*: 4. 767–822; or *Claudii Galeni Pergameni Scripta Minora*, ed. Mueller, 2. 32–79.

52. Padel, *In and Out of Mind*, 27, n. 60; see also 76.

53. Ibid., 39.

54. This is what Laqueur calls the "fungibility of fluids" in the ancient body. See *Making Sex*, 19–20, and Chap. 2.

55. Solmsen, "Greek Philosophy," 153; see also Longrigg, "Philosophy and Medicine," 154. According to the Hippocratic *Sacred Disease* 19, air gives the brain its intelligence.

56. Hahm, "Early Hellenistic Theories," 66–67. The quotations are from Hahm's

translation of *SVF*, vol. 2, frg. 471; see also frg. 442. For other Stoic theories of *pneuma* and perception see *SVF* 2. 697, 841, 310.

57. Hahm, "Early Hellenistic Theories," 85; see also *Herophilus*, ed. von Staden, 466. Philo also assumes that all other forms of stuff may be pervaded by pneuma (*On the Creation* 131) and that pneuma is the substance of all sense perception (*On Flight and Finding* 182, note *to horatikon pneuma*).

58. Von Staden, "Stoic Theory of Perception," 97.

59. Plutarch *Placita* 5. 15 (*Moralia* 907C–D); see *Herophilus*, ed. von Staden, frg. 202a–b, p. 372. For a Jewish text underlain by the same assumptions, see 2 Maccabees 14:46.

60. *Herophilus*, ed. von Staden, 173; the belief was not limited to physicians: it was held by Pliny the Elder *Natural History* 11. 89. 219; see *Herophilus*, ed. von Staden, 360; Kleinknecht, "*Pneuma, pneumatikos, ktl.*"

61. Scarborough, *Roman Medicine*, 35, 119.

62. Temkin, *Double Face of Janus*, 155.

63. Woollam, "Concepts of the Brain," 17.

64. Aetius 4. 21. 1–4 (fragments of Aetius are edited in Diels, *Doxographi Graeci*, see pp. 410–411; this passage is also in *SVF* 2. 836); *HP* 53H. As already noted above, Philo attributed hearing to the agency of pneuma.

65. Hahm, "Early Hellenistic Theories," 61, 65; for Plato, see Turnbull, "Role of 'Special Sensibles,'" 9.

66. Hahm, "Early Hellenistic Theories," 87.

67. Von Staden, "Stoic Theory of Perception," 105.

68. *Herophilus*, ed. von Staden, 204.

69. Solmsen, "Greek Philosophy," 150, speaking of Herophilus and Erasistratus. The belief, however, was more widespread.

70. Temkin, *Double Face of Janus*, 303.

71. Hippocrates *Breaths* 8; cf. Padel, *In and Out of Mind*, 81; for influences of different winds as causing illnesses, see

Hippocrates *Humors* 14–19; *Sacred Disease* 14–16.

72. Hippocrates *Nature of Man* 9, my trans. At about the same time as the genesis of the Hippocratic medical traditions, Greek tragedians could speak of pneuma as "gusts" of passion that buffet the innards of a tragic character (Aeschylus *Prometheus Bound* 883–884, Sophocles *Antigone* 137; see Padel, *In and Out of Mind*, 92). The way these playwrights speak of emotions is structurally identical, as Padel argues, with the way the medical theorists explain the dynamics of disease.

73. Galen *De sanitate tuenda* 1. 4, 8; 3. 12; Greek text in *Opera Omnia*, ed. Kühn; English: *Galen's Hygiene*, trans. Green; Galen *On the Affected Parts* 3. 11 (p. 95); see also Temkin, *Double Face of Janus*, 159. Elsewhere Galen notes that the psychic pneuma must be "pure and excellent" and that it can be adversely affected by "nasty vapors" (*On Respiration and the Arteries* 5. 5 (p. 129). For fascinating parallels (with important differences) in ancient Chinese systems, see Kuriyama, "Imagination of Winds."

74. Siegel, *Galen's System*, 192.

75. Siegel, *Galen on Psychology*, 137–138; Galen *On the Affected Parts* 3. 10: the "humoral mixture" of the brain can be altered by vile humors.

76. Temkin, *Double Face of Janus*, 159, citing *Methodus medendi*, bk. 12, chap. 5; see also *Galen's Hygiene*, trans. Green, 1. 4 and 1. 11. For the pneuma as the substance enabling intelligence and sense, see Hippocrates *Sacred Disease* 19; intelligence "comes from air" (*phronēsios tou ēeros*): 20. 30.

77. According to Temkin, Galen considered the psychic pneuma "the indispensable organ of the rational soul and the medium by which the function of the senses as well as nerves can be explained" (*Double Face of Janus*, 160). The concept was especially employed by, but not limited to, the Stoics; Galen was not, after all, a Stoic; see Frede, "On Galen's Epistemology," 68–69; de

Lacy, "Galen's Platonism." Philo speaks of the pneuma as the stuff that constitutes the soul or mind (R. A. Horsley, "Pneumatikos vs. Psychikos," 272). For other examples of the role played by (or upon) pneuma in disease, see Longrigg, *Greek Rational Medicine*, 37, 173.

78. See Tanner, "St. Paul and Panaetius," 364. For an account of the importance of pneuma in ideas of sympathy even outside Stoicism, see Rist, "On Greek Biology," esp. 40.

79. Lee, "Sense of an Object," 51–52.

80. Scarborough, *Roman Medicine*, 143. On the medical importance of the doctrine of sympathy in Galen's thought (he uses the term *koinōnia*), see Siegel, *Galen's System of Physiology and Medicine*, 360–382.

81. Hahm maintains that the Platonic (and later, more general Hellenistic) theory of vision "reduces vision to a tactile sensation." He adds: "Yet the proponents of the theory reduce tactile sensation as well to the same mechanical interaction of particles" (75, citing Democritus, according to Theophrastus *Concerning Odors* 61–66, and Plato *Timaeus* 61D–64D; see also Hahm, "Early Hellenistic Theories," 84, for comments about Stoics).

82. Temkin, *Double Face of Janus*, 316.

83. Aristotle *Meteorologica* 3. 4. 373b2–10; Hahm, "Early Hellenistic Theories," 78.

84. Hahm, "Early Hellenistic Theories," 79.

85. Lucretius *De rerum natura* 4. 337–352; Hahm, "Early Hellenistic Theories," 76.

86. Tarrant, "Pneuma-Related Concepts in Platonism."

87. Re beauty as infallible sign of nobility and even divinity, see Chariton *Chaereas and Callirhoe* 5. 9; Xenophon of Ephesus *An Ephesian Tale* 1. 1, 1. 2; Heliodorus *An Ethiopian Story* 1. 2, 1. 7, 1. 19–20, 2. 19, 7. 12, 7. 19; Achilles Tatius *Leucippe and Clitophon* 1. 4; Edwards, "Surviving the Web of Roman Power," 193, n. 6, 194. True servility likewise always reveals itself; see,

e.g., Heliodorus *Ethiopian Story* 1. 4 (the master—i.e., the one who has captured the hero and heroine—resembles the servant in the presence of the truly noble people he holds in bondage), 3. 3, 7. 26.

88. See Temkin's Introduction to Soranus, *Gynecology*, xxxviii. For the Greek text, see *Sorani Gynaeciorum libri IV*, ed. Ilberg, or *Sorani Gynaeciorum*, ed. Rose.

89. Soranus *Gynecology* 1. 10. 39. (Numbers refer to book, chapter, and article, with the articles numbered consecutively throughout each book, not beginning again with each chapter.)

90. Ibid., 2. 16. 32–33 [36. 101–102]. (Numbers in brackets refer to the enumeration in Rose's edition, which divides the text into two books [rather than four] and numbers the articles consecutively through those two divisions.)

91. Galen, *Hygiene*, trans. Green. References include book and chapter followed by page number in Green's translation.

92. For powder and oil as toughening agents, see 1. 7, p. 22; 3. 13, p. 138.

93. MacMullen, *Roman Social Relations*, 88–94.

94. Douglas, *Rules and Meanings*, 93.

95. *SVF* 2. 879; *HP* 53G.

96. Ptolemy, "On the *Kriterion* and *Hegemonikon*," 14.5.

97. See D. B. Martin, *Slavery as Salvation*, 71–74. For the various meanings of the penis, see Artemidorus *Oneirocritica* 1. 2, 1. 45; for the head as representing the master, see Introduction to bk. 4 (p. 185). Page numbers refer to the translation by White.

98. Galen, *Hygiene*, trans. Green, 6. 13 (p. 271).

99. Ibid., (pp. 51–52); Galen believes it is possible, though difficult, for a laborer, or even a slave, to follow a modified regimen to preserve good health: 6. 5 (pp. 248–249); 6. 7 (pp. 253–255).

100. Laqueur, *Making Sex*, 5–6.

101. Hippocrates *Regimen* 1. 34; see

Horowitz, "Aristotle and Women"; Allen, *Concept of Woman*, 95–97. Clement of Alexandria combines the familiar notion that women's bodies are cool while men's are hot with the theme that the female is an "imperfect" male (*Paedagogus* 3. 3).

102. See Lloyd, "Hot and Cold," 102–104. As Lloyd notes, "Thus it was widely assumed that the difference between the two sexes was in some way to be connected with a difference between hot and cold (and sometimes, too, between dry and wet), though there was no general agreement as to which opposites corresponded to which sex" (102).

103. Hippocrates *Regimen* 1. 27; see McLaren, *History of Contraception*, 22, 24.

104. Hippocrates, "On Generation," 18. 1, trans. Lonie. McLaren, *History of Contraception*, 31.

105. Soranus *Gynecology* 2. 21. 46 (41. 115).

106. Ptolemy, "On the *Kriterion* and *Hegemonikon*," 13. 2–4.

107. See n. 87 above. The most traditional Greek figure embodying this assumption was Thersites, the character in the *Iliad* who is despicable, ugly, and obnoxious, and who becomes, in later Greek tradition and rhetoric, the typical lower-class caricature.

108. See Pseudo-Aristotle *Physiognomics* 2. For a similar physiognomic ideology among Jews, see Vermes, *Dead Sea Scrolls in English*, 268–269 (4Q186[1]; 4Q186[2]).

109. Maximus of Tyre, "Dissertation," 25. 3 (Dissertation 15 in trans. by Taylor).

110. Evans, *Physiognomics*, 12.

111. Ibid., 59; see also 12–13, 40–41.

112. Ibid., 26–27. In moral philosophy this link between wisdom and beauty was altered somewhat to emphasize the beauty of the "inner" man even if the "outer" man was not beautiful (see Cicero *Pro Murena* 29. 61, *De Finibus* 3. 75). This was an alteration *by philosophers*, however, of the more popular rhetorical common sense that beauty of

body was a natural expression of beauty of character.

113. Galen *Peri kraseōn* (*De temperamentis*) 2. 1 (in *Opera Omnia*, ed. Kühn 1. 576; trans. Evans, *Physiognomics*, 75); see Evans, "Galen as Physiognomist," 298, for the whole passage.

114. Galen *On the Passions*, chap. 3, trans. Harkins, p. 32.

115. Galen, *Hygiene*, trans. Green, 6. 14 (p. 275).

Chapter 2: The Rhetoric of the Body Politic

1. Dio Chrysostom *Discourse* 34. 20, trans. Cohoon and Crosby.

2. M. M. Mitchell, *Paul and the Rhetoric of Reconciliation*, 65–66. Ignorant of Mitchell's work, I noted the importance of homonoia speeches for the study of 1 Corinthians in my 1988 dissertation, published in 1990 as *Slavery as Salvation* (see 143–145). Mitchell's research has superseded all previous studies on the subject, but one may compare Kramer, *Quid valeat homonoia*; Tarn, *Alexander the Great*, 2. 399–449; Romilly, "Vocabulaire et propagande"; Ferguson, *Moral Values*, 118–132.

3. Aelius Aristides *Oration* 23. 31. For a modern physician's reading of Aelius, popularly written, see London, "Was That Old Greek a Hypochondriac?"

4. An analysis of the different portrayals of disease will be pursued in Chap. 6.

5. See Isocrates *On the Peace* 109; Dio Chrysostom *Discourses* 34. 17, 20, 22; 38. 12, 14; 39. 5; 41. 9; 48. 12; Aelius Aristides *Oration* 24. 16, 18.

6. Incidentally, whereas moderns would normally make a dichotomy between the individual and society, for the ancients the comparable dichotomy is between the private and the public. Men in their "private" lives (*tōn idiōtōn*) have different interests than do cities, which must give attention to what

is "common" (*koinē;* see Dio Chrysostom *Discourse* 38. 30). What Dio contrasts here is not the modern notion of the individual psyche as opposed to the social entity but rather the realm of the household versus that of the polis. Modern individualism is remarkably absent from ancient concepts, in spite of misleading modern references to the "individualism" of ancient Greek thought.

7. For speeches addressing the conflicts between the Assembly and the Council, see *Discourse* 43 (addressed to the Assembly); *Discourse* 50 (to the Council).

8. See also Philo *On Joseph* 145; 1 *Clement* 20; Marcus Aurelius *Meditations* 5. 30; Aelius Aristides *Oration* 24. 42, 27. 35.

9. This interpretation contradicts that of M. M. Mitchell, *Paul and Rhetoric of Reconciliation*, 127, that "the whole purpose of a concordant political body is to make all members strong." Indeed, the sources she cites in support, including this one by Pseudo-Aristotle, all assume maintenance of the hierarchy, not its abolition in a universal strength of all members.

10. 1 *Clement* 21. 7–8; Dio Chrysostom *Discourse* 24. 24; 38. 15; Aelius Aristides *Oration* 24. 7.

11. See Dio Chrysostom *Discourse* 40. 34; Demosthenes *Epistle* 3. 45, quoted by Aelius Aristides *Oration* 23. 71; M. M. Mitchell, *Paul and Rhetoric of Reconciliation*, 130–132.

12. Gerd Theissen, in a series of ground-breaking articles (see *Social Setting of Pauline Christianity*), proposed that Paul himself advocated "love-patriarchalism" (what I have called "benevolent patriarchalism") to the Corinthians. I critique Theissen's position in my *Slavery as Salvation*, 26–30, 88–91, 126–129. I use the term *benevolent* with some irony here, since patriarchalism may be characterized as benevolent only in the minds of the deluded. But the oxymoronic term "benevolent patriarchalism" reflects the terminology used by the Greco-Roman writers themselves (see, e.g., Philo's *patēr eunous*, *On Joseph* 67–69).

13. Cassius Dio *Roman History* 4. 17, trans. Cary.

14. Even when placed in a more democratic context, this theme of yielding to the other can function conservatively. Josephus, for example, places a homonoia speech on the lips of the dying Mattathias, who urges his sons to continue the fight (later known as the Maccabean War) against the Greco-Syrians. He urges his sons, "In whatever respect one of you is superior to the others, in that yield to one another, and so make the best use of your several abilities" (*Antiquities* 12. 283, trans. Marcus). The cooperative rule of equal brothers is usually the symbol for democratic constitutions in Greco-Roman political philosophy (see Aristotle *Nichomachean Ethics* 8. 10. 6; *Politics* 1. 2. 3). Nevertheless, benevolent patriarchalism still interjects itself: each brother is assumed to be superior to the others in some way, and it is in that aspect of strength that the weaker brothers are to yield to the stronger. The weaker is still urged to yield to the stronger, and thus no disruption of "natural" status is envisioned.

15. Plutarch *Lycurgus* 7. 2, trans. Perrin.

16. Demosthenes *Epistle* 3. 45; 2. 2, trans. Goldstein.

17. Dionysius Halicarnassus *Roman Antiquities* 6. 36. 1–37. 2, trans. Cary.

18. Ibid., 6. 71. 1–86. 5; the quotation is from 6. 85. 1.

19. Note the many commonplaces of homonoia speeches found in *Discourse* 34: Dio urges their *true* advantage (34. 6–7; cf. 28); discord arises when the weak are oppressed by the strong (10–11). Note also the typical models of concord: the ship (16, 32), the healthy body (17, 20, 22), and the household (24).

20. See *Discourse* 38. 28, and note Dio's rejection of "false glory" in 38. 29.

21. See R. A. Horsley, "Wisdom of Word and Words of Wisdom."

22. This and the other references to rhetoric in 1 Cor. 1–4 are fully examined in a study by Stephen Pogoloff (*Logos and Sophia*, see esp. 108–127), on which my treatment relies.

23. Ibid., 158–172.

24. Cicero *De Oratore* 1. 11. 47.

25. Ibid., 1. 31. 137–1. 32. 145; 2. 18. 75–76; 3. 19. 70–73.

26. Isocrates *On the Peace* 38.

27. Isocrates *Antidosis* 200–204; quotation from 204, trans. Norlin.

28. Isocrates *Against the Sophists* 14.

29. Dio Chrysostom *Discourse* 42. 2; see also Plutarch *On Brotherly Love* (*Moralia*) 478C; Sextus Empiricus *Against the Professors* (*Mathematikos*) 2. 76–83; Pogoloff, *Logos and Sophia* 136, 148–153.

30. See Fish, *Doing What Comes Naturally*, 471–475.

31. D. A. Russell, *Greek Declamation*, 76.

32. Gwynn, *Roman Education from Cicero to Quintilian*, 246; Bonner, *Education in Ancient Rome*, 48; Marrou, *History of Education*, 271 (see also 265–291 for an entertaining description of Roman education). For discussion of literary levels and how extensive education was in the population at large, see Harris, *Ancient Literacy*.

33. Suetonius *On Grammarians* 4; Quintilian *Rhetoric* 2. 1. 1–6.

34. Quintilian *Rhetoric* 2. 4. 1–3.

35. The terms "sophist" and "rhetor" overlap (at least during the second century C.E., the time of the "Second Sophistic," and possibly earlier). According to E. L. Bowie ("Importance of Sophists"), sophists were expected to be both teachers and virtuoso speakers, whereas the word *rhetor* could designate a public speaker or perhaps simply a teacher of rhetoric. On upward mobility due to rhetorical training, see Stambaugh, "Social Relations," 80.

36. Bouvier, "Hommes de lettres." Eight rhetors or orators are listed, six "sophists." The sophists are all from the second century C.E., perhaps indicating the revived popularity of the term with the so-called Second Sophistic?

37. Chaniotis, "Als die Diplomaten noch tanzten und sangen." See also Bowie, "Importance of Sophists." According to Bowie, rhetors were ambassadors because they came from the upper class, not because they were accomplished as rhetors (55–56). For rhetors as political leaders and ambassadors in democratic Athens (403–322 B.C.E.), see M. H. Hanson, "*Rhetores* and *Strategoi* in Fourth-Century Athens." For the Antioch inscription honoring Diotrephes, see C. P. Jones, "Diotrephes of Antioch." For the family of sophists, see Pouilloux, "Une famille de sophistes thessaliens à Delphes au II^{e}s. ap. J.-C."

38. Bowie, "Importance of Sophists," 32.

39. G. Anderson, "Julianus of Laodicea," 202.

40. Plutarch *On Brotherly Love* (*Moralia*) 485A, D, trans. Helmbold.

41. Plutarch *On Tranquility of Mind* (*Moralia*) 472A, trans. Helmbold.

42. Ijsseling, *Rhetoric and Philosophy in Conflict*, 10. As Carlin Barton notes, "Walking, sitting, reclining, facial expressions and gestures, and above all, speech—its tone and tenor, rhythm and accent—were subject to regulation according to a set of increasingly refined stylistic models" (*Sorrows of the Ancient Romans*, 115). See also Ramage, *Urbanitas*, 115, 117, *et passim;* Grant, *Ancient Rhetorical Theories*, 121–125; David, "Les Orateurs."

43. Among the many recent studies emphasizing Paul's use of Greco-Roman rhetoric, see M. M. Mitchell, *Paul and the Rhetoric of Reconciliation*, and Pogoloff, *Logos and Sophia;* P. Lampe, "Theological Wisdom"; Smit, "Genre of 1 Corinthians 13," and "Two Puzzles."

44. Hock, "Paul's Tentmaking," and *Social Context of Paul's Ministry.*

45. D. B. Martin, *Slavery as Salvation*, 123; Malherbe, *Paul and Thessalonians*, 55.

46. See also Malherbe, "Beasts at Ephesus," 81.

47. D. B. Martin, *Slavery as Salvation*, 69–70, 77–85.

48. Note, e.g., Isocrates *Nicocles, or The Cyprians* 45.

49. Possibly Paul's reference to a "painful visit" that occurred between the writing of 1 and 2 Corinthians implies an open confrontation between himself and some members of the church there (2:1). Certainly, by the time he wrote 2 Cor. 10–13 Paul has had to deal with open opposition (see 10:1, 10–11; 12:11; 13:1–3).

50. On 2 Cor. 10–13 as part of a separate letter, see Barrett, *Second Epistle*, 10–21; Héring, *Second Epistle*, xi–xv; Best, *Second Corinthians*, 91–92; Georgi, *Opponents of Paul*, 9–14.

51. Demetrius *On Style* 4. 227; Seneca *Letter* 75. 1; Stowers, *Letter Writing*, 32–35, 62; White, *Light from Ancient Letters*, 190–191. On letter writing as part of rhetorical education, see Stowers, 32–35; White, 189–190.

52. For the common topos of "word" and "deed" in moral philosophy, see Malherbe, *Moral Exhortation*, 38–39, and index under "word . . . and deed."

53. D. A. Russell, *Greek Declamation*, 82. Russell is here speaking of the Second Sophistic (mainly second century C.E.), but rhetorical interest in the body, though perhaps greater in the period of the Second Sophistic, was an element of rhetoric in previous centuries too. See, for example, the Odyssean speech of Antisthenes, in which Odysseus must defend himself against charges that he is low-class because of his clothing and appearance: Caizzi, ed., *Antisthenis Fragmenta;* Giannantoni, ed., *Socraticorum reliquiae;* D. B. Martin, *Slavery as Salvation,* 105–107.

54. It should be clear from this section— in which I repeatedly attempt to read the themes of 1 Cor. 5–15 as foreshadowed in 1 Cor. 1–4—why I remain unconvinced by Martinus DeBoer's fascinating suggestion

that the first four chapters were originally intended by Paul to stand on their own as a complete letter. See his "Composition of 1 Corinthians."

55. See Amos 5:18–20; Joel 2:31; Aus, "Comfort in Judgment"; Kuck, "Judgment and Community Conflict," 77.

56. Bakhtin, "Problem of the Text in Linguistics," in *Speech Genres.*

57. M. M. Mitchell, *Paul and Rhetoric of Reconciliation,* 83–86.

58. Theissen, *Social Setting;* see also N. A. Dahl, "Paul and the Church at Corinth"; Welborn, "On Discord in Corinth"; Plunkett, "Sexual Ethics and the Christian Life," 231.

59. 1 Cor. 4:15. On the pedagogue in antiquity, see Lull, "'The Law Was Our Pedagogue,'" 489, n. 44. I disagree with Lull that the role of pedagogue was generally considered an honorable one. Perhaps it was by other slaves or members of the lower classes, but to the educated (the target of Paul's rhetoric here) the pedagogue was a slave of especially low status. I believe Lull's positive construction of the ancient pedagogue's reputation is too affected by his attempt to read Galatians as assigning a positive role to the Law. A more balanced account is that of Young ("*Paidagogos*"), which highlights the low-status connotations of the word while admitting that "the role of the pedagogue was . . . ambivalent; attracting ridicule and scorn on the one hand, but praise and appreciation on the other" (168); to which I would add only that the appreciation expressed to pedagogues was that appropriate for slaves, not free teachers. See also Longenecker, "Pedagogical Nature of the Law."

60. See M. M. Mitchell, *Paul and Rhetoric of Reconciliation,* 47–50.

61. Hengel, *Crucifixion.*

62. I would take the following texts as indicating a traditional, ongoing Jewish use of apocalypticism to resist Greek and Roman imperialism, *regardless* of whether

the social groups using these texts actually armed themselves and mounted a rebellion: Dan. 11–12; the "War Scroll" from the Qumran documents; Josephus's accounts of eschatological prophets in Palestine (especially *War* 2. 258–260 and *Antiquities* 20. 167–168; *War* 2. 261–263; 6. 283–287; even John the Baptist, according to Josephus's account, is viewed as a revolutionary figure by the authorities: *Antiquities* 18. 118). For a discussion of these and other prophetic figures, see Gray, *Prophetic Figures in Late Second Temple Jewish Palestine.* My analysis differs somewhat from Gray's in that I believe she underplays the political significance of some of these figures and their movements. On the political significance of Jewish apocalyptic, see P. R. Davies, "Daniel in the Lion's Den"; Hengel, "Messianische Hoffnung"; A. Y. Collins, "Persecution and Vengeance"; J. J. Collins, *Apocalyptic Vision of the Book of Daniel,* 191–218.

63. Theissen, *Social Setting,* 72.

64. The Greek *doxa* did not simply mean "glory" in a modern, theologized sense; it referred to what we would call "fame," and that is the promise offered to Christians by Paul's message.

65. See Carr, "Rulers of this Age," for a history of different interpretations; my conclusions differ, however, from Carr's; see also his *Angels and Principalities.* Carr denies that Paul is here referring to superhuman powers, but his argument depends on his unsubstantiated claim that Greco-Roman society was religiously more traditional and less gullible when it came to astrology, mystery cults, etc., in the mid-first century than it was before and after. Carr's case is weak because, in the first place, he argues from silence: because Luke in Acts does not mention mystery religions, astrology, or "men bound by decrees of Fate," Asia and Greece (Carr believes) must have been relatively free of these religious phenomena during that time. Carr also draws on very different kinds of sources

(contrasting Epictetus's insistence that real peace cannot be had by means of politics with epigraphical propaganda of a later period praising the *pax Romana*) as evidence of a chronological development in beliefs throughout society, rather than recognizing that all these different views could have been (certainly *were*) held by different people during the same era. Philosophers were *expected* to have rather pessimistic views, and the propagandists of Rome, such as Aelius Aristides, were *expected* to praise the benefits of Empire!

66. Dibelius, *Die Geisterwelt*, 90; B. A. Pearson, *Pneumatikos-Psychikos Terminology*, 33; Wink, *Naming the Powers*, 40–45; Koenig, "Christ and the Hierarchies."

67. Pneumatic epistemology is very important for Paul's position throughout 1 Corinthians. As Louis Martyn notes, "What justification by faith is to Galatians and Romans, the epistemological issue is to 1 and 2 Corinthians" ("Epistemology at the Turn of the Ages," 276).

68. Several scholars have studied the *pneumatikos–psychikos* terminology of 1 Corinthians and have suggested, probably correctly, that the distinction is one used by the Corinthians and thence adopted by Paul (see B. A. Pearson, *Pneumatikos–Psychikos Terminology*; R. A. Horsley, "How can some of you say 'There is no Resurrection of the Dead?'"). Precisely what *psychē* refers to, though, is not clear. At any rate, in Paul's system, and probably that assumed by the Strong at Corinth also, psyche is the stuff of the self (both human and animal) responsible for animation, movement, indeed life. It is lower on the hierarchy of essences than pneuma, the stuff of higher life, perception, cognition, and rationality. However we regard psyche in 1 Corinthians, I would insist that we *not* translate it as "nature" or the "natural" (as scholars do when translating the *psychikos* body of 1 Cor. 15 as the "natural" body opposed to the "spiritual" or "supernatural" body of the resurrection) or

as "physical" as opposed to "spiritual" (as in the misleading translation of the terms of 1 Cor. 15 found in many modern English versions).

69. On Paul's apocalyptic opposition of pneuma to sarx, see Martyn, "Apocalyptic Antinomies." For one history of scholarship on the question, see Brandenburger, *Fleisch und Geist*.

70. D. B. Martin, *Slavery as Salvation*, 15–17, 80.

71. The meaning of *peripsēma*, here translated as "residue" or "scapegoat," is debated. It is actually not very different from the preceding word *perikatharma*; both refer, on the most basic level, to the dirt or scum that is wiped off something and thrown away. *Peripsēma*, however, is sometimes used to refer to an expiatory sacrifice, as when a criminal is condemned to death as a sacrifice for the salvation or purification of a city. Some commentators reject such an interpretation in this context as introducing a narrower meaning than would normally be assigned to the word by hearers of Paul's day. See Conzelmann, *1 Corinthians*, 90, n. 49; Theissen, *Social Setting*, 58, and 111, n. 7.

72. See Castelli, *Imitating Paul*, 98–111; Lassen, "Use of the Father Image in Imperial Propaganda and 1 Corinthians 4:14–21."

Chapter 3: The Body's Economy

1. In the nineteenth century, F. C. Baur argued that Paul's opponents were Judaizers ("Die Christus Partei"). Wilhelm Lütgert and Adolf Schlatter opposed the "Judaizers" hypothesis, arguing that the opponents were hyper-paulinists, pneumatics, and Gnostics (Lütgert, *Freiheitspredigt und Schwarmgeister in Korinth;* Schlatter, *Die korinthische Theologie*). R. Reitzenstein implied that it was Paul who was more "gnostic" (*Die hellenistischen Mysterien-religion*, 75–79, 333–396; see also

the cautious remarks by Pagels, *The Gnostic Paul*). T. W. Manson argues that Paul is fighting on two fronts, opposing the "Cephas party" (Palestinian Jewish Christianity) and the "Christ party" (Hellenistic and libertarian); ("Corinthian Correspondence (1)"). Walter Schmithals maintains that Paul is opposing both a general enthusiasm and Gnosticism (*Gnosticism in Corinth*), a position less nuanced than that of Conzelmann, who claims that Paul's opponents are only "proto-Gnostics" (*1 Corinthians*, 15). C. K. Barrett, building on the work of Manson, postulates four parties corresponding to the divisions of 1 Cor. 1:12 ("Christianity at Corinth").

2. See 1:26–27; 4:10; 8:9; 10:22; Theissen, *Social Setting;* Meeks, *First Urban Christians;* P. Lampe, "Das korinthische Herrenmahl."

3. It is sometimes disputed whether the sentence in brackets is part of the Corinthians' slogan or Paul's answer. I take it to be part of their slogan, to which Paul responds by emphasizing the resurrection of the body in opposition to the destruction of it. Mark Plunkett notes, for example, that the literary structure suggests a two-part slogan and a two-part response. Furthermore, explanations as to why Paul would have taught a total destruction of "food and the belly" are inadequate and not consonant with Paul's generally *redemptive* apocalypticism ("Sexual Ethics and the Christian Life," 73–76, 110–111; see 110, n. 21 for other references supporting the claim that 6:13b is part of the Corinthian slogan).

4. See n. 1 above.

5. For a study that questions whether "libertine Gnostics" actually existed, see Wisse, "Die Sextus-Sprüche und das Problem der gnostischen Ethik;" see also *idem*, " 'Opponents' in the New Testament in Light of the Nag Hammadi Writings."

6. Such as Conzelmann, *1 Corinthians*, 15; R. A. Horsley, "Gnosis in Corinth." One of the most influential proponents of a first-century gnosticism is Rudolph, *Gnosis*.

For surveys of the debate (and refutation of claims for a Gnostic movement in the first century), see Yamauchi, *Pre-Christian Gnosticism;* Perkins, *Gnosticism and the New Testament*. Birger Pearson has argued that Paul's Corinthian opponents were not Gnostics, though he reserves judgment about the possible existence of Gnosticism in the first century ("Philo, Gnosis, and the New Testament," 166, n. 5).

7. Dupont, *Gnosis;* Plunkett, "Sexual Ethics"; Deming, *Paul on Marriage and Celibacy*. A classic account similarly arguing for a Stoic "background" to the Corinthian slogans is J. Weiss, *Der erste Korintherbrief*.

8. Philo *Quod omnis;* see also *idem, Posterity and Exile of Cain*, 133. Deming insists that Cynic and Stoic influences are behind the Corinthian slogans, but even some of the parallels he cites, on the Stoic commonplaces on marriage, for instance, are from writers like Plutarch (Deming, *Paul on Marriage and Celibacy*, chap. 3; see Plutarch *Moralia* 142F–143A).

9. On the general eclecticism and in some cases dilettantism of Greco-Roman educated men, see Long, "Ptolemy *On the Criterion*," 182; Malherbe, *Moral Exhortation*, 12; Meeks, *Moral World*, 41. Galen, for example, rejects any *one* school allegiance: *Diagnosis and Cure of the Soul's Passions* 8. 59. In a famous passage, Justin Martyr (*Dialogue with Trypho* 2) portrays himself (in what was probably a typical topos) as having sampled all the major philosophical schools before settling on the "philosophy" of Christianity.

10. See Introduction to the Loeb edition by Oldfather, viii.

11. Another case of upward mobility by means of education may be Lucian if we take his essay on his decision not to be a stone mason as truly autobiographical; see Lucian *The Dream, or Lucian's Career*. Lucian was a rhetor rather than a philosopher, but his writings show extensive knowledge of at least the basic philosophy of the main schools, especially Epicureanism. For the

assumption that manual labor effectively precludes getting an education and is evidence of a lack of one, see Lucian *The Runaways* 12.

12. A comic presentation of such situations is found in Lucian *On Salaried Posts in Great Houses* (see esp. 4).

13. Theissen, *Social Setting*, 96, 106.

14. Pliny *Epistles* 2. 6; cf. Martial *Epigrams* 3. 60; Theissen, *Social Setting*, 153–158; see also P. Lampe, "Das korinthische Herrenmahl"; D. E. Smith, "Social Obligation," 36–38; Smith and Taussig, *Many Tables*, 33–34.

15. The different meanings of "discerning the body" are explored in Chap. 7.

16. See Bookidis and Fischer, "Sanctuary of Demeter and Kore."

17. I am quite willing to grant Richard Horsley's argument ("Gnosis in Corinth") that the Corinthian view of idols had been mediated to them mainly via Hellenistic Jewish appropriation of Greco-Roman philosophical arguments, as long as that is not taken to mean that these Corinthians were themselves Jews. It should further be noted that an argument about the impotence of idols need not be a Jewish versus Gentile argument at all but could be conducted within either a Greek context or a Jewish one.

18. This is pursued further in Chap. 7.

19. This is argued extensively in my *Slavery as Salvation*.

20. Winter, "Civil Litigation in Secular Corinth and the Church;" A. Mitchell, "Rich and Poor in the Courts of Corinth"; see also Mitchell's dissertation on the subject: "I Corinthians 6:1–11: Group Boundaries and the Courts of Corinth."

21. Winter, "Civil Litigation," 561.

22. "It is especially important to examine the status of each man, to see whether he is a decurion or a commoner; to ask whether his life is virtuous or marred by vice, whether he is rich or poor (for poverty might imply that he is out for gain), and whether he is

personally hostile to the man against whom he is witnessing or friendly to the man whose cause he is advocating" (*Digest* 22. 5. 3; quoted in Garnsey, "Legal Privilege in the Roman Empire," 145–146).

23. A. C. Mitchell, "Rich and Poor"; see also Chow, *Patronage and Power*, 75–80, on the importance of patronage for access to legal redress and protection in Roman Corinth.

24. Seneca *Controversiae* 10. 1. 2 and 7; see the discussion in Winter, "Civil Litigation," 565.

25. Petronius *Satyricon* 14, trans. Rouse.

26. A. C. Mitchell, "Rich and Poor," 9; he is referring primarily to the work of Black, *Behavior of Law*; see also Nader, "Anthropological Study of Law."

27. For the text, see Lutz, *Musonius Rufus*, 76–81. See A. C. Mitchell, "Rich and Poor."

28. A. C. Mitchell, "Rich and Poor," 6.

29. On the importance of shame for Mediterranean cultures in general, see Gilmore, *Honor and Shame*.

30. See A. C. Mitchell, "I Corinthians 6.1–11."

31. See the discussion of this term in A. C. Mitchell, "Rich and Poor."

32. For similar analyses, see Clarke, "Secular and Christian Leadership in Corinth"; and Chow, *Patronage and Power*, 182.

33. More will be found on the boundary-setting issues of this passage in Chap. 7.

34. Of these, the following are representative. Barrett, *First Epistle*, 207: Paul believed it was incongruous with the sacrifice of Jesus for preachers to make money from the gospel. Dautzenburg, "Der Verzicht," 224, 231–232: Paul's rejection of support is an imitation of the weakness of Christ. Hock, *Social Context*, 48–49: Paul, like Socrates on the Cynic depiction, rejected using his divine commission for personal gain. J. Weiss, *Der erste Korintherbrief*, 238: Paul did not want to burden the poor (cf. Dungan, *Sayings of Jesus*, 15, 30–

31). Betz, *Apostel Paulus*, 115–117: Paul used traditional Socratic rhetoric, distinguishing philosophers from sophists, who charged fees (cf. Holmberg, *Paul and Power*, 91). Hock, *Social Context*, 48–49; Malherbe, *Paul and the Thessalonians*, 16, 99; Dautzenburg, "Der Verzicht," 222–224: Paul refused money and worked for his living to set an example to converts. Marshall, *Enmity in Corinth*, 397 *et passim*: Paul refused money in order to avoid the obligations that accepting it would entail.

35. Malherbe, *Paul and the Thessalonians*, 15.

36. It is unclear whether Paul means that they should need nothing or no one; nor is it clear whether Paul is advocating independence from "outsiders" or if he also wants the Thessalonians to avoid dependence on wealthier Christians. I think he would be concerned about either situation.

37. See Lucian *Runaways* for the upper-class insinuation that some Cynics pursued philosophy only as a pretext for social disruption and radicalism—and to escape the workbench.

38. See Marshall, *Enmity in Corinth*, 158–164.

39. Ibid., 161–164.

40. Judge, "Cultural Conformity and Innovation in Paul," 15. For comparison with gift giving and status in modern cultures, see Wolf, "Kinship, Friendship, and Patron–Client Relations."

41. For a similar analysis of the social expectations of gift giving and receiving, see Peterman, "'Thankless Thanks.'" I disagree, however, with Peterman's conclusion: "It should not be expected that Paul would owe a material return to the Philippians. Paul has not become socially obligated by accepting their gifts. Rather, because he has accepted their gifts, they have been elevated to the unique place of partnership in the gospel; for no other congregation had attempted to share in giving and receiving as the Philippians" (270). Peterman's own analysis belies his conclusion: the regular expectation was that gifts would be repaid or a debt incurred that would translate into status differentiation. *Paul* reinterprets the gift as not a gift; Peterman is too uncritical in accepting Paul's construal of the transaction as *the* correct one. Indeed, Paul must insist that the gift is not a gift precisely because it would normally have been perceived as one—with all the attending debt and status implications.

42. D. B. Martin, *Slavery as Salvation*, 117–135.

43. Marshall, *Enmity in Corinth*.

44. Paul refers to the financial "abundance" of the Corinthian Christians, when compared with the Macedonian Christians, in 2 Cor. 8:14. For further evidence regarding the socioeconomic level of the Corinthian Christians, see Theissen, *Social Setting*, 69–119; Meeks, *First Urban Christians*, 67–72. Some Corinthian Christians were already supporting other "apostles" (2 Cor. 11:20) and seem upset that Paul will not take their money (11:7–12; 12:13–15), indicating that they had money for him to refuse.

Chapter 4: Tongues of Angels in the Body of Christ

1. D. B. Martin, "Tongues of Angels and Other Status Indicators."

2. Scholars sometimes point to the following accounts as containing parallels of early Christian glossolalia, none of which fits my definition: Plato *Phaedrus* 244; Herodotus *History* 8. 135; Heraclitus, quoted in Plutarch *Oracles at Delphi* 397A; see also 406F, 412A. See Forbes, "Early Christian Inspired Speech." For a critique of the method and conclusions of Forbes's dissertation ("Prophecy and Inspired Speech in Early Christianity and its Hellenistic Environment"), see my "Tongues of Angels," 558, n. 22.

3. I accept recent scholars' arguments that there is no need to posit a Montanist redaction of the *Testament of Job;* it represents a form of Judaism independent of direct Christian influence (see J. J. Collins, "Structure and Meaning in the Testament of Job," 49–51; Kraft, *Testament of Job,* 17–20; van der Horst, "Images of Women"). Forbes rejects the interpretation that Paul is referring to glossolalia as angelic language in 1 Cor. 13:1, insisting that such an exegesis rests on too flimsy evidence ("Prophecy and Inspired Speech," 75–76, 228). Inexplicably, he takes "tongues of men" as referring to glossolalia, thereby assuming that Paul considered glossolalia as including unlearned human languages (187). Forbes claims: "Neither in the Hellenistic nor the Jewish background have we found sufficient evidence to overthrow the case that early Christians almost uniformly believed glossolalia to be the power to speak in otherwise unlearned human languages" (228). Forbes has in no way established such a case, however. There is no indication that Paul viewed glossolalia as human language. Contrary to Forbes's exegesis, Paul's statement about "tongues of men" in 1 Cor. 13:1 is in opposition to "tongues of angels." The latter refers to glossolalia, the former to normal speech. The construction is the rhetorical commonplace "from the lesser to the greater" and may be paraphrased as follows: "Even if I have power to speak all human languages— or, to mention something more impressive, even *angelic* languages— . . . I am nothing." The first refers to human (normal) language, the latter to heavenly (esoteric)—that is, glossolalic—language.

4. See also "Book of the Resurrection of Jesus Christ by Bartholomew the Apostle" (ed. Budge, 3. 11–12 and 189), where women sing hymns in the language of cherubim. In the *Apocalypse of Abraham* 17 an angel teaches Abraham a heavenly song, but there is no indication that it is in a special language. According to P. Alexander

(Introduction to "3 Enoch," 1. 234), glossolalia may have been a feature of Merkabah mysticism, in messages from "the heavenly world" (citing *Heikhalot Rabbati* 18:4; see also Scholem, *Jewish Mysticism,* 133–135). Roy Harrisville ("Speaking in Tongues") cites several other texts as Jewish instances of glossolalia or heavenly languages (*Jubilees* 25:14; *Testament of Judah* 25:3; *1 Enoch Similitudes* 40; 70:11; *4 Maccabees* 10:21; *Martyrdom of Isaiah* 5:14). But in each case, the actual language spoken seems to have been normal, not esoteric. I have therefore left them out of consideration.

5. Eusebius (*Ecclesiastical History* 5. 16. 7) uses the phrase *te lalein kai xenophonein* in describing Montanus's speech, which Kirsopp Lake translates "to speak and to talk strangely." I would translate it "to babble and speak foreign speech."

6. Tertullian *On the Soul* 9. Tertullian probably knew the *Testament of Job* (Spittler, Introduction to "Testament of Job," 1. 834, 836; 847, n. 20).

7. Dio Chrysostom *Discourses* 10. 23 and 11. 22.

8. For that reason I have quoted the translation by Scott, p. 129, 26a. For a different translation, which I cannot explain, see Layton, ed., *Gnostic Scriptures,* 458. One might include here, though I do not, the function of "nonsense" terms (at least to outsiders if not to insiders) in Gnostic literature and magical papyri. See, e.g., *The Egyptian Gospel (The Holy Book of the Great Invisible Spirit)* 54 (Layton, ed., 107); 78:10ff. (Layton, ed., 119); *PGM* 1. 76– 79 (Luck, *Arcana Mundi,* 94–95); Betz, ed., *Greek Magical Papyri,* xxxii *et passim.*

9. As noted above, I find Forbes's dismissal of these parallels unpersuasive ("Prophecy and Inspired Speech," 197–199).

10. *Contra Celsum* 7. 10, trans. Chadwick. The argument by Robeck, ed., *Charismatic Experiences,* 118, that Origen's response to Celsus demonstrates that Celsus was *not* referring to glossolalia, is not convincing. It is

true that Origen takes Celsus to mean simply that he was unable to interpret the import of the prophecies, not that he was unable to understand the actual language. But I see no reason to allow Origen's understanding of Celsus's terminology to rule our own interpretation. In the first place, Celsus's terms fit a description of prophetic esoteric speech, especially when compared with the account of Alexander mentioned above. Secondly, Celsus's reference to "sorcerers" suggests that he took the esoteric speech to resemble the incantations of sorcerers, who, as the magical papyri show abundantly, used esoteric speech quite similar to glossolalia.

11. Irenaeus *Against the Heresies* 5. 6. 1.

12. Iamblicus *De Mysteriis Aegyptorum* 3. 8, trans. Taylor. In 3. 5 Iamblicus also uses terminology (specifically *ēchē*) which may be taken to indicate glossolalic speech. The term *mainomenō stomati* refers elsewhere to the Sybil and other mantic-style speakers: Plutarch *De Pythiae oraculis* 397A (Heraclitus, frg. 92).

13. The image has been traced as far back as 900 B.C.E. and recurs in political rhetoric through the Middle Ages and into modern political theory. Geographically, the analogy has been noted from India, Iran, and Russia, as well as from the ancient Mediterranean (Lincoln, *Myth, Cosmos, and Society*, 1–15, 141–148).

14. Lincoln, *Myth, Cosmos, and Society;* Wikenhauser, *Die Kirche*, 130–143; Barkan, *Nature's Work of Art;* Ellen, "Anatomical Classification"; Hainz, *Ekklesia*, 260, n. 2.

15. Dio Chrysostom, for example, can compare the parts of the body to one's friends when he points out that the friends, because more mobile, are more useful than even the members of one's own body (*Discourse* 3. 104–107; see also 1. 31–32). But more often the analogy occurs in Dio's homonoia speeches or when he is addressing the subject of homonoia in other kinds of speeches (39. 5ff.; 34. 22; 9. 2; 33. 44; and esp. 40. 21; 41. 9; 50. 3). Dio does not

do much with the image but, rather, cites it like an overused metaphor (which label Dio explicitly applies to the "ship of state" comparison: 34. 16; also 38. 14). See also Cicero *De officiis* 3. 5. 22–23; 3. 6. 26–27; Seneca *On Anger* 2. 31. 7; Philo *On Dreams* 1. 27f.; *idem, Special Laws* 3. 131. These are only a few of many such occurrences; for others, see M. M. Mitchell, *Paul and Rhetoric of Reconciliation*, 218–226.

16. The function of the body analogy in Aristotle's *Politics* is a good example. Just as body members are defined by their existence within the body, so the individual is defined by his or her place within society. The "givenness" or "naturalness" of hierarchy is thus reinforced in opposition to any possibility of change, equality, or "communism" in Plato's sense. See *Politics* 1. 1. 11 (1253a19ff.), 3. 1. 1–3 (1276b21ff.), and 2. 1. 4 (1261a18ff.); also *idem, Movement of Animals* 10 (703a29–703b2). In *On Anger* 2. 31. 7, Seneca is concerned primarily with the virtue of the individual, not the state, but the way he introduces the body analogy reveals its background in political rhetoric about homonoia.

17. For the traditional nature of the story see Ogilvie, *Commentary on Livy*, 312–313; Nestle, "Die Fabel." See also Hausrath, ed., *Corpus Fabularum Aesopicarum*, fasc. 1, pp. 157–158 (§132) and fasc. 2, p. 169 (Fab. Synt. §35); Jacobs, *Fables of Aesop*, 82–88, and 247; Dionysius Halcarnassus *Antiquities of the Romans* 6. 86, 6. 54. 2; Josephus *Jewish War* 4. 406. For occurrences of the analogy in Rabbinic literature, see Schwarzbaum, "Talmudic-Midrashic Affinities," 432–433.

18. A similar ideological move is made by Cicero, though he does not make explicit use of the hierarchy of the body members: *De officiis* 3. 5. 22–23. Cicero's body analogy is made to serve the opposite end to what one might expect. One could argue that the body is quintessentially "communistic," with all the goods distributed from a common source. But Cicero, the Roman

conservative, makes the analogy support the necessity of carefully guarded private property.

19. Greek text of Polyaenus: *Strategemata in lucem prolata curis Julii;* the English translation used here is by R. Shepherd. Marsilius of Padua in the fourteenth-century *Defensor pacis* uses the analogy to maintain the structures of society (conservatively), but in a way that challenges the papal attempt to control all society directly. Marsilius argues that the head cannot control the foot directly but must go through the proper channels; otherwise it would be as if the foot (or finger, etc.) were joined directly to the head—a monstrosity! Thus, Marsilius's use of the analogy limits the power of the "head"—that is, the papacy— while remaining nonetheless conservative (326–327).

20. In vv. 8–11, for example, Paul uses words connoting "otherness" nine times (*allos,* "other," is used six times; *heteros,* "the other," twice; and *hekastos,* once, v. 11), and terms connoting unity or sameness five times (*to auto* and *to hen*).

21. John Chrysostom also takes Paul to be referring here to genitalia (*Homilies on 1 Corinthians* 31. 425–426).

22. See esp. Artemidorus *Dream Handbook* 1. 45, 79, 80. Paul uses the plural *anagkaia,* whereas Artemidorus uses the singular when referring to the penis. This difference may be explained by either of two suggestions: (1) Paul is speaking of lower-status *members* of the body, not of one individual, and the plural is therefore more suited to his use of the analogy; (2) Paul is probably thinking of the genitals as understood generically, rather than of the penis in particular, and therefore the plural (if not the dual, which is hardly ever used in early Christian writings) is more appropriate. In any case, I am less concerned with Paul's intentions than with the multiple ways in which the language would have been heard by Paul's audience. Thus, I think it likely that his hearers would

have recognized some degree of ambiguous punning here. Significantly, Bruce Lincoln points out that in uses of the body analogy in other cultures the genitals represent the peasants as the most productive and reproductive class (142 and 145).

23. As noted in Chap. 2, "weaker" is unambiguously a low-status term, often referring in political rhetoric to the lower class: Plato *Republic* 569B; Euripides *Suppliant Women,* lines 433–438; Theissen, *Social Setting,* 70–73; Marshall, *Enmity in Corinth,* 290.

24. See Chap. 1 above.

25. J. Rodman Williams's argument that the lists of gifts in 1 Cor. 12 are not hierarchical—and that the hierarchical list is one of offices, not charismata—is to me unconvincing ("Greater Gifts").

26. The problem of the category of rationality when used by modern scholars can be illustrated by E. R. Dodds's classic work *The Greeks and the Irrational.* "Rational" seems to mean something like bourgeois individualism or "democracy" (34); "rationalism" means antisupernaturalism (189–190). Magic, on the other hand, is "irrational" (194, 212). It seems that "irrational" can refer to actions not proceeding from conscious intention, actions that are not planned but that, instead, spring from external agency (38). An "irrational" force, though, may be understood to proceed either from the "supernatural" or from some part of the self (186). Dodds recognizes that Plato, though a rationalist in his terminology, admits supernatural revelation. But this seems irrational to Dodds and thus requires explanation. I believe that Dodds himself creates the problem by introducing the modern categories of rational/irrational and natural/supernatural, neither of which would have found any place in the thinking of the ancients.

27. "Ruling agent": *On Dreams* 1. 30, 128; *Allegorical Interpretation* 3. 80. Father of the senses: *On Dreams* 1. 88. The strict

but gentle father: *Allegorical Interpretation* 3. 80–84. Richard Horsley's claim that *psychē, pneuma*, and *nous* are "largely parallel or interchangeable" in Philo is not entirely correct ("*Pneumatikos* vs. *Psychikos*," 271–272).

28. In human beings the nous is a divine fragment (*apospasma theion ōn: On Dreams* 1. 34), but it needs guidance from the divine pneuma if it is to be able to ascertain spiritual truth (*Moses* 2. 264). Indeed, one can say that there are two different kinds of nous: one that partakes of pneuma, which connotes "strength and vigor and power," and one that is simply made out of firmer matter (*hylē*), which is less powerful and discerning (*Allegorical Interpretation* 1. 42).

29. For active and passive sex roles in Greco-Roman conceptions, see Foucault, *Care of the Self*, 19–25, 32–36, *et passim*; Halperin, *One Hundred Years of Homosexuality*, 23–24, 30–35, 47; Winkler, *Constraints of Desire*, 40, and index under "Penetration."

30. Similar references to the esoteric significance of divine language can be found in Artemidorus and Dio Chrysostom, both more nearly contemporaneous with Paul (Artemidorus, *Dream Handbook* 2. 37; Dio Chrysostom *Discourses* 10. 23; 11. 22).

31. Plutarch also shares the theory: *Dialogue on Love* 755E–763A, esp. 758D.

32. We should not suppose that the Platonic theory of inspiration is *the* Greek understanding. It seems to have been only one of many possible theoretical explanations of what happens in inspiration. Aristotle, for example, has somewhat different ideas (*Rhetoric* 1408B; *Poetics* 1455A).

33. I am in no way claiming a direct literary influence of any of these authors on Paul or others at Corinth. In fact, I think it unlikely that Paul ever studied philosophy or read Plato, much less Philo. And, of course, Iamblicus is much later than Paul. What I do want to suggest, however, is that much of the conceptualization of glossolalia by

Paul (and probably the Corinthians) partook of categories of thought that were available even in popular conceptions and appropriations of Platonism (or Platonisms) in the first century. Paul's language should be heard as belonging to a common conceptual schema informed by popular, first-century Platonic theory.

34. For a modern, psychological understanding of tongues as "nonrational" and "experiential," see Tappeiner, "Function of Tongue-Speaking." It should be clear by now that my analysis is at odds with that of Theissen, though using many of the same texts (see his *Psychological Aspects*, see esp. 282–288). His insinuations that glossolalia is "ecstatic" speech (it often is not), that it represents an upsurge of the natural "irrational" within human beings (note his phrases like "creative impulses emerge from unconscious depths within human beings," 282; "a transformed psychic state," 290), that it expresses previously suppressed or repressed emotions and thoughts (310–311) and constitutes "a regression to a-dual experience of the world" (313) all seem to me inappropriately modern—especially in their presupposition of basically universal psychodynamics and realities (such as the modern category of the unconscious). I find Theissen's conclusion—"In glossolalia, unconscious interpretation of the normative and demanding tribunals according to the pattern of hostility is overcome" (335)— anachronistic, culturally hegemonic, and presumptuously omniscient.

35. For the argument that this political image (of leaders who give up high status and claims to hierarchical superiority) is part of a topos associated with demagogues in Greco-Roman rhetoric, see my *Slavery as Salvation*, 86–116, and Chap. 3 above.

36. D. B. Martin, *Slavery as Salvation*.

37. Note, for example, Plato's disgust when lower-status beings (including horses!) do not yield the right of way to their social superiors (*Republic* 563A–D).

38. D. B. Martin, *Slavery as Salvation*, 110–116, 128–129.

39. Ibid., 121–124.

Chapter 5: *The Resurrected Body*

1. See von Soden, "Sacrament and Ethics in Paul"; Schniewind, "Die Leugner der Auferstehung in Korinth"; Barrett, *First Corinthians*, 109; Güttgemanns, *Der leidende Apostel*, 67–72; Becker, *Auferstehung der Toten im Urchristentum*, 55, 69–76; Thiselton, "Realized Eschatology at Corinth"; Malherbe, "Beasts at Ephesus," 88. John Chrysostom believed that the Corinthian view was that the resurrection had already happened; see "Homily on 1 Corinthians," 38 (*Patrologiae Graeca* [Migne] 61, col. 321); English: *Homilies*, 529. For a survey of many theories regarding the eschatological beliefs of the Corinthians, see Sellin, *Der Streit um die Auferstehung der Toten*, 17–37; Moiser, "1 Corinthians 15."

2. So also Barclay, "Thessalonica and Corinth," 64.

3. Delobel, "Fate of the Dead According to 1 Thes 4 and 1 Cor 15"; for other rejections of the realized eschatology hypothesis, see B. A. Pearson, *Pneumatikos–Psychikos Terminology*, 15; R. A. Horsley, "How can some of you say?"; Sellin, *Der Streit*, 23–30; Plunkett, "Sexual Ethics," 122–123.

4. Thus Francis Glasson, for instance, believes that Platonism was what influenced the Corinthians ("2 Corinthians v. 1–10 *versus* Platonism"). Glasson is mistaken when he claims that Platonism was "flourishing at the Academy in Athens" at this time. In the first place, the Academy, as such, had ceased to function as a philosophical school in the previous century; see Glucker, *Antiochus and the Late Academy*; and Chap. 1, n. 24 above. In the second place, the kind of philosophy presented even then at the Academy (i.e., before it closed) was Skepticism, not traditional Platonism. As I have already argued,

the body/soul dualism identified by Glasson as particularly Platonic could readily be found among many (non-Platonic) educated persons in Paul's day.

5. For a popular account of the deconstruction of the concept "matter" that has taken place in physics during the twentieth century, see Davies and Gribbin, *Matter Myth*.

6. See, e.g., Plunkett, "Sexual Ethics," 149–151.

7. MacMullen, *Paganism in the Roman Empire*, 51–57.

8. W. D. Davies also remarks that the Corinthians could have acquired a distaste for resurrection simply from "popular philosophy" (*Paul and Rabbinic Judaism*, 304).

9. The most common translation of *nekros*, especially in classical Greek but also later, is "corpse," although the term has hardly ever been translated that way in the New Testament. See LSJ, "*nekros*"; see also, e.g., Epictetus *Discourses* 1. 5. 7; 1. 9. 33; Lucian *Menippus* 17, 18; Sextus Empiricus *Against the Professors* 1. 261. In inscriptions too the term *nekros* (or sometimes *nekys*) usually refers to the corpse: "Blessed and beloved Sabinus, it is sleep that holds you; you live as a hero and have not turned into a corpse [*nekys*] . . ." (Syria, second century C.E.; *EG* 433; trans. in Lattimore, *Themes in Greek and Latin Epitaphs*, 49); "Corpse [*nekys*] though I am I thank you for your great gifts. . . . In this tomb I have some deliverance from the bitterness of death" (Cos, Roman period; *EG* 200. 2. 4; trans. in Lattimore, 57). *Sōma*, on the other hand, could be used in inscriptions (as in philosophical statements, as we will presently see) to refer to the immortal, heavenly body: "Untouched and not concerned with a husband you made haste to join the immortals, purifying your body with the stars of heaven" (Neoclaudianopolis; *SEG* 4. 727; trans. in Lattimore, 50).

10. R. A. Horsley ("How can some of you say?") suggests that the Corinthian

position stems from Platonic dualism mediated by Hellenistic Judaism as found in the philosophy of Philo (see also Sellin, *Der Streit*, 24–25). I would differ by insisting that the sort of dualism implied here was not limited in the first century to Platonists, that it need not imply a matter/nonmatter dichotomy, and that the Corinthians need not have come by it via any form of Judaism. Hellenistic Jews such as Philo expressed such dualistic notions for the same reason that many other intellectuals did: it was simply "in the air" in first-century popular philosophy.

11. Many Jewish texts omit any mention of an afterlife: Tobit, Baruch (which in 2:17 seems to *deny* any afterlife except the "life" of the dead in Hades, who in that state will not be able to glorify God), 1 Maccabees, 3 Maccabees, Judith, *Letter of Aristeas*. Some Jewish texts express a belief in the immortality of the soul: Wisdom 1:15 (cf. 9:15); *Testament of Asher* 6:5–6; 4 Maccabees 14:5–6; 18:23; see also the Jewish tombstone inscription of Arsinoe (Leontopolis, Egypt, 5 B.C.E.; *CIJ* 1510). Some texts even seem to reject a belief in immortality—*Baruch* 2:17?—while others seem to reject the resurrection of the body—see Wisdom 9:15 (by comparison with 3:1–4). Philo would doubtless reject the resurrection of the body, although he never actually mentions it; see *On the Creation* 77; *Moses* 2. 288. Philo does say that a "corpse" (*nekron*) cannot come into the sight of God (*On Flight* 10–11, §§55–59; see Downing, "Resurrection of the Dead"). *2 Baruch* 30:1–5 mentions a resurrection of the soul but not of the body. The Sadducees seem to have rejected any belief in an afterlife or resurrection (Josephus *War* 2. 165; *Antiquities* 18. 16; Mark 12:18–27 and parallels; Acts 4:2, 23:8). I would imagine that other Jews lost to history were similarly skeptical. Pseudo-Phocylides uncritically juxtaposes different views: resurrected and deified corpses, the immortality of souls,

Hades as the common home of all the dead (*Sentences*, vv. 97–115). As Hans Cavallin says, "There is obviously no single Jewish doctrine about life after death in the period under consideration; there is rather a great variety and pluralism of ideas both about the end of world history and about death and about that which follows the death of the individual person" (*Life after Death*, 199). Cavallin's conclusions are also found in his "Leben nach dem Tode." See also Nickelsburg, *Resurrection*, esp. 180; Sanders, *Judaism*, 284–301; Perkins, *Resurrection*, 37.

12. MacMullen, *Paganism*, 51. See M. Smith, "Salvation in the Gospels"; G. H. R. Horsley, *New Documents 1978*, 29.

13. Lattimore, *Themes*, 84. Greek versions of this phrase could also be found, as in an inscription from second-century Rome: "I, Nicomedes, am happy. I was not, and I became, I am not, and nothing hurts me" (*EG* 595; trans. in Lattimore, 84; see other examples given by Lattimore). Cf. MacMullen, 57.

14. Rome, third–fourth century C.E.; *EG* 646; trans. in Lattimore, 75.

15. Lattimore, *Themes*, 68, 71 and n. 379.

16. As Lattimore puts it, people could imagine an afterlife "as a shadowy ghost, as a citizen of Hades' world or of Elysium, as nothing at all" (*Themes*, 74).

17. Note, for example, Meeks's caveat concerning MacMullen's presentation (*First Urban Christians*, 241, n. 44). Meeks points out that hopes of an afterlife occur in some literature apparently composed for something like popular consumption, such as rhetorical handbooks and set consolation pieces. Though Meeks's point is well-taken, it must be remembered that the "popular consumption" of any textually embodied expression in a largely illiterate society such as the Roman Empire would have been limited.

18. *SEG* 3. 612. 4; trans. in Lattimore, *Themes*, 29.

19. Sabine countryside, second century C.E.; *EG* 651; trans. in Lattimore, *Themes*, 33–34.

20. Though the reader may wish to question some of Lattimore's interpretations, his book is still a valuable anthology of inscriptions and well repays perusal for its demonstration of the remarkable diversity of beliefs surrounding death. In a more recently published inscription, several beliefs are combined: the soul of a six-year-old girl is said to have been kept from Hades and sent to "flight in the sky"; she dwells among the "heroines"; yet she is also spoken of as "enclosed in the tomb" (G. H. R. Horsley, *New Documents 1977*, no. 14. 5; pp. 51–52). Theological consistency was seldom aimed for in popular beliefs—then as now.

21. Lucian *Menippus* 10–11, 15; see 20 for the idea that the bodies of the dead are punished in Hades while their souls may be sent back to occupy other bodies on earth—in this case, the bodies of donkeys. For a range of descriptions of the underworld in inscriptions, see Lattimore, *Themes*, 87–90.

22. See, e.g., Cullmann, "Immortality of the Soul," 24–25.

23. Apollodorus *Library* 1. 9. 15; see also Hyginus *Fabulae* 51; Plato *Symposium* 179B.

24. Euripides *Madness of Hercules* 616.

25. Hyginus *Fabulae* 251 (*Myths of Hyginus*, trans. Grant).

26. Pliny *Natural History* 29. 1. 3; Lucian *Dance* 45.

27. Pausanias *Description of Greece* 2. 27. 4; see also 2. 26. 5; 2. 32. 1–2.

28. Ovid *Fasti* 6. 733–762.

29. Apollodorus *Library* 3. 3. 1–2; see p. 312, n. 2, of the Loeb edition for other references to the story; Hyginus *Fabulae* 49; idem, *Astronomica* 2. 14 (*De Astronomia*, ed. Viré, 2. 14. 577–598).

30. Apollodorus *Library* 3. 10. 3; see vol. 2, pp. 16–18, n. 2–4, for other references to the resurrections attributed to Asclepius; see also appendix 7, "Resurrec-

tion of Glaucus," in the Loeb edition of *Library*, vol. 2, pp. 363–370, by Frazer.

31. *PGM* IV. 154–285 (Betz, ed., p. 42).

32. *PGM* IV. 296–466 (Betz, ed., p. 44).

33. *PGM* IV. 1990; IV. 2140–2144 (Betz, ed., pp. 73, 76).

34. Lucian *Lover of Lies* 13, trans. Harmon, slightly modified.

35. See also ibid. 25 and 27.

36. As Wedderburn notes, "Heracles' fate may suggest ascension or apotheosis rather than resurrection to us, but how did it appear to the ancient world?" (*Baptism and Resurrection*, 192–193). For accounts of resuscitations in Greek and Near Eastern myth, see Paraskos, "Biblical Accounts of Resuscitation." Paraskos's analysis is uncritical and unhelpful; he tries to argue, along the lines of eighteenth-century rationalists, that the raisings performed by Elijah and Elisha were, to all intents and purposes, mouth-to-mouth resuscitations.

37. Sextus Empiricus *Against the Professors* 1. 263; Plutarch *The E in Delphi* (*Moralia* 389A), trans. Babbitt.

38. For differences in beliefs about an afterlife among different classes, see Dodds, *Greeks and the Irrational*. On the "universalizing" education of upper-class males (*paideia*), see Brown, *Power and Persuasion in Late Antiquity*, 4, 53, *et passim*.

39. Cicero *Tusculan Disputations* 1. 11. 23–24. See also Marcus Aurelius *Meditations* 5. 24. 107.

40. Plutarch *Consolation to his Wife* 611E.

41. Attica; *EG* 21b; in Lattimore, *Themes*, 31; my trans.

42. *EG* 156. 1–2; trans. in Lattimore, *Themes*, 32.

43. Quoted in MacMullen, *Paganism in the Roman Empire*, 13; see Robert, "Trois oracles."

44. The problem here, as I have already noted in Chap. 1, is that the English word *matter*, at least today, includes things that the Greek word *hylē*, which is the one most

often translated "matter," would not include, such as air, fire, ether, or sometimes even water. Thus, some ancient philosophers insist that the soul is not composed of hyle but nevertheless believe it to be composed of air or fire.

45. Cicero *Tusculan Disputations* 1. 17. 41; 1. 19. 43.

46. Seneca *Consolation to Marcia* 25. 3; 26. 6; *Moral Epistle* 102. 28–30.

47. Philo *Special Laws* 4. 122; see *idem*, *Allegorical Interpretation* 3. 161.

48. See Philo *On Dreams* 1. 135, 138–142; *On Giants* 6–8, 10–11. Philo seems to modern readers self-contradictory, at times appearing to hold a materialist view of the soul and pneuma and at other times insisting that the soul was not created at all but came directly from God and is naturally immortal, or arguing that the mind of man is *not* made of ether, since it is made of "no created thing" and that the "reasonable soul" is made of the divine and invisible spirit (*pneuma*). But here again we must be careful about Cartesian categories: does Philo mean by "invisible" what we mean by "immaterial"? We moderns certainly do not equate invisibility with immateriality. (Oxygen and other gases are still, for us, "matter," even though we cannot see them.) Perhaps we need a more nuanced vocabulary to unravel Philo's apparent contradictions.

49. Carales, Sardinia; *EG* 547. 7–8; trans. in Lattimore, *Themes*, 30; cf. an inscription from Sidyma; *TAM* 2. 203. 1–4; trans. in Lattimore, 56.

50. Lattimore, *Themes*, 31–33.

51. See Evans, *Physiognomics*, 11.

52. For an interesting parallel in Indian religion, see Flood, "Techniques of Body and Desire in Kashmir Saivism," 48.

53. A. Scott, *Origen and the Life of the Stars*.

54. Ibid., 4, 11; Plato *Timaeus* 32B–C2.

55. See esp. Scott, *Life of the Stars*, 24–26, 34, 38, for a discussion of Aristotle's

views and how they were sometimes misunderstood by later philosophers.

56. Arcesine; *IG* 12, 7, 123, 5–6; trans. in Lattimore, *Themes*, 35.

57. Wisdom 3:7, about the souls of the righteous: "In the time of their visitation they will shine forth" (NRSV). *1 Enoch* 62:15: "The righteous and elect ones shall rise from the earth and shall cease being of downcast face. They shall wear the garments of glory" (trans. Isaac). *2 Enoch* 66:7: "They will be made to shine seven times brighter than the sun" (trans. Andersen). *Testament of Moses* 10:9: "And God will raise you to the heights. Yea, he will fix you firmly in the heaven of the stars, in the place of their habitation" (trans. Priest). *4 Maccabees* 17:5: "The moon in heaven, with the stars, does not stand so august as you, who, after lighting the way of your star-like seven sons to piety, stand in honor before God and are firmly set in heaven with them" (NRSV).

58. Philo *On the Creation* 144; *On Dreams* 1. 135–137, 138–145; *On the Giants* 7; *Questions on Exodus* 2. 114; *Moses* 2. 108.

59. Cumont, *After Life in Roman Paganism*, 198; Hengel, *Judaism and Hellenism*, 1. 197; Cavallin, *Life after Death*.

60. Cicero *De natura deorum* 2. 15. 42.

61. Philo *Noah's Work as a Planter* 12, trans. Colson and Whitaker; Philo repeats, sometimes almost verbatim, these ideas several times: *On Dreams* 1. 141; 1. 135; *Giants* 6–11.

62. Cicero *De natura deorum* 2. 15. 42.

63. Philo *Allegorical Interpretation* 3. 161; *Who is the Heir?* 283 (cf. 57); *Worse Attacks Better* 84; *Special Laws* 4. 122 (cf. 4. 217). In the end, Philo abstains from speculation on the subject, insisting that humans cannot know the real nature of the heavens or the stars: *On Dreams* 1. 22. For a discussion of Philo's contradictory statements on the subject, see A. Scott, *Life of the Stars*, 65–67. On the confusion of fire and ether, see Gersh, *Middle Platonism and Neoplatonism*, 1. 305 and n. 323.

64. Birger Pearson notes that Hellenistic Jewish texts tend to refer to pneuma as the highest part of the human being, whereas non-Jewish philosophers assign nous that status (*Pneumatikos–Psychikos Terminology*, 11–12). While I agree with this observation in general, I would nonetheless point out that non-Jews too could refer to this higher part of the self as *pneuma*, due probably to the common belief that pneuma was the stuff that enabled perception, cognition, and contemplation—activities of the nous. Note, for example, the remarks on Epictetus above, contrasting pneuma with flesh, and funeral inscriptions that speak of the pneuma as leaving the body at death (Lattimore, *Themes*, 30, discussed above).

65. Aristotle *On the Heavens* 2. 8, 290a9; note that for Aristotle the "first body" of the universe—that is, the first sphere—can be spoken of as a "body" even though it is not composed of hyle; it is composed, rather, of ether: 1. 3, 270a25.

66. Plutarch *On the Face on the Moon* (*Moralia* 928A–C; 929A).

67. Clement of Alexandria *Eclogae Propheticae* 55. 1, ed. Früchtel, 3. 152; A. Scott, *Life of the Stars*, 108. Clement, significantly, is not simply trying to defend Paul's language but is speaking of references to stars in the Old Testament.

68. Wedderburn, *Baptism and Resurrection*, 211, 231, 332–342; MacMullen, *Paganism*, 55.

69. See also Lucian *Lover of Lies* 11.

70. *PGM* 4. 195; for "wake" as the dominant meaning of *egeirein*, see LSJ.

71. See also 2 *Baruch* 49:1–51:12 and *Testament of Job* 4:9, 40:4 for resurrection of the body.

72. Cavallin, *Life after Death*, 173; *Genesis Rabbah* 14:5 and *Leviticus Rabbah* 14:9. (The texts do not explicitly speak of resurrection but only of the formation of the body or fetus in the "next world." Cavallin maintains that this is an aspect of a dispute about the resurrection of the body.)

73. This connection is evident in more

ways than one; see Rev. 1:5; Col. 1:18; *1 Clement* 24; Ignatius *Letter to the Trallians* 9:2; *To the Smyrneans* 5:3; *Letter to Diognetus* 9:2.

74. "Flesh": Hermas *Shepherd: Similitudes* 5:6–7; 2 *Clement* 9:2, 14:5; Irenaeus *Against the Heresies* 5. 33. 1; *idem, Proof of the Apostolic Preaching* 39; Athenagoras *Plea regarding Christians* 31; Tertullian *On the Resurrection of the Flesh* 28:6, 57:13; Tatian *Address to the Greeks* 25. "Body": Justin Martyr *1 Apology* 18. The use of both is found in Irenaeus *Against the Heresies* 1. 10. 3; Clement of Alexandria *Paidagogos* 9.

75. Athenagoras *Resurrection of the Dead* 12.

76. Tertullian, *On the Resurrection of the Flesh*, trans. Evans.

77. Ibid., 63:1. According to Tertullian, Christians will be raised with hair, eyes, and teeth. Cyprian taught that women should not wear cosmetics lest God be unable to recognize them at the resurrection (*On the Dress of Virgins* 17 [*ANF* 5. 434]); see Barnard, "Athenagoras: *De Resurrectione*."

78. This example is from the letter of the churches of Lyons and Vienne (Eusebius *Ecclesiastical History* 1:61–63); see Musurillo, ed., *Acts of Christian Martyrs*, 81–83.

79. Incidentally, one line in this last argument seems initially out of place. Paul quotes a cliché from the poet Menander: "Evil companions corrupt good morals" (15:33). The abrupt interjection of the saying in Paul's argument may indicate that he believes the Corinthians' skepticism to be due to influences from other sources—in fact, from persons who have only "ignorance of God" (v. 34), a designation often used by Jews to refer to Gentiles. He then uses "shaming" language to attempt to change their position (v. 34: "I say this to your shame" [*entropē*]). All this suggests that Paul attributes the Corinthians' doubts to Greek philosophy, especially, perhaps, the skepticism of Epicureanism. See Malherbe, "Beasts at Ephesus," for the argument that Paul uses traditional moral-philosophical arguments that are often turned against

Epicureans (or, more precisely, caricatures of Epicurean views). For the suggestion that Paul is attacking (or thinks he is attacking) some form of Epicureanism, see M. E. Dahl, *Resurrection of the Body*, 12 and n. 4.

80. Scroggs, *The Last Adam*, 66. Scroggs assumes that the opposite of "spiritual" is "physical" (92–94). But, as the list of terms given in the text shows, the opposite of "spiritual" in Paul's system is not "physical" but "psychical," quite a different thing.

81. I am in disagreement with a stream of New Testament scholarship illustrated by the following quotation from Adela Yarbro Collins, who is here reflecting a tradition best represented by Bultmann and E. Schweizer: "The term [*sarx*] was not, however, used by Paul to describe a *part* of the human person as opposed to other parts, but rather to indicate the whole person from the material point of view. Likewise, the human 'spirit' (*pneuma*) is not some part of the human being which can exist independently, but represents the whole person viewed under a particular aspect" ("Function of Excommunication," 257–258; see also Sand, *Der Begriff "Fleisch,"* 143–145). I agree that it is misleading to speak of "flesh" or "spirit" as representing "parts" of the human person in Paul's view; but it is just as misleading to use terms like "aspect" or, as Collins later says, "different attitudes, different orientations of life" in describing the function of Paul's categories of sarx and pneuma, as if those terms could be boiled down to modern psychological notions. To be sure, sarx and pneuma represent "attitudes" and "orientations," but they are also (*always*, as far as we can tell from Paul's text) "stuff." That is why I say that the resurrection of a pneumatic body in Paul refers not to an immaterial "thing" but to a body constituted by its pneumatic part or aspect.

82. Eduard Schweizer is unconvincing when he claims, in reference to 1 Cor.

15:47, that "the first clause with *gēs* ['earth'] denotes the stuff from which the first man is made, while the second clause characterises the second man, not by the substance of which he consists but by his origin" (*"pneuma, ktl"*). I see nothing in the text to indicate that the modifier of "body" is to be interpreted in one clause as denoting "substance" and in the parallel clause as denoting origin, not substance. Schweizer may simply be uncomfortable with the notion that Paul thought of the resurrected body as a body composed of pneumatic stuff. Moreover, I am in complete disagreement with accounts of 1 Corinthians 15 that insist that Paul is not concerned here with the "stuff" of resurrection (e.g., Gooch, *Partial Knowledge*, 69–70). Paul explicitly contrasts an "earthy," "dusty," "psychic" body with a celestial, pneumatic body. Just as the former terms refer to both stuff and cosmic location, so do the latter. Much of the confusion of such scholars comes from their indefensible translation of *psychē* as "nature" or "physical" and their confusion in taking *pneumatikos* as "spiritual" in the sense of "immaterial." Gooch's treatment is also marred by the fact (evident at 70–72) that he is not so much concerned with ancient concepts of embodiment as with making Paul's resurrected body palatable to modern (but now old-fashioned) philosophy.

83. The classic, and still impressive, exposition is that by Albert Schweitzer, *Mysticism of Paul*, see esp. 115–125; see also Sanders, *Paul and Palestinian Judaism*, 453–463. Earle Ellis says, "The corporate body represents no mere metaphor but a reality no less ontological than the individual body. It is a conception difficult to comprehend in modern Western culture, with our nominalist mindset and our exaltation of the individual, but it is a *sine qua non* for understanding the apostle Paul" ("*Sōma* in First Corinthians," 138).

84. John Chow relates (and rejects) various proposals designed to distance Paul

from any approval of baptism for the dead: *Patronage and Power*, 158–159.

85. The classic passage demonstrating this assumption of identity through participation is Romans 6, which merits a study in its own right. As we will see in Chap. 8 below, this connection between the bodies of human beings in relationship informs Paul's teaching that the non-Christian spouse is "sanctified" by association with the Christian spouse.

86. Bakhtin, *Speech Genres;* see also Holquist, *Dialogism*, 60; Todorov, *Mikhail Bakhtin.*

87. See Räisänen, *Paul and the Law*, 143.

Chapter 6: The Body, Disease, and Pollution

1. The most thorough study to date of the notion of pollution in Greek culture is Parker, *Miasma.* Although Parker's concern is preclassical and classical Greece, his study repeatedly refers to Greek texts of the Hellenistic and Roman periods as well.

2. Though related in methodology, my conclusions differ in important ways from those of Neyrey, *Paul, In Other Words.* In my view, Neyrey's analysis does not sufficiently take into account differences in ideological constructions of the body, especially as related to purity issues, in Greco-Roman culture. For example, he claims that "purity" systems reflect an attempt to "order" the universe, implying that those ideological constructs not concerned with purity are thereby less concerned with order (see 24–25). In my view, purity systems vary considerably from one another, reflecting different contingent and ideological situations; also "purity" is only *one* way of expressing anxiety about "order." I see the Strong at Corinth as very concerned about order (as expressed in the hierarchical body) but not about purity.

3. Dubos, *Mirage of Health*, 90.

4. Farquhar, "Objects, Processes, and Female Infertility in Chinese Medicine," 371. For a different classification system, one that compares modern and early Christian notions of *health* rather than *disease*, see Pilch, "Understanding Healing."

5. See, for example, the historical survey provided by Wellin, "Theoretical Orientations in Medical Anthropology."

6. George Peter Murdoch, for example, writes that as early as 1932 modern science "clearly demonstrated that the explanations of illness current among most of the peoples of the world have little in common with those recognized by modern medical science and relate much more closely to the ideology of primitive religion" (*Theories of Illness*, 3). Modern science is thus placed on one side, and all "primitive" notions on the other, grouped with the discarded superstitions of "primitive religion." Murdoch's conclusion should not surprise us, however, since he gathers together everything that is "supernatural" in the camp of the "other."

7. Bonnie Glass-Coffin describes a disease called *daño* (found in North Coastal Peru), which is experienced as an attack by a nonhuman being who captures the person's soul and is expelled by a healer who functions as something like a broker in a complicated series of economic-sounding transactions involving evil spirits and Satan. The disease etiology is fashioned on the market and debt system of the local livestock economy ("Discourse, *Daño*, and Healing," 43). Shigehisa Kuriyama describes several different ancient Chinese disease etiologies. According to one, small creatures (*shi*) inhabit the body and report periodically to the heavenly emperor (*shangdi*) about the misdeeds of the victim. Disease is construed as a bureaucratic system ruled by an internal espionage network presided over by a ledger-keeping emperor ("Changing Concepts of Disease in East Asia," 56). A brief comparison of only these two studies demonstrates the wide variety of ways,

sometimes even in the same society, that diseases operate socially.

8. Lock, *East Asian Medicine in Urban Japan*, see esp. 3; Dubos, *Man Adapting*, 319–321.

9. Lock, *East Asian Medicine*, 25.

10. Ibid., 29.

11. Ibid., 37.

12. Ibid., 37; see also Kuriyama, "Changing Concepts."

13. Lock, *East Asian Medicine*, 45.

14. I also build somewhat on an article by George Foster, "Disease Etiologies in Non-Western Medical Systems." Foster's article helped me focus my ideas about ancient disease etiologies, but his classification system, while promising in terms of the article, is ultimately not as useful for my purposes, since his later treatment of the subject with Anderson confuses the issues by falling back into the naturalist/supernaturalist dichotomy (though he uses the term "personalistic" rather than "supernaturalistic" in opposition to "natural" causation). See Foster and Anderson, *Medical Anthropology*, 53–55. I am interested in comparing systems that posit disease as a result of imbalance with those that attribute disease to an invasive agent, regardless of whether or not that agent is a personalized force such as a daimon/demon or a natural force that is nevertheless spoken of in agential terms, such as a germ or a pollutant.

15. Glick, "Medicine as an Ethnographic Category." Glick seems to assume that all folk medicine construes illness as due to such hostile agents, but, as I will note presently, some kinds of traditional medicine ("folk" or "primitive") adopt the imbalance logic and are less concerned with hostile agents. Re the Tuareg, see Rasmussen, "Veiled Self, Transparent Meanings," esp. 106; *idem*, "Reflections on *Tamazai*, a Tuareg Idiom of Suffering." I pursue the significance of veiling for pollution issues in 1 Cor. 11 in Chap. 9.

16. See the discussion, for example, in McGill, "Structures of Inhumanity," esp. 118–125. McGill insightfully connects popular concepts of disease causation with ideology supporting American militarism.

17. Kuriyama, "Changing Concepts," 53; see also his "Pulse Diagnosis in the Greek and Chinese Traditions."

18. Kuriyama, "Changing Concepts," 54.

19. The logic of imbalance is not limited to the highly developed, sophisticated systems of classical Asian or Greek medicine. Other studies indicate an imbalance logic for diseases in India (Alter, *Wrestler's Body*, esp. 38); Mexico (Foster, "Disease Etiologies"; Foster and Anderson, *Medical Anthropology*, 60); and Hispanic America (Rubel, "Epidemiology of a Folk Illness," esp. 126).

20. Laderman, "Malay Medicine, Malay Person," esp. 84, 87, 91. For another case of the coexistence of different disease etiologies, see Nuckolls, "Divergent Ontologies of Suffering in South Asia."

21. Kuriyama, "Changing Concepts," 55.

22. Dubos, *Mirage of Health*, 136.

23. B. Weiss, "Plastic Teeth Extraction"; see also his *Making and Unmaking of the Haya Lived World*.

24. Hippocrates *On Affections* 1, trans. Potter; see also Hippocrates *Nature of Man* 3–4. I have altered Potter's translation of *lagneiē* from "venery" to "sexual intercourse," as sounding less prudish. The term refers simply to sexual intercourse or emission of semen; in fact, a form of the word (*lagneuma*) occurs as a word for semen itself: LSJ; see also Hippocrates *Internal Affections* 47.

25. Miller, "'Airs, Waters, and Places,' in History." See also the statements of Aetius (5. 30. 1): W. H. S. Jones, *Philosophy and Medicine in Ancient Greece, with an Edition of Peri archaiēs iētrikēs*, 4.

26. Celsus *On Medicine*, Prooemium 14–15, trans. Spencer (slightly modified). For a recent study of Celsus's social role as physician and author, see Spivack, "A. C. Celsus: Roman Medicus." For a fuller study

of Asclepiades, who often seems like a maverick among ancient medical theorists, see Vallance, *Lost Theory of Asclepiades*. In spite of Asclepiades' radical differences from many ancient medical theorists, his etiology of disease is still ruled by an imbalance logic; see ibid., 93–122.

27. Celsus *On Medicine*, Prooemium 55–56.

28. Ibid., 56.

29. Galen *Hygiene* 6. 15; quoted and trans. in Vallance, *Lost Theory*, 41.

30. Hippocrates *On Affections* 4; see also *idem*, *Diseases IV* 51. 1.

31. See, for example, the comments by Aelius Aristides, who reasonably thinks that he should take a "hot" drug (meaning a drug that causes heat, not just one that is itself heated) for his "cold": *Sacred Tales* 1. 26.

32. Galen, *Hygiene* 1. 5; see also Galen *On the Passions and Errors of the Soul* 13.

33. Galen *Hygiene* 1. 4, trans. Green, 13.

34. Greek: *ta enantia tōn enantiōn estin iēmata* (Hippocrates *Breaths* 1. 30).

35. Jackson, "Use of Passions in Psychological Healing," 152–153.

36. Celsus *On Medicine* 1. 3. 14, trans. Spencer.

37. Hippocrates *On Affections* 19; see 18–22 for concerns about impurities and cleansing treatments.

38. Ibid., 20.

39. Ibid., 29–31 *et passim*.

40. Celsus *On Medicine* 1. 3. 19.

41. Hippocrates *On Affections* 36.

42. Aelius Aristides *Sacred Tales* 2. 38, trans. Behr.

43. Pseudo-Aristotle *Problems* 1. 7, 859b15. (Book 1 is entirely devoted to medical questions.)

44. Sextus Empiricus *Against the Professors* 5. 2.

45. Philo *On the Giants* 10; Galen *Hygiene* 1. 4; 1. 11.

46. Galen *On Respiration and the Arteries* 5. 5 (trans. Furley and Wilke, 129).

47. Celsus *On Medicine*, Prooemium 70; see also 1. 2. 3; 1. 10; 2. 1. 10–11.

48. Thucydides *History* 2. 51. 4–6.

49. Poole and Holladay, "Thucydides and the Plague of Athens," 298. Note that Sophocles speaks of corpses as "death-carriers" (*thanatophora*) in plague (*Oedipus the King* 181); but, as will be noted below, a disease etiology different from that of medical theorists, including notions of invasion, attack, and contagion, seems to have been predominant in Greek tragedy. Joanne Phillips notes Varro's theory that some diseases were caused by "tiny animals" that bred in swamps; she argues that this was a confused misinterpretation of Lucretius and that the theory (which resembles modern ideas of infection) was "unique in antiquity" ("On Varro's *animalia quaedam minuta*," 16). See also Temkin, "Historical Analysis of the Concept of Infection," in *Double Face of Janus*, 460.

50. Poole and Holladay, "Thucydides," 299; see also the remarks of Lucretius on the plague of Athens: *De rerum natura* 6. 1090–1286. (Although apparently following Thucydides' account, Lucretius uses an etiology of "bad air" and "climatic change" to explain the spread of the disease.) Eusebius has a statement, quoted from the Hippocratic work *Flatulence*, that might signify a notion of dangerous contagion: *Ecclesiastical History* 10. 4. 11.

51. Plato *Timaeus* 64–65A, 86A, 82A.

52. Epictetus *Discourse* 3. 16. 12.

53. Artemidorus *Oneirocritica* (*Dream Handbook*) 3. 51; 4. 45; 1. 33.

54. Aelius Aristides *Sacred Tales* 1. 9, trans. Behr.

55. Ibid., 1. 26; 2. 22.

56. Ibid., 2. 38.

57. Edelstein, "Greek Medicine in its Relation to Religion and Magic," 220–221.

58. Celsus *On Medicine*, Prooemium 4.

59. "For Homer as well as the culture represented by him, internal diseases are

usually caused by supernatural beings":
Kudlein, "Early Greek Primitive Medicine,"
312.

60. Hesiod *Works and Days* 90–105, trans.
Evelyn-White.

61. Prioreschi, "Supernatural Elements
in Hippocratic Medicine," 396. Prioreschi's
comment here is accurate, though much
of the way he conceptualizes the situation
(using the problematic notion of the supernatural) is anachronistic and inaccurate. He
means by "supernatural" any activity of the
divine (in causing illness, in particular), even
though he realizes that many ancients would
include divinities within "nature" or would
call "nature" itself "divine." He would be
more correct to refer to the ancient dichotomies as divine/human or divine/nondivine,
for supernatural/natural is misleading.
For example, *contra* Prioreschi's statement,
the medical writers have not "merged the
natural and the supernatural" (400). They
do not speak in such categories at all; since
they have never divided the natural from the
supernatural, they cannot be said to merge
them. On this, compare the much better
statements by Padel, *In and Out of Mind*, 39,
quoted in Chap. 1 above.

62. See also the account of the purifying
of Athens from the plague by Epimenides:
Diogenes Laertius *Lives* 1. 110. Many Jews
of the Hellenistic period, though certainly
not all, held similar views: *Jubilees* 10, 17,
says that good angels taught Moses medicine
in order to protect human beings from the
diseases of demons. Philo, as representative
of a more educated perspective of the time,
attributes disease to an imbalance etiology
(see, e.g., *Every Good Man is Free* 76; *On the
Giants* 10).

63. *Sacred Disease* 4; see also §§1 and 21.

64. A typical misreading is that of James
Longrigg ("Philosophy and Medicine,"
149–150), who is contradicted by his own
quotations from the Hippocratic text.
He quotes a passage to demonstrate its
"rationality"—that is, its denial of "divine

origin" for the "sacred disease" and its
alleged attribution of the disease instead to
"natural causes." (See also Longrigg, *Greek
Rational Medicine*.) In fact, the quotation
makes no such point; it simply says that the
disease is no *more* divine than any other: "So
that there is no need to put the disease in a
special class and to consider it more divine
than the others; they are all divine and all
human."

65. *On Decorum* 6, trans. Jones. The
author of *Sacred Disease* says that it would be
reasonable to bring the sick to sanctuaries
and offer sacrifice and prayers. But he complains about the elaborate "purifications"
prescribed by the "magicians, purifiers,
and charlatans" that take place *outside* the
traditional cultic institutions (§§2 and 4).
The gods may *purify* but not *defile*.

66. *Airs, Waters, Places* 22. The second-
century C.E. medical writer Aretaeus
(probably a contemporary of Galen) is still
willing to ascribe *one* form of madness to
"divine origin"—that of devotees to certain
divinities (probably referring to priests of
Cybele). He says that they rave madly and
cut themselves under the influence of divine
forces but are otherwise sane. See Aretaeus
On the Causes and Symptoms of Chronic Diseases
1. 6 Greek text: *Aretaeus* ed. Hude. English:
Extant Works of Aretaeus, the Cappodocian, ed.
and trans. Adams.

67. It was common in Greco-Roman
medicine to link semen or sperm (they
were not differentiated in ancient theory)
to the brain; the brain either produced or
controlled the seed. See, e.g., Ptolemy, "On
the *Kriterion* and *Hegemonikon*," 15. 3. On the
involvement of the gods, note Edelstein's
astute statement: "All these instances reveal
how utterly different are the ancients' conceptions of natural phenomena from those
of modern times. . . . Natural and religious
expressions are used as equivalents" ("Greek
Medicine," 209).

68. The translation of Galen is by
Edelstein, "Greek Medicine," 231; see also

Kudlein, "Galen's Religious Belief"; Riddle, *Dioscorides on Pharmacy and Medicine*, 88; Pliny *Natural History* 19. 62. 189; Herophilus, quoted in Plutarch *Moralia* 663B–C, and Galen *De compositione medicamentorum secundum locos* 6. 8 (XII, pp. 965–966K); *Herophilus*, ed. von Staden, 417–418.

69. Prioreschi, "Supernatural Elements," 400; see *Sacred Disease* 4.

70. Lucian *Lover of Lies* 19, 16.

71. Ibid., 8–9. On the relationship between medicine and magic, see Riddle, *Dioscorides*, 82–88. As will become evident in the following paragraphs, I believe that linking "magic" to "the supernatural" and "medicine" to "the natural," as Riddle and many other historians of medicine do, is uncritical and misleading. Riddle's confusion is evident, for example, when he is puzzled that Pliny the Elder "denounced magic but he related considerable supernatural information," such as the idea that kissing a mule's muzzle would heal a cold (Riddle, *Dioscorides*, 137; Pliny *Natural History* 30. 1. 1–3; 30. 11. 51). This should have led Riddle to realize that the charge of "magic" has nothing to do with the (totally modern) category of "the supernatural."

72. Lucian *Lover of Lies* 10.

73. Plutarch *On Superstition* (*Moralia* 164E–171F), 164B.

74. Ibid., 166A–167A.

75. Ibid., 168B.

76. Ibid., 171B.

77. Theophrastus *Characters* 16. 2, 7, 9.

78. Ibid., 16. 14.

79. Plutarch *Sayings of Spartans* 11 (*Moralia* 223E).

80. Plutarch *On Tranquility of Mind* (*Moralia*) 465D; *On the Sign of Socrates* (*Moralia*) 579F–580B. A full ideological analysis of attacks on "superstition" would be interesting, though out of place here. Speaking of a different time and place, for example, Michel de Certeau says, "Totalitarianism attacks what it quite correctly calls *superstitions*: supererogatory semantic

overlays that insert themselves 'over and above' and 'in excess,' and annex to a past or poetic realm a part of the land the promoters of technical rationalities and financial profitabilities had reserved for themselves" (*Practice of Everyday Life*, 106). On such a reading, "superstition" may be construed as insubordination and an insinuation of a space alternative to that controlled by the dominant ideology.

81. Plutarch *On Isis and Osiris* 383B–C.

82. Ibid., 383D.

83. Parker, *Miasma*, 57.

84. Diogenes Laertius *Lives* 6. 61, 63.

85. Betz, ed., *Greek Magical Papyri*, xlv.

86. See, e.g., *PGM* II. 147, and Betz, ed. *passim*. All the examples given here are available in English translation in Betz, ed.

87. G. H. R. Horsley, *New Documents 1977*, no. 12.

88. *PGM* IV. 2441–2621, see 2515ff. for the prophylactic part of the spell.

89. *PGM* IV. 296–466; IV. 1496–1595; for the "sadistic" aspect of love charms, see Winkler, *Constraints of Desire*, 86–96. Winkler notes that in some charms a female statuette is "pierced" in order to elicit love and loyalty. Note the aspect of penetration as well as the notion that pain and disease, here as inflamed passion, invade the body from without.

90. Theocritus 2 ("The Spell"), 55, 85, trans. Edmonds.

91. See esp. Celsus *On Medicine* 5. 27. 2; Aristotle *Historia animalium* 4. 8, 604a; Pliny *Natural History* 29. 32. 98–102; Lucian *Lover of Lies* 40; but see Wilkinson, "Development of the Virus Concept," who notes that in spite of these occasional hints, the actual concept of viral contagion does not appear until Fracastoro in the sixteenth century, and even this later date is disputed by Howard-Jones, "Fracastoro and Henle."

92. Aeschines ("Against Ctesiphon") 3. 114, 157.

93. Demosthenes ("On the Crown") 18. 159, trans. Vince and Vince.

94. Plato *Cratylus* 396D–E. As this section has demonstrated, Edelstein was mistaken to say that the "demonic" etiology of disease was due to "the Christians and Jews who propagated these ideas at the end of Greek and Roman history" ("Greek Medicine," 222). Edelstein too often takes upper-class writings as representing all Greco-Roman society.

95. Hippocrates *Diseases* IV. 51. 1–7, trans. Lonie, *Hippocratic Treatises "On Generation," "On the Nature of the Child," "Diseases IV,"* 34–35.

96. Hippocrates *Diseases* IV. 51. 7, trans. Lonie.

97. Betz, ed., *Greek Magical Papyri*, xlvii.

Chapter 7: Sex, Food, and the Pollution of the Corinthian Body

1. The texts speak of the agents of disease as *daimones* or *pneumata* apparently indiscriminately. We must remember that in this case ancient Greek speakers probably recognized no difference between concepts that we modern English speakers would distinguish: for example, between "spirit," "demon," and "daimon" (which connotes for us the benign image of a demigod more than the evil image of a "demon"). Likewise, as we will see when looking at Paul's terminology, the term *aggelos* ("angel") referred to a morally ambiguous agent very much like *daimones*, not at all like the English "angel," which is usually understood as the opposite of "demon." Throughout my treatment in this chapter I render the Greek *daimōn* "daimon" rather than "demon" in order to highlight the normally ambiguous function of the term in Greek and to remind readers that the entities referred to in this chapter are like those semi-divine agents studied in the previous chapter as a cause of disease.

2. See also Mark 3:11; 5:2; Luke 9:42.

3. As will be clear by now, I am skeptical of modern accounts that dichotomize ancient experience into physiological as opposed to psychological or religious categories. I am also wary of attempts to divide ancient discourses regarding purity into opposing categories of ontology and morality. When Jacob Neusner and Bruce D. Chilton argue that virtue and holiness constitute separate classifications in a certain strand of first-century Judaism and that "uncleanness formed an ontological category, not a moral one at all," I suspect that they have posited a false, modern either/or. See their "Uncleanness: A Moral or an Ontological Category in the Early Centuries A.D.?," 65.

4. Here I disagree with John Pilch, who claims that in the Gospel accounts of exorcism "the demon is not the 'cause' but rather the manifestation of the misfortune, the symptoms. Jesus' exorcisms are thus symptomatic therapies rather than aetiological therapies" ("Understanding Healing," 31). I believe this is an unsupportable either/or. Contrary to Pilch's claims, ancient persons, educated and uneducated alike, *were* concerned with the causes of disease. In fact, one sect of medical theorists (the Empiricists) was noted for its *peculiar* rejection of much contemporary speculation about hidden causes of disease (see Celsus *On Medicine*, Prooemium 27–40).

5. Jewish attribution of disease to daimonic activity was fairly widespread. Before the Hellenistic period, Israelite beliefs resemble the "invasion" etiology, not surprisingly, given contemporaneous and earlier assumptions about disease in ancient Mesopotamian cultures, which point to gods and demons and use exorcisms and antidemonic prophylactics (both materials and incantations) for disease therapy. See Nash, "Devils, Demons, and Disease," esp. 64, for talismans and prophylactic drugs and objects, and 74 for prophylactic house cleaning after the exorcism of a disease-demon (Lev. 14:33–57). In the same volume, see Martinez, "Epidemic Disease,

Ecology, and Culture in the Ancient Near East," esp. 423–428, for plague caused by gods or disease-demons. Josephus also tells tales of Jewish exorcists who use esoteric knowledge from "books of Solomon" to cast out daimons (*daimonia*); he mentions a Palestinian Jew named Eleazer who cast out a daimon in the presence of Vespasian (*Antiquities* 8. 45–49).

6. I am using the NRSV, which reflects the Hebrew original (when it can be reconstructed) rather than the later Greek Septuagint version. The Greek version of 38:15, rather than praising the physician, contains the curse: "May [the sinner] fall into the hands of the physician," a sentiment also known from Greek and Latin sources.

7. Philo *On the Giants* 10–11. Philo condemns *deisidaimonia* ("superstition" or "fear of daimons"), but he nonetheless believes in the existence of daimons (as did many Greek theorists; see *Giants* 16).

8. Celsus *On Medicine* 5. 19. 11; see Stern, *Greek and Latin Authors on Jews and Judaism*, 1. 369. For Galen and Damascius, see Stern, 2. 309, n. 7; 2. 679.

9. Baumgarten, "The 4Q Zadokite Fragments on Skin Disease," 162.

10. Ibid., 162. Another Qumran document, a fragment called the "Prayer of Nabonidus" (4QPrNab), speaks of a disease being healed by an exorcist. At Qumran both basic medical procedures and exorcisms were probably practiced, reflected in the fact that some Qumran documents evince one etiology, some the other. For the text, see Fitzmyer and Harrington, *Manual of Palestinian Aramaic Texts*, 2–3.

11. See the several references in Kottek, "Concepts of Disease in the Talmud," 14–18.

12. Preuss, *Biblical and Talmudic Medicine*, 167; Preuss claims that this is the only instance in the entire Talmud of "a teaching of body temperaments," a claim disputed by more recent scholars.

13. Neumyer, "Talmudic Medicine and Greek Sources." Neumyer and Kottek are especially concerned to correct the statements of Preuss (*Biblical and Talmudic Medicine* 142), and Muntner, Introduction to Preuss, *Biblisch-talmudische Medizin*, xxiv.

14. See "Asaph Ha-Rofe," in *Encyclopedia Judaica*; see also Baumgarten, "4Q Zadokite Fragments," 163–164. Earlier claims by James Charlesworth that a scroll from Qumran is a medical document and predates "the heretofore oldest known Hebrew medical manuscript by fourteen centuries" are apparently inaccurate; see *Discovery of a Dead Sea Scroll (4Q Therapeia)*, iii. The original publication of the scroll and the claim that it was a medical document were made by J. M. Allegro, *Dead Sea Scrolls and the Christian Myth*, 235–240. Joseph Naveh later demonstrated that the scroll was merely the scratch paper of a scribe practicing writing by means of the alphabet and a few biblical Hebrew names ("Medical Document or Writing Exercise?"). Charlesworth has since retracted his earlier claims (without, however, mentioning the work of Naveh): "A Misunderstood Recently Published Dead Sea Scroll (4QM130)," 2. For a dated, but still useful, bibliography of ancient Hebrew medicine, see Friedenwald, *Jews and Medicine*, 2. 99–145.

15. In Phil. 2:26–27 Paul mentions that Epaphroditus has been ill; the cause is not mentioned, but the cure is expected to come through prayer and the mercy of God.

16. See the survey and references in Woods, "Opposition to a Man and his Message." I am not persuaded by Woods's argument that Paul here refers to social opposition and hence not to a physical ailment. Woods does not take into account the social implications and cultural meanings of illness and physical weakness pervasive in ancient ideologies of the body.

17. Paul constructs the scene in 1 Cor. 5 as a courtroom. He says that he has already passed judgment on the offender (making himself either a judge or a prosecutor), and

he calls on the Corinthians, in the role of co-judges or the jury, to concur with his judgment and turn the man over to Satan. For the occurrence of *paradidonai* ("turn over") in court cases to refer to the delivery of a condemned person for punishment or torture, see Antiphon *Prosecution for Poisoning* 20; Isocrates *Speech* 17. 15; Demosthenes *Speech* 45. 61. With regard to handing someone over for trial, see Andocides *Speech* 1. 17; Demosthenes *Speech* 49. 9; to imprisonment. Demosthenes *Speech* 51. 8; for execution, Lysias *Speech* 14. 17. In the previous chapter Paul used the term *hēmera* unambiguously to indicate a human court (4:3; in 1:8 and 3:13 also it would be as easy to translate the term "court" as "day"). In Paul's constructed court, interestingly enough, neither God nor Christ play any role. Satan is the torturer, the *basanistēs*.

18. So Campbell, "Flesh and Spirit in 1 Cor. 5:5." Campbell perhaps goes too far the other way, insisting that Paul is *only* concerned with the church's "flesh" and "spirit." For a variety of views about the individual man's fate, see Joy, "Is the Body Really to be Destroyed?"; G. W. H. Lampe, "Church Discipline and the Epistles to the Corinthians"; Barrett, *First Epistle*, 126–127; Conzelmann, *1 Corinthians*, 97–98.

19. This has been argued especially by A. Y. Collins, "Function of 'Excommunication' in Paul." I believe that Collins, who argues that Paul is concerned about the fate of the communal body and says nothing about the fate of the man's body, has gone too far in the other direction. Besides the fact that Paul does not explicitly address the communal pollution until vv. 6–8, Collins's interpretation splits the phrase of v. 5b into two parts with different referents: it takes the "destruction" to apply to the individual man but the "salvation" to apply to the church and not to the man. It is better not to try to make a decision as to whether Paul is referring to the body of the individual man or the church body; both are implicated

throughout—as required by Paul's logic of participation and his ignorance of modern notions of individualism.

20. Note 1 Thess. 4:5; Col. 3:5–10; 1 Pet. 4:3; see also Stambaugh and Balch, *New Testament in its Social Environment*, 57; Zass, "Catalogues and Context."

21. Mitton, "New Wine in Old Wine Skins"; for Jewish texts, see Forkman, *Limits of the Religious Community*, 147–149; also Neyrey, *Paul, In Other Words*, esp. 117. See too Rosner, "Temple and Holiness," for the Jewish background to Paul's concerns about the purity of the church as the "Temple of God."

22. Meeks, *First Urban Christians*, 97–107; *idem, Moral World*, 98–108.

23. Brian Rosner is right to emphasize the "corporate responsibility" and hence shared guilt of the Corinthian church in Paul's view ("*'ouchi mallon epenthēsate'*"). But he does not stress sufficiently the importance of communal *pollution* among Paul's concerns.

24. See Chap. 6; Padel, *In and Out of Mind*, 95; Hippocrates *Breaths* 6–7, 9–10; Galen *On Respiration and the Arteries* 5. 5; Temkin, *Hippocrates in a World of Pagans and Christians*, 12.

25. Padel, *In and Out of Mind*, 81; Hippocrates *Breaths* 8.

26. Aretaeus *On the Causes and Symptoms of Acute Diseases* 1. 7. Galen *On the Affected Parts* 3. 9, trans. Siegel; see also Siegel, *Galen on Sense Perception*. According to Plutarch, "fullness in the body" puts pressure on the pneuma "around" the nerves(?), thereby causing diseases (*Advice about Keeping Well* 127E); activity after eating should be gentle to avoid "oppressing" the pneuma (133D). Bad dreams are due to disturbances of pneuma and may presage disease (129B), and straining the pneuma by loud speaking produces "ruptures and strains" (130D). Note that these very "materialistic"-sounding remarks about the pneuma come from someone who considers himself a good Platonist.

27. Hippocrates *Affections* 18–22.

28. Plutarch *Dinner of the Seven Wise Men* (*Moralia*) 159B.

29. See Sevenster, *Paul and Seneca*, 81–83; Martyn, "Apocalyptic Antinomies." I am here in some disagreement with Paul Meyer ("The Holy Spirit in the Pauline Letters," 11–12) when he claims that Paul does not hypostatize the flesh as a demonic power in opposition to God and the Spirit. Paul does speak of Sarx as possessing "thoughts" that are "enemies" of God (Rom. 8:7); the "flesh" has its own passions and desires in opposition to the pneuma (Gal. 5:17); it has its own "works" (Gal. 5:19). Rather than take all this to be mere metaphor, I prefer to allow Paul's personification of sarx its full force.

30. Exegetes frequently take 1 Cor. 5:1–2 as certain evidence that the entire Corinthian church not only tolerated sexual immorality but *boasted* about it (see, e.g., Daube, "Pauline Contributions to a Pluralistic Culture," 224). But this is to take *Paul's* rhetoric as completely and accurately reflecting other people's attitudes, surely a precarious (though too common) practice, to say the least. 1 Cor. 5, despite Paul's insinuations, provides no evidence that the Corinthian Strong *approved* of the man's behavior, much less boasted about it. All it suggests is that they were of high status and that they failed openly to condemn offending Christians. I take 1 Cor. 7 as giving a more accurate picture of their views about sex— and from that discussion it is clear that they were ascetics, not libertarians. But their asceticism was not regarded as universally applicable. Weak, ignorant persons were not expected to have the same kind of self-control as those with stronger characters who had had proper philosophical training. The Strong do not react as strongly as Paul to sexual immorality because they do not fear pollution of the whole church (or themselves!) due to the sexual misdeeds of weaker Christians. I take 1 Cor. 5 to be

Paul's exaggeration (certainly not rare with him) of their position.

31. Robert Parker (*Miasma*, 96) remarks on the importance of social status for concerns about sexual continence: "That there should be unchaste women and boys in the world is no matter for concern; they provide, indeed, a useful outlet for the not unreasonable desires of honest men. It is only among the possessors of 'honour' (full citizen rights) that they are out of place. Offenders are not exiled or put to death but deprived of 'honour' and forced to find a place amid the flotsam of foreignness and vice that laps around the citizen body." I do not suggest that the Strong at Corinth shared precisely this view of sexual activity but rather that they shared an assumption that what constituted proper sexual control depended on the social status of the person; likewise, they had little fear of pollution through proximity.

32. See, e.g., Zass, "'Cast out the Evil Man from your Midst,'" 260; Neyrey, *Paul, In Other Words*, 124–125 *et passim*.

33. For the curious (and quite non-modern) function of Paul's "spirit" in the condemnation of the man from a distance, see Ellis, "*Sōma* in First Corinthians," 137. I agree with Ellis that Paul's reference here to his pneuma "offers no support to an anthropological dualism in which Paul's 'spirit' (his 'real self') is active, separated and distant from his body."

34. For one analysis suggesting different views about boundaries between Paul and the Corinthians, see Barclay, "Thessalonica and Corinth."

35. See Chap. 3 and A. Mitchell, "I Corinthians 6:1–11."

36. I take the primary context to be one of *male* Christians visiting *female* prostitutes only because Paul here uses the feminine form of the word for prostitute. Of course, female Christians may have gone to male prostitutes, in which case Paul's point about the penetration of the Christian's body by

the cosmos (discussed below) would have been much more pertinent, though perhaps less striking and ironic.

37. Winkler, *Constraints of Desire*, 39; see also 37 and 41 for *synousia*.

38. See ibid., 67–70.

39. Aeschines, "Against Timarchos," 1. 159; see the discussion in Winkler, *Constraints of Desire*, 63.

40. I have translated *hyperbainein* as "step on," although it more accurately means "step over," as in "to surpass, transgress, trespass," in order to bring out its status aspects. The word means to overreach someone, putting oneself above the other in doing so. The term translated "vessel" may refer to the man's wife, his own body, or particularly his sexual organ; I have left it ambiguous. See Ellicott, *Commentary*, 61, for a list of patristic sources; see also Carros, "Jewish Ethics," 308–310; Wanamaker, *Thessalonians*, 151–153; Best, *Commentary*, 161–163.

41. Pierce, *Conscience in the New Testament*, 50; see also 44–50, from which the points made in this paragraph are taken. Of course, the pain from past transgressions will have some effect on future action, but the emphasis is on the past and the pain caused by misdeeds rather than on some abstract guide to future action. See also R. A. Horsley, "Consciousness and Freedom among the Corinthians." Horsley translates *syneidēsis* as "consciousness" rather than "conscience" in order to avoid the misleading connotations of the latter word in modern conceptions (581). See also Tomson, *Paul and Jewish Law*, 195.

42. Pierce, *Conscience in the New Testament*, 66; R. A. Horsley, "Consciousness," 586; Maurer, "*synoida, syneidēsis*," *TDNT* 7. 914.

43. Maurer, "*synoida, syneidēsis*," 917.

44. Paul's term in 1 Cor. 4:4 is *synoida*, which is from the same word-group as *syneidēsis* and refers to the same faculty or process.

45. R. A. Horsley, "Consciousness," 582.

Horsley is here referring to Philo's *On the Decalogue.*

46. Maurer, "*synoida, syneidēsis*," 914.

47. For the traditional Jewish association of idols with daimons, see Tomson, *Paul and Jewish Law*, 156–159. The ambivalence found in Paul (are they *daimons* or just "nothings"?) is reflected in other Jewish sources.

48. The position is well stated, and rejected, by Cope, "First Corinthians 8–10." Some scholars argue that the only possible recourse is to partition theories according to which the different parts of Paul's argument come from what were originally different letters. See discussion (and counter-arguments) in Hurd, *Origin of I Corinthians*, 42–47, and Willis, "An Apostolic Apologia?" I am unpersuaded by Cope's argument that 10:1–22 is an interpolation. Paul's different statements do not seem to me so contradictory. It is simply that his position is not rigorously consistent. He does believe that idols have no true existence and are "nothings" in the sense that they lack any real power before the greater power of God; but he also believes that they represent daimonic beings that may under certain circumstances pollute weak Christians. Since one cannot tell by looking at a person whether he or she is susceptible to pollution, precautions are thus in order in every case. This, I believe, explains Paul's confusing and apparently dual position.

49. Willis, *Idol Meat in Corinth*, 49; Smith and Taussig, *Many Tables*, 22–24. In spite of 8:10, Tomson (*Paul and Jewish Law*, 195) denies that Paul seriously entertains the idea that a Christian would be present at a cultic activity in a temple. I believe Tomson's analysis of this passage is marred by his *presupposition* (which I think is questionable) that Paul, as a Jew, *could not conceivably* have condoned the consumption of idol-food or attendance at an idolatrous ritual.

50. It is important to realize that this is

not simply the Greek view as opposed to Paul's Jewish fears of pollution from idols. As some Rabbinic texts show, even Jews could use philosophical-sounding arguments to insist that a Jew would not be defiled by proximity to Greek "divinities," by using water from a "bath of Aphrodite," or even by participating in the manufacture of idols. Most Jews would have avoided idol-meat, but not necessarily because of fears of pollution: see Winter, "Theological and Ethical Responses to Religious Pluralism," 217, 219–222; Tomson, *Paul and Jewish Law*, 159–160, 162, 167.

51. I believe this is what Theissen (*Psychological Aspects*) and Via (*Self-Deception*, see esp. 47–52) do. Though we may speak of Paul as doing something "unconsciously," any use of that kind of language to posit an actual arena of the mind or personality that has ontological status but is closed to conscious analysis seems to me too modern relative to ancient categories of mind, thought, and self.

52. Diogenes Laertius *Lives* 6. 61; this and similar passages are discussed in Chap. 6.

53. Plutarch, *Advice to Bride and Groom* (*Moralia*) 145C. For Cynic and Stoic emphases on knowledge as providing *exousia*, see Conzelmann, *1 Corinthians*, 142, 108–109; Niederwimmer, *Der Begriff der Freiheit*, 28–68, 196–212.

54. Galen *On the Passions and Errors of the Soul* 28; also 31. See too Lucretius *De rerum natura* 1. 62–79, where the culprit defeated by philosophy is *religio*. Similar notions of knowledge occur in Jewish texts: Wisdom 7:17–30.

55. I disagree with William Countryman, who attempts to distinguish pollution (what he calls, in a modern way, "physical impurity") from "acting contrary to one's conscience" (*Dirt, Greed, and Sex*, 103–104). He argues throughout his study that Paul is *not* really concerned about pollution at all (see 104–105, 107, 120); he also problematically separates purity issues (as

being somehow physical) from moral issues (such as those dealing with sin as a moral but not a physiological category; see 105, 122). Once we get beyond the modern dichotomy between physiological and psychological, all such interpretations are suspect.

56. Bultmann, *"ginōskō, ktl,"* *TDNT* 1.689–719.

57. Betz, ed., *Greek Magical Papyri in Translation*, xlvii.

58. *PGM* VIII. 1–63, trans. O'Neil.

59. *PGM* XIII. 783–806, trans. Morton Smith and quoted in his "Salvation in the Gospels, Paul, and the Magical Papyri," 71.

60. Theophrastus *Enquiry into Plants* 7. 13. 4.

61. Scarborough and Nutton, "Preface of Dioscorides' *Materia Medica*," 223. For the text of Dioscorides, see *Pedanii Dioscuridis Anazarbei De materia medica*, ed. Wellmann.

62. *PGM* VII. 579–590; IV. 3007–3086; other spells, of course, were designed to send daimons into the bodies of other people: *PGM* VII. 429–458.

63. *PGM* IV. 2967–2975, trans. O'Neil (Betz, ed., 95); for a discussion see Scarborough, "Pharmacology of Sacred Plants, Herbs, and Roots." For one recipe for *kyphi*, see Riddle, *Dioscorides on Pharmacy and Medicine*, 90 (taken from Dioscorides).

64. *PGM* I. 21; I. 85–90; for other references to eating with deities, see *PGM* I. 1–42; III. 424–430; IV. 750–775; VII. 644–651; Klauck, *Herrenmahl und hellenistischer Kult*, esp. 156–158, 190.

65. See, e.g., Pierce, *Conscience in the New Testament*, 77; B. A. Pearson, "Philo, Gnosis, and the New Testament," 168.

66. See Theissen, *Social Setting*. For a good recent reconstruction of the situation along these lines, including a useful comparison with other sorts of Greco-Roman social meals, see P. Lampe, "Das korinthische Herrenmahl."

67. See, for example, the translation by Charles Perrot: "ils mangent leur condamnation" ("Lecture de 1 Co 11, 17–34"); and the

statement by Grosheide, *Commentary*, 275:
"a figurative expression in which 'judgment'
is treated as if it were food."

68. Héring, *First Epistle*, 119.

69. Earle Ellis notes that the same logic
and realism underlie Paul's concerns about
prostitutes and the Lord's Supper: the
"body of Christ" is no mere metaphor, nor a
simple theological conception, but is at least
as real as any other body: "*Sōma* in First
Corinthians," 140–141.

70. Parry, *Thelxis*, 25.

71. See ibid., 161, and Winnington-
Ingram, *Euripides and Dionysus*, 115–117,
157–158.

72. Sophocles *Trachiniae* 572–574; Parry,
Thelxis, 266.

73. Antiphon *Prosecution for Poisoning*.

74. It was also recognized that the
same drug (such as parts of the orchid
bulb) used one way might function as an
aphrodisiac, increasing desire, but used
another way might work as an anaphrodi-
siac, diminishing desire or even leading to
impotence. The condition of the patient was
important: drugs from India were reputed
to enable a man to have sex twelve times
in quick succession; for a strong man his
performance could be increased to seventy
times. Happily, the modern translator of
the passage promises, "An active search for
plants which possess these activities is being
carried out at the present time" (Gemmill,
"Missing Passage in Hort's Translation of
Theophrastus").

75. Riddle, *Dioscorides*, 139. Of course,
one can hardly help remembering here
Jacques Derrida's fascinating study of the
pharmakon in "Plato's Pharmacy" (see
Dissemination).

76. Dioscorides *Materia medica* 3. 63.
Likewise, mandrake cures but can kill in
large doses (4. 76). Nicander also mentions
korion as a poison in his *Alexipharmaka* 157
and as a curative in *Theriaka* 874.

77. The precautions are also passed on by
Dioscorides (first century C.E.); Dioscorides

is not as disdainful of some of these beliefs
as Theophrastus, but he nevertheless tends
to distance himself from them, citing them
as the practices and beliefs of "some people."
See *Materia medica* 4. 151. For this reading
of Dioscorides as relating popular remedies
while distancing himself from them, see
Riddle, *Dioscorides*, 84.

78. Pliny *Natural History* 25. 11. 30, trans.
Jones.

79. Ibid., 25. 21. 50.

80. See, e.g., *PGM* II. 147; see also
Scarborough, "Pharmacology of Sacred
Plants, Herbs, and Roots," 157.

81. Pliny *Natural History* 25. 17. 37.
Cato is the typically anti-Greek Roman
in his opposition to Greek medicine. He
thus provides an example of an upper-
class person who embraced folk medicine
over professional medicine. As John Riddle
writes, "Folk medicine was superior medicine to him, because he distrusted Hellenic
ways and trusted things that sprang from
the soil of the Roman farm" ("Folk Tradition
and Folk Medicine," 41).

82. *Contra*, e.g., Cornelius à Lapide, *Great
Commentary*, 296–297; Godet, *Commentary*,
2. 167; Héring, *First Epistle*, 120; Fisher,
Commentary, 189; Green, *To Corinth with
Love*, 45.

83. *Contra*, e.g., Moffatt, *First Epistle*,
174; Higgins, *Lord's Supper in the New
Testament*, 72–73. See H. A. W. Meyer,
Critical and Exegetical Handbook, 270, for a
list of German supporters of this view and a
rejection of it.

84. The Strong at Corinth would probably have found Paul's fears embarrassing,
just as they would his anxieties about
pollutions from sex or idol-meat. My
position differs from an older view that the
Corinthians were "super-sacramentalists"
(von Soden, "Sakrament und Ethik bei
Paulus"). As Richard Horsley says, "It was
Paul, not the Corinthians, who introduced
the notion of an almost magical influence of
a cultic meal" ("Gnosis in Corinth," 48).

Chapter 8: The Dangers of Desire

1. D. B. Martin, *Slavery as Salvation*, 63–68.

2. For an interpretation of Rom. 16:7, see Brooten, "'Junia . . . Outstanding among the Apostles.'" I take 1 Cor. 14:34–35 to be a non-Pauline interpolation; see Fee, *First Epistle*, 699–708. But even if it is authentic, one must interpret it in the context of Paul's other statements about women, which do allow them a voice in the church, especially 1 Cor. 11, which assumes that women will pray and prophesy in church (on which, see Chap. 9 below). On Gal. 3:28, as I will argue in Chap. 9, "egalitarian" interpretations do not adequately recognize the function of androgynous mythology in the ancient world.

3. See esp. Foucault, *Care of the Self;* Rousselle, *Porneia;* Laqueur, *Making Sex;* Halperin et al., eds., *Before Sexuality.*

4. Soranus reports that according to one medical view, people who have never had sex are unacquainted with desire (*Gynecology* 1. 7. 30). Greek text: Ilberg, ed., *Sorani Gynaeciorum libri IV;* Rose, ed., *Sorani Gynaeciorum.*

5. Ibid.

6. Ibid.

7. Aristotle had taught that only the male produces seed and that the female body is merely the soil in which the seed is nourished and grows into a human being. But Aristotle was reacting to older Hippocratic theory, and he did not win the day (*Generation of Animals* 728a; see 763b for the views of Aristotle's predecessors). Galen agreed with Aristotle that the female is an imperfect male but parted company in his belief (which he shared with most people of his day) that the female produced seed also (see Allen, *Concept of Woman*, 187–189 and 83–103). See also Horowitz, "Aristotle and Women"; Preus, "Science and Philosophy in Aristotle's *Generation of Animals.*"

8. For Aristotle's theories in the context of the more dominant medical tradition that both men and women produced sperm, see Sissa, "Sexual Philosophies of Plato and Aristotle," 72–73, 77–79; McLaren, *History of Contraception*, 19. There were some disagreements as to whether sperm was the foam of boiling blood or simply of bodily fluids or humors in general. The Hippocratic *On Generation* (1. 1; 8. 1) maintains the latter, whereas the former view is held by Aristotle, Erasistratus, and Herophilus, among others. For Aristotle, see *Generation of Animals* 721a26–727b30; for the other two, see the fragments of Herophilus in *Herophilus*, ed. von Staden, frg. 104, p. 213; see also the excellent summary of the evidence by von Staden, pp. 288–296.

9. See also the later Christian writer Methodius of Olympus, who is parroting the medical opinions of previous centuries: "The marrow-like generative part of the blood, which is liquid bone, gathers from all parts of the body, curdled and worked into a foam, and then rushes through the generative organs into the living soil of the woman" (*Symposium* 2. 2, trans. Musurillo).

10. Oribasius *Collectionum Medicarum Reliquiae* 22. 2. 19–21. This English translation is by Felicia Pheasant, translator of Rousselle, *Porneia*, and is found on pp. 14–15. The word "moderately" should be "immoderately," as it is in the Greek and the French. Rousselle is here quoting from the French edition of Oribasius: *Oeuvres*, ed. and trans. Daremberg and Bussemaker, 3. 46–47. The more recent edition of the Greek by Raeder places this portion of the text in the section *Libri Incerti* 9 (4. 92–93).

11. For the woman as an imperfect male, see Aristotle *Generation of Animals* 728a18; Clement of Alexandria *Paedagogus* 3. 3; Sissa, "Sexual Philosophies of Plato and Aristotle," 65. On the proper way to accustom an adolescent to the regimen of the cold bath, see Galen *Hygiene* 3. 4 and Chap. 1 above.

12. Galen *On the Affected Parts* 6. 5, trans. Siegel.

13. Rousselle, *Porneia*, 19, citing Oribasius *Collectionum Medicarum Reliquiae* 14. 66 and 6. 3. See also Aretaeus *On the Causes and Symptoms of Acute Diseases* 2. 12 for other views on male and female illness due to sexual urges.

14. For a survey of philosophical opposition to marriage, see Yarbrough, *Not Like the Gentiles*, 32–36; also Balch, "Backgrounds of I Cor. VII," 351; idem, "1 Cor. 7:32–35 and Stoic Debates," 429–435. Of course, opposition to marriage did not mean opposition to sexual activity for most of these writers. For Orphics and Pythagoreans as advocating some form of asceticism and disciplined life, see Stambaugh and Balch, *New Testament in its Social Environment*, 45.

15. Diogenes *Epistle* 47 (on the dating, see Malherbe, *Cynic Epistles*, 14–15). According to Diogenes Laertius *Lives* 6. 29 and 6. 54, Diogenes praised those who refrained from marriage and family. On the other hand, one tradition indicates that he had sons of his own (6. 31), and another that he advocated communal wives (6. 72). He seems not to condemn sex—or even marriage—as long as the man retains complete self-mastery. Galen cites a tradition that Diogenes disdained marriage but without disdaining sex (*Affected Parts* 6. 5). For a survey of philosophical positions on marriage and sex, see Deming, *Paul on Marriage and Celibacy*, chap. 2.

16. See Diogenes Laertius. *Lives* 6. 46, 69.

17. Epictetus *Discourse* 3. 22. See Balch, "1 Cor 7:32–35 and Stoic Debates."

18. In fact, the majority opinion even among philosophers seems to have been that marriage and procreation, under certain circumstances (a good wife, for instance), were desirable. See Yarbrough, *Not Like the Gentiles*, 31–53. Roy Bowen Ward ("Musonius and Paul on Marriage") offers a correction of the position of Balch

("1 Cor 7:32–35 and Stoic Debates"), who perhaps overplays the similarities between the positions of Musonius Rufus and Paul.

19. Rousselle, *Porneia*, 170.

20. Hurd, *Origin of 1 Corinthians*, 67; Schrage, "Zur Frontstellung der paulinischen Ehebewertung"; Phipps, "Paul's Attitude," 125–130; Fee, *First Epistle*, 270–271.

21. Fee, *First Epistle*, 269.

22. Balch, "Backgrounds."

23. Philo *Questions and Answers on Genesis* 2. 49; *Moses* 2. 66–70.

24. Balch, "Backgrounds," 360, 361. Balch notes that these ideals are not original with Philo but are part of Hellenistic Judaism in general.

25. For asceticism in first-century Judaism, see Boyarin, *Carnal Israel*.

26. Philo *Moses* 2. 68, trans. Colson; see Balch, "Backgrounds," 359.

27. I agree with Antoinette Clark Wire that the sexual ascetics at Corinth are *not* concerned about pollution (see *Corinthian Women Prophets*, 96); but I disagree with her claim that it is the women prophets in particular who are advocating sexual abstinence. Sexual control was a symbol of strength (especially claimed by men for themselves) in Greco-Roman upper-class ideology; therefore I think that men were included among the Corinthian ascetics.

28. See Galen's *Hygiene* for such dietary regimens. As Lonie observes, Greek medical dietary control was implicated in the cosmological theories of balance of the elements of the body, since a proper diet maintains the balanced body and counteracts the disrupted state of the sick body ("A Structural Pattern," 237–239).

29. This also makes more sense of the Corinthians' position, given that most of them would probably have been Gentiles by birth rather than Jews.

30. See M. Y. MacDonald, "Women Holy in Body and Spirit," 162. Some commentators point out that both prac-

tices could conceiveably spring from one theological (Gnostic) position; see Lütgert, *Freiheitspredigt und Schwärmgeister*, 123–128; Schlatter, *Die korinthische Theologie*, 36–45. But many others have noted difficulties with this view: (1) we have no evidence of actual social groups (not even Gnostic ones) that combine asceticism with libertinism (see Plunkett, "Sexual Ethics," 296); (2) Gnostic libertinism seems, in the end, to have been mostly an invention of Gnosticism's enemies (see F. Wisse, "Die Sextus-Sprüche").

31. I disagree, therefore, with the suggestion of Gordon Fee: "Paul seems concerned to shift the problem from one of individual freedom to one of relational responsibility" (*First Epistle*, 501–502). In my opinion, the Strong at Corinth probably had just as much sense of "relational responsibility" as Paul; they simply construed the proper expressions of that responsibility differently.

32. Moiser, "A Reassessment of Paul's View of Marriage," 110. For other attempts to redeem Paul for sexuality (or at least heterosexuality), see Garland, "The Christian's Posture toward Marriage and Celibacy"; Phipps, "Paul's Attitude."

33. See Marr, *Sex in Religion*, 75–77, and Bertrand Russell, *Marriage and Morals*, 48, both of which are cited and rejected by Phipps.

34. Note the plural. It is unclear precisely what Paul means here by *porneiai*. Indeed, scribes, recognizing the strangeness of the term, altered it to the singular. The term may mean something like "all situations of pagan sexual activity."

35. Yarbrough, *Not Like the Gentiles*, 99–100.

36. *Agamos* may here refer more particularly to "widowers," but there is no way to limit the term to that referent. Its normal meaning includes all unmarried persons, and this is probably the way most of Paul's Greek readers would have taken it. Paul specifies "widows" here because they occupied a special social position among all "unmarried persons."

37. See above, and Balch, "1 Cor 7:32–35 and Stoic Debates."

38. Foucault, *Care of the Self*; Sedgwick, *Epistemology of the Closet*; Greenberg, *Construction of Homosexuality*; Winkler, *Constraints of Desire*; Halperin, *One Hundred Years of Homosexuality*; Halperin et al., eds., *Before Sexuality*.

39. See Garland, "Christian's Posture toward Marriage and Celibacy," 361, n. 29; see also the discussion in Fee, *First Epistle*, 289; Barrett, *First Epistle*, 161. The view that "burn" here refers to eschatological judgment has been most vividly argued by Michael L. Barré, "To Marry or to Burn." Of course, the reference to burning could be taken to refer to *both* the fire of desire and the fire of judgment; one could read both senses in Sirach 23:16: "Hot passion that blazes like a fire will not be quenched until it burns itself out; one who commits fornication with his near of kin will never cease until the fire burns him up" (NRSV). Although it is not entirely clear what the second "burns" refers to (and it could simply be a parallel to the first), it could have been read, especially by an apocalyptic Jew, as promising the fires of eschatological judgment.

40. *PGM* IV. 1505, 1530; see also VII. 467–477; VII. 593–619 (the beloved victim is also cursed with being "seized by a daimon"); VII. 981–993. See also Rousselle, *Porneia*, 21, 123, 135; John Chrysostom *Instruction and Refutation Directed Against Those Men Cohabiting with Virgins* 2, quoted in Clark, *Jerome, Chrysostom, and Friends*, 168.

41. Hippocrates, "Generating Seed/Nature of the Child," quoted in A. E. Hanson, "Hippocrates: Diseases of Women 1," 583.

42. Marcus Aurelius speaks of himself as being "cured" (*hygianai*) of "amatory passions" (recall that *pathē* here is the Greek

word for disease as well as the English "passions"): *Meditations* 1. 17. 6. A later Christian writer, Pseudo-Fastidius, speaks of marriage as a "medicine" prescribed by Paul (in 1 Cor. 7) for the disease of fornication; see "A Letter on Chastity" (VI) 10. 1, ed. and trans. Haslehurst, *Works of Fastidius;* the letter has been variously attributed to Fastidius, Pelagius, or to an unknown Pelagian writer. For the Latin, see *Patrologiae Cursus Completus, Series Latina, Supplementum* (Paris: Garnier Frères, 1958), 1464–1505.

43. See Plutarch *Demetrius* 38. 4; Grmek, *Diseases in the Ancient Greek World,* 43; Archilochus, frg. 245, 249, 266L-B (ed. Lasserre); Sappho, frg. 2; see also Grmek, *Diseases,* 368, n. 175; Mesulan, "Diagnosis of Love-Sickness"; Clavolella, *La malattia d'amore dall'antichità al Medioevo;* Giedke, *Die Liebeskrankheit in der Geschichte der Medizin.*

44. In Chariton's romance *Chareas and Callirhoe,* desire (*pathos erōtikos*) is spoken of as a wound or disease (1. 1. 6; 1. 1. 7; 1. 1. 10; see Edwards, "Surviving the Web of Roman Power," 198).

45. Padel, *In and Out of Mind,* 54; see ref., esp. to Greek tragedy, given there; see also 116: desire is fire and burning; fire is daemonic, as is passion.

46. Oribasius *Libri Incerti* 18. 16; more on Rufus and the regimen for virgins below. See also Rousselle, *Porneia,* 35.

47. Soranus *Gynecology* 1. 7; 1. 9. 35.

48. Galen *Hygiene* 1. 8. Galen also refers to desire as "burning" in *On the Affected Parts* 6. 6. Thomas Laqueur notes that the twelfth-century physician Tortulla taught that barrenness could result from a lack of heat (lust); but it could also be the result of too *much* ("Orgasm, Generation, and the Politics of Reproductive Biology," 9).

49. Note that Pliny the Elder and Lucretius, like Soranus and Galen, assume that women's desire and pleasure are necessary for successful impregnation: Pliny *Natural History* 10. 83; 24. 11; 28. 30, 80; 20. 263;

Lucretius *De rerum natura* 4. 1190–1270; Soranus *Gynecology* 1. 3. 10; McLaren, *History of Contraception,* 48–49. We know of a *few* cases of female doctors, who seem to have been wives of male physicians: Pleket, *Epigraphica II,* nos. 1, 12, 20, 26, 27; G. H. R. Horsley, *New Documents 1977,* 16–17.

50. Soranus *Gynecology* 1. 9. 35.

51. Clement of Alexandria *Stromata* 3. 7. 58, my trans.; see Noonan, *Contraception,* 76. Greek and Roman authors preceded Christians in raising the possibility of the absence of desire in marriage. As Roy Bowen Ward remarks, "The Roman poet Ovid had opined that there could be no erotic pleasure (*amor*) between husband and wife because it was a relationship of duty; Musonius, in a normative vein, taught that there *should* be no erotic pleasure between husband and wife" ("Musonius and Paul"). Musonius probably believed that *some* desire was necessary for procreation, but he wanted it *limited* to the purpose of procreation. Paul wants it precluded entirely.

52. Clement of Alexandria *Stromata* 3. 7. 57; Noonan, *Contraception,* 77.

53. Ambrose, *Traité sur l'évangile de S. Luc,* 1, 69; Jerome *Patrologia Latina* 26. 415; Noonan, *Contraception,* 80.

54. See Pagels, *Adam, Eve, and the Serpent,* esp. 111–112. For Augustine's view that sex without desire is the ideal, though humanly unattainable since the Fall, see *City of God* 14. 16, 23, 26. Galen knows that animals (and some very controlled persons) have sex not for pleasure but to relieve the pressure stemming from a need to expel semen (*On the Affected Parts* 6. 5).

55. *Contra* Ward, "Musonius and Paul," 285. Noting that Paul advocates marriage rather than burning, Ward says, "from which we may infer that he advised marriage as the context for satisfying that desire." Such an inference is not at all called for and indeed contradicts the logic of Paul's

position, by which marriage is designed to *preclude* desire, not "satisfy" it.

56. Plutarch, for example, in the words of Angus McLaren, "hailed marriage as a brake on the sexual passions and a school for order and domestication" (*History of Contraception,* 44). As I pointed out, n. 51 above, Greco-Roman authors occasionally mention the possibility of sex or marriage without desire; they probably do not mean, however, a complete absence of desire; and they are a small minority in any case.

57. This concept of purification by proximity is not unique to Paul. An analogous concept seems to be at work in the teaching of the rabbis (and perhaps the Pharisees) that "unclean" water may be purified simply by contact with "clean" water before being introduced into a *miqveh;* see Sanders, *Judaism,* 226.

58. I accept the modern consensus that the situation refers to an engaged couple, and that Paul is addressing the man. The view dominant in the early church, that Paul is here addressing a father who must decide whether or not to give his daughter in marriage, was popular, I believe, because the Church Fathers from the second century on wanted to exclude any possibility that Paul would be condoning the practice of "spiritual marriage" (*subintroductae*), the actual structure of which was probably not established until the second century. By reading Paul's statements as addressed to a father, the Church Fathers could advocate celibacy while simultaneously claiming that Paul's letters provide no warrant for spiritual marriage. For a quite different reading of this passage, which I find fascinating but ultimately unconvincing, see Wire, *Corinthian Women Prophets;* I see no evidence in 1 Corinthians, for example, that virgins constitute a delineable social group which enjoys strong "community support" (see 89).

59. For examples of modern interpretations, see Moiser, "Paul's View of Marriage," 116–117. Versions that take

the phrase to refer to the man's passion include the Revised Standard Version, New English Bible, Today's English Version, and Moffatt. Those taking it to refer to the virgin's age are the King James Version, New International Version, Jerusalem Bible, and Douay Version. I know of none that translates it as indicating either the man's age or the virgin's passion.

60. There are two occurrences in *Praecepta Salubria,* ed. Bussemaker, in *Poetae bucolici et didactici.* Athenaeus *Deipnosophistae* 14. 657d (quoting Myron of Priene, *Messenian History*) uses the term *hyperakmazoien* to refer to slaves whose appearance "exceeds in vigor" that expected of a slave. Late uses of the term by Eustathius, archbishop of Thessalonica, seem not to be helpful; see, e.g., his *Commentarii ad Homeri Iliadem Pertinentes,* 3. 486, line 25.

61. Caelius Aurelianus *Gynaecia* 8, lines 194–195.

62. See the fuller discussion of these ideas below.

63. For Soranus's views on the age of first menses, see *Gynecology* 1. 8. 33. For the age of girls at marriage, see Hopkins, "The Age of Roman Girls at Marriage"; Shaw, "The Age of Roman Girls at Marriage: Some Reconsiderations." Hopkins has been convinced by Shaw's arguments and now agrees with his conclusions.

64. Epiphanius *Panarion (Adversus Octaginta Haereses)* 61. 5. 1–8.

65. "A Letter on Chastity" (VI) 10. 15 (see n. 42 above). See also John Chrysostom's treatise *On Virginity* 78. 1. Greek text: *La Virginité,* text and introduction by Musurillo with French trans. by Grillet, 368; English trans.: John Chrysostom *On Virginity: Against Remarriage,* trans. Shore, 116. The French translator takes *hyperakmos* chronologically as "passer l'âge." The English translator nicely preserves the ambiguity: "If anyone thinks he is behaving dishonorably toward his virgin *because a critical moment has come . . .*" Pelagius also

takes the problem to be the girl's desire due to her increasing age; see his *Expositions of Thirteen Epistles of St. Paul*, I, vol. 9. 2, p. 169. I am indebted to Elizabeth Clark for alerting me to these references.

66. Carson, "Putting Her in Her Place: Women, Dirt, and Desire," 138–139. For similar beliefs among Jews of the first century, see Kottek, "The Essenes and Medicine," 86.

67. For class indicators of Galen's expected readership, see his *Hygiene* 3. 10; 6. 14. For the audience of Soranus's *Gynecology*, see the Introduction by Temkin, xxxviii.

68. A. E. Hanson, "Hippocrates: Diseases of Women 1," 572 (*Dis.* 1. 1).

69. Ibid., §7 (p. 576).

70. Ibid., §1 (p. 573).

71. Ibid., §2 (p. 573).

72. Hippocrates, "Generating Seed/Nature of the Child," 4. 3, trans. Hanson; see A. E. Hanson, "Diseases of Women 1," p. 583. See also Lonie, *Hippocratic Treatises*, 122.

73. Galen *On the Affected Parts* 6. 5, trans. Siegel, 187–188; before Galen, Soranus also discounted popular ideas about the wandering womb; see *Gynecology* 3. 4. 29. For more on the "wandering womb," see Chap. 9.

74. Galen *On the Affected Parts* 6. 5, trans. Siegel, 184.

75. Ibid., trans. Siegel, 185.

76. Soranus *Gynecology*, 1. 7. 31, trans. Temkin, p. 28.

77. Oribasius *Libri Incerti* 18. 1–2, my trans. The fragment of Rufus is found in a collection of medical texts made in the late Empire by Oribasius. Greek text: Oribasius, *Collectionum medicarum reliquiae*, vol. 4, ed. Raeder, 106–109.

78. The term used by Rufus is *proakmazō*, translated "arrive at puberty too early" in LSJ. But Rufus wants to delay the entire complex of processes that make desire dangerous for a virgin: puberty and the

beginning of menstruation, the heat that comes from "fullness," and the desire that would compel a girl to engage in sexual intercourse before her body is able to bear a child.

79. McLaren notes also the ancient fear that while lack of intercourse strengthens men, it may lead to barrenness in women (*History of Contraception*, 24–25).

80. See, for example, the representation of a *malakos* (soft man) in the Pseudo-Aristotelian *Physiognomy* 808a9–13 and 808a34–38 and the portrait of the effeminate man who seduces women in Chariton's novel *Chaereas and Callirhoe* 1. 4: the man is dressed in soft, fine clothes, wears perfume, and minces his steps *in order to attract women*.

Chapter 9: Prophylactic Veils

1. Meeks, "Image of the Androgyne."

2. Ibid., 194.

3. Ibid., 200.

4. Ibid., 208. For a similar view of androgyny as implying equality, in this case in nonbiblical early Christian and Jewish texts, see Scholer, "'And I was a Man.'" Scholer mistakenly takes several texts as teaching the "transcendence" of sexuality, whereas what they imply is a swallowing up of the feminine by the superior masculine. This is not the transcendence of female sexuality but its denial. Meeks has since changed his mind and now recognizes that androgyny does not imply equality in Paul's conception (private conversation).

5. Laqueur, *Making Sex*, 62.

6. Soranus *Gynecology*, trans. Temkin, 3 prooemium 3 (for the Aristotelian reference see *On the Generation of Animals* 1. 20, 728a17ff.). Soranus makes this comment in a discussion of whether there exist particularly female diseases, a notion he himself generally rejects except for diseases that affect only female organs or conditions. He does not disagree with the claim that

females are imperfect males, only with the inference that all their diseases will differ from those of men.

7. Dean-Jones, "The Cultural Construct of the Female Body in Classical Greek Science," 115. According to these scientists, presumably, the surfeit of blood interfered with the mechanisms of rationality; since many people believed the pneuma to be the material of rationality, too much blood could be thought of as drowning out the optimal function of pneuma.

8. Ibid., 134, n. 31. Plutarch devotes a whole section (3. 4) of *Table Talk* (*Quaestionum Convivialium*) to the debate (*Moralia* 650F–651E).

9. Gilhus, "Male and Female Symbolism in the Gnostic *Apocryphon of John*," 40.

10. Ibid., 42–43; see also Buckley, "An Interpretation of Logion 114 in *The Gospel of Thomas*," 246: "Female followers will have to attain maleness *before* they may become 'living spirits.' Male disciples, then, appear to have to make only one step: from maleness to the spiritual level. So, the hierarchy of salvation here is: female–male–living spirit.'" As Buckley later remarks, "Therefore, the woman's salvation is more complicated than that of the male devotee" (272).

11. Tertullian, "On the Apparel of Women," 1. 2, trans. Thelwall, in *ANF*.

12. Jerome *Commentariorum in Epistolam ad Ephisios libri III* (*Patrologiae Latina* [Migne] 26 (1884). 567, trans. in Bullough, "Medieval Medical and Scientific Views of Women," 499. On the use of these ancient views by medieval authors, see also Beier, *Sufferers and Healers*; Maclean, *Renaissance Notion of Woman*.

13. D. R. MacDonald, "Corinthian Veils and Gnostic Androgynes," 285. Most editions print *heis* as the supposedly original reading. Alternative readings from some manuscripts, including a few that have the neuter *hen* in place of the masculine *heis*, are perhaps evidence that scribes noticed

Paul's use of the masculine and thought it, for some reason, problematic. See also *idem, There is no Male and Female*. The point about the masculinity of *heis* was made earlier by Ben Witherington, "Rite and Rights for Women," 597. I disagree with Witherington's claim (603, n. 22) that Paul is arguing *against* androgyny by emphasizing that "Christ was a male and we are united to Him." As I have argued, this is precisely the way androgyny functioned in ancient culture. Gael Hodgkins, comparing initiation rites in southwest Africa, Australia, and New Guinea, makes a statement about those cultures that is equally applicable to Greco-Roman culture: ". . . in some instances the final object of initiations seems to be a repudiation of the feminine rather than affirmation of it, and therefore the emphasis in interpretation should not be on the desire of one sex to incorporate the powers of the other but rather on the nearly universal viewpoint that there is something 'better' about maleness than femaleness" ("Androgynous Initiation Rites," 57).

14. The link between origin and hierarchy can be seen in various aspects of Greco-Roman culture, one of which is the tendency of Greeks to claim higher status than Romans due to acknowledged Roman borrowing of older Greek things. Jews made much the same claims; Philo and Josephus, for example, attempt to prove that everything that is of value in Greek culture was prefigured in Hebrew sources: Solon (or whoever) simply stole his ideas from Moses. This idea is also reflected in the commonplace that the imitator is inferior to the original; see, e.g., Diogenes Laertius *Lives* 6. 84.

15. See my *Slavery as Salvation*, 123, 152. Attempts to read 1 Cor. 11:11–12 as Paul's egalitarian "correction" of his "apparent" subordination of women are unconvincing (see, e.g., Murphy-O'Connor, "Sex and Logic," 496). Those verses teach the interdependence of man and woman,

not their equality. It was acknowledged that slaves needed masters and masters needed slaves and that neither could exist without the other, but this did not mean that they were equal in ancient ideology. (See Chap. 2, in which I point out that mutual dependence in the household and polis did not imply equality in homonoia speeches.) While respecting attempts to read Paul as less misogynist than much Christian tradition has been, I am more impressed by the hermeneutical approach put forward by Francis Watson ("Strategies of Recovery and Resistance"). A critical stance vis-à-vis the sexism of traditional Christianity might better begin with a frank confession of the sexism reflected in biblical texts rather than attempting to reread those texts to de-emphasize the sexism.

16. Fee, *First Epistle*, 502–503; see 502, n. 42 and 503, n. 44 for bibliography supporting the reading. For the opposing argument, see Grudem, "Does *kephale* ('Head') Mean 'Source' or 'Authority over' in Greek Literature?"; Fitzmyer, "*Kephalē* in I Corinthians 11:3."

17. See, e.g., the note to 1 Cor. 11:11–12 in The New Oxford Annotated Bible, 241NT.

18. Ann Jervis's claim that Paul's language does *not* present a "chain of command" implies (mistakenly, in my view) that Paul's language does not promote patriarchal hierarchy (see her "'But I Want You to Know . . .'" 241). For one clear instance of Paul's subordination of Christ to God, see 1 Cor. 15:24–28. John Chrysostom goes out of his way to insist that this passage does *not* implicate the apostle Paul in a problematic subordinationist Christology; but his very protestations highlight Paul's innocent and unreflected subordinationism (see *Homilies on First Epistle* 26 [Homily on 1 Cor. 11]).

19. Fiorenza, *In Memory of Her*, 226–233; Padgett, "Paul on Women in the Church." For one rejection of such arguments, see Oster, "When Men Wore Veils to Worship."

On the significance of hairstyles in ancient cultic activity, see Lösch, "Christliche Frauen in Korinth"; R. and K. Kroeger, "An Inquiry into Evidence of Maenadism in the Corinthian Congregation"; Heyob, *The Cult of Isis among Women in the Greco-Roman World*, 60. For those who believe that the problem is one of veils rather than hairstyles, see Jaubert, "Le Voile des femmes (1 Cor. xi.2–16)"; Feuillet, "La Dignité et le rôle de la femme d'après quelques textes pauliniens"; Scroggs, "Paul and the Eschatological Woman." Murphy-O'Connor suggests that the women are cutting their hair and the men growing theirs ("Sex and Logic"). I think this is an extreme case of "mirror-reading"—that is, taking a statement by Paul that serves as only an example of behavior that he assumes both he and they reject to reflect actual behavior at Corinth. Murphy-O'Connor's attempt to see homosexuality as also implicated is modern fantasy: it confuses effeminacy with homosexuality (inaccurate for both modern and ancient situations) and interjects the concepts of effeminacy and mannishness into a text that hints at neither.

20. For a brief survey of hairstyles and head-coverings for both men and women, including helpful photographs of archeological evidence, see Thompson, "Hairstyles, Head-Coverings, and St. Paul." On honor and shame in connection with this text, see Neyrey, *Paul, In Other Words*, 67; Malina, *New Testament World*, 25–50; Corrington, "'Headless Woman,'" 224–225; Wire, *Corinthian Women Prophets*, 118–120. For Jewish references to female veiling, see Tomson, *Paul and Jewish Law*, 133. It should be noted that Paul does not use the term *kalymma* (veil) in the pericope; he refers rather to the *action* of veiling.

21. Irenaeus *Against the Heresies* 1. 8. 2 (*ANF* 1. 327); Clement of Alexandria *Paidagogos* 3. 11 (*ANF* 2. 290); Tertullian *The Chaplet (De Corona)*, chap. 14 (*ANF* 3. 102); *On Prayer*, chaps. 21–22 (*ANF* 3. 687–

688); *Against Marion* 5. 9 (*ANF* 3. 446); "On the Apparel of Women," 2. 7 (*ANF* 4. 21–22); "On the Veiling of Women"; Augustine *Letters* CCXLV (*Nicene and Post-Nicene Fathers*, 1. 588); Jerome *Letters* CXL VII. 5 (*Nicene and Post-Nicene Fathers*, second series, 6. 292). Ambrose takes the reference to covering to be to hair; but it is uncertain whether this excludes taking it also to refer to veils (see *Duties of the Clergy* 1. 46. 232 [*Nicene and Post-Nicene Fathers*, second series, 10. 37–38]).

22. Sutton, "Interaction between Men and Women Portrayed on Attic Red-Figure Pottery," 156, see also n. 130; Hague, "Marriage Athenian Style," 35.

23. Patterson, "Marriage and the Married Woman in Athenian Law," 54; see also Oakley, "Anakalypteria," 113, n. 1.

24. See also Sutton, "On the Classical Athenian Wedding"; Carson, "Putting Her in Her Place," esp. 160, 163. For references to possible marriage scenes on funerary reliefs in which the women are veiled, see Gill, "Importance of Roman Portraiture for Head-Coverings," 253.

25. Homer *Odyssey* 3. 392. The connection is made by Eustathius *Commentarii ad Homeri Odysseam*, commenting on 3. 392 (vol. 1, p. 135). See A. E. Hanson, "Medical Writers' Woman," 325–326, also n. 80.

26. Nagler, *Spontaneity and Tradition*, 45, 53, 60; Carson, "Putting Her in Her Place," 160.

27. A. E. Hanson, "Medical Writers' Woman," 326.

28. Nagler, *Spontaneity and Tradition*, 45, 49, 66–67. My analysis throughout this chapter is quite similar to, and dependent upon, that of Gail Paterson Corrington, "'Headless Woman.'" See, for example, her suggestion that the unveiled female head was thereby rendered "open" to the penetration of prophecy (225, 227).

29. Thus Dio Chrysostom, at a very different time and place from the Homeric referents, knows the important signifi-

cances of veiling: *Discourse* 33. 48–49. See also Plutarch *Moralia* 138D, 139C, 232C, 267B; Lucian *The Carousal, or the Lapiths (Symposium)* 8. These references show the inadequacies of analyses by biblical scholars claiming that the significance of veiling in Corinth comes from particularly *Jewish* (or "eastern") culture; see, e.g., Hooker, "Authority on her Head," 413.

30. Carson, "Putting Her in Her Place," 160.

31. Crawley, *Mystic Rose*, 2. 42–45.

32. Papanek, "Purdah," 296.

33. Berg, *Unconscious Significance of Hair*; see critique by Leach, "Magical Hair," 149.

34. Leach, "Magical Hair," 153; see also 156. The importance of hiding the mouth, even for men when confronting women, is noted by J. W. Anderson, "Social Structure and the Veil," 402.

35. Mason, "Sex and Symbol in the Treatment of Women," 650.

36. Mernissi, *Beyond the Veil*, 41.

37. Mason, "Sex and Symbol," 650; see also 657.

38. Ibid., 650; Makhlouf, *Changing Veils*, 38; Macleod, *Accommodating Protest*, 83, 155.

39. Mernissi, *Beyond the Veil*, 44.

40. Makhlouf, *Changing Veils*, 38.

41. Anderson, "Social Structure," 405; see also Rasmussen, "Veiled Self, Transparent Meanings," 105: Tuareg men veil themselves as protection against "the spirits called *el Essuf* (People of Solitude)," and women veil themselves as protection from invasion by spirits (106, 113, 115).

42. Makhlouf, *Changing Veils*, 38; see also Crawley, *Mystic Rose*, 2. 45, where mention is made of a "sacred umbrella" held over the head in a society in China, in order to "prevent evil coming down upon that sensitive part of the body."

43. Leach, "Magical Hair," 156; Renée Hirschon ("Open Body/Closed Space") notes a parallel connection with regard to Greeks living in Turkey in the early twentieth century.

44. Euripides *Baccanals* 695. For the *binding* of hair as a symbol of virginity and purity, see *Greek Anthology* 6. 275, 276, 280; for loosened hair as a sign of abandonment in "Phrygian" ecstasy, see ibid., 6. 281. See also Carson, "Putting Her in Her Place," 152; n. 19 above.

45. Hierocles *The Philogelos or Laughter-Lover* 235; Greek: *Philogelos. Der Lachfreund.* See also Dean-Jones, "Cultural Construct," 136, n. 68; on the religious significance (in popular belief) of hair coverings, see Dibelius, *Die Geisterwelt im Glauben des Paulus,* 19–20.

46. This is true in Greek as well as Latin. *Stoma* is used for the mouth of the womb, *cheilos* for the labia, and *trachēlos* for the cervix: see LSJ, *stoma* II. 2; *cheilos* II; *trachēlos* II. 2.

47. Laqueur, *Making Sex,* 36.

48. Aristotle *Historia animalium* 10. 3. 635b19–24; Laqueur, *Making Sex,* 50.

49. Soranus *Gynecology* 1. 10. 37; Laqueur, *Making Sex,* 51.

50. Hippocrates *Diseases of Women* 1. 11; see A. E. Hanson, "Hippocrates: Diseases of Women 1," 579.

51. Dean-Jones, "Cultural Construct," 125 and 136, n. 70; see Aristotle *Generation of Animals* 2. 7, 747a7–23. In a study of traditional wrestling in modern India, Joseph S. Alter notes connections between the head and the genitals, in that "semen is said to be located in a reservoir in the head." Thus a wrestler who engages in too much sex will manifest symptoms in the face and, especially, the eyes: "I think it is clear that the eyes are sunken and the complexion pallid because the head has been drained of semen" (*Wrestler's Body,* 154).

52. A. E. Hanson, "Continuity and Change," 85; Hippocrates *Aphorisms* 5. 33.

53. Soranus *Gynecology* 3. 4. 29. See A. E. Hanson, "Continuity and Change," 82–83.

54. Helen King, "From *parthenos* to *gynē*"; cited in A. E. Hanson, "Continuity and Change," 105, n. 73; and Dean-Jones,

"Cultural Construct," 124. Hanson disagrees that women had a special tube connecting mouth to vagina but says that Hippocratics thought that there was a "central tube" in both men and women connecting the nose and mouth to the anus (105, n. 73).

55. See, e.g., Plutarch *Oracles at Delphi* (*Moralia*) 397C.

56. Plutarch *Obsolescence of Oracles* (*Moralia*) 414E.

57. See the remarks by Ruth Padel: "The implications of physical pain and erotic penetration here helped to establish in the tradition the idea that prophetic possession by a male god involved pain, which the priestess naturally resisted" ("Women: Model for Possession by Greek Daemons," 14). For an interesting parallel in the Hebrew prophetic tradition, see the analysis of Jer. 20:7 by Abraham Heschel, *The Prophets,* 1. 113–114; in Heschel's translation, Jeremiah complains that the Lord has "seduced" and "raped" him. (I am grateful to Mary Hinkle for this reference.)

58. Soranus *Gynecology* 1. 9. 34.

59. Plutarch *Moralia* 438B; for the view that the woman's desire and receptivity are essential for fertilization, see Soranus *Gynecology* 1. 10. 37.

60. A. E. Hanson, "Hippocrates: Diseases of Women 1," 572. See also *idem,* "Medical Writers' Woman," 317; Dean-Jones, "Cultural Construct," 114.

61. Carson, "Putting Her in Her Place," 153, see also 136, 163.

62. The connotations of a shaved head for women in Greco-Roman culture have been debated, but with few firm conclusions; see Fee, *First Epistle,* 510–511; Grosheide, *Commentary on First Epistle,* 253–254; W. J. Martin, "I Corinthians 11:2–16." Although the *explicit* meaning of shaving the head in Greco-Roman culture is unclear, it doubtless connotes the shameful uncovering of the genitals—symbolized by the head. For connections of a shaved head with shameful, sometimes sexual, states, see Plutarch *Roman*

Questions 267B; Dio Chrysostom *Discourse* 64. 2–3; Gill, "Importance of Roman Portraiture for Head-Coverings," 256.

63. For suggestions that the word translated here "authority" (*exousia*) actually refers to the veil itself, see Kittel, "Die 'Macht' auf dem Haupt (I Cor. xi.10)," 20. See also Fitzmyer, "A Feature of Qumrân Angelology and the Angels of I Cor. XI.10," 52, n. 3.

64. The primary advocate of the idea that angels are here understood as protectors of the order of creation is Moffatt, *First Epistle*, 152.

65. Fitzmyer, "A Feature of Qumrân Angelology," 56–57; see also Jervis, "But I Want You to Know," 244 and n. 53. The main problem with Fitzmyer's argument in my opinion is his insistence that *if* the mention of angels refers to their role as enforcers of proper worship, *then* the other interpretation (that they pose a sexual threat) is necessarily excluded. This sort of either/or argument is due to a philosophical mistake about how language functions, in my view, and has wreaked havoc in biblical scholarship. Fitzmyer's other argument against the "sexual angels" interpretation (that Paul never means "bad" or "fallen" angels when he uses the article before the noun) is specious; we have too little written material from Paul, comparatively speaking, and too few references to angels even there, for such arguments to carry any weight.

66. Besides the ancient witnesses to this reading, several scholars in the late nineteenth and early twentieth century promoted it; see Everling, *Die paulinische Angelologie und Dämonologie*, 37; Dibelius, *Die Geisterwelt im Glauben des Paulus*, 13–23; Lietzmann, *An die Korinther*, 55; Tomson, *Paul and Jewish Law*, 136; see also the comments by Fitzmyer, "A Feature of Qumrân Angelology," 52. Fitzmyer's criticism of the view (that there is no evidence "that a woman's veil was ever thought of as having such a function [prophylactic?] in

antiquity") should be discounted, given the evidence marshaled in this chapter. The current consensus, according to which, as noted by Winandy ("Un curieux *casus pendens*"), the "sexual threat" reading has been "practically abandoned" by most New Testament commentators, is due, in my opinion, to the mistaken notion that *if* the angels are taken to be protectors of order or enforcers of the Law, *then* they cannot also constitute a sexual threat. As I argue in this chapter, comparative anthropological studies of veiling cultures reveal this to be a false either/or.

67. See Dimant, "'The Fallen Angels' in the Dead Sea Scrolls and in the Apocryphal and Pseudepigraphic Books Related to Them." See also *The Testament of Reuben* 5.

68. See Gilhus, "Male and Female Symbolism in the Gnostic *Apocryphon of John*," 37.

69. See also Corrington, "Headless Woman," 230.

70. Kittel, "*Aggelos, ktl,*" *TDNT* 1. 86. See also Richardson, *Introduction to the Theology of the New Testament*, 209; Jung, *Fallen Angels in Jewish, Christian and Mohammedan Literature*, 90. For a contextualization of the roles of angels in Jewish and non-Jewish ("pagan") concepts, see M. Smith, "Pagan Dealings with Jewish Angels." I disagree with Morna Hooker that angels are never given such negative roles in the New Testament ("Authority on her Head").

71. Besides Tertullian's texts on veiling discussed below, see his *Against Marcion* 5. 8; *On Prayer* 22. Clement of Alexandria assumes that one function of veiling is to avoid sexual temptation of men (*Paedagogus* 3. 11); he also reads Genesis 6 as referring to sexual angels (*Paedagogus* 3. 2). See also Justin Martyr *Second Apology* 10. In a fascinating, though sometimes confusing, text, Paulinus of Nola (ca. 400 C.E.) mingles the issues of authority, hierarchy, and sexual seduction (precisely as I wish to read Paul's text). The "pride" manifested by unveiled

women renders them even more desirable to the lustful angels, who will seduce them. On the other hand, if the angels see the women veiled, humble, and modest, they will be "confused" (Paulinus of Nola, *Letters*, 23. 24).

72. Corrington, "'Headless Woman,'" 227. Paulinus even interprets "inspiration" as "impregnation" when reading 1 Cor. 11:10. When prophesying, a woman "becomes pregnant with the spirit, and accordingly rouses the hatred of the tempter all the more when she leaves behind the boundaries of her womanly weakness, and aspires to human perfection." Likewise in prayer: "So because a woman becomes spiritually pregnant also when she prays, Paul desires her appearance to reveal that she has *a power over her head*, so that the wiles and snares of the enemy may not confront her if she steps beyond what Scripture calls her vessel" (*Letters*, 23. 25). Though much of Paulinus's exposition of this passage is confusing, it shows how a man of his culture could assume the connections I have argued for between angels, sexual penetration in prophecy, and the function of veiling both to protect the woman's body and to maintain gender-cosmic hierarchy.

73. I hesitate to speculate about the point of view of the Corinthian women prophets themselves. (I think that Paul's rhetoric—which is, after all, all we possess—gives us very little, if anything, to go on as regards how the women would have construed their own activity.) I would imagine that both they and certain men of the congregation would have rejected Paul's fears of angelic invasion as low-class superstition, needless anxiety, or lack of faith. For one

possible reconstruction of the women's point of view, see Wire, *Corinthian Women Prophets*, esp. 131. Ann Jervis believes the problem has to do with both male and female activity, and that it results from the Corinthians' misappropriation of Paul's eschatological statements about male and female "in Christ" (see "'But I Want You to Know . . .'"). I see Jervis's position as resulting from too much mirror-reading of Paul's own statements. I see no evidence that the Corinthians' position stemmed from a misunderstanding of Pauline doctrine. Furthermore, I believe that Paul's references to appropriate attire, hairstyle, and demeanor for men do not indicate any particular behavior on the part of the Corinthian men but are simply the result of Paul taking examples "from nature" about *men* that he assumes will be convincing to his auditors, in order to influence their ideas about women.

74. See discussion in Foerster, "*Exestin, exousia, ktl.*;" Bruce, *1 and 2 Corinthians*, 106.

75. *Contra* Bruce, *1 and 2 Corinthians*.

76. Tertullian, "On the Veiling of Virgins," 1. 2; "On the Apparel of Women," 2. 7, trans. Thelwall, *ANF* (all the translations of these works given here are those of Thelwall unless otherwise noted).

77. Woman also represents a primary location for all sorts of social disruption in ancient ideology; see M. Y. MacDonald, "Woman Holy in Body and Spirit," 178–179.

Postscript

1. Note Barrett, *Second Epistle*, 6.

Bibliography

Aelius Aristides and the Sacred Tales. Trans. C. A. Behr. Amsterdam: Adolf M. Hakkert, 1968.

Alexander, Loveday, ed. *Images of Empire.* Sheffield: JSOT Press, 1991.

Alexander, P. Introduction to "3 (Hebrew Apocalypse of) Enoch." In *The Old Testament Pseudepigrapha,* ed. James H. Charlesworth, 1: 223–254. Garden City, N.Y.: Doubleday, 1983.

Allegro, J. M. *The Dead Sea Scrolls and the Christian Myth.* Buffalo: Prometheus Books, 1984.

Allen, Prudence. *The Concept of Woman: The Aristotelian Revolution 750 BC–AD 1250.* Montreal: Eden Press, 1985.

Alter, Joseph S. *The Wrestler's Body: Identity and Ideology in North India.* Berkeley: University of California Press, 1992.

Ambrose. *Traité sur l'évangile de S. Luc.* Ed. and trans. Gabriel Tissot. Paris: Editions du Cerf, 1956.

Anderson, Graham. "Julianus of Laodicea: Rhetor or Trader?" *Journal of Hellenic Studies* 102 (1982): 202.

Anderson, Jon W. "Social Structure and the Veil: Comportment and the Composition of Interaction in Afghanistan." *Anthropos* 77 (1982): 397–420.

Archilochus. *Archiloque Fragments.* Ed. François Lasserre. Paris: Belles Lettres, 1958.

Aretaeus the Cappadocian. *Aretaeus.* Ed. Carolus Hude. Berlin: In aedibus Academiae scientiarum, 1958.

———. *The Extant Works of Aretaeus, the Cappadocian.* Ed. and trans. Francis Adams. London: Sydenham Society, 1856.

Artemidori Daldiani Onirocriticon Libri V. Ed. Roger A. Pack. Leipzig: Teubner, 1963.

Artemidorus, *The Interpretation of Dreams (Oneirocritica).* Trans. and commentary by Robert J. White. Park Ridge, N.J.: Noyes Press, 1975.

"Asaph Ha-Rofe," *Encyclopedia Judaica,* 3: 673–675. Jerusalem: Keter, 1972.

Aus, Roger David. "Comfort in Judgment: The Use of Day of the Lord and Theophany Traditions in Second

Thessalonians 1." Ph.D. diss., Yale University, 1971.

Bakhtin, M. M. *Speech Genres and Other Late Essays.* Austin: University of Texas Press, 1986.

Balch, David L. "1 Cor 7:32–35 and Stoic Debates about Marriage, Anxiety, and Distraction." *Journal of Biblical Literature* 102 (1983): 429–439.

———. "Backgrounds of I Cor. VII: Sayings of the Lord in Q, Moses as an Ascetic *Theios Anēr* in II Cor. III." *New Testament Studies* 18 (1971/72): 351–364.

Barclay, John M. G. "Thessalonica and Corinth: Social Contrasts in Pauline Christianity." *Journal for the Study of the New Testament* 47 (1992): 49–74.

Barkan, Leonard. *Nature's Work of Art: The Human Body as Image of the World.* New Haven: Yale University Press, 1975.

Barnard, L. W. "Athenagoras: De Resurrectione: The Background and Theology of a Second-Century Treatise on the Resurrection." *Studia Theologica* 30 (1976): 1–42.

Barré, Michael L. "To Marry or to Burn: *porousthai* in 1 Cor. 7:9." *Catholic Biblical Quarterly* 36 (1974): 193–202.

Barrett, C. K. *A Commentary on the First Epistle to the Corinthians.* New York: Harper and Row, 1968.

———. *A Commentary on the Second Epistle to the Corinthians.* New York: Harper and Row, 1973.

———. "Christianity at Corinth." In *Essays on Paul,* 1–27. Philadelphia: Westminster, 1982.

Barton, Carlin A. *The Sorrows of the Ancient Romans: The Gladiator and the Monster.* Princeton: Princeton University Press, 1993.

Baumgarten, Joseph M. "The 4Q Zadokite Fragments on Skin Disease." *Journal of Jewish Studies* 41 (1990): 153–165.

Baur, F. C. "Die Christus Partei in der korinthischen Gemeinde." *Tübinger Zeitschrift für Theologie* 5 (1831): 61–206. Also

in *Ausgewählte Werke in Einzelausgaben,* ed. Klaus Scholder, 1. 1–146. Stuttgart and Bad Canstatt: Frommann (Halzboog).

Beck, L. J. *The Metaphysics of Descartes: A Study of the Meditations.* Oxford: Clarendon, 1965.

Becker, Jürgen. *Auferstehung der Toten im Urchristentum.* Stuttgart: Verlag Katholisches Bibelwerk, 1976.

Beier, Lucinda McCray. *Sufferers and Healers: The Experience of Illness in Seventeenth-Century England.* London: Routledge and Kegan Paul, 1987.

Berchman, Robert M. *From Philo to Origen: Middle Platonism in Transition.* Brown Judaic Studies 69. Chico, Calif.: Scholars Press, 1984.

Berg, Charles. *The Unconscious Significance of Hair.* London: Allen and Unwin, 1951.

Best, Ernest. *A Commentary on the First and Second Epistles to the Thessalonians.* London: Adam and Charles Black, 1977.

———. *Second Corinthians.* Atlanta: John Knox, 1987.

Betz, Hans Dieter. *Der Apostel Paulus und die sokratische Tradition.* Tübingen: Mohr (Siebeck), 1972.

Betz, Hans Dieter, ed. *The Greek Magical Papyri in Translation, Including the Demotic Spells.* 2d ed. Chicago: University of Chicago Press, 1992.

Black, Donald. *The Behavior of Law.* New York: Academic Press, 1976.

Bonner, Stanley F. *Education in Ancient Rome: From the Elder Cato to the Younger Pliny.* Berkeley: University of California Press, 1977.

Bookidis, N., and J. E. Fischer. "The Sanctuary of Demeter and Kore on Acrocorinth." *Hesperia* 41 (1972): 283–331.

Bottomley, Frank. *Attitudes to the Body in Western Christendom.* London: Lepus Books, 1979.

Bouvier, Henri. "Hommes de lettres dans les inscriptiones Delphiques." *Zeitschrift für Papyrologie und Epigraphik* 58 (1985): 119–135.

Bowie, E. L. "The Importance of Sophists." *Yale Classical Studies* 27 (1982): 29–59.

Boyarin, Daniel. *Carnal Israel: Reading Sex in Talmudic Culture.* Berkeley: University of California Press, 1993.

Brandenburger, Egon. *Fleisch und Geist: Paulus und die dualistische Weisheit.* Neukirchen-Vluyn: Neukirchener, 1968.

Brooten, Bernadette. "'Junia . . . Outstanding among the Apostles' (Romans 16:7)." In *Women Priests: A Catholic Commentary on the Vatican Declaration*, ed. L. Swidler and A. Swidler, 141–144. New York: Paulist, 1977.

Brown, Peter. *Power and Persuasion in Late Antiquity: Toward a Christian Empire.* Madison: University of Wisconsin Press, 1992.

Bruce, F. F. *1 and 2 Corinthians.* Grand Rapids, Mich.: Eerdmans, 1971.

Buckley, Jorunn Jacobsen. "An Interpretation of Logion 114 in *The Gospel of Thomas.*" *Novum Testamentum* 27 (1985): 245–272.

Budge, E. A. Wallis, ed. and trans. "The Book of the Resurrection of Jesus Christ by Bartholomew the Apostle." In *Coptic Apocrypha in the Dialect of Upper Egypt*, 3. 1–48, 179–230. London: British Museum, 1913.

Bullough, Vern L. "Medieval Medical and Scientific Views of Women." *Viator* 4 (1973): 485–501.

Bultmann, R. "*ginōskō, ktl.*" *TDNT* 1: 689–719.

Burnyeat, M. F. "Idealism and Greek Philosophy: What Descartes Saw and Berkeley Missed." *Philosophical Review* 41 (1982): 3–40.

Caelius Aurelianus. *Gynaecia: Fragments of a Latin Version of Soranus' Gynaecia from a Thirteenth Century Manuscript.* Supplements to the Bulletin of the History of Medicine, no. 13. Ed. Miriam F. Drabkin and Israel E. Drabkin. Baltimore: Johns Hopkins University Press, 1951.

Cagnat, René Louis Victor. *Cours d'épigraphie latine.* 3d ed. Paris: A. Fontemoing, 1898.

Caizzi, Fernanda Decleva, ed. *Antisthenis Fragmenta.* Milan-Varese: Istituto Editoriale Cisalpino, 1966.

Campbell, Barth. "Flesh and Spirit in 1 Cor. 5:5: An Exercise in Rhetorical Criticism of the NT." *Journal of the Evangelical Theological Society* 36 (1993): 331–342.

Carr, Wesley. *Angels and Principalities: The Background, Meaning and Development of the Pauline Phrase hai archai kai hai exousiai.* Cambridge: Cambridge University Press, 1981.

———. "The Rulers of This Age—I Corinthians II.6–8." *New Testament Studies* 23 (1976–77): 20–25.

Carros, George P. "Jewish Ethics and Gentile Converts: Remarks on 1 Thes. 4, 3–8." In *The Thessalonian Correspondence*, ed. Raymond F. Collins, 306–315. Leuven: Leuven University Press, 1990.

Carson, Anne. "Putting Her in Her Place: Women, Dirt, and Desire." In *Before Sexuality*, ed. Halperin et al., 135–169.

Castelli, Elizabeth A. *Imitating Paul: A Discourse of Power.* Louisville, Ky.: Westminster/John Knox, 1991.

Cavallin, Hans C. C. "Leben nach dem Tode in Spätjudentum und im frühen Christentum, I: Spätjudentum." In *Aufstieg und Niedergang der römischen Welt* 2. 19. 1. 240–345. Berlin/New York: Walter de Gruyter, 1979.

———. *Life after Death: Paul's Argument for the Resurrection of the Dead in I Cor. 15: Pt. I: An Enquiry into the Jewish Background.* Lund: Gleerup, 1974.

Chaniotis, Angelos. "Als die Diplomaten noch tanzten und sangen: zu zwei Dekreten kretischer Städte in Mylasa." *Zeitschrift für Papyrologie und Epigraphik* 71 (1988): 154–156.

Charlesworth, James H. "A Misunderstood Recently Published Dead Sea Scroll (4QM130)." *Explorations* (American

Institute for the Study of Religious
Cooperation, Philadelphia) 1 (1987): 2.
———. *The Discovery of a Dead Sea Scroll
(4Q Therapeia): Its Importance in the History
of Medicine and Jesus Research.* Lubbock:
Texas Tech University, 1985.

Chow, John K. *Patronage and Power: A
Study of Social Networks in Corinth.* JSNT
Supplement Series 75. Sheffield: JSOT
Press, 1992.

Clark, Elizabeth A. *Jerome, Chrysostom, and
Friends: Essays and Translations.* New York:
Edwin Mellen, 1979.

Clarke, Andrew D. "Secular and Christian
Leadership in Corinth." Ph.D. diss.,
Cambridge University, 1991. Abstract in
Tyndale Bulletin 43 (1992): 395–398.

Clavolella, Massimo. *La malattia d'amore
dall' antichità al Medioevo.* Rome: Bulzoni,
1976.

Clement of Alexander. *Clemens Alexandri-
nus.* Ed. Ludwig Früchtel. Berlin:
Akademie-Verlag, 1970.

Collins, Adela Yarbro. "The Function of
'Excommunication' in Paul." *Harvard
Theological Review* 73 (1980): 251–263.
———. "Persecution and Vengeance in the
Book of Revelation." In *Apocalypticism in
the Mediterranean World and the Near East,*
ed. Hellholm, 729–749.

Collins, John J. *The Apocalyptic Vision of the
Book of Daniel.* Missoula, Mont.: Scholars
Press, 1977.
———. "Structure and Meaning in the
Testament of Job." *Society of Biblical
Literature Seminar Papers* (1974): 35–52.

Conzelmann, Hans. *1 Corinthians.* Philadelphia: Fortress, 1975.

Cope, Lamar. "First Corinthians 8–10:
Continuity or Contradiction?" *Anglican
Theological Review* Supplement 11 (1990):
114–123.

Corrington, Gail Paterson. "The 'Headless
Woman': Paul and the Language of the
Body in 1 Cor. 11:2–16." *Perspectives in
Religious Studies* 18 (1991): 223–231.

Countryman, L. William. *Dirt, Greed, and
Sex: Sexual Ethics in the New Testament and
Their Implications for Today.* Philadelphia:
Fortress, 1988.

Crawley, Ernest. *The Mystic Rose: A Study of
Primitive Marriage and of Primitive Thought
in its Bearing on Marriage.* 2d ed. 2 vols.
London: Methuen, 1927.

Cullmann, Oscar. "Immortality of the
Soul or Resurrection of the Dead." In
Immortality and Resurrection, ed. Krister
Stendahl, 9–53. New York: Macmillan,
1965.

Cumont, Franz V. M. *After Life in Roman
Paganism.* New Haven: Yale University
Press, 1922.

Dahl, M. E. *The Resurrection of the Body: A
Study of I Corinthians 15.* London: SCM,
1962.

Dahl, Nihls A. "Paul and the Church
at Corinth according to 1 Corinthians
1:10–4:21." In *Studies in Paul,* 40–61.
Minneapolis: Augsburg, 1977.

Daube, David. "Pauline Contributions to
a Pluralistic Culture: Re-Creation and
Beyond." In *Jesus and Man's Hope,* ed.
Donald G. Miller and Kikran Y. Ha-
didian, 2: 223–245. Pittsburgh: Pittsburgh
Theological Seminary, 1971.

Dautzenberg, G. "Der Verzicht auf das
apostolische Unterhaltsrecht. Eine exege-
tische Untersuchung zu 1 Kor 9." *Biblica*
50 (1969): 212–232.

David, Jean-Michel. "Les Orateurs des
municipes à Rome: intégration, réticences
et snobismes." In *Les 'Bourgeoisies' muni-
cipales italiennes aux IIe et Ier siècles av.
J.-C.,* 309–323. Paris: Editions du Centre
national de la recherche scientifique,
1983.

Davies, Paul, and John Gribbin. *The Matter
Myth.* New York: Simon and Schuster,
1992.

Davies, Philip R. "Daniel in the Lion's
Den." In *Images of Empire,* ed. L.
Alexander, 160–178.

Davies, W. D. *Paul and Rabbinic Judaism:*

Some Rabbinic Elements in Pauline Theology.
Philadelphia: Fortress, 1980.

De Boer, Martinus C. "The Composition of
1 Corinthians." *New Testament Studies* 40
(1994): 229–245.

De Certeau, Michel. *The Practice of Everyday
Life.* Berkeley: University of California
Press, 1984.

De Lacy, Phillip. "Galen's Platonism."
American Journal of Philology 93 (1972):
27–39.

Dean-Jones, Lesley. "The Cultural Con-
struct of the Female Body in Classical
Greek Science." In *Women's History and
Ancient History*, ed. Sarah B. Pomeroy,
111–137. Chapel Hill: University of
North Carolina Press, 1991.

Delobel, Joël. "The Fate of the Dead
according to 1 Thes 4 and 1 Cor 15."
In *The Thessalonian Correspondence*, ed.
Raymond F. Collins, 340–347. Leuven:
Leuven University Press, 1990.

Deming, Will. *Paul on Marriage and Celibacy:
The Hellenistic Background of 1 Corinthians
7.* Cambridge: Cambridge University
Press, forthcoming.

Derrida, Jacques. *Dissemination.* Chicago:
University of Chicago Press, 1981.

Descartes, René. *A Discourse on Method and
Selected Writings.* Trans. John Veitch.
New York: E. P. Dutton, 1951.

Dibelius, Martin. *Die Geisterwelt im Glauben
des Paulus.* Göttingen: Vandenhoeck und
Ruprecht, 1909.

Diels, Hermann. *Doxographi Graeci.* Berlin
and Leipzig: Walter de Gruyter, 1929.

Dillon, John M. *The Middle Platonists: A
Study of Platonism 80 B.C. to A.D. 220.*
London: Duckworth, 1977.

———. "'Orthodoxy' and 'Eclecti-
cism': Middle Platonists and Neo-
Pythagoreans." In *The Question of
"Eclecticism": Studies in Later Greek Phi-
losophy*, ed. John M. Dillon and A. A.
Long, 103–125. Berkeley: University of
California Press, 1988.

Dimant, D. "'The Fallen Angels' in the

Dead Sea Scrolls and in the Apocryphal
and Pseudepigraphic Books Related to
Them." Ph.D. diss., Hebrew University,
1974.

Dioscorides. *Pedanii Dioscuridis Anazarbei
De materia medica.* Ed. Max Wellmann.
Berlin: Weidmannos, 1907–14; rpt. 1958.

Dodds, E. R. *The Greeks and the Irrational.*
Boston: Beacon, 1957.

Donini, Pierluigi. "Science and Meta-
physics: Platonism, Aristotelianism, and
Stoicism in Plutarch's *On the Face in the
Moon.*" In *The Question of "Eclecticism,"* ed.
Dillon and Long, 126–144.

Douglas, Mary. *Rules and Meanings.*
Harmondsworth: Penguin Education,
1973.

Downing, F. Gerald. "The Resurrection
of the Dead: Jesus and Philo." *Journal for
the Study of the New Testament* 15 (1982):
42–50.

Dubos, René. *Man Adapting.* Enlarged ed.
New Haven: Yale University Press, 1980.

———. *Mirage of Health: Utopias, Progress,
and Biological Change.* New York: Harper
and Brothers, 1959.

Dungan, David L. *The Sayings of Jesus in the
Churches of Paul.* Philadelphia: Fortress,
1971.

Dupont, Jacques. *Gnosis: La connaissance
religieuse dans les Epîtres de Saint Paul.*
Universitas Catholica Lovaniensis Disser-
tationes Series II, Tomus 40. Louvain:
Nauwelaerts; Paris: Gabalda, 1949.

Edelstein, Ludwig. "Greek Medicine in
Its Relation to Religion and Magic." In
*Ancient Medicine: Selected Papers of Ludwig
Edelstein*, ed. Owsei Temkin and C. Lilian
Temkin, 205–246. Baltimore: Johns
Hopkins University Press, 1967.

Edwards, Douglas R. "Surviving the Web
of Roman Power: Religion and Politics
in the Acts of the Apostles, Josephus,
and Chariton's *Chaereas and Callirhoe.*"
In *Images of Empire*, ed. L. Alexander,
179–201.

Ellen, Roy F. "Anatomical Classification

and the Semiotics of the Body." In *The Anthropology of the Body*, ed. John Blacking, 343–373. New York: Academic Press, 1977.

Ellicott, Charles J. *Commentary on St. Paul's Epistles to the Thessalonians*. Andover: Warren F. Draper, 1865.

Ellis, E. Earle. "*Sōma* in First Corinthians." *Interpretation* 44 (1990): 132–144.

Epiphanius. *Panarion (Adversus Octaginta Haereses)*. Ed. Karl Holl. 3 vols. Leipzig: J. C. Hinrichs, 1915.

Eustathius, Archbishop of Thessalonica. *Commentarii ad Homeri Iliadem Pertinentes*. Ed. Marchinus van der Valk. Leiden: Brill, 1971–87.

———. *Commentarii ad Homeri Odysseam*. Leipzig: Wiegel, 1825.

Evans, Elizabeth C. "Galen the Physician as Physiognomist." *Transactions of the American Philological Association* 76 (1945): 287–298.

———. *Physiognomics in the Ancient World*. Philadelphia: American Philosophical Society, 1967.

Everling, O. *Die paulinische Angelologie und Dämonologie*. Göttingen: Vandenhoeck and Ruprecht, 1888.

Farquhar, Judith. "Objects, Processes, and Female Infertility in Chinese Medicine." *Medical Anthropology Quarterly* n.s. 5 (1991): 370–399.

Fee, Gordon D. *The First Epistle to the Corinthians*. Grand Rapids, Mich.: Eerdmans, 1987.

Ferguson, John. *Moral Values in the Ancient World*. London: Methuen, 1958.

Feuillet, A. "La Dignité et le rôle de la femme d'après quelques textes pauliniens." *New Testament Studies* 21 (1975): 157–191.

Fish, Stanley. *Doing What Comes Naturally*. Durham, N.C.: Duke University Press, 1989.

Fisher, Fred. *Commentary on 1 and 2 Corinthians*. Waco, Tex.: Word, 1975.

Fitzmyer, Joseph A. "A Feature of Qumrân Angelology and the Angels of I Cor. XI.10." *New Testament Studies* 4 (1957–58): 48–58.

———. "*Kephalē* in I Corinthians 11:3." *Interpretation* 47 (1993): 52–59.

Fitzmyer, Joseph A., and D. J. Harrington. *A Manual of Palestinian Aramaic Texts*. Rome: Biblical Institute Press, 1978.

Flood, Gavin D. "Techniques of Body and Desire in Kashmir Saivism." *Religion* 22 (1992): 47–62.

Foerster, Werner. "*Exestin, exousia, ktl.*" *TDNT* 2: 560–574.

Forbes, Christopher. "Early Christian Inspired Speech and Hellenistic Popular Religion." *Novum Testamentum* 28 (1986): 257–270.

———. "Prophecy and Inspired Speech in Early Christianity and Its Hellenistic Environment." Ph.D. diss., Macquarie University, 1987.

Forkman, Göran. *The Limits of the Religious Community: Expulsion from the Religious Community within the Qumran Sect, within Rabbinic Judaism, and within Primitive Christianity*. Lund: Gleerup, 1972.

Foster, George M. "Disease Etiologies in Non-Western Medical Systems." *American Anthropologist* 78 (1976): 773–782.

Foster, George M., and Barbara Gallatin Anderson. *Medical Anthropology*. New York: John Wiley and Sons, 1978.

Foucault, Michel. *The Care of the Self*. New York: Pantheon Books, 1986.

Frede, M. "On Galen's Epistemology." In *Galen: Problems and Prospects*, ed. Nutton, 68–69.

Friedenwald, Harry. *The Jews and Medicine*. 2 vols. Baltimore: Johns Hopkins University Press, 1944.

Galen, Claudius. *Claudii Galeni Pergameni Scripta Minora*. Ed. Iwani Mueller. Leipzig: Teubner, 1891.

———. *Hygiene: A Translation of Galen's Hygiene (De sanitate tuenda)*. Trans. Robert

Montraville Green. Springfield, Ill.: Charles C. Thomas, 1951.

———. *On Respiration and the Arteries*. Ed. and trans. David J. Furley and J. S. Wilke. Princeton: Princeton University Press, 1984.

———. *On Semen*. Ed. Phillip de Lacy. *Corpus Medicorum Graecorum* 3/1. Berlin: Akademie-Verlag, 1992.

———. *On the Affected Parts*. Trans. Rudolph E. Siegel. Basel and New York: Karger, 1976.

———. *On the Passions and Errors of the Soul*. Trans. Paul W. Harkins. Introduction and Interpretation by Walter Riese. Columbus: Ohio State University Press, 1963.

———. *Opera Omnia*. Ed. C. G. Kühn. Leipzig: C. Knobloch, 1821–33.

Garland, David E. "The Christian's Posture toward Marriage and Celibacy: 1 Corinthians 7." *Review and Expositor* 80 (1983): 351–362.

Garnsey, Peter. "Legal Privilege in the Roman Empire." In *Studies in Ancient Society*, ed. Moses I. Finley, 141–165. London: Routledge and Kegan Paul, 1974.

Gemmill, Chalmers L. "The Missing Passage in Hort's Translation of Theophrastus." *Bulletin of the New York Academy of Medicine* 49 (1973): 127–129.

Georgi, Dieter. *The Opponents of Paul in Second Corinthians*. Philadelphia: Fortress, 1986.

Gersh, Stephen. *Middle Platonism and Neoplatonism: The Latin Tradition*. 2 vols. Notre Dame, Ind.: University of Notre Dame Press, 1986.

Giannantoni, G., ed. *Socraticorum reliquiae*. Collana Elenchos 6–7. Naples: Bibliopolis, 1983–85.

Giddens, Anthony. "Four Theses On Ideology." *Canadian Journal of Political and Social Theory/Revue canadienne de théorie politique et sociale* 7 (1983): 8–21.

Giedke, Adelheid. *Die Liebeskrankheit in der Geschichte der Medizin*. Düsseldorf: Institut für Geschichte der Medizin, 1983.

Gilhus, Ingvild Saelid. "Male and Female Symbolism in the Gnostic *Apocryphon of John*." *Temenos* 19 (1983): 33–43.

Gill, David W. J. "The Importance of Roman Portraiture for Head-Coverings in 1 Corinthians 11:2–16." *Tyndale Bulletin* 41 (1990): 245–260.

Gilmore, David D. *Honor and Shame and the Unity of the Mediterranean*. Washington, D.C.: American Anthropological Association, 1987.

Glass-Coffin, Bonnie. "Discourse, *Daño*, and Healing in North Coastal Peru." *Medical Anthropology* 13 (1991): 33–55.

Glasson, T. Francis. "2 Corinthians v. 1–10 *versus* Platonism." *Scottish Journal of Theology* 43 (1990): 145–155.

Glick, Leonard B. "Medicine as an Ethnographic Category: The Gimi of the New Guinea Highlands." In *Culture, Disease and Healing*, ed. Landy, 58–70; rpt. with abridgments from *Ethnology* 6 (1967): 31–56.

Glucker, John. *Antiochus and the Late Academy*. Göttingen: Vandenhoeck and Ruprecht, 1978.

Godet, F. *Commentary on St. Paul's First Epistle to the Corinthians*. Edinburgh: T. and T. Clark, n.d.

Goldstein, Jonathan A. *The Letters of Demosthenes*. New York: Columbia University Press, 1968.

Gooch, Paul W. *Partial Knowledge: Philosophical Studies in Paul*. Notre Dame, Ind.: University of Notre Dame Press, 1987.

Grant, Mary A. *The Ancient Rhetorical Theories of the Laughable*. University of Wisconsin Studies in Language and Literature, no. 21. Madison: University of Wisconsin Press, 1924.

Gray, Rebecca. *Prophetic Figures in Late Second Temple Jewish Palestine: The Evidence from Josephus*. New York: Oxford University Press, 1993.

Green, Michael. *To Corinth with Love.*
London: Hodder and Stoughton, 1982.
Greenberg, David F. *The Construction of
Homosexuality.* Chicago: University of
Chicago Press, 1988.
Griffin, Miriam. "*Urbs Roma, Plebs,* and
Princeps." In *Images of Empire,* ed.
L. Alexander, 19–46.
Grmek, Mirko D. *Diseases in the Ancient
Greek World.* Baltimore: Johns Hopkins
University Press, 1989.
Grosheide, F. W. *Commentary on the First
Epistle to the Corinthians.* Grand Rapids,
Mich.: Eerdmans, 1953.
Grudem, W. "Does *kephale* ('Head') Mean
'Source' or 'Authority over' in Greek
Literature? A Survey of 2,336 Examples."
Trinity Journal n.s. 6 (1985): 38–59.
Güttgemanns, Erhardt. *Der leidende Apostel
und sein Herr: Studien zur paulinischen
Christologie.* Göttingen: Vandenhoeck and
Ruprecht, 1966.
Gwynn, Aubrey. *Roman Education from
Cicero to Quintilian.* Oxford: Clarendon,
1926.
Hague, Rebecca. "Marriage Athenian
Style." *Archaeology* 41 (1988): 32–36.
Hahm, David E. "Early Hellenistic Theo-
ries of Vision and the Perception of
Color." In *Studies in Perception,* ed.
Machamer and Tumbull, 60–95.
Hainz, J. *Ekklesia: Strukturen paulinischer
Gemeinde-Theologie und Gemeinde-Ordnung.*
Biblische Untersuchungen 9. Regens-
burg: Pustet, 1972.
Halperin, David. *One Hundred Years of
Homosexuaity and Other Essays on Greek
Love.* New York: Routledge, 1990.
Halperin, David, John J. Winkler, and
Froma Zeitlin, eds. *Before Sexuality: The
Construction of Erotic Experience in the
Ancient Greek World.* Princeton: Princeton
University Press, 1990.
Hanson, Ann Ellis. "Continuity and
Change: Three Case Studies in Hip-
pocratic Gynecological Therapy and
Theory." In *Women's History and Ancient
History,* ed. Sarah B. Pomeroy, 73–
110. Chapel Hill: University of North
Carolina Press, 1991.
———. "Hippocrates: Diseases of Women
1." *Signs* 1 (1975): 567–584.
———. "The Medical Writers' Woman."
In *Before Sexuality,* ed. Halperin et al.,
309–337.
Hanson, Mogen Herman. "*Rhetores* and
Strategoi in Fourth-Century Athens."
Greek, Roman, and Byzantine Studies 24
(1983): 151–180.
Harris, William V. *Ancient Literacy.* Cam-
bridge: Harvard University Press,
1989.
Harrisville, Roy A. "Speaking in Tongues:
A Lexicographical Study." *Catholic
Biblical Quarterly* 38 (1976): 35–48.
Hausrath, A., ed. *Corpus Fabularum Ae-
sopicarum.* Vol. 1. Leipzig: Teubner,
1970.
Hellholm, David, ed. *Apocalypticism in the
Mediterranean World and the Near East.*
Tübingen: Mohr (Siebeck), 1983.
Hengel, Martin. *Crucifixion in the Ancient
World and the Folly of the Message of the
Cross.* Philadelphia: Fortress, 1977.
———. *Judaism and Hellenism.* Philadelphia:
Fortress, 1974.
———. "Messianische Hoffnung und
politischer 'Radikalismus' in der
'jüdisch-hellenistischen Diaspora'." In
*Apocalypticism in the Mediterranean World
and the Near East,* ed. Hellholm, 655–686.
Heraclitus. *Fragments.* Ed. T. M. Robinson.
Toronto: University of Toronto Press,
1987.
Héring, Jean. *The First Epistle of Saint Paul to
the Corinthians.* London: Epworth, 1962.
———. *The Second Epistle of Saint Paul to the
Corinthians.* London: Epworth, 1967.
Herophilus. *Herophilus: The Art of Medicine
in Alexandria.* Ed. and trans. Heinrich
von Staden. Cambridge: Cambridge
University Press, 1989.
Heschel, Abraham. *The Prophets.* New York:
Harper and Row, 1962.

Heyob, S. Kelly. *The Cult of Isis among Women in the Greco-Roman World*. Leiden: Brill, 1975.

Hierocles. *Philogelos. Der Lachfreund*. Ed. Andreas Thierfelder. Munich: Heimeran, 1968.

————. *The Philogelos or Laughter-Lover*. Trans. Barry Baldwin. Amsterdam: J. C. Gieben, 1983.

Higgins, A. J. B. *The Lord's Supper in the New Testament*. London: SCM, 1952.

Hippocrates. *The Hippocratic Treatises "On Generation," "On the Nature of the Child," "Diseases IV."* Trans. Iain M. Lonie. Berlin and New York: Walter de Gruyter, 1981.

Hirschon, Renée. "Open Body/Closed Space: The Transformation of Female Sexuality." In *Defining Females: The Nature of Women in Society*, ed. Shirley Ardener, 66–88. London: Croom Helm, 1978.

Hock, Ronald F. "Paul's Tentmaking and the Problem of His Social Class." *Journal of Biblical Literature* 97 (1978): 555–564.

————. *The Social Context of Paul's Ministry: Tentmaking and Apostleship*. Philadelphia: Fortress, 1980.

Hodgkins, Gael. "Androgynous Initiation Rites: Incorporation or Repudiation of the Feminine?" *Anima* 1 (1974): 56–63.

Holmberg, Bengt. *Paul and Power*. Philadelphia: Fortress, 1980.

————. *Sociology and the New Testament: An Appraisal*. Minneapolis: Fortress, 1990.

Holquist, Michael. *Dialogism: Bakhtin and His World*. London: New Accents, 1990.

Hooker, Morna D. "Authority on her Head: An Examination of I Cor. xi.10." *New Testament Studies* 10 (1964): 410–416.

Hopkins, Keith. "The Age of Roman Girls at Marriage." *Population Studies* 18 (1965): 309–327.

Horowitz, Maryanne Cline. "Aristotle and Women." *Journal of the History of Biology* 9 (1976): 183–214.

Horsley, G. H. R. *New Documents Illustrating Early Christianity: A Review of the Greek Inscriptions and Papyri Published in 1977*. North Ryde, Australia: Macquarie University, 1982.

————. *New Documents Illustrating Early Christianity: A Review of the Greek Inscriptions and Papyri Published in 1978*. North Ryde, Australia: Macquarie University, 1983.

Horsley, Richard A. "Consciousness and Freedom among the Corinthians: 1 Corinthians 8–10." *Catholic Biblical Quarterly* 40 (1978): 574–589.

————. "Gnosis in Corinth: I Corinthians 8.1–6." *New Testament Studies* 27 (1980): 32–51.

————. "'How Can Some of You Say 'There Is No Resurrection of the Dead?' Spiritual Elitism in Corinth." *Novum Testamentum* 20 (1978): 203–231.

————. "*Pneumatikos* vs. *Psychikos*: Distinctions of Spiritual Status among the Corinthians." *Harvard Theological Review* 69 (1976): 269–288.

————. "Wisdom of Word and Words of Wisdom in Corinth." *Catholic Biblical Quarterly* 39 (1977): 224–239.

Howard-Jones, Norman. "Fracastoro and Henle: A Re-appraisal of their Contribution to the Concept of Communicable Diseases." *Medical History* 21 (1977): 61–68.

Hurd, John Coolidge, Jr. *The Origin of 1 Corinthians*. New York: Seabury, 1965.

Hyginus. *De Astronomia*. Ed. Ghislaine Viré. Stuttgart: Teubner, 1992.

————. *The Myths of Hyginus*. Trans. and ed. Mary Grant. Lawrence: University of Kansas Press, 1960.

Iamblicus. *De Mysteriis Aegyptorum*. English translation: *On the Mysteries of the Egyptians, Chaldeans, and Assyrians*. Trans. Thomas Taylor. Chiswick: C. Whittingham, 1821.

Ijsseling, Samuel. *Rhetoric and Philosophy in Conflict: An Historical Survey*. The Hague: Martinus Nijhoff, 1976.

Jackson, Stanley W. "The Use of Passions in Psychological Healing." *Journal of the*

History of Medicine and Allied Sciences 45 (1990): 150–175.

Jacobs, Joseph. *The Fables of Aesop.* New York: Burt Franklin, [1889] 1970.

Jaubert, A. "Le Voile des femmes (1 Cor xi.2–16)." *New Testament Studies* 18 (1972): 419–430.

Jervis, L. Ann. "'But I Want You to Know . . .': Paul's Midrashic Intertextual Response to the Corinthian Worshipers (1 Cor 11:2–16)." *Journal of Biblical Literature* 112 (1993): 231–246.

John Chrysostom. *The Homilies of St. John Chrysostom on the First Epistle of St. Paul the Apostle to the Corinthians.* Oxford: John Henry Parker, 1854.

———. *La Virginité.* Text and introduction by Herbert Musurillo, general introduction and French translation by Bernard Grillet. Paris: Editions du Cerf, 1966.

———. *On Virginity: Against Remarriage.* Trans. Sally Rieger Shore, introduction by Elizabeth A. Clark. Studies in Women and Religion, 9. New York: Edwin Mellen, 1983.

Jones, C. P. "Diotrephes of Antioch." *Chiron* 13 (1983): 369–380.

Jones, W. H. S. *Philosophy and Medicine in Ancient Greece, with an Edition of Peri archaiēs iētrikēs.* Supplements to the *Bulletin of the History of Medicine* no. 8. Baltimore: Johns Hopkins University Press, 1946.

Joy, N. George. "Is the Body Really to Be Destroyed? (1 Corinthians 5.5)." *The Bible Translator* 39 (1988): 429–436.

Judge, E. A. "Cultural Conformity and Innovation in Paul: Some Clues from Contemporary Documents." *Tyndale Bulletin* 35 (1984): 3–24.

Jung, Leo. *Fallen Angels in Jewish, Christian and Mohammedan Literature.* New York: KTAV, 1926; rpt. 1974.

Kaibel, G. "Inschriften aus Pisidien." *Hermes* 23 (1888): 532–545.

Kenny, Anthony. *The Anatomy of the Soul: Historical Essays in the Philosophy of Mind.* Oxford: Basil Blackwell, 1973.

Kittel, Gerhard. "*Aggelos, ktl.*" *TDNT* 1: 74–87.

———. "Die 'Macht' auf dem Haupt (I Cor. xi.10)." *Rabbinica; Arbeiten zur Vorgeschichte des Christentums,* 1/3, 20. Leipzig: J. Hinrichs, 1920.

Klauck, Hans-Josef. *Herrenmahl und hellenistischer Kult, Neitestamentliche Abhandlungen, N.F.15.* Münster: Aschendorff, 1982.

Kleinknecht, Hermann. "*Pneuma, pneumatikos, ktl.*" *TDNT* 6: 355–356.

Koenig, John. "Christ and the Hierarchies in First Corinthians." *Anglican Theological Review* Supplement 11 (1990): 99–113.

Kottek, Samuel J. "Concepts of Disease in the Talmud." *Koroth* 9, nos. 1–2, *International Symposium on Medicine in Bible and Talmud (2d, December 18–20, 1984):* 7–33. Jerusalem: Israel Institute of Medical History, 1985.

———. "The Essenes and Medicine." *Clio Medica* 18 (1983): 81–99.

Koyré, Alexandre. *From the Closed World to the Infinite Universe.* Baltimore: Johns Hopkins University Press, 1957.

Kraft, Robert. *The Testament of Job according to the SV Text.* Missoula, Mont.: Scholars Press, 1974.

Kramer, H. *Quid valeat homonoia in litteris Graecis.* Göttingen: Officina Academia Dieterichiana, 1915.

Kroeger, R., and K. Kroeger. "An Inquiry into Evidence of Maenadism in the Corinthian Congregation." *SBL Seminar Papers* 14 (1978): 2. 331–346.

Kuck, David William. "Judgment and Community Conflict: Paul's Use of Apocalyptic Judgment Language in 1 Corinthians 3:5–4:5." Ph.D. diss., Yale University, 1989.

Kudlein, Fridolf. "Early Greek Primitive Medicine." *Clio Medica* 3 (1968): 305–336.

———. "Galen's Religious Belief." In *Galen: Problems and Prospects,* ed. Nutton, 117–127.

Kümmel, Werner George. *The New Testament: The History of the Investigation of Its*

Problems. Nashville, Tenn.: Abingdon, 1972.

Kuriyama, Shigehisa. "Changing Concepts of Disease in East Asia." In *The Cambridge World History of Disease*, ed. Kenneth F. Kiple, 52–59. Cambridge: Cambridge University Press, 1993.

———. "The Imagination of Winds and the Development of the Chinese Conception of the Body." In *Body, Subject, and Power in China*, ed. Angela Zito and Tani Barlow, 23–41. Chicago: University of Chicago Press, 1994.

———. "Pulse Diagnosis in the Greek and Chinese Traditions." In *History of Diagnostics: Proceedings of the 9th International Symposium on the Comparative History of Medicine—East and West*, ed. Yosio Kawakita, 43–67. Osaka: Taniguchi Foundation, 1987.

Laderman, Carol. "Malay Medicine, Malay Person." *Medical Anthropology* 13 (1991): 83–97.

Lampe, G. W. H. "Church Discipline and the Epistles to the Corinthians." In *Christian History and Interpretation: Studies Presented to John Knox*, ed. W. R. Farmer et al., 337–361. Cambridge: Cambridge University Press, 1967.

Lampe, Peter. "Das korinthische Herrenmahl im Schnittpunkt hellenistisch-römischer Mahlpraxis und paulinischer Theologie Crucis (1 Kor 11,17–34)." *Zeitschrift für die neutestamentliche Wissenschaft* 82 (1991): 183–213.

———. "Theological Wisdom and the 'Word about the Cross': The Rhetorical Scheme of I Corinthians 1–4." *Interpretation* 44 (1990): 117–131.

Landy, David, ed. *Culture, Disease, and Healing: Studies in Medical Anthropology*. New York: Macmillan, 1977.

Lapide, Cornelius à. *The Great Commentary of Cornelius à Lapide: I Corinthians*. Ed. W. F. Cobb. London: John Hodges, 1896.

Laqueur, Thomas. *Making Sex: Body and Gender from the Greeks to Freud*. Cambridge: Harvard University Press, 1990.

———. "Orgasm, Generation, and the Politics of Reproductive Biology." In *The Making of the Modern Body: Sexuality and Society in the Nineteenth Century*, ed. Catherine Gallagher and Thomas Laqueur, 1–41. Berkeley: University of California Press, 1987.

Lassen, Eva Maria. "The Use of the Father Image in Imperial Propaganda and 1 Corinthians 4:14–21." *Tyndale Bulletin* 42 (1991): 127–136.

Lattimore, Richard. *Themes in Greek and Latin Epitaphs*. Illinois Studies in Language and Literature, vol. 28, nos 1–2. Urbana: University of Illinois Press, 1942.

Layton, Bentley, ed. *The Gnostic Scriptures*. Garden City, N.Y.: Doubleday, 1987.

Leach, E. R. "Magical Hair." *Journal of the Royal Anthropological Institute of Great Britain and Ireland* 88 (1958): 147–164.

Lee, Edward N. "The Sense of an Object: Epicurus on Seeing and Hearing." In *Studies in Perception*, ed. Machamer and Turnbull, 27–59.

Lietzmann, H. *An die Korinther I–II*. 4th ed. Tübingen: Mohr, 1949.

Lincoln, Bruce. *Myth, Cosmos, and Society: Indo-European Themes of Creation and Destruction*. Cambridge: Harvard University Press, 1986.

Lloyd, G. E. R. "The Hot and the Cold, the Dry and the Wet in Greek Philosophy." *Journal of Hellenic Studies* 84 (1964): 92–106.

Lock, Margaret M. *East Asian Medicine in Urban Japan*. Berkeley: University of California Press, 1980.

London, Oscar. "Was That Old Greek a Hypochondriac?" *Washington Post*, Health Section, 1 Jan. 1991, pp. 10–12.

Long, A. A. "Ptolemy *On the Criterion*: An Epistemology for the Practicing Scientist." In *The Question of "Eclecticism,"* ed. Dillon and Long, 176–207.

Long, A. A., and D. N. Sedley. *The Hellenistic Philosophers*. 2 vols. Cambridge: Cambridge University Press, 1987.

Longenecker, Richard N. "The Pedagogical Nature of the Law in Galatians 3:19–4:7." *Journal of the Evangelical Theological Society* 25 (1982): 53–61.

Longrigg, James. *Greek Rational Medicine: Philosophy and Medicine from Alcmaeon to the Alexandrians*. London: Routledge, 1993.

———. "Philosophy and Medicine: Some Early Interactions." *Harvard Studies in Classical Philology* 67 (1963): 147–175.

Lonie, Iain M. "Medical Theory in Heraclides of Pontus." *Mnemosyne* ser. 4, vol. 18 (1965): 125–143.

———. "A Structural Pattern in Greek Dietetics and the Early History of Greek Medicine." *Medical History* 21 (1977): 235–260.

Lösch, S. "Christliche Frauen in Korinth." *Theologische Quartalschrift* 127 (1947): 216–261.

Luck, George. *Arcana Mundi*. Baltimore: Johns Hopkins University Press, 1985.

Lull, David J. "'The Law Was Our Pedagogue': A Study in Galatians 3:19–25." *Journal of Biblical Literature* 105 (1986): 481–498.

Lütgert, Wilhelm. *Freiheitspredigt und Schwärmgeister in Korinth*. Gütersloh: Bertelsmann, 1908.

Lutz, Cora. *Musonius Rufus: The Roman Socrates*. New Haven: Yale University Press, 1947.

Lynch, John. *Aristotle's School: A Study of a Greek Educational Institution*. Berkeley: University of California Press, 1972.

MacDonald, Dennis Ronald. "Corinthian Veils and Gnostic Androgynes." In *Images of the Feminine in Gnosticism*, ed. Karen L. King, 276–292. Philadelphia: Fortress, 1988.

———. *There Is No Male and Female: The Fate of a Dominical Saying in Paul and Gnosticism*. Harvard Dissertations in Religion, no. 20. Philadelphia: Fortress, 1987.

MacDonald, Margaret Y. "Women Holy in Body and Spirit: The Social Setting of 1 Corinthians 7." *New Testament Studies* 36 (1990): 161–181.

Machamer, Peter K., and Robert G. Turnbull, eds. *Studies in Perception: Interrelations in the History of Philosophy and Science*. Columbus: Ohio State University Press, 1978.

Maclean, Ian. *The Renaissance Notion of Woman: A Study in the Fortunes of Scholasticism and Medical Science in European Intellectual Life*. Cambridge: Cambridge University Press, 1980.

Macleod, Arlene Elowe. *Accommodating Protest: Working Women, the New Veiling, and Change in Cairo*. New York: Columbia University Press, 1991.

MacMullen, Ramsay. *Paganism in the Roman Empire*. New Haven: Yale University Press, 1981.

———. *Roman Social Relations 50 B.C. to A.D. 284*. New Haven: Yale University Press, 1974.

Maddalena, A. "L'ENNOIA e l'EPISTEME THEOU in Filone Ebreo." *Revista di Filosofia e de Istruzione Classica* 96 (1968): 5–27.

Makhlouf, Carla. *Changing Veils: Woman and Modernization in North Yemen*. Austin: University of Texas Press, 1979.

Malherbe, Abraham J. "The Beasts at Ephesus." In *Paul and the Popular Philosophers*, 79–89. Minneapolis: Fortress, 1989.

———. *The Cynic Epistles*. Missoula, Mont.: Scholars Press, 1977.

———. *Moral Exhortation: A Greco-Roman Sourcebook*. Philadelphia: Westminster, 1986.

———. *Paul and the Thessalonians: The Philosophic Tradition of Pastoral Care*. Philadelphia: Fortress, 1987.

Malina, Bruce J. *The New Testament World: Insights from Cultural Anthropology*. Atlanta: John Knox, 1981.

Mansfeld, Jaap. "Philosophy in the Service of Scripture: Philo's Exegetical Strategies." In *The Question of "Eclecticism,"* ed. Dillon and Long, 70–102.

Manson, T. W. "The Corinthian Correspondence (1)." In *Studies in the Gospels and Epistles,* ed. Matthew Black, 190–210. Philadelphia: Westminster, 1962.

Marr, G. Simpson. *Sex in Religion: An Historical Survey.* London: Allen and Unwin, 1936.

Marrou, Henri I. *A History of Education in Antiquity.* New York: Sheed and Ward, 1956.

Marshall, Peter. *Enmity in Corinth: Social Conventions in Paul's Relations with the Corinthians.* Wissenschaftliche Untersuchungen zum Neuen Testament 2/23. Tübingen: Mohr (Siebeck), 1987.

Martin, Dale B. "Ancient Slavery, Class, and Early Christianity." *Fides et Historia* 23 (1991): 105–113.

———. Review of Robert G. Hamerton-Kelly, *Sacred Violence. Modern Theology* 9 (1993): 225–228.

———. *Slavery as Salvation: The Metaphor of Slavery in Pauline Christianity.* New Haven: Yale University Press, 1990.

———. "Social-Scientific Criticism." In *Treating the Text: An Introduction to Biblical Criticisms and Their Application,* ed. Stephen R. Haynes and Steven L. McKenzie, 103–119. Louisville, Ky.: Westminster/John Knox, 1993.

———. "Tongues of Angels and Other Status Indicators." *Journal of the American Academy of Religion* 59 (1991): 547–589.

Martin, W. J. "I Corinthians 11:2–16: An Interpretation." In *Apostolic History and the Gospel,* ed. W. Ward Gasque and Ralph P. Martin, 231–241. Grand Rapids, Mich.: Eerdmans, 1970.

Martinez, Robert M. "Epidemic Disease, Ecology, and Culture in the Ancient Near East." In *The Bible in the Light of Cuneiform Literature,* Scripture in Context III, Ancient Near Eastern Texts and Studies

8, ed. William W. Hallo et al., 413–457. Lewiston, N.Y.: Edwin Mellen, 1990.

Martyn, J. Louis. "Apocalyptic Antinomies in Paul's Letter to the Galatians." *New Testament Studies* 31 (1985): 410–424.

———. "Epistemology at the Turn of the Ages: 2 Corinthians 5:16." In *Christian History and Interpretation: Studies Presented to John Knox,* ed. W. R. Farmer et al., 269–287. Cambridge: Cambridge University Press, 1967.

Mason, John P. "Sex and Symbol in the Treatment of Women: The Wedding Rite in a Libyan Oasis Community." *American Ethnologist* 2 (1975): 649–661.

Maurer, C. *"Synoida, syneidēsis." TDNT* 7: 898–919.

Maximus of Tyre. *The Dissertations of Maximus Tyrius.* Trans. Thomas Taylor. London: Evans, 1804.

McGill, Arthur C. "Structures of Inhumanity." In *Disguises of the Demonic: Contemporary Perspectives on the Power of Evil,* ed. Alan M. Olson, 116–133. New York: Association Press, 1975.

McLaren, Angus. *A History of Contraception: From Antiquity to the Present Day.* Oxford: Basil Blackwell, 1990.

Meeks, Wayne A. *The First Urban Christians.* New Haven: Yale University Press, 1983.

———. "The Image of the Androgyne: Some Uses of a Symbol in Earliest Christianity." *History of Religions* 13 (1974): 165–208.

———. *The Moral World of the First Christians.* Philadelphia: Westminster, 1986.

Mernissi, Fatima. *Beyond the Veil: Male–Female Dynamics in Modern Muslim Society.* Rev. ed. Bloomington: Indiana University Press, 1987.

Mesulan, M. M. "The Diagnosis of Love-Sickness: Experimental Psychopathology without a Polygraph." *Psychophysiology* 9 (1972): 546–551.

Methodius of Olympus. *The Symposium.* Ancient Christian Writers, no. 27. Trans.

Herbert Musurillo. Westminster, Md.: Newman Press, 1958.

Meyer, Heinrich August Wilhelm. *Critical and Exegetical Handbook to the Epistles to the Corinthians*. New York: Funk and Wagnalls, 1884.

Meyer, Paul W. "The Holy Spirit in the Pauline Letters: A Contextual Exploration." *Interpretation* 33 (1979): 3–18.

Miller, G. "'Airs, Waters, and Places,' in History." *Journal of the History of Medicine* 17 (1962): 129–140.

Mitchell, Alan C. "I Corinthians 6:1–11: Group Boundaries and the Courts of Corinth." Ph.D. diss., Yale University, 1986.

———. "Rich and Poor in the Courts of Corinth: Litigiousness and Status in 1 Corinthians 6.1–11." *New Testament Studies*, forthcoming.

Mitchell, Margaret Mary. *Paul and the Rhetoric of Reconciliation: An Exegetical Investigation of the Language and Composition of 1 Corinthians*. Tübingen: Mohr (Siebeck), 1991.

Mitton, C. Leslie. "New Wine in Old Wine Skins: IV Leaven." *Expository Times* 84 (1972–73): 339–343.

Moffatt, James. *The First Epistle of Paul to the Corinthians*. London: Hodder and Stoughton, 1947.

Moiser, Jeremy. "1 Corinthians 15." *Irish Biblical Studies* 14 (1993): 10–30.

———. "A Reassessment of Paul's View of Marriage with Reference to 1 Cor. 7." *Journal for the Study of the New Testament* 18 (1983): 103–122.

Muntner, Süssman. Introduction to *Biblisch-talmudische Medizin*, by Julius Preuss. New York: KTAV, 1971.

Murdoch, George Peter. *Theories of Illness: A World Survey*. Pittsburgh: University of Pittsburgh Press, 1980.

Murphy-O'Connor, Jerome. "Sex and Logic in 1 Corinthians 11:2–16." *Catholic Biblical Quarterly* 42 (1980): 482–500.

Musurillo, Herbert, ed. *The Acts of the Christian Martyrs*. Oxford: Clarendon, 1972.

Nader, Laura. "The Anthropological Study of Law." *American Anthropologist* 67 (1965): 3–32.

Nagler, Michael N. *Spontaneity and Tradition: A Study in the Oral Art of Homer*. Berkeley: University of California Press, 1974.

Nash, Tom. "Devils, Demons, and Disease: Folklore in Ancient Near Eastern Rites of Atonement." In *The Bible in the Light of Cuneiform Literature*, ed. Hallo et al., 57–88. (See Martinez.)

Naveh, Joseph. "A Medical Document or a Writing Exercise? The So-called 4Q Therapeia." *Israel Exploration Journal* 36 (1986): 52–55.

Nestle, W. "Die Fabel des Menenius Agrippa." *Klio* 21 (1927): 350–360.

Neumyer, Stephen. "Talmudic Medicine and Greek Sources." *Koroth* 9 (1985): 34–57.

Neusner, Jacob, and Bruce D. Chilton. "Uncleanness: A Moral or an Ontological Category in the Early Centuries A.D.?" *Bulletin for Biblical Research* 1 (1991): 63–88.

New Oxford Annotated Bible. Ed. Bruce M. Metzger and Roland E. Murphy. New York: Oxford University Press, 1991.

Neyrey, Jerome H. *Paul, in Other Words: A Cultural Reading of His Letters*. Louisville, Ky.: Westminster/John Knox, 1990.

Nickelsburg, George W. E., Jr. *Resurrection, Immortality, and Eternal Life in Intertestamental Judaism*. Cambridge: Harvard University Press, 1972.

Niederwimmer, Kurt. *Der Begriff der Freiheit im Neuen Testament*. Berlin: Alfred Töpelmann, 1966.

Noonan, John Thomas. *Contraception: A History of its Treatment by the Catholic Theologians and Canonists*. Cambridge: Belknap, 1965.

Nuckolls, Charles W. "Divergent Ontologies of Suffering in South Asia." *Ethnology* 31 (1992): 57–74.

Nutton, Vivian. *Galen: Problems and Prospects*. London: Wellcom Institute for the History of Medicine, 1981.

Oakley, John H. "The Anakalypteria." *Archäologischer Anzeiger* 8 (1982): 113–118.

Ogilvie, R. M. *A Commentary on Livy, Books I–V*. Oxford: Clarendon, 1965.

Oribasius. *Oeuvres*. Ed. and trans. C. Daremberg and U. C. Bussemaker. Paris: Impr. nationale, 1858.

———. *Oribasii collectionum medicarum reliquiae*. Ed. Raeder, Ioannes. Amsterdam: Adolf M. Hakkert, 1964.

Oster, Richard. "When Men Wore Veils to Worship: The Historical Context of 1 Corinthians 11.4." *New Testament Studies* 34 (1988): 481–505.

Padel, Ruth. *In and Out of the Mind: Greek Images of the Tragic Self*. Princeton: Princeton University Press, 1992.

———. "Women: Model for Possession by Greek Daemons." In *Images of Women in Antiquity*, ed. Averil Cameron and Amélie Kuhrt, 3–19. Detroit: Wayne State University Press, 1983.

Padgett, Alan. "Paul on Women in the Church. The Contradictions of Coiffure in I Corinthians 11.2–16." *Journal for the Study of the New Testament* 20 (1984): 69–86.

Pagels, Elaine. *Adam, Eve, and the Serpent*. New York: Random House, 1988.

———. *The Gnostic Paul: Gnostic Exegesis of the Pauline Letters*. Philadelphia: Fortress, 1975.

Papanek, Hanna. "Purdah: Separate Worlds and Symbolic Shelter." *Comparative Studies in Society and History* 15 (1973): 289–325.

Paraskos, John A. "Biblical Accounts of Resuscitation." *Journal of the History of Medicine and Allied Sciences* 47 (1992): 310–321.

Parker, Robert. *Miasma: Pollution and Purification in Early Greek Religion*. Oxford: Clarendon, 1983.

Parry, Hugh. *Thelxis: Magic and Imagination in Greek Myth and Poetry*. Lanham, Md.: University Press of America, 1992.

Patrologiae Cursus Completus, Series Latina, Supplementum. Paris: Garnier Frères, 1958.

Patterson, Cynthia B. "Marriage and the Married Woman in Athenian Law." In *Women's History and Ancient History*, ed. Sarah B. Pomeroy, 48–72. Chapel Hill: University of North Carolina Press, 1991.

Paulinus of Nola. *The Letters of St. Paulinus of Nola*. Ancient Christian Writers, no. 36. Trans. P. G. Walsh. New York: Newman Press, 1967.

Pearson, A. C. *The Fragments of Zeno and Cleanthes*. New York: Arno, 1973.

Pearson, Birger A. "Philo, Gnosis, and the New Testament." In *Gnosticism, Judaism, and Egyptian Christianity*, 165–182. Minneapolis: Fortress, 1990. First published in *The New Testament and Gnosis: Essays in Honour of Robert McL. Wilson*, ed. A. H. B. Logan and A. J. M. Wedderburn, 73–89. Edinburgh: T. and T. Clark, 1983.

———. *The Pneumatikos–Psychikos Terminology in 1 Corinthians: A Study in the Theology of the Corinthian Opponents of Paul and Its Relation to Gnosticism*. Missoula, Mont.: Scholars Press, 1973.

Pelagius, *Expositions of Thirteen Epistles of St. Paul. I: Texts and Studies*, vol. 9/2. Ed. Alexander Souter. Cambridge: Cambridge University Press, 1926.

Perkins, Pheme. *Gnosticism and the New Testament*. Minneapolis: Fortress, 1993.

———. *Resurrection: New Testament Witness and Contemporary Reflection*. Garden City, N.Y.: Doubleday, 1984.

Perrot, Charles. "Lecture de 1 Co 11,17–34." In *Le Corps et le corps du Christ dans la première épître aux Corinthiens*, ed. Victor Guénel, 94–96. Paris: Editions du Cerf, 1983.

Peterman, Gerald W. "'Thankless Thanks': The Epistolary Social Convention in Philippians 4:10–20." *Tyndale Bulletin* 42 (1991): 261–270.

Phillips, Joanne H. "On Varro's *animalia quaedam minuta* and Etiology of Disease." *Transactions and Studies of the College of Physicians of Philadelphia* ser. 5, vol. 4 (1982): 12–25.

Phipps, W. E. "Is Paul's Attitude towards Sexual Relations Contained in 1 Cor. 7.1?" *New Testament Studies* 28 (1982): 125–131.

Pierce, C. A. *Conscience in the New Testament.* London: SCM, 1955.

Pilch, John. "Understanding Healing in the Social World of Early Christianity." *Biblical Theology Bulletin* 22 (1992): 26–33.

Pleket, H. W. *Epigraphica II, Texts on the Social History of the Greek World.* Textus Minores 41. Leiden: Brill, 1969.

Plunkett, Mark Allen. "Sexual Ethics and the Christian Life: A Study of 1 Corinthians 6:12–7:7." Ph.D. diss., Princeton Theological Seminary, 1988.

Pogoloff, Stephen. *Logos and Sophia: The Rhetorical Situation of 1 Corinthians.* Atlanta: Scholars Press, 1992.

Polyaenus. *Strategemata in lucem prolata curis Julii.* Ed. Julius A. de Foucault. Paris: Belles Lettres, 1949.

———. *Stratagems of War.* Trans. R. Shepherd. London: George Nicol, 1793.

Poole, J. C. F., and A. J. Holladay, "Thucydides and the Plague of Athens." *Classical Quarterly* n.s. 29 (1979): 282–300.

Pouilloux, Jean. "Une famille de sophistes thessaliens à Delphes au IIe s. ap. J.-C." *Revue de études greques* 80 (1967): 379–384.

Praecepta Salubria. Ed. U. Cats. Bussemaker. In *Poetae bucolici et didactici: Fragmenta Poematum Rem Naturalem vel medicinam Spectantium,* 132–134. Paris: Ambrosio Firmin Didot, 1851.

Preus, Anthony. "Science and Philosophy in Aristotle's *Generation of Animals.*" *Journal of the History of Biology* 3 (1970): 1–52.

Preuss, Julius. *Biblical and Talmudic Medicine.* New York: Sanhedrin, 1978; original German, 1911.

Prioreschi, Plinio. "Supernatural Elements in Hippocratic Medicine." *Journal of the History of Medicine and Allied Sciences* 47 (1992): 389–404.

Pseudo-Fastidius. *The Works of Fastidius.* Ed. and trans. R. S. T. Haslehurst. London: Society of SS. Peter and Paul, 1927.

Pseudo-Phocylides. *The Sentences of Pseudo-Phoeylides: with Introduction and Commentary.* Ed. and trans. P. W. van der Horst. Leiden: Brill, 1978.

Ptolemy, Claudius. "On the *Kriterion* and *Hegemonikon.*" Text and trans. in Pamela Huby and Gordon Neal, eds., *The Criterion of Truth: Essays Written in Honour of George Kerford Together with a Text and Translation (with Annotations) of Ptolemy's On the Kriterion and Hegemonikon,* 179–230. Liverpool: Liverpool University Press, 1989.

Räisänen, Heikki. *Paul and the Law.* Tübingen: Mohr (Siebeck), 1983.

Ramage, Edwin S. *Urbanitas: Ancient Sophisticatio and Refinement.* Norman: University of Oklahoma Press, 1973.

Rasmussen, Susan J. "Reflections on *Tamazai,* a Tuareg Idiom of Suffering." *Culture, Medicine and Psychiatry* 16 (1992): 337–365.

———. "Veiled Self, Transparent Meanings: Tuareg Headdress as Social Expression." *Ethnology* 30 (1991): 101–117.

Reitzenstein, Richard. *Die hellenistischen Mysterien-religion.* 3d ed. Leipzig: Teubner, 1927. Rpt. Darmstadt: Wissenschaftliche Buchgesellschaft, 1967.

Richardson, Alan. *An Introduction to the Theology of the New Testament.* New York: Harper and Row, 1958.

Riddle, John M. *Dioscorides on Pharmacy and Medicine.* Austin: University of Texas Press, 1985.

———. "Folk Tradition and Folk Medicine: Recognition of Drugs in Classical Antiquity." In *Folklore and Folk Medicine*, ed. John Scarborough, 33–45. Madison, Wis.: American Institute of the History of Pharmacy, 1987.

Riese, Walter. "Descartes' Ideas of Brain Function." In *The Brain and Its Functions*, ed. Woollam, 115–134.

Rist, John. "On Greek Biology, Greek Cosmology and Some Sources of Theological Pneuma." *Prudentia* supplementary number 1985 (1985): 27–47.

———. *The Use of Stoic Terminology in Philo's Quod Deus Immutabilis Sit 33–50*. Berkeley: Center for Hermeneutical Studies in Hellenistic and Modern Culture, 1976.

Robeck, Cecil M., Jr., ed. *Charismatic Experiences in History*. Peabody, Mass.: Hendrickson, 1985.

Robert, Louis. "Trois oracles de la Théosophie et un prophète d'Apollon." *Comptes rendus de l'Académie des Inscriptions et Belles-Lettres* (1968): 568–599. Paris: De Boccard, 1968.

Roberts, Alexander, and James Donaldson, eds. *The Ante-Nicene Fathers*, vol. 2. Buffalo: Christian Literature Publishing, 1885.

Robinson, John A. T. *The Body: A Study in Pauline Theology*. London: SCM, 1952.

Romilly, Jacqueline de. "Vocabulaire et propagande, ou les premiers emplois du mot *homonoia*." In *Mélanges de Linguistique et de Philologie Grecques offerts à Pierre Chantraine*, Etudes et commentaires, 79, pp. 199–209. Paris: Klincksieck, 1972.

Rosner, Brian S. " '*Ouchi mallon epenthēsate*': Corporate Responsibility in 1 Corinthians 5." *New Testament Studies* 38 (1992): 470–473.

———. "Temple and Holiness in 1 Corinthians 5." *Tyndale Bulletin* 42 (1991): 137–145.

Rousselle, Aline. *Porneia: On Desire and the Body in Antiquity*. Oxford: Basil Blackwell, 1988.

Rubel, Arthur J. "The Epidemiology of a Folk Illness: *Susto* in Hispanic America." In *Culture, Disease, and Healing*, ed. Landy, 119–128. Rpt. (abridged) from *Ethnology* 3 (1964): 268–283.

Rudolph, Kurt. *Gnosis: The Nature and History of Gnosticism*. San Francisco: Harper and Row, 1983.

Runia, David T. *Philo of Alexandria and the Timaeus of Plato*. Leiden: Brill, 1986.

Russell, Bertrand. *Marriage and Morals*. New York: Liveright, 1957.

Russell, D. A. *Greek Declamation*. Cambridge: Cambridge University Press, 1983.

Ste. Croix, G. E. M. de. *The Class Struggle in the Ancient Greek World*. Ithaca, N.Y.: Cornell University Press, 1989.

Sand, Alexander. *Der Begriff "Fleisch" in den paulinischen Hauptbriefen*. Regensburg: Pustet, 1967.

Sanders, E. P. *Judaism: Practice and Belief 63 BCE–66 CE*. Philadelphia: Trinity, 1992.

———. *Paul and Palestinian Judaism: A Comparison of Patterns of Religion*. Philadelphia: Fortress, 1977.

Scarborough, John. "The Pharmacology of Sacred Plants, Herbs, and Roots." In *Magika Hiera: Ancient Greek Magic and Religion*, ed. Christopher A. Faraone and Dirk Obbink, 138–174. New York and Oxford: Oxford University Press, 1991.

Scarborough, John, and Vivian Nutton. "The Preface of Dioscorides' *Materia Medica*: Introduction, Translation, and Commentary." *Transactions and Studies of the College of Physicians of Philadelphia*, ser. 5, vol. 4 (1982): 187–227.

———. *Roman Medicine*. Ithaca, N.Y.: Cornell University Press, 1969.

Schlatter, Adolf. *Die korinthische Theologie*. Gütersloh: Bertelsmann, 1914.

Schmithals, Walter. *Gnosticism in Corinth*. New York: Abingdon, 1971.

Schniewind, Julius. "Die Leugner der Auferstehung in Korinth." In *Nachgelassene*

Reden und Aufsätze, 110–39. Berlin: Alfred Töpelmann, 1952.

Scholem, Gershom G. *Major Trends in Jewish Mysticism*. New York: Schocken, 1941.

Scholer, David M. "'And I was a Man': The Power and Problem of Perpetua." *Daughters of Sarah* 15 (Sept.–Oct. 1989): 10–14.

Schrage, Wolfgang. "Zur Frontstellung der paulinischen Ehebewertung in 1 Cor 7,1–7." *Zeitschrift für die neutestamentliche Wissenschaft* 67 (1976): 214–234.

Schüssler Fiorenza, Elisabeth. *In Memory of Her: A Feminist Theological Reconstruction of Christian Origins*. New York: Crossroad, 1983.

Schwarzbaum, Haim. "Talmudic-Midrashic Affinities of Some Aesopic Fables." In *Essays in Greco-Roman and Related Talmudic Literature*, ed. H. A. Fischel, 425–442. New York: KTAV, 1977.

Schweitzer, Albert. *The Mysticism of Paul the Apostle*. New York: Henry Holt, 1931.

Schweizer, Eduard. *"Pneuma, ktl." TDNT* 6: 421.

Scott, Alan. *Origen and the Life of the Stars: A History of an Idea*. Oxford: Clarendon, 1991.

Scott, Walter, trans. *Hermetica*. Oxford: Clarendon, 1924.

Scroggs, Robin. *The Last Adam: A Study in Pauline Anthropology*. Philadelphia: Fortress, 1966.

Sedgwick, Eve Kosofsky. *Epistemology of the Closet*. Berkeley: University of California Press, 1990.

———. "Paul and the Eschatological Woman." *Journal of the American Academy of Religion* 40 (1972): 283–303.

Sellin, Gerhard. *Der Streit um die Auferstehung der Toten*. Göttingen: Vandenhoeck and Ruprecht, 1986.

Sevenster, J. N. *Paul and Seneca*. Leiden: Brill, 1961.

Shaw, Brent D. "The Age of Roman Girls at Marriage: Some Reconsiderations." *Journal of Roman Studies* 77 (1987): 30–46.

Siegel, Rudolph E. *Galen on Psychology, Psychopathology, and Function and Diseases of the Nervous System*. Basel: S. Karger, 1973.

———. *Galen on Sense Perception*. Basil: S. Karger, 1970.

———. *Galen's System of Physiology and Medicine: An Analysis of His Doctrines and Observations on Bloodflow, Respiration, Humors and Internal Diseases*. New York: S. Karger, 1968.

Sissa, Guilia. "The Sexual Philosophies of Plato and Aristotle." In *A History of Women in the West. I: From Ancient Goddesses to Christian Saints*, ed. Pauline Schmitt Pantel, 46–81. Cambridge: Belknap, 1992.

Smit, J. F. "The Genre of 1 Corinthians 13 in the Light of Classical Rhetoric." *Novum Testamentum* 33 (1991): 193–216.

———. "Two Puzzles: 1 Corinthians 12.31 and 13.3, A Rhetorical Solution." *New Testament Studies* 39 (1993): 246–264.

Smith, Dennis E. "Social Obligation in the Context of Communal Meals: A Study of the Christian Meal in 1 Corinthians in Comparison with Graeco-Roman Communal Meals." Th.D. diss., Harvard Divinity School, 1980.

Smith, Dennis E., and Hal E. Taussig. *Many Tables: The Eucharist in the New Testament and Liturgy Today*. Philadelphia: Trinity, 1990.

Smith, Morton. "Pagan Dealings with Jewish Angels: P. Berlin 5025b, P. Louvre 2391." *Studii Clasice* 24 (1986): 175–179.

———. "Salvation in the Gospels, Paul, and the Magical Papyri." *Helios* 13 (1986): 63–74.

Solmsen, Friedrich. "Greek Philosophy and the Discovery of the Nerves." *Museum Helveticum* 18 (1961): 150–197.

Soranus. *Gynecology*. Trans. Owsei Temkin. Baltimore: Johns Hopkins University Press, 1956.

———. *Sorani Gynaeciorum*. Ed. Valentino Rose. Leipzig: Teubner, 1882.

———. *Sorani Gynaeciorum libri IV, De signis*

Fracturarum, De fasciis, Vita Hippocratis secundum Soranum. Ed. Ilberg, Johannes. *Corpus Medicorum Graecorum* 4. Leipzig: Teubner, 1927.

Spittler, R. P. Introduction to "Testament of Job." In *The Old Testament Pseudepigrapha*, ed. Charlesworth, 1: 829–868. (See P. Alexander.)

Spivack, Betty S. "A. C. Celsus: Roman Medicus." *Journal of the History of Medicine and Allied Sciences* 46 (1991): 143–157.

Stacey, David. *The Pauline View of Man in Relation to Its Judaic and Hellenistic Background.* London: Macmillan, 1956.

Stambaugh, John E. "Social Relations in the City of the Early Principate." In *Society of Biblical Literature 1980 Seminar Papers*, ed. Paul J. Achtemeier, 75–99. Chico, Calif.: Scholars Press, 1980.

Stambaugh, John E., and David Balch. *The New Testament in Its Social Environment.* Philadelphia: Westminster, 1986.

Stern, Menahem. *Greek and Latin Authors on Jews and Judaism.* 2 vols. Jerusalem: Israel Academy of Sciences and Humanities, 1976.

Sterrett, J. R. S. *The Wolfe Expedition to Asia Minor. Papers of the American School of Classical Studies at Athens* 3 (1884–85). Boston: Damrell and Upham, 1888.

Stowers, Stanley K. *Letter Writing in Greco-Roman Antiquity.* Philadelphia: Westminster, 1986.

Sutton, Robert F., Jr. "The Interaction between Men and Women Portrayed on Attic Red-Figure Pottery." Ph.D. diss., University of North Carolina–Chapel Hill, 1981.

———. "On the Classical Athenian Wedding: Two Red-Figure Loutrophoroi in Boston." In *Daidalikon: Studies in Memory of Raymond V. Schoder, S.J.*, ed. Robert F. Sutton, Jr., 331–359. Wauconda, Ill.: Bolchazy-Carducci, 1989.

Tanner, R. G. "St. Paul and Panaetius." *Studia Biblica 1978.* III: *Papers on Paul and Other New Testament Authors*, ed. E. A.

Livingstone, 361–375. Sheffield: JSOT Press, 1980.

Tappeiner, Daniel A. "The Function of Tongue-Speaking for the Individual: A Psycho-Theological Method." *Journal of the American Scientific Affiliation* 26 (1974): 29–32.

Tarn, W. W. *Alexander the Great.* 2 vols. Cambridge: Cambridge University Press, 1948.

Tarrant, H. A. S. "Pneuma-Related Concepts in Platonism." *Prudentia* supplementary number 1985 (1985): 55–60.

Temkin, Owsei. *The Double Face of Janus and Other Essays in the History of Medicine.* Baltimore: Johns Hopkins University Press, 1977.

———. *Hippocrates in a World of Pagans and Christians.* Baltimore: Johns Hopkins University Press, 1991.

Tertullian. *On the Resurrection of the Flesh.* Trans. and ed. Ernest Evans. London: SPCK, 1960.

Theissen, Gerd. *Psychological Aspects of Pauline Theology.* Philadelphia: Fortress, 1987.

———. *The Social Setting of Pauline Christianity.* Philadelphia: Fortress, 1982.

Thiselton, Anthony C. "Realized Eschatology at Corinth." *New Testament Studies* 24 (1977): 510–526.

Thompson, Cynthia L. "Hairstyles, Head-Coverings, and St. Paul: Portraits from Roman Corinth." *Biblical Archaeologist* 51 (1988): 99–115.

Thompson, John B. *Ideology and Modern Culture, Critical Theory in the Era of Mass Communication.* Stanford: Stanford University Press, 1990.

Todorov, Tzvetan. *Mikhail Bakhtin: The Dialogical Principle.* Minneapolis: University of Minnesota Press, 1984.

Tomson, Peter J. *Paul and the Jewish Law: Halakha in the Letters of the Apostle to the Gentiles.* Assen, Netherlands: Van Gorcum; Minneapolis: Fortress, 1990.

Turnbull, Robert G. "The Role of the 'Special Sensibles' in the Perception Theories of Plato and Aristotle." In *Studies in Perception*, ed. Machamer and Turnbull, 3–26.

Vallance, J. T. *The Lost Theory of Asclepiades of Bithynia*. Oxford: Clarendon, 1990.

Van der Horst, Pieter W. "Images of Women in the Testament of Job." In *Studies on the Testament of Job*, ed. Michael A. Knibb and Pieter W. van der Horst, 93–116. Cambridge: Cambridge University Press, 1989.

Verbeke, G. *L'Évolution de la doctrine du pneuma du Stoïcisme à S. Augustin*. Paris: Desclée de Brouwer, 1945.

Vermes, Geza. *The Dead Sea Scrolls in English*. New York: Penguin, 1975.

Via, Dan O. *Self-Deception and Wholeness in Paul and Matthew*. Minneapolis: Fortress, 1990.

Von Arnim, Johannes, ed. *Stoicorum Veterum Fragmenta*. Leipzig: Teubner, 1921–24.

Von Soden, Hans Freiherr. "Sakrament und Ethik bei Paulus." In *Marburger theologische Studien (Rudolf Otto Festgruss) (1931)*, vol. 1. Rpt. in *Urchristentum und Geschichte*, 239–75. Tübingen: Mohr (Siebeck), 1951. Abridged and trans. as "Sacrament and Ethics in Paul," in *The Writings of St. Paul*, ed. Wayne A. Meeks, 257–68. New York: Norton, 1972.

Von Staden, Heinrich. "The Stoic Theory of Perception and its 'Platonic' Critics." In *Studies in Perception*, ed. Machamer and Turnbull, 96–136.

Wanamaker, Charles A. *The Epistles to the Thessalonians*. Grand Rapids, Mich.: Eerdmans, 1990.

Ward, Roy Bowen. "Musonius and Paul on Marriage." *New Testament Studies* 36 (1990): 281–289.

Watson, Francis. "Strategies of Recovery and Resistance: Hermeneutical Reflections on Genesis 1–3 and Its Pauline Reception." *Journal for the Study of the New Testament* 45 (1992): 79–103.

Wedderburn, A. J. M. *Baptism and Resurrection: Studies in Pauline Theology against Its Graeco-Roman Background*. Tübingen: Mohr (Siebeck), 1987.

Weiss, Brad. *The Making and Unmaking of the Haya Lived World: Consumption, Commodities, and Everyday Practice*. Durham, N.C.: Duke University Press, forthcoming.

———. "Plastic Teeth Extraction: The Iconography of Haya Gastro-Sexual Affliction." *American Ethnologist* 19 (1992): 538–552.

Weiss, Johannes. *Der erste Korintherbrief*. Kritisch-exegetischer Kommentar 5. 9th ed. Göttingen: Vandenhoeck and Ruprecht, 1910.

Welborn, L. L. "On the Discord in Corinth: 1 Corinthians 1–4 and Ancient Politics." *Journal of Biblical Literature* 106 (1987): 85–111.

Wellin, Edward. "Theoretical Orientations in Medical Anthropology: Continuity and Change over the Past Half-Century." In *Culture, Disease, and Healing*, ed. Landy, 47–58.

White, John L. *Light from Ancient Letters*. Philadelphia: Fortress, 1986.

Wikenhauser, Alfred. *Die Kirche als der mystische Leib Christi nach dem Apostel Paulus*. Münster in Westphalen: Aschendorff, 1937.

Wilkie, J. S. "Body and Soul in Aristotelian Tradition." In *The Brain and Its Functions*, ed. Woollam, 19–28.

Wilkinson, Lise. "The Development of the Virus Concept as Reflected in Corpora of Studies on Individual Pathogens: 4. Rabies—Two Millennia of Ideas and Conjecture on the Aetiology of a Virus Disease." *Medical History* 21 (1977): 15–31.

Williams, J. Rodman. "The Greater Gifts." In *Charismatic Experiences in History*, ed. Robeck, 44–65.

Willis, Wendell L. "An Apostolic Apologia? The Form and Function of 1 Corinthians 9." *Journal for the Study of the New Testament* 24 (1985): 33–48.

———. *Idol Meat in Corinth.* Chico, Calif.: Scholars Press, 1985.

Winandy, Jacques. "Un curieux *casus peudens:* 1 Corinthians 11:10 et son interpretation." *New Testament Studies* 38 (1992): 621–629.

Wink, Walter. *Naming the Powers: The Language of Power in the New Testament.* Philadelphia: Fortress, 1984.

Winkler, John J. *The Constraints of Desire: The Anthropology of Sex and Gender in Ancient Greece.* New York: Routledge, 1990.

Winnington-Ingram, R. P. *Euripides and Dionysus: An Interpretation of the* Bacchae. Cambridge: Cambridge University Press, 1948.

Winter, Bruce W. "Civil Litigation in Secular Corinth and the Church: The Forensic Background to 1 Corinthians 6.1–8." *New Testament Studies* 37 (1991): 559–572.

———. "Theological and Ethical Responses to Religious Pluralism—1 Corinthians 8–10." *Tyndale Bulletin* 41 (1990): 209–226.

Wire, Antoinette Clark. *The Corinthian Women Prophets: A Reconstruction through Paul's Rhetoric.* Philadelphia: Fortress, 1990.

Wisse, Frederik. "The 'Opponents' in the New Testament in Light of the Nag Hammadi Writings." In *Colloque Internationale sur les Textes de Nag Hammadi (Quebec, 22–25 août 1978),* ed. Bernard Barc, 99–120. Quebec: L'Université Laval, 1981.

———. "Die Sextus-Sprüche und das Problem der gnostischen Ethik." In *Zum Hellenismus in den Schriften von Nag Hammadi,* Göttinger Orientforschungen VI. Reihe: Hellenistica 2, ed. Alexander Bölig and Frederik Wisse, 55–86. Wiesbaden: Harrassowitz, 1975.

Witherington, Ben. "Rite and Rights for Women—Galatians 3.28." *New Testament Studies* 27 (1981): 593–604.

Wolf, Eric. "Kinship, Friendship, and Patron–Client Relations." In *The Social Anthropology of Complex Societies,* ed. Michael Banton, 1–22. New York: Frederick A. Praeger, 1966.

Woods, Laurie. "Opposition to a Man and His Message: Paul's 'Thorn in the Flesh' (2 Cor. 12:7)." *Australian Biblical Review* 39 (1991): 43–53.

Woollam, D. H. M. "Concepts of the Brain and Its Functions in Classical Antiquity." In *The History and Philosophy of Knowledge of the Brain and Its Functions,* 5–18. Amsterdam: B. M. Israël, 1973.

Yamauchi, Edwin M. *Pre-Christian Gnosticism: A Survey of the Proposed Evidence.* 2d ed. Grand Rapids, Mich.: Baker, 1983.

Yarbrough, O. Larry. *Not Like the Gentiles: Marriage Rules in the Letters of Paul.* Atlanta: Scholars Press, 1985.

Young, Norman H. "*Paidagogos:* The Social Setting of a Pauline Metaphor." *Novum Testamentum* 29 (1987): 150–176.

Zass, Peter S. "'Cast Out the Evil Man from Your Midst' (1 Cor. 5:13b)." *Journal of Biblical Literature* 103 (1984): 260.

———. "Catalogues and Context: 1 Corinthians 5 and 6." *New Testament Studies* 34 (1988): 622–629.

Index of Scripture Citations

General Index